The anime's begun.
It's all thanks to you readers that we've
come this far, so thank you very much!

KOHEI HORIKOSHI

MY HERO ACADEMIA

8

SHONEN JUMP Manga Edition

STORY & ART KOHEI HORIKOSHI

TRANSLATION & ENGLISH ADAPTATION **Caleb Cook**
TOUCH-UP ART & LETTERING **John Hunt**
DESIGNER **Shawn Carrico**
SHONEN JUMP SERIES EDITOR **John Bae**
GRAPHIC NOVEL EDITOR **Mike Montesa**

BOKU NO HERO ACADEMIA © 2014 by Kohei Horikoshi
All rights reserved.
First published in Japan in 2014 by SHUEISHA Inc., Tokyo.
English translation rights arranged by SHUEISHA Inc.

The stories, characters and incidents mentioned in this publication are entirely fictional.

Printed in the U.S.A.

Published by VIZ Media, LLC
P.O. Box 77010
San Francisco, CA 94107

10 9 8 7 6 5
First printing, May 2017
Fifth printing, November 2018

PARENTAL ADVISORY
MY HERO ACADEMIA is rated T for Teen
and is recommended for ages 13 and up.
This volume contains fantasy violence.

shonenjump.com

MY HERO ACADEMIA

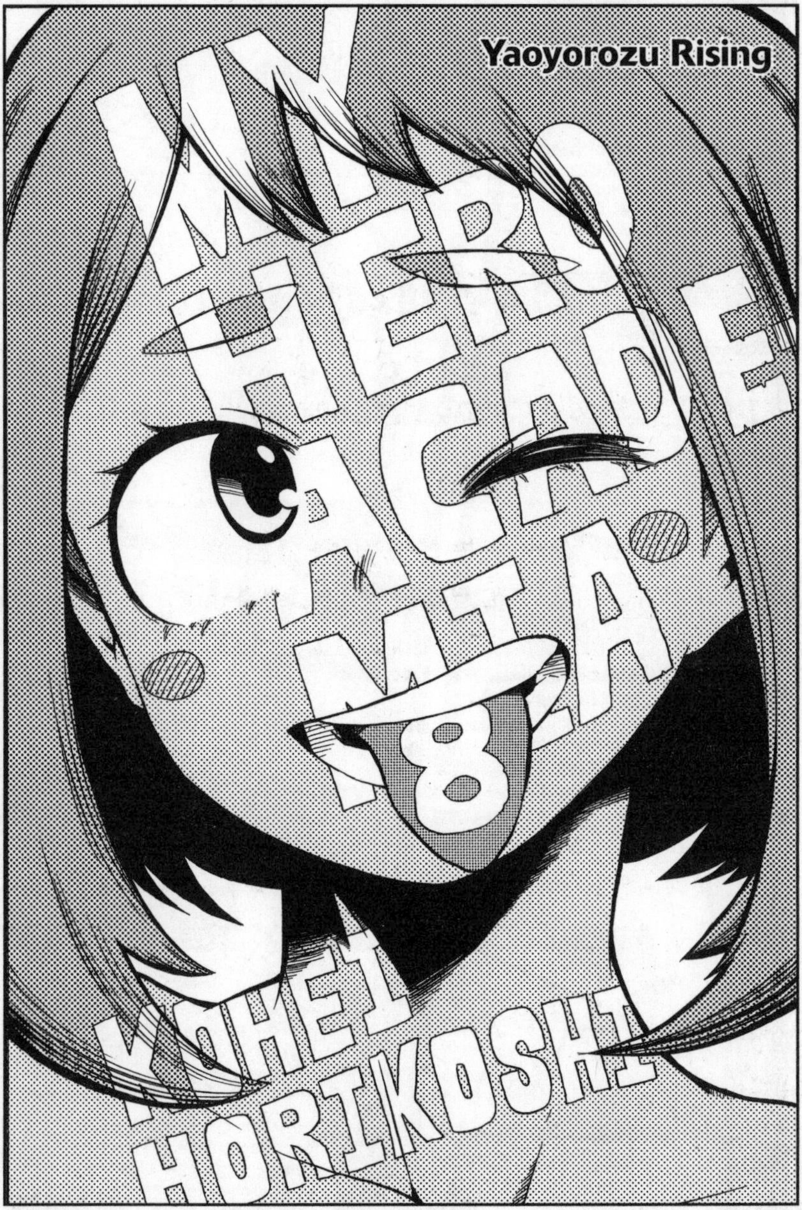
Yaoyorozu Rising
MY HERO ACADEMIA
8
KOHEI HORIKOSHI

KOHEI HORIKOSHI

*SHONEN**JUMP** MANGA*

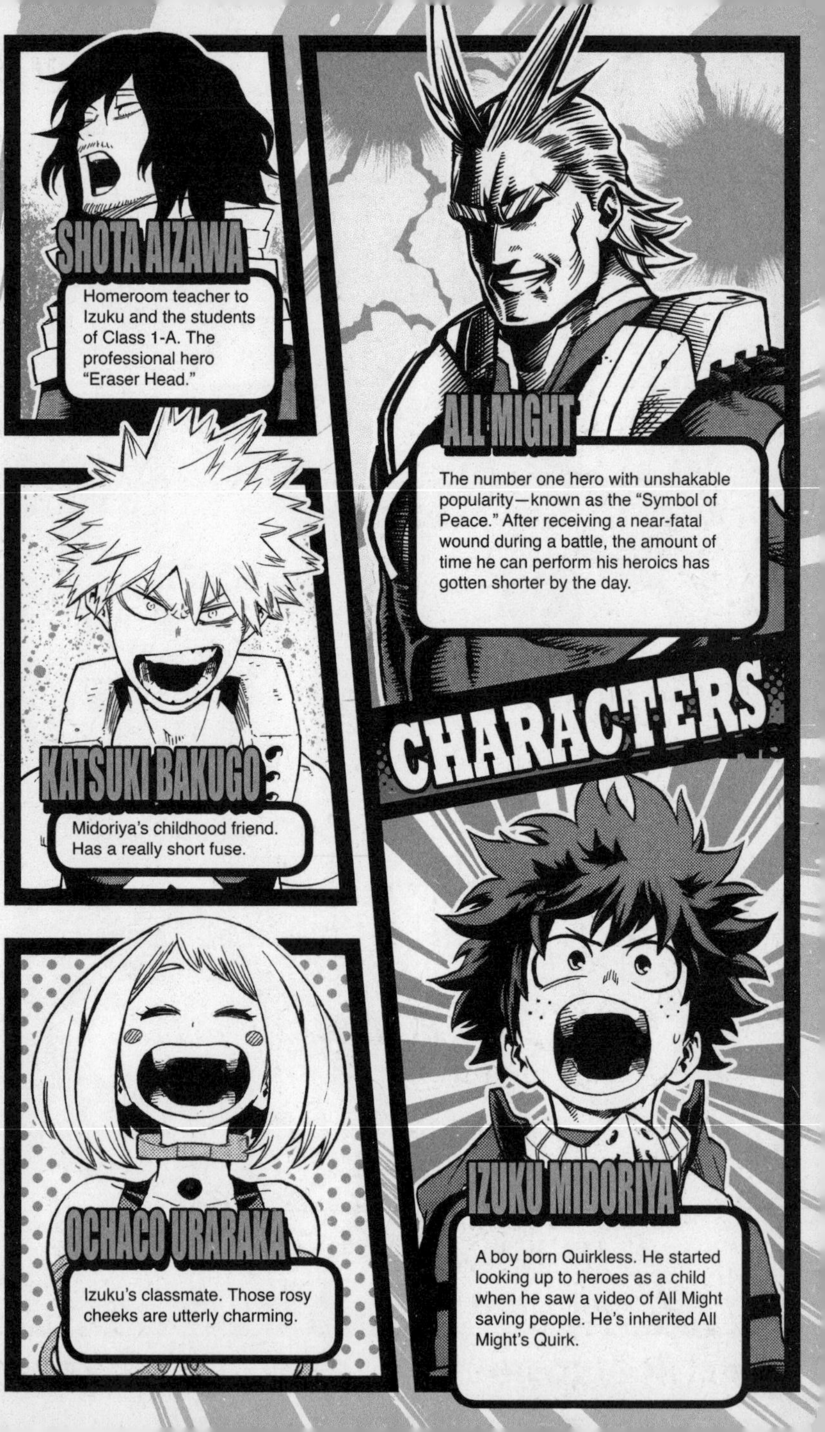
ALL MIGHT
The number one hero with unshakable popularity—known as the "Symbol of Peace." After receiving a near-fatal wound during a battle, the amount of time he can perform his heroics has gotten shorter by the day.
CHARACTERS
IZUKU MIDORIYA
A boy born Quirkless. He started looking up to heroes as a child when he saw a video of All Might saving people. He's inherited All Might's Quirk.
SHOTA AIZAWA
Homeroom teacher to Izuku and the students of Class 1-A. The professional hero "Eraser Head."
KATSUKI BAKUGO
Midoriya's childhood friend. Has a really short fuse.
OCHACO URARAKA
Izuku's classmate. Those rosy cheeks are utterly charming.

STORY

One day, people began manifesting special abilities that came to be known as "Quirks," and before long, society became full of these superpowered humans. But with the advent of these exceptional individuals came an increase in crime, and governments were unable to deal with the situation. At the same time, others emerged to oppose the spread of evil! As if straight from the comic books, these heroes keep the peace and are even officially authorized to fight crime. Our story begins when a certain Quirkless boy and lifelong hero fan meets the world's number one hero, starting him on his path to becoming the greatest hero ever!

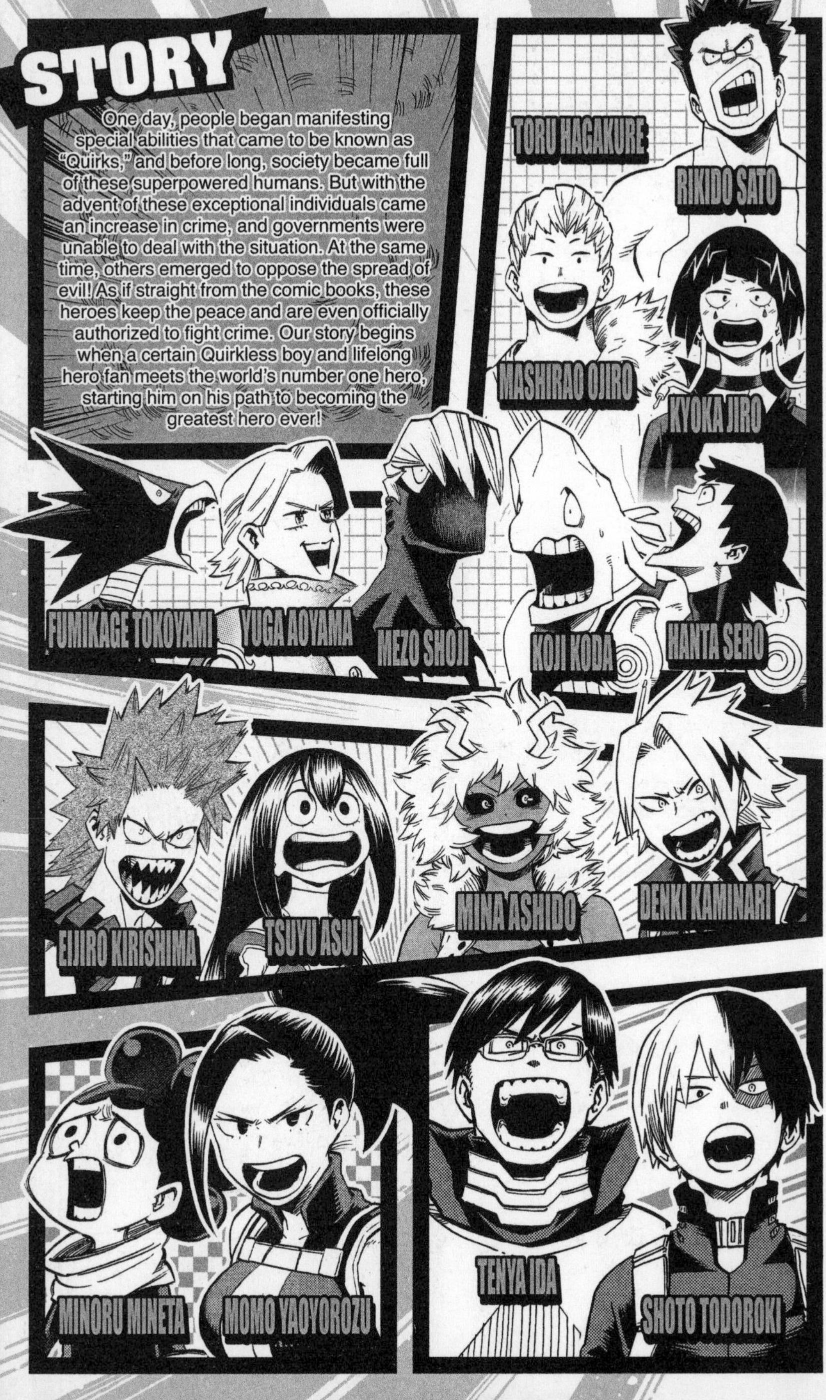
TORU HAGAKURE
RIKIDO SATO
KYOKA JIRO
MASHIRAO OJIRO
HANTA SERO
KOJI KODA
MEZO SHOJI
YUGA AOYAMA
FUMIKAGE TOKOYAMI
DENKI KAMINARI
MINA ASHIDO
TSUYU ASUI
EIJIRO KIRISHIMA
SHOTO TODOROKI
TENYA IDA
MOMO YAOYOROZU
MINORU MINETA

MY HERO ACADEMIA

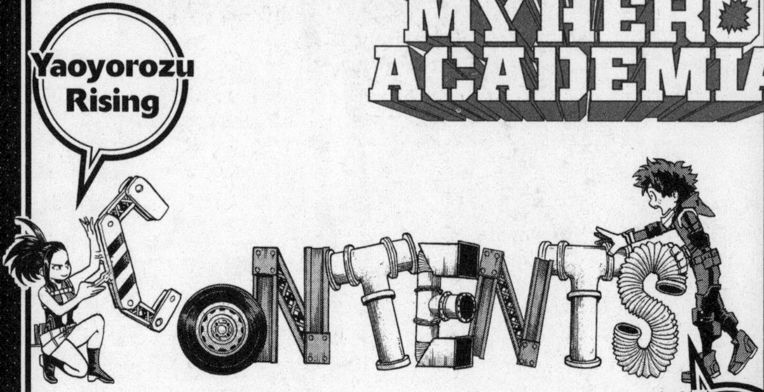
Yaoyorozu Rising
CONTENTS

Vol. 8

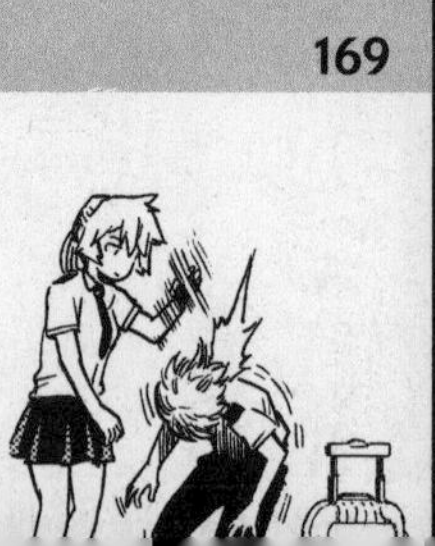

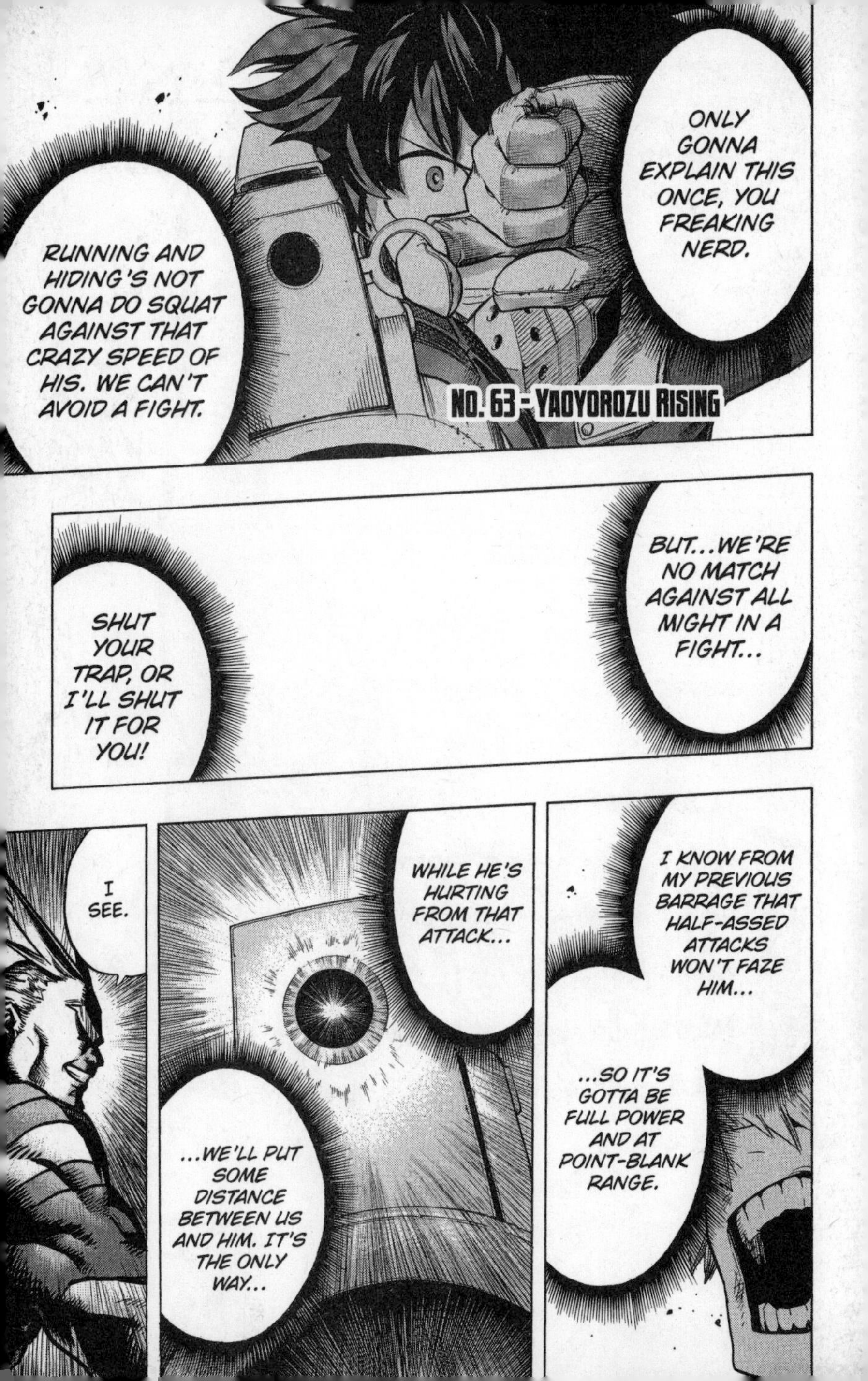
ONLY GONNA EXPLAIN THIS ONCE, YOU FREAKING NERD.
RUNNING AND HIDING'S NOT GONNA DO SQUAT AGAINST THAT CRAZY SPEED OF HIS. WE CAN'T AVOID A FIGHT.
NO. 63 - YAOYOROZU RISING
BUT...WE'RE NO MATCH AGAINST ALL MIGHT IN A FIGHT...
SHUT YOUR TRAP, OR I'LL SHUT IT FOR YOU!
I KNOW FROM MY PREVIOUS BARRAGE THAT HALF-ASSED ATTACKS WON'T FAZE HIM...
...SO IT'S GOTTA BE FULL POWER AND AT POINT-BLANK RANGE.
WHILE HE'S HURTING FROM THAT ATTACK...
...WE'LL PUT SOME DISTANCE BETWEEN US AND HIM. IT'S THE ONLY WAY...
I SEE.

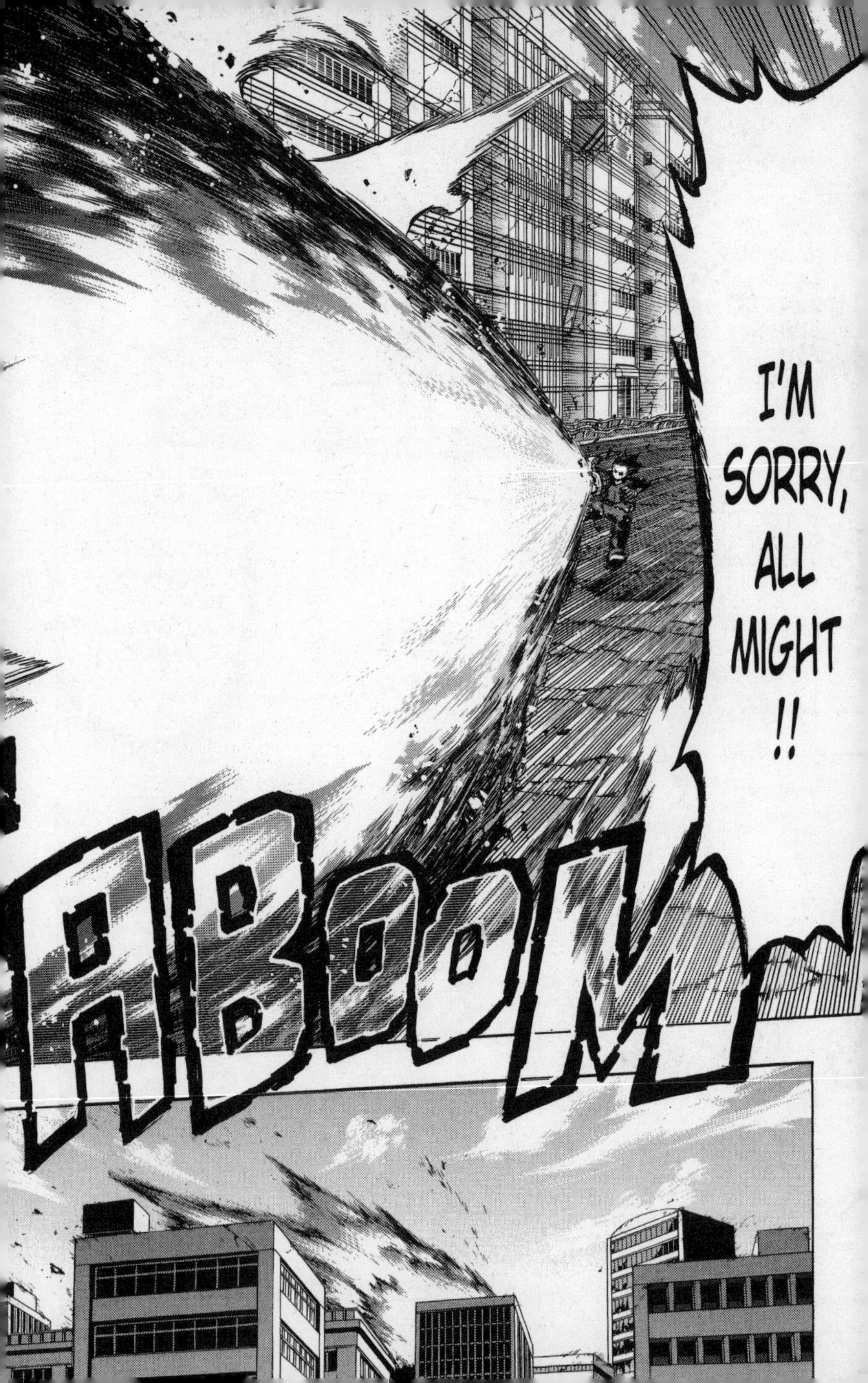
I'M SORRY, ALL MIGHT!!
KABOOM

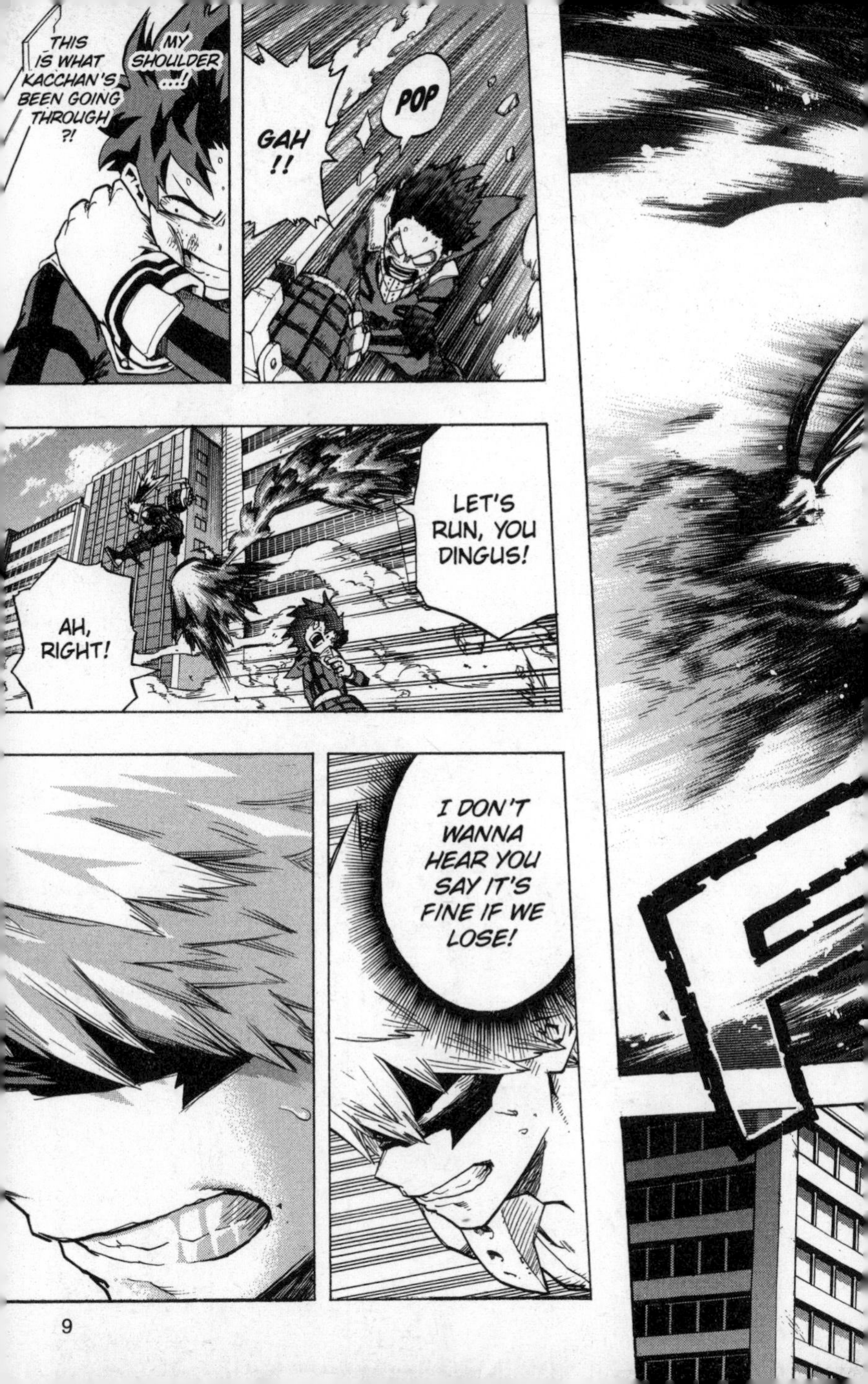
POP
GAH!!
MY SHOULDER...!
THIS IS WHAT KACCHAN'S BEEN GOING THROUGH?!
LET'S RUN, YOU DINGUS!
AH, RIGHT!
I DON'T WANNA HEAR YOU SAY IT'S FINE IF WE LOSE!

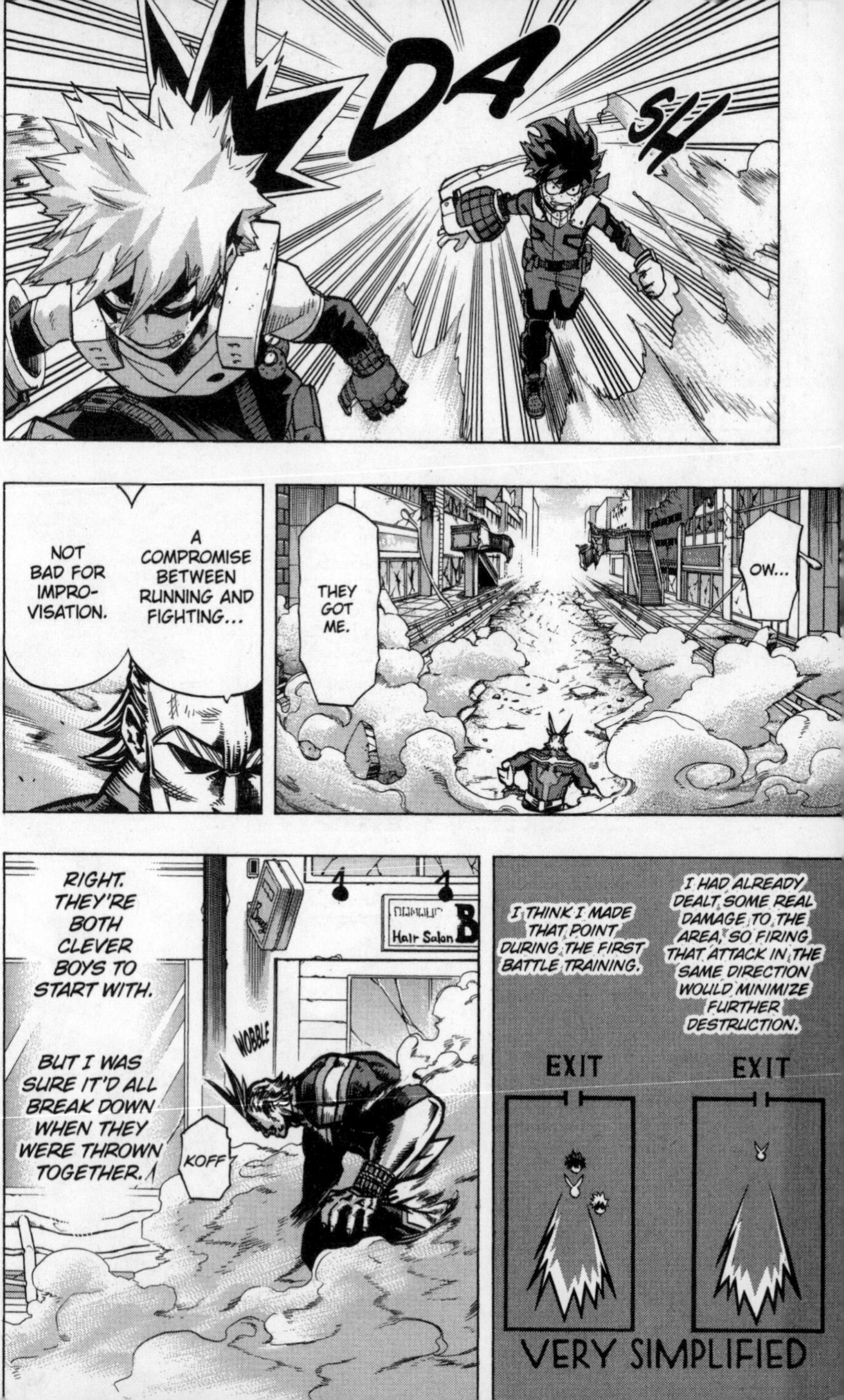
DASH
OW...
THEY GOT ME.
A COMPROMISE BETWEEN RUNNING AND FIGHTING...
NOT BAD FOR IMPRO-VISATION.
I HAD ALREADY DEALT SOME REAL DAMAGE TO THE AREA, SO FIRING THAT ATTACK IN THE SAME DIRECTION WOULD MINIMIZE FURTHER DESTRUCTION.
I THINK I MADE THAT POINT DURING THE FIRST BATTLE TRAINING.
EXIT
EXIT
VERY SIMPLIFIED
Hair Salon
RIGHT. THEY'RE BOTH CLEVER BOYS TO START WITH.
WOBBLE
BUT I WAS SURE IT'D ALL BREAK DOWN WHEN THEY WERE THROWN TOGETHER.
KOFF

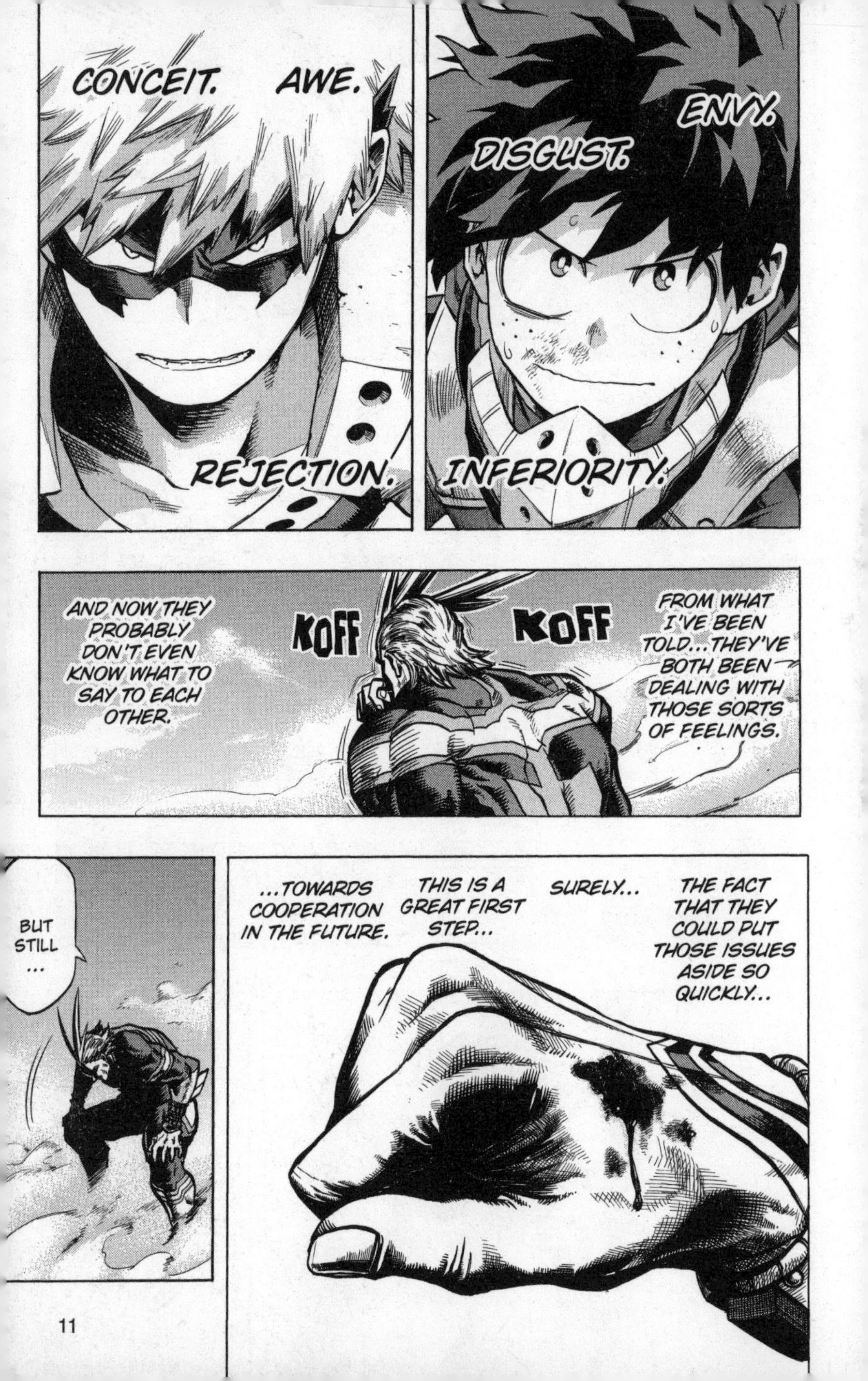
ENVY.
DISGUST.
INFERIORITY.
AWE.
CONCEIT.
REJECTION.
FROM WHAT I'VE BEEN TOLD...THEY'VE BOTH BEEN DEALING WITH THOSE SORTS OF FEELINGS.
KOFF
KOFF
AND NOW THEY PROBABLY DON'T EVEN KNOW WHAT TO SAY TO EACH OTHER.
THE FACT THAT THEY COULD PUT THOSE ISSUES ASIDE SO QUICKLY...
SURELY...
THIS IS A GREAT FIRST STEP...
...TOWARDS COOPERATION IN THE FUTURE.
BUT STILL ...

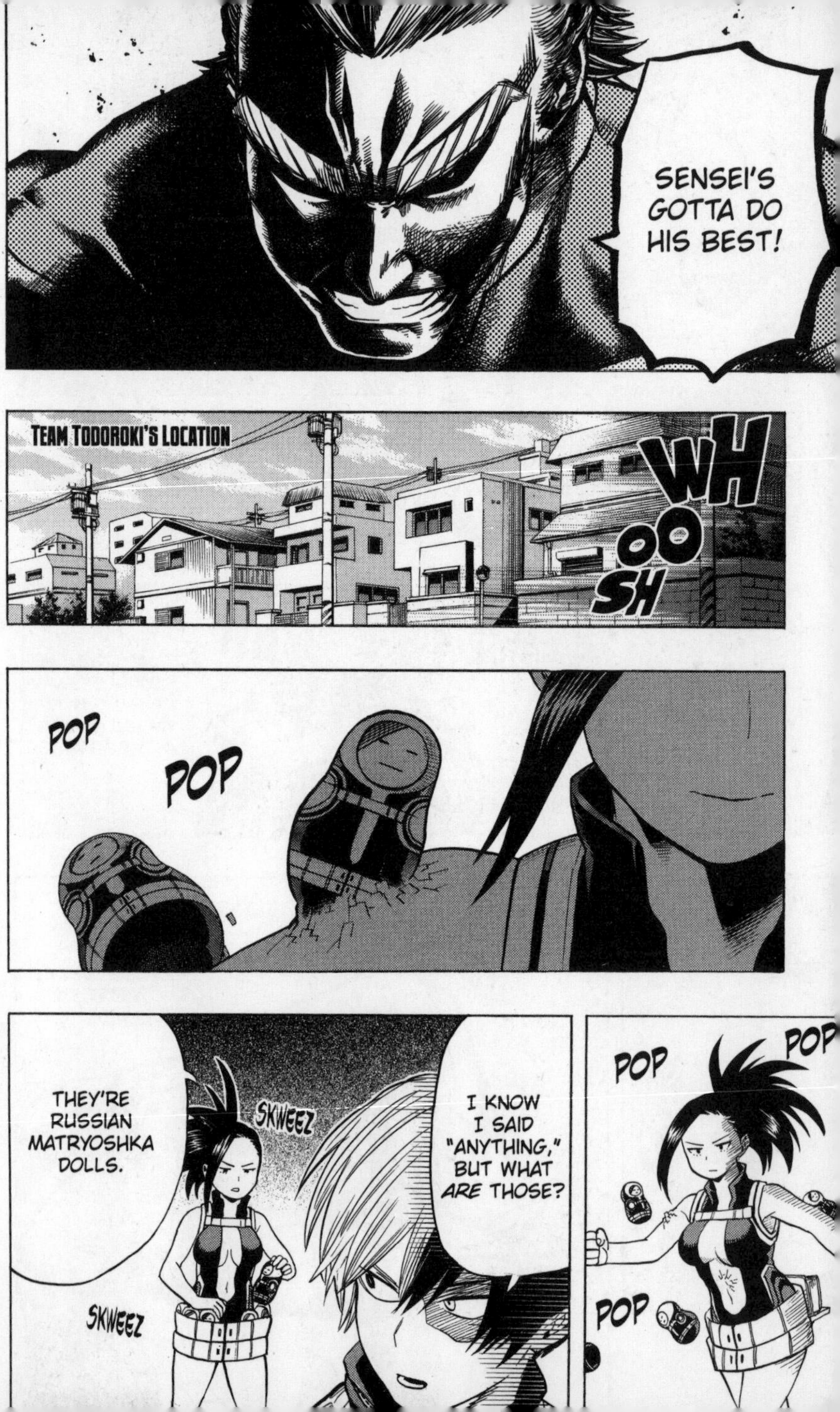
SENSEI'S GOTTA DO HIS BEST!
TEAM TODOROKI'S LOCATION
WHOOSH
POP
POP
POP
POP
POP
I KNOW I SAID "ANYTHING," BUT WHAT ARE THOSE?
SKWEEZ
THEY'RE RUSSIAN MATRYOSHKA DOLLS.
SKWEEZ

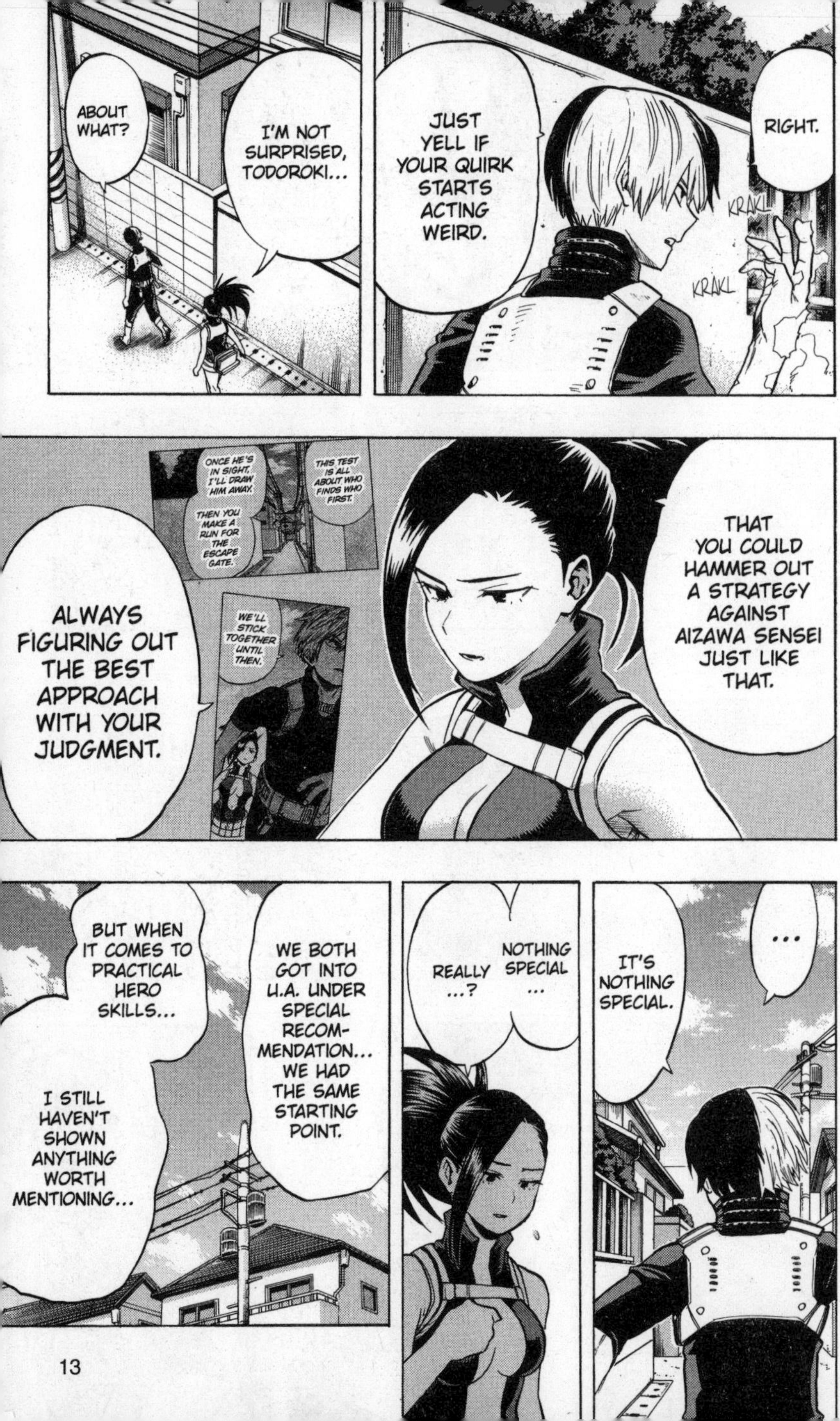
RIGHT.
JUST YELL IF YOUR QUIRK STARTS ACTING WEIRD.
KRAKL
KRAKL
I'M NOT SURPRISED, TODOROKI...
ABOUT WHAT?
THAT YOU COULD HAMMER OUT A STRATEGY AGAINST AIZAWA SENSEI JUST LIKE THAT.
THIS TEST IS ALL ABOUT WHO FINDS WHO FIRST.
ONCE HE'S IN SIGHT, I'LL DRAW HIM AWAY.
THEN YOU MAKE A RUN FOR THE ESCAPE GATE.
WE'LL STICK TOGETHER UNTIL THEN.
ALWAYS FIGURING OUT THE BEST APPROACH WITH YOUR JUDGMENT.
...
IT'S NOTHING SPECIAL.
NOTHING SPECIAL ...
REALLY ...?
WE BOTH GOT INTO U.A. UNDER SPECIAL RECOM-MENDATION... WE HAD THE SAME STARTING POINT.
BUT WHEN IT COMES TO PRACTICAL HERO SKILLS...
I STILL HAVEN'T SHOWN ANYTHING WORTH MENTIONING...

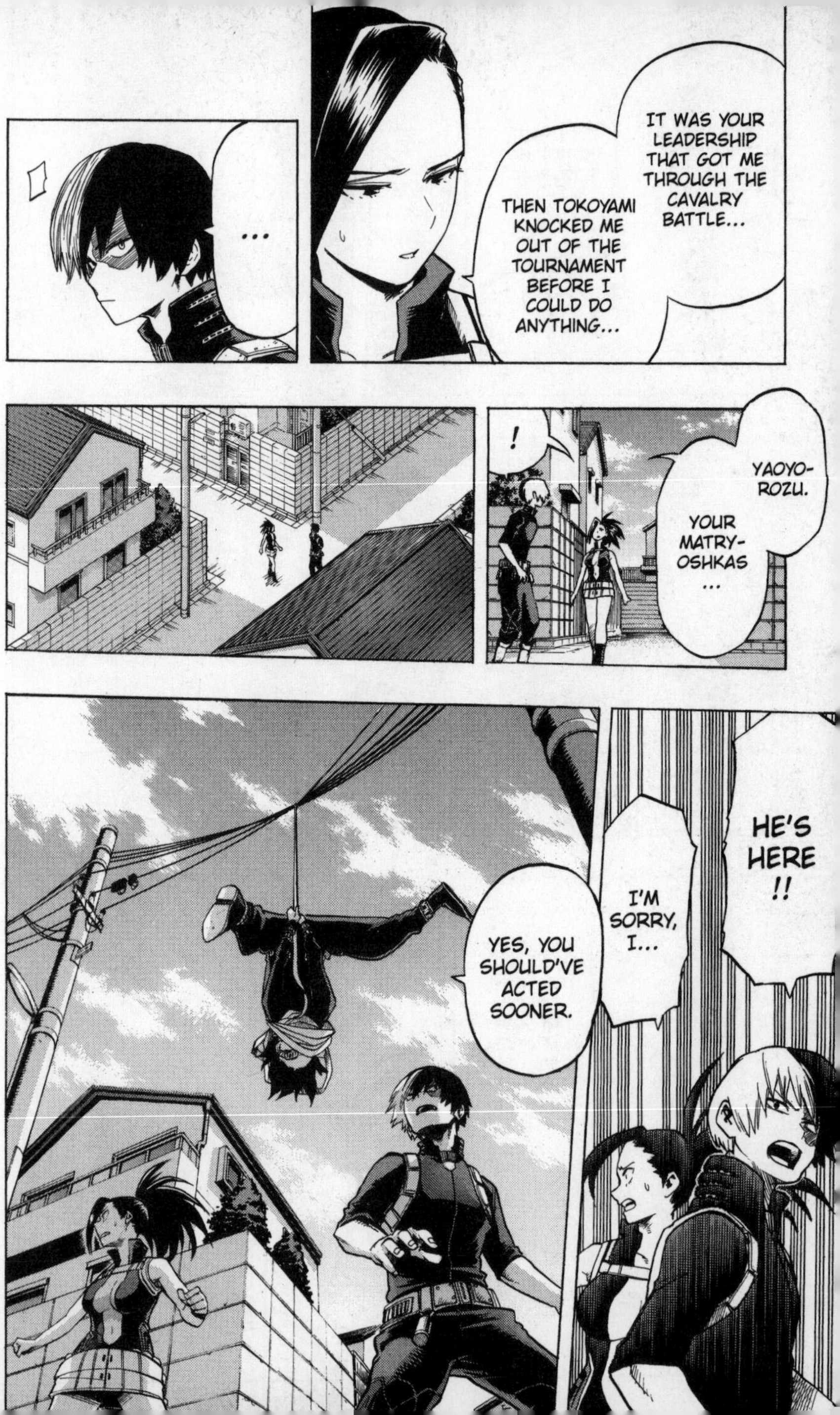
IT WAS YOUR LEADERSHIP THAT GOT ME THROUGH THE CAVALRY BATTLE...
THEN TOKOYAMI KNOCKED ME OUT OF THE TOURNAMENT BEFORE I COULD DO ANYTHING...
...
YAOYO-ROZU.
YOUR MATRY-OSHKAS ...
!
HE'S HERE !!
I'M SORRY, I...
YES, YOU SHOULD'VE ACTED SOONER.

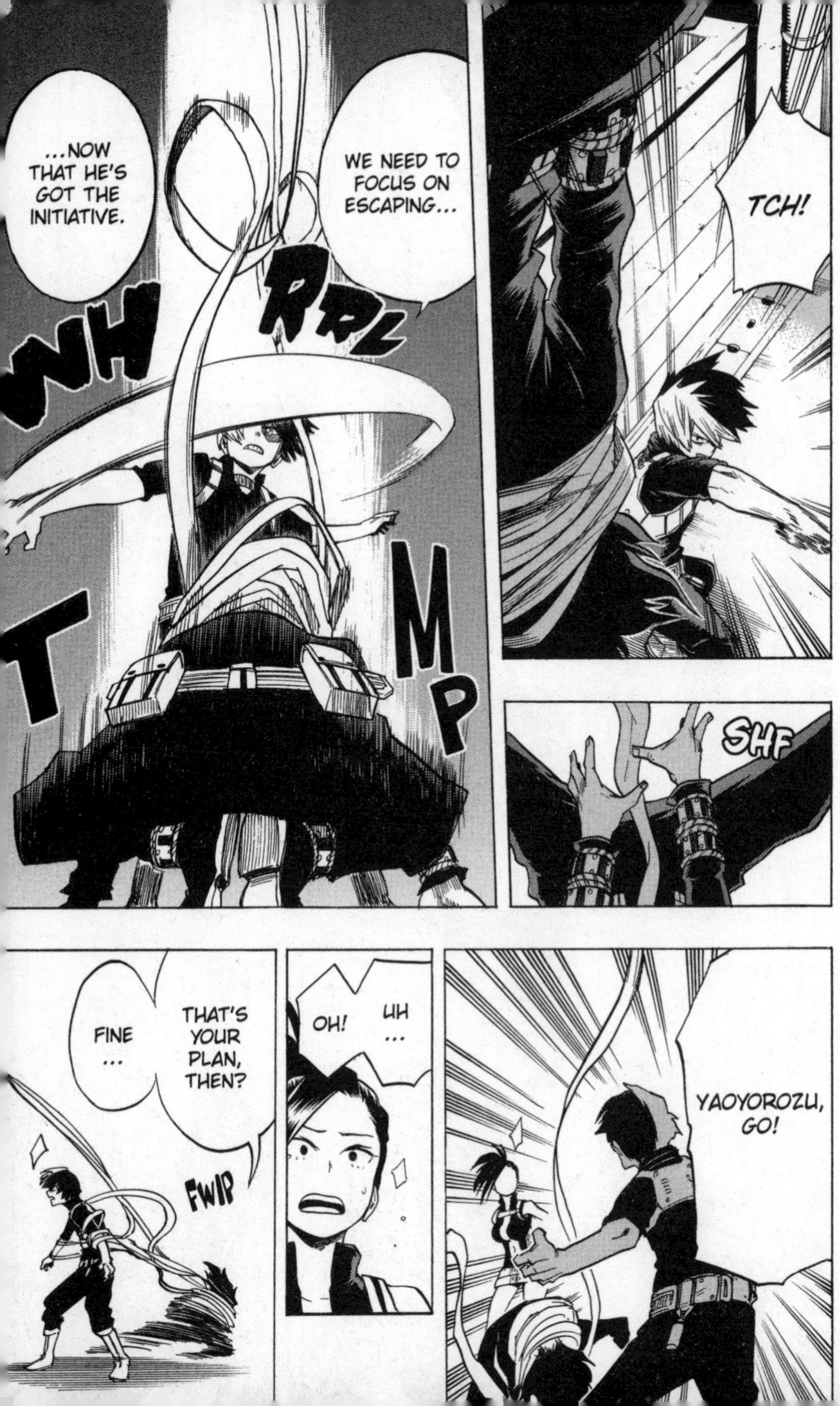
TCH!
SHF
WE NEED TO FOCUS ON ESCAPING...
...NOW THAT HE'S GOT THE INITIATIVE.
WH RRL
T MP
YAOYOROZU, GO!
UH ...
OH!
THAT'S YOUR PLAN, THEN?
FINE ...
FWIP

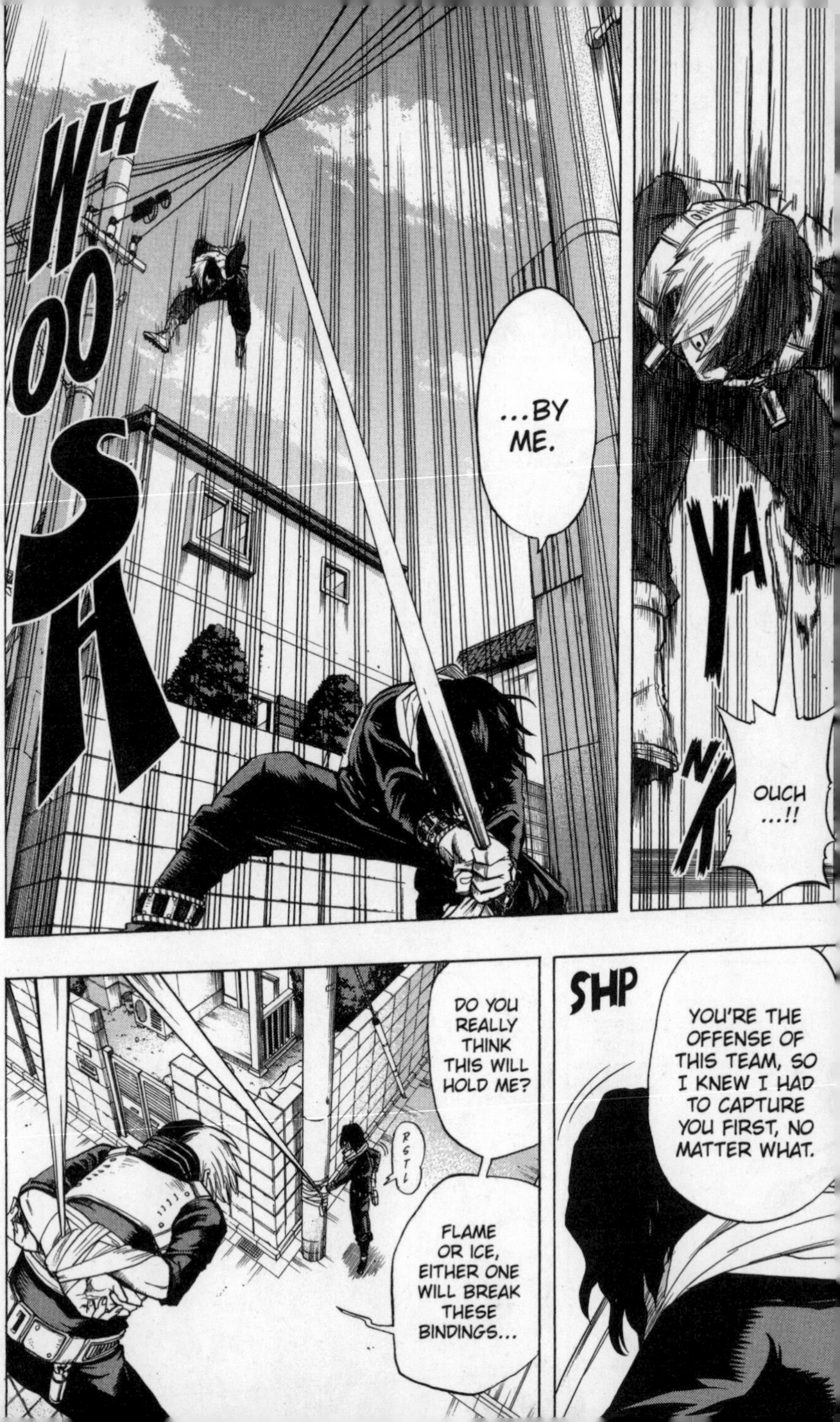

YANK
OUCH ...!!
WHOOSH
...BY ME.
SHP
YOU'RE THE OFFENSE OF THIS TEAM, SO I KNEW I HAD TO CAPTURE YOU FIRST, NO MATTER WHAT.
DO YOU REALLY THINK THIS WILL HOLD ME?
RSTL
FLAME OR ICE, EITHER ONE WILL BREAK THESE BINDINGS...

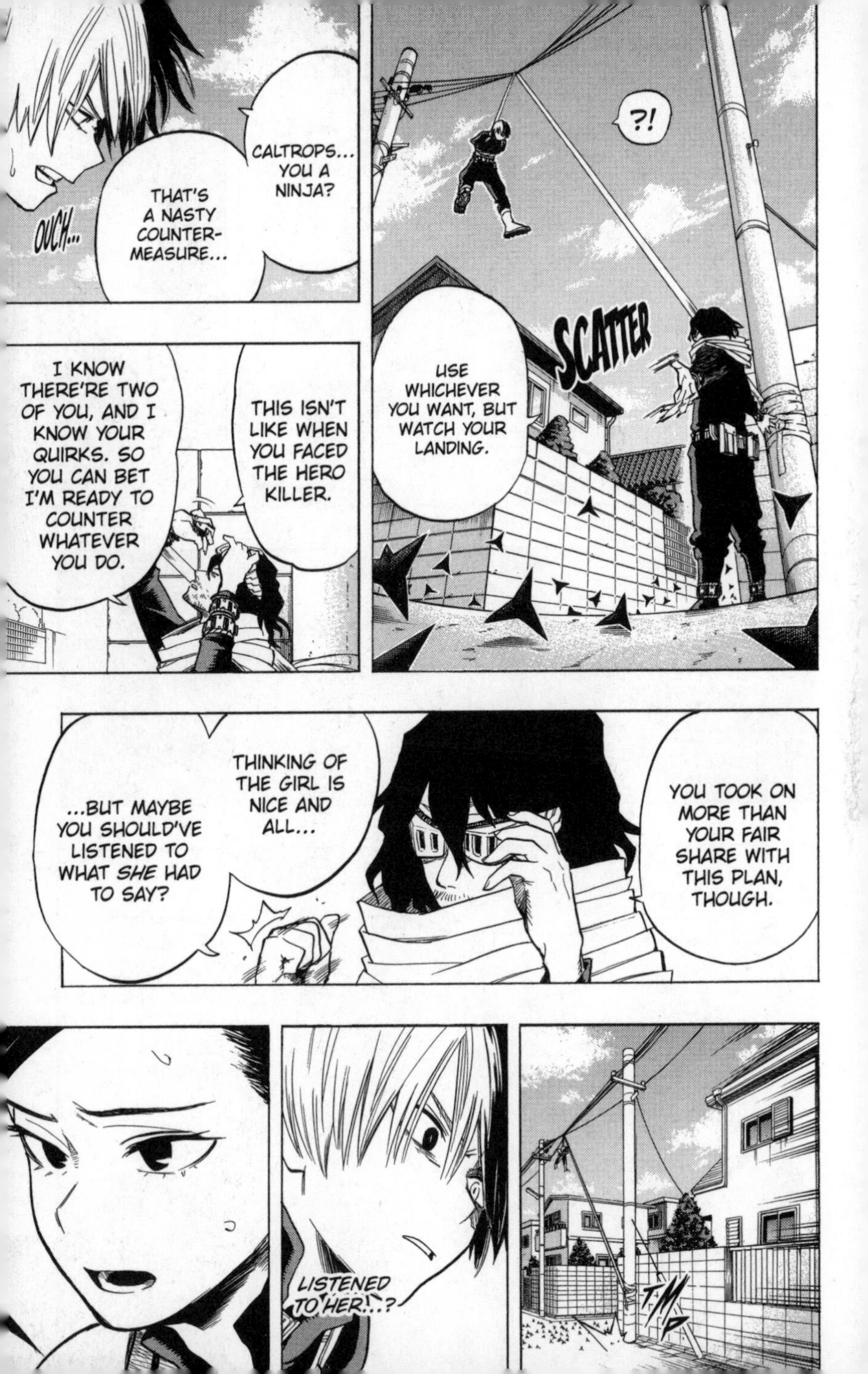
?!
SCATTER
USE WHICHEVER YOU WANT, BUT WATCH YOUR LANDING.
CALTROPS... YOU A NINJA?
THAT'S A NASTY COUNTER-MEASURE...
OUCH...
THIS ISN'T LIKE WHEN YOU FACED THE HERO KILLER.
I KNOW THERE'RE TWO OF YOU, AND I KNOW YOUR QUIRKS. SO YOU CAN BET I'M READY TO COUNTER WHATEVER YOU DO.
YOU TOOK ON MORE THAN YOUR FAIR SHARE WITH THIS PLAN, THOUGH.
THINKING OF THE GIRL IS NICE AND ALL...
...BUT MAYBE YOU SHOULD'VE LISTENED TO WHAT *SHE* HAD TO SAY?
TMP
LISTENED TO HER...?

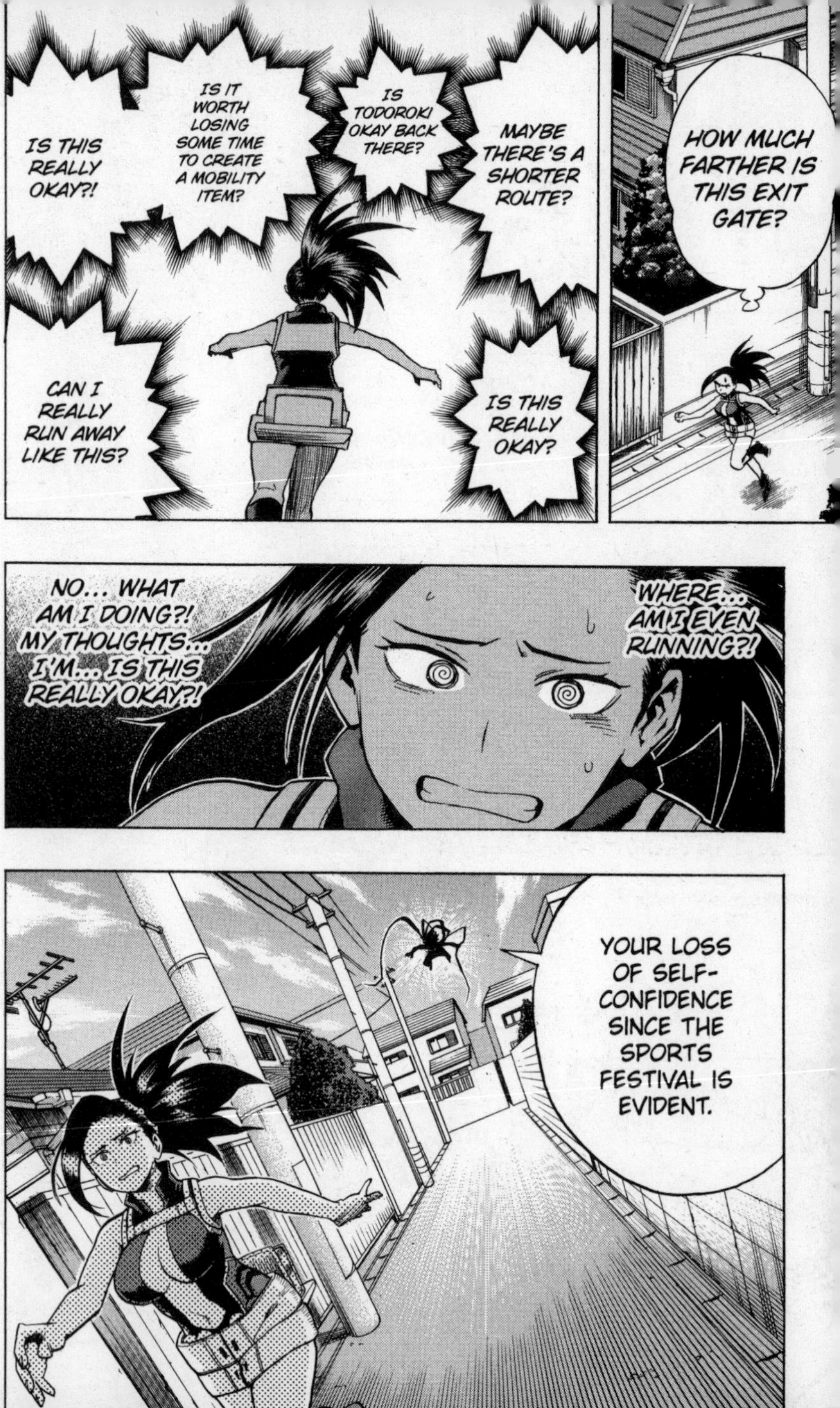
HOW MUCH FARTHER IS THIS EXIT GATE?
MAYBE THERE'S A SHORTER ROUTE?
IS TODOROKI OKAY BACK THERE?
IS IT WORTH LOSING SOME TIME TO CREATE A MOBILITY ITEM?
IS THIS REALLY OKAY?!
IS THIS REALLY OKAY?
CAN I REALLY RUN AWAY LIKE THIS?
WHERE... AM I EVEN RUNNING?!
NO... WHAT AM I DOING?! MY THOUGHTS... I'M... IS THIS REALLY OKAY?!
YOUR LOSS OF SELF-CONFIDENCE SINCE THE SPORTS FESTIVAL IS EVIDENT.

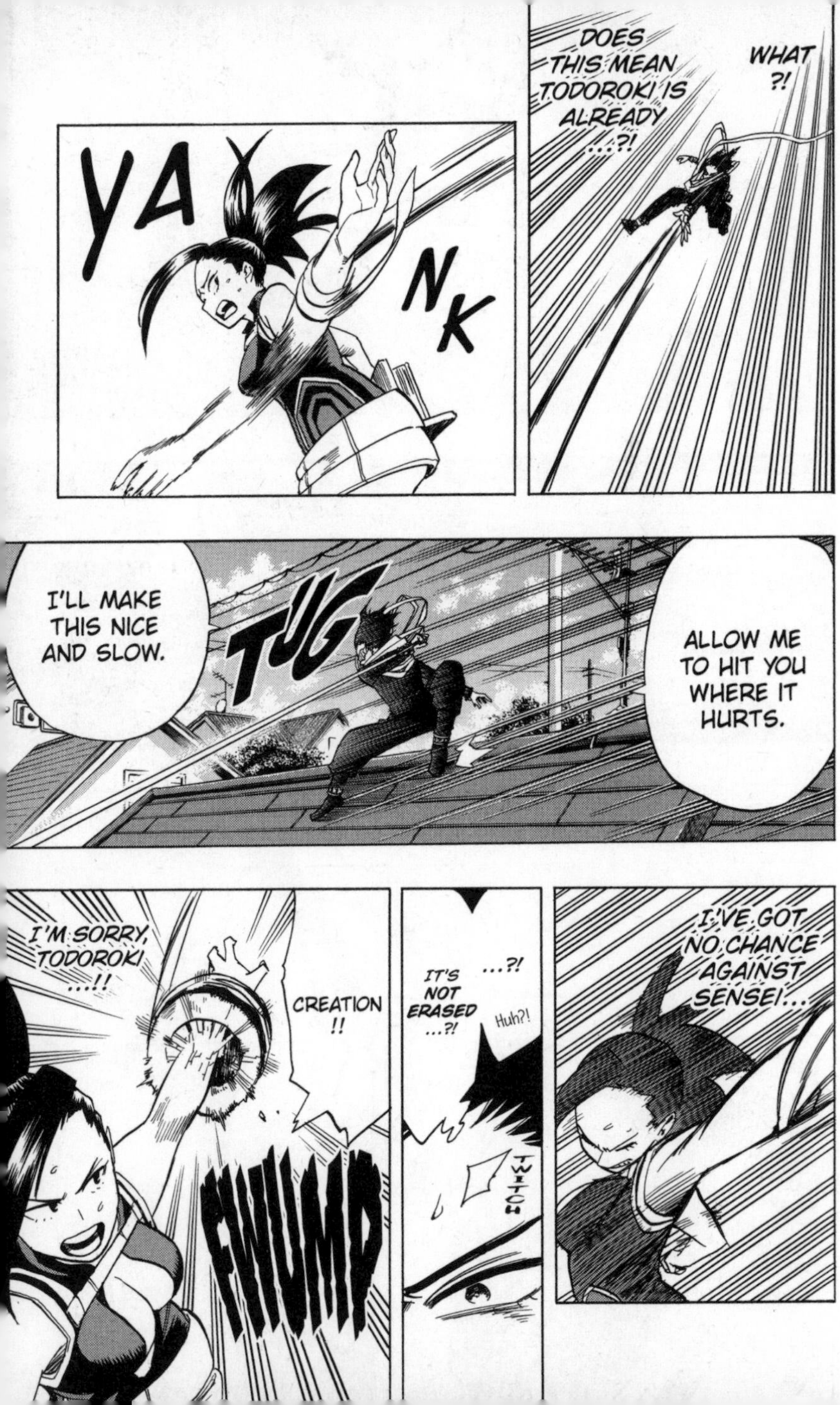
WHAT ?!
DOES THIS MEAN TODOROKI IS ALREADY ...?!
YANK
ALLOW ME TO HIT YOU WHERE IT HURTS.
TUG
I'LL MAKE THIS NICE AND SLOW.
I'VE GOT NO CHANCE AGAINST SENSEI...
...?!
Huh?!
IT'S NOT ERASED ...?!
TWITCH
I'M SORRY, TODOROKI ...!!
CREATION !!
FWUMP

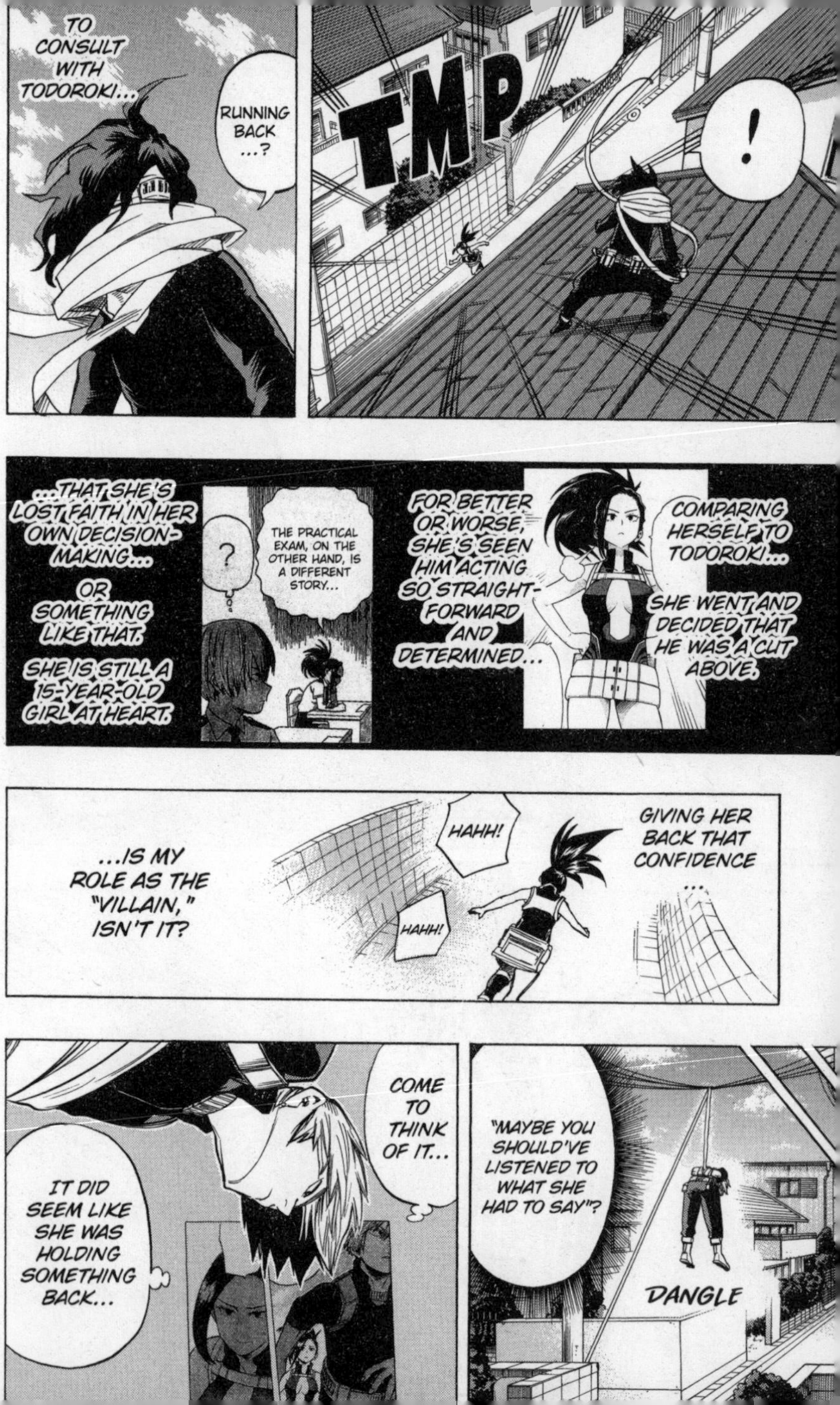
TMP
!
RUNNING BACK ...?
TO CONSULT WITH TODOROKI...
COMPARING HERSELF TO TODOROKI...
SHE WENT AND DECIDED THAT HE WAS A CUT ABOVE.
FOR BETTER OR WORSE, SHE'S SEEN HIM ACTING SO STRAIGHT-FORWARD AND DETERMINED...
THE PRACTICAL EXAM, ON THE OTHER HAND, IS A DIFFERENT STORY...
?
...THAT SHE'S LOST FAITH IN HER OWN DECISION-MAKING...
OR SOMETHING LIKE THAT.
SHE IS STILL A 15-YEAR-OLD GIRL AT HEART.
GIVING HER BACK THAT CONFIDENCE ...
HAHH!
HAHH!
...IS MY ROLE AS THE "VILLAIN," ISN'T IT?
"MAYBE YOU SHOULD'VE LISTENED TO WHAT SHE HAD TO SAY"?
DANGLE
COME TO THINK OF IT...
IT DID SEEM LIKE SHE WAS HOLDING SOMETHING BACK...

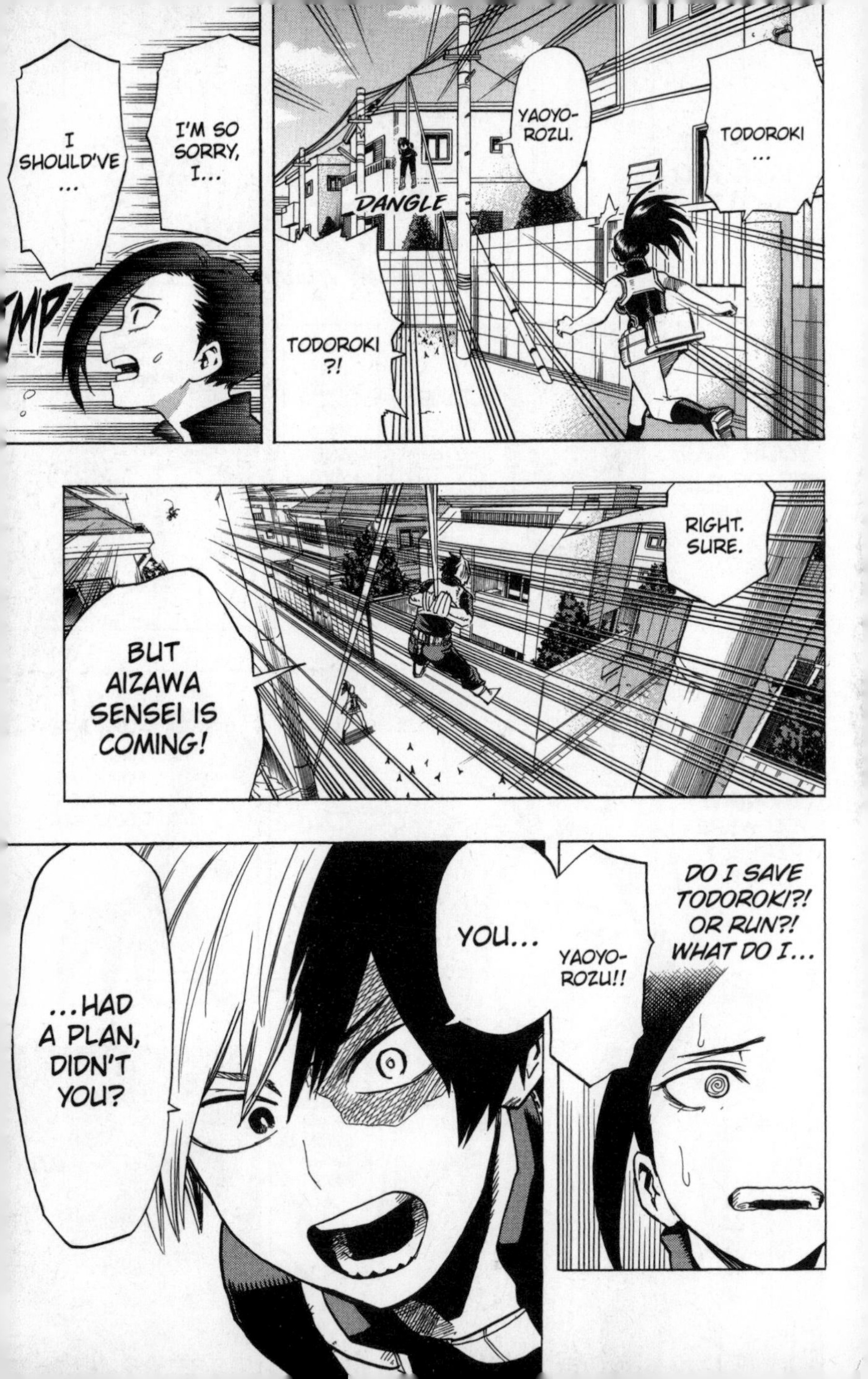
TODOROKI ...
YAOYO-ROZU.
DANGLE
TODOROKI ?!
I'M SO SORRY, I...
I SHOULD'VE ...
RIGHT. SURE.
BUT AIZAWA SENSEI IS COMING!
DO I SAVE TODOROKI?! OR RUN?! WHAT DO I...
YAOYO-ROZU!!
YOU...
...HAD A PLAN, DIDN'T YOU?

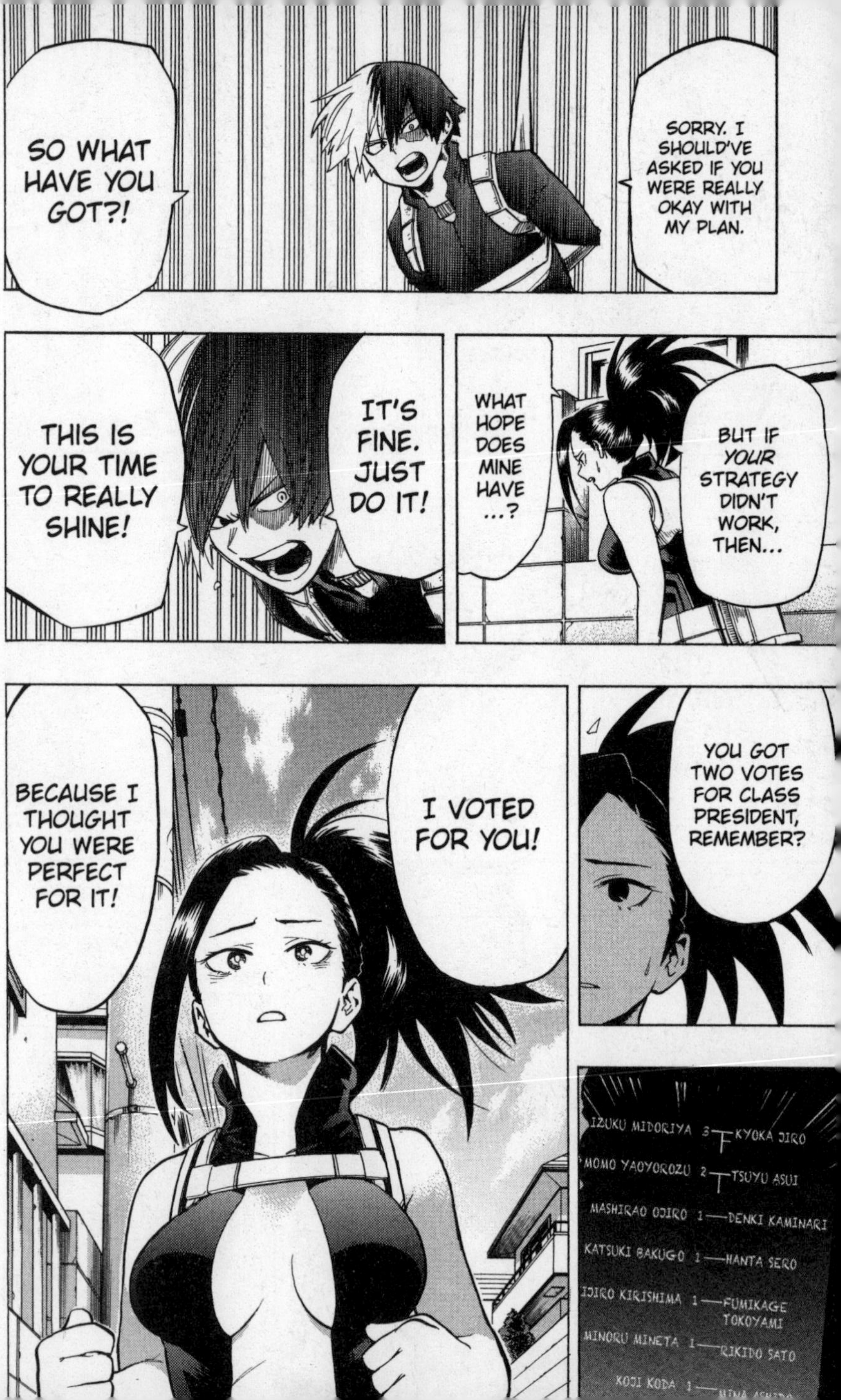
SORRY. I SHOULD'VE ASKED IF YOU WERE REALLY OKAY WITH MY PLAN.
SO WHAT HAVE YOU GOT?!
BUT IF *YOUR* STRATEGY DIDN'T WORK, THEN...
WHAT HOPE DOES MINE HAVE ...?
IT'S FINE. JUST DO IT!
THIS IS YOUR TIME TO REALLY SHINE!
YOU GOT TWO VOTES FOR CLASS PRESIDENT, REMEMBER?
IZUKU MIDORIYA 3 KYOKA JIRO
MOMO YAOYOROZU 2 TSUYU ASUI
MASHIRAO OJIRO 1—DENKI KAMINARI
KATSUKI BAKUGO 1—HANTA SERO
IJIRO KIRISHIMA 1—FUMIKAGE TOKOYAMI
MINORU MINETA 1—RIKIDO SATO
KOJI KODA 1
I VOTED FOR YOU!
BECAUSE I THOUGHT YOU WERE PERFECT FOR IT!

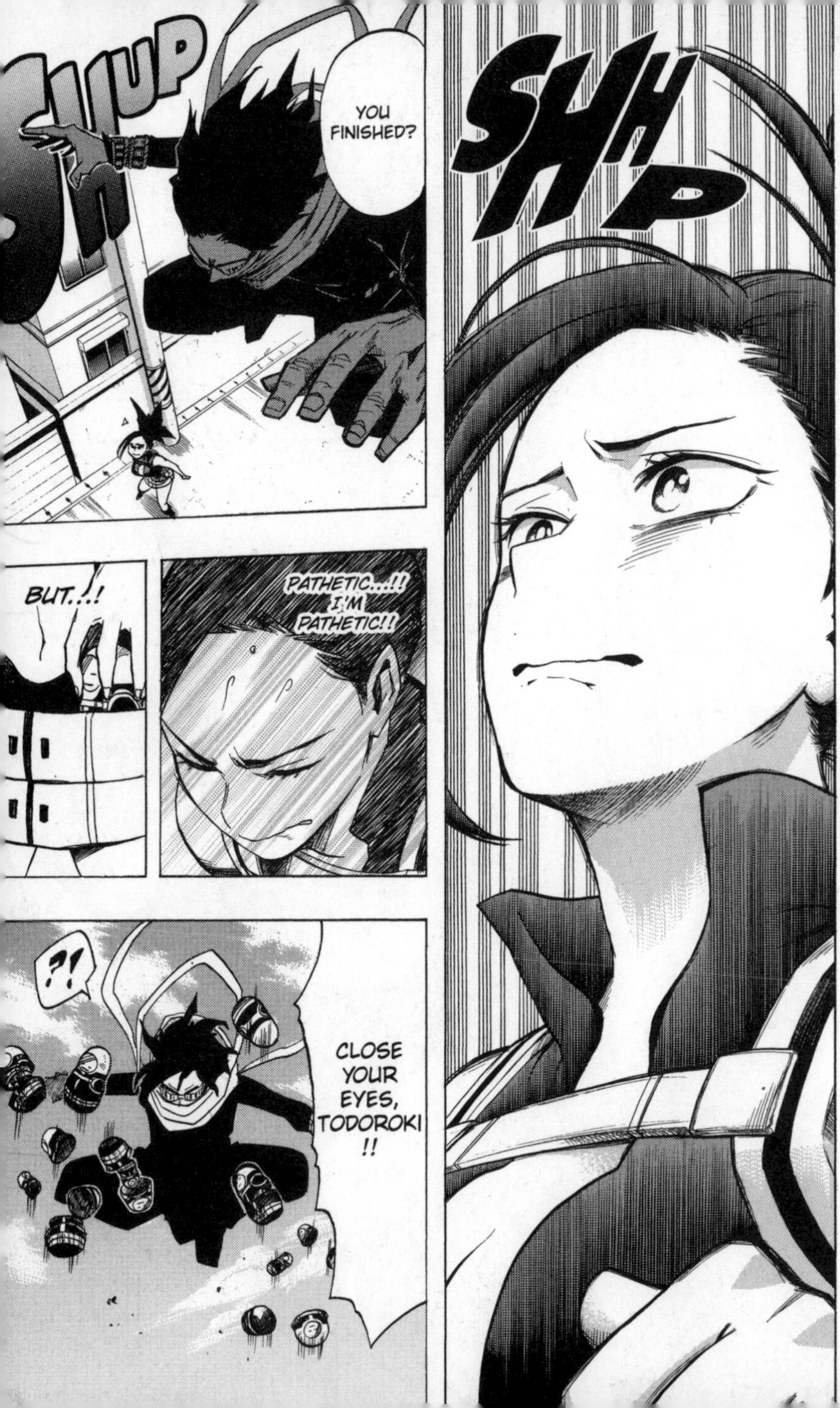
SHHP
YOU FINISHED?
SHUP
PATHETIC...!!
I'M PATHETIC!!
BUT...!
CLOSE YOUR EYES, TODOROKI!!
?!

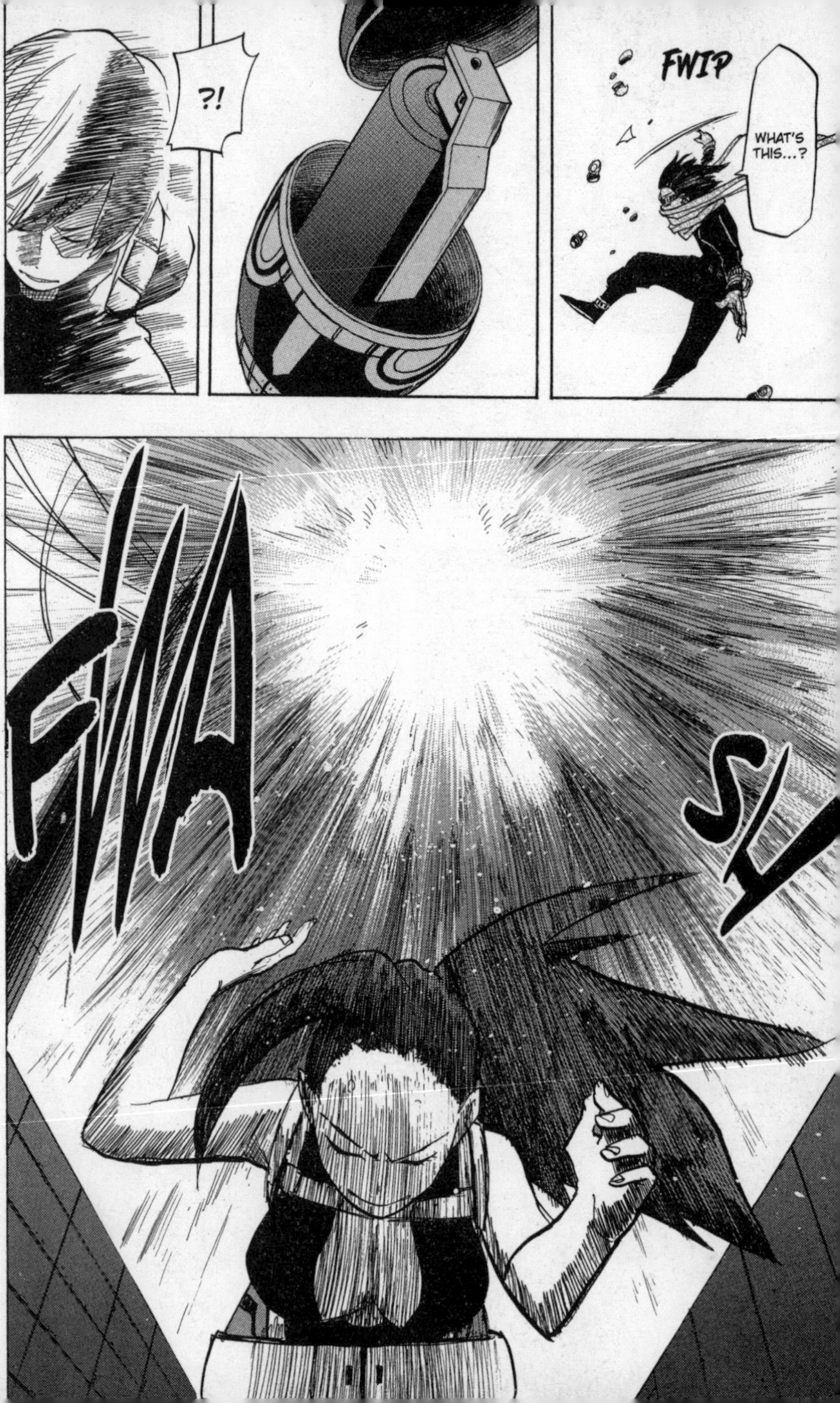
FWIP
WHAT'S THIS...?
?!
FWA

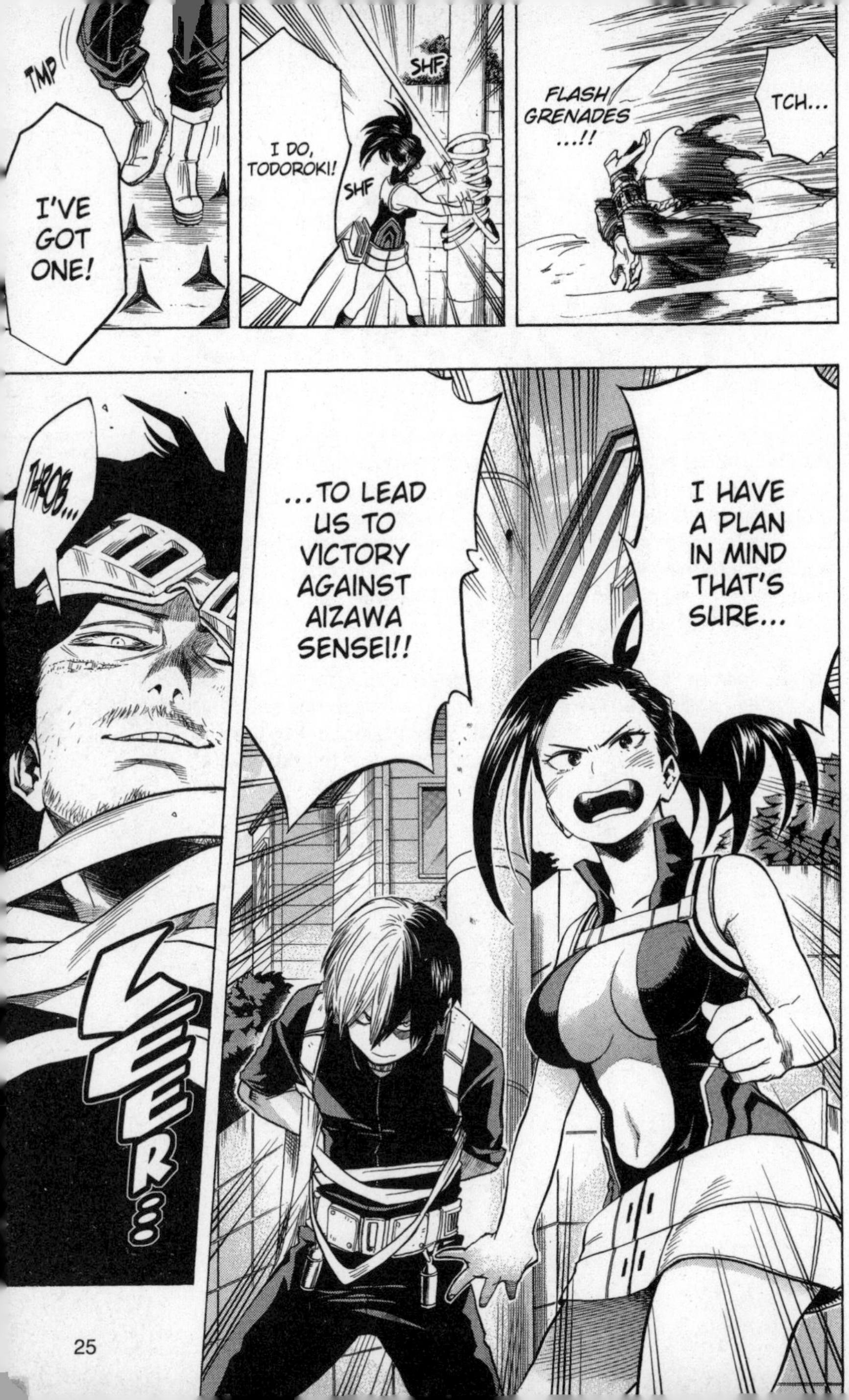
TCH...
FLASH GRENADES ...!!
SHF
I DO, TODOROKI!
SHF
TMP
I'VE GOT ONE!
I HAVE A PLAN IN MIND THAT'S SURE...
...TO LEAD US TO VICTORY AGAINST AIZAWA SENSEI!!
THROB...
LEER...

MYSTERY OF THE YAOYOSHKAS

When creating complex objects, there are a number of things Yaoyorozu needs to keep in mind. There are the necessary parts, the optimal materials, method of assembly, and if necessary, an outer coat of paint. She has to understand the object on an intimate level before creating it, but luckily for her, she grew up in a wealthy household that provided her with plenty of resources to learn from. The environment was a perfect one to help cultivate her knowledge.

Matryoshka dolls were Yaoyorozu's go-to item for practicing her Quirk as a child. She remembers them being the first things she learned to produce accurately and on the spot. She practiced with them so much that, nowadays, she can pop them out one after the other without even thinking about it.

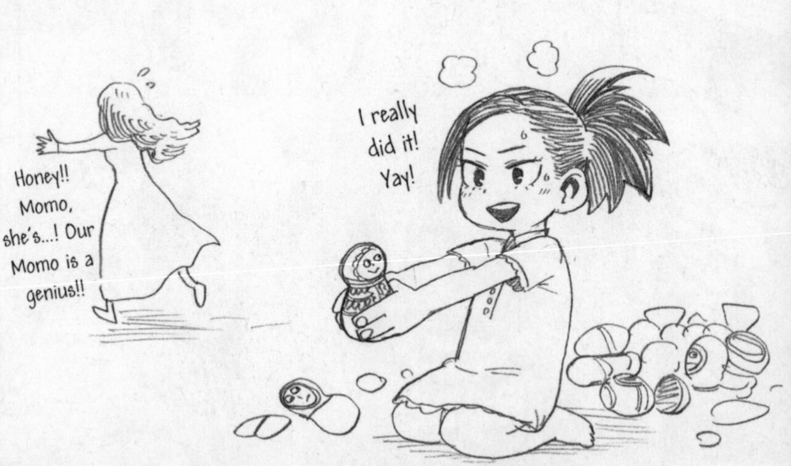
I really did it! Yay!
Honey!! Momo, she's...! Our Momo is a genius!!

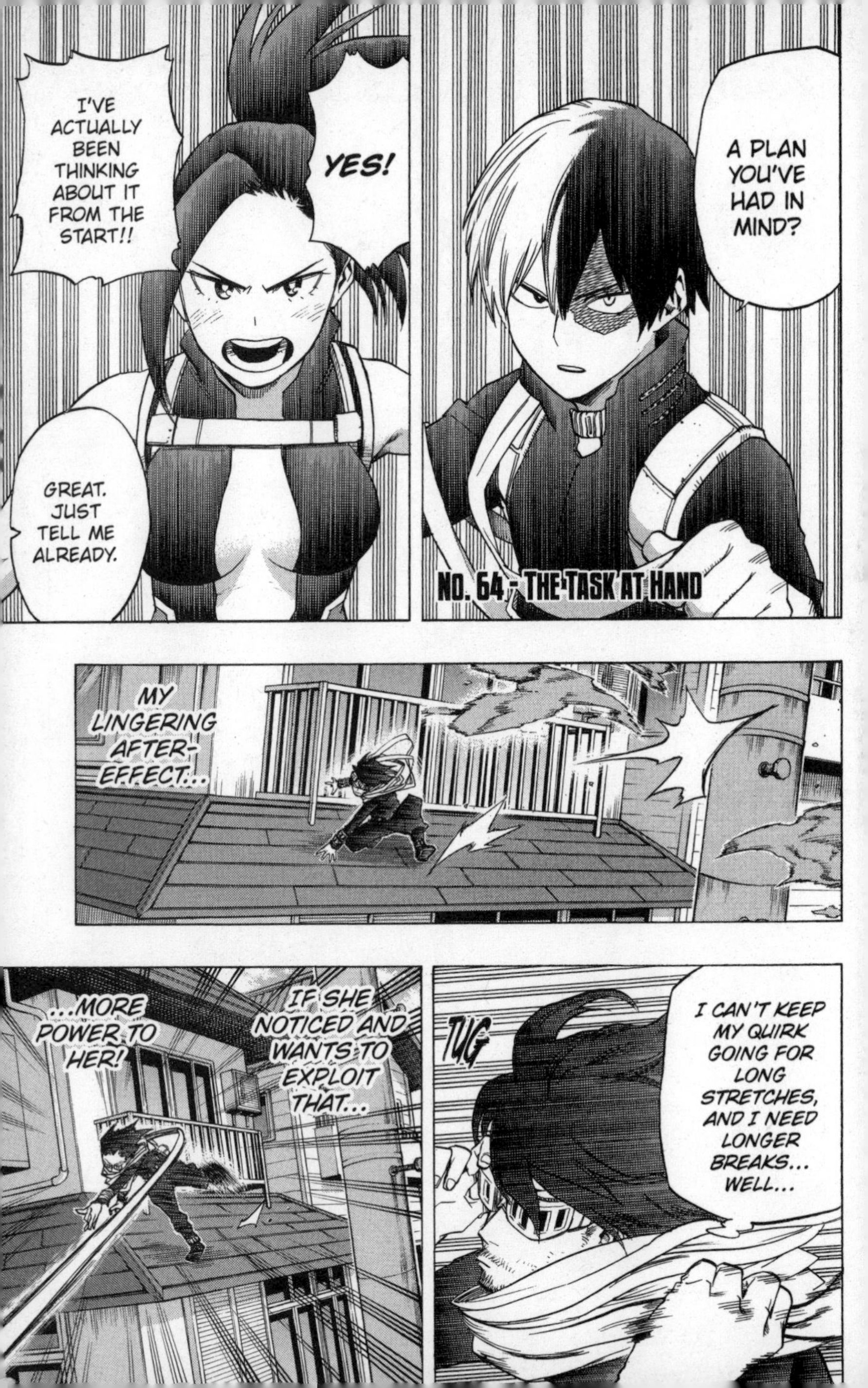
A PLAN YOU'VE HAD IN MIND?
NO. 64 - THE TASK AT HAND
YES!
I'VE ACTUALLY BEEN THINKING ABOUT IT FROM THE START!!
GREAT. JUST TELL ME ALREADY.
MY LINGERING AFTER-EFFECT...
TUG
I CAN'T KEEP MY QUIRK GOING FOR LONG STRETCHES, AND I NEED LONGER BREAKS... WELL...
IF SHE NOTICED AND WANTS TO EXPLOIT THAT...
...MORE POWER TO HER!

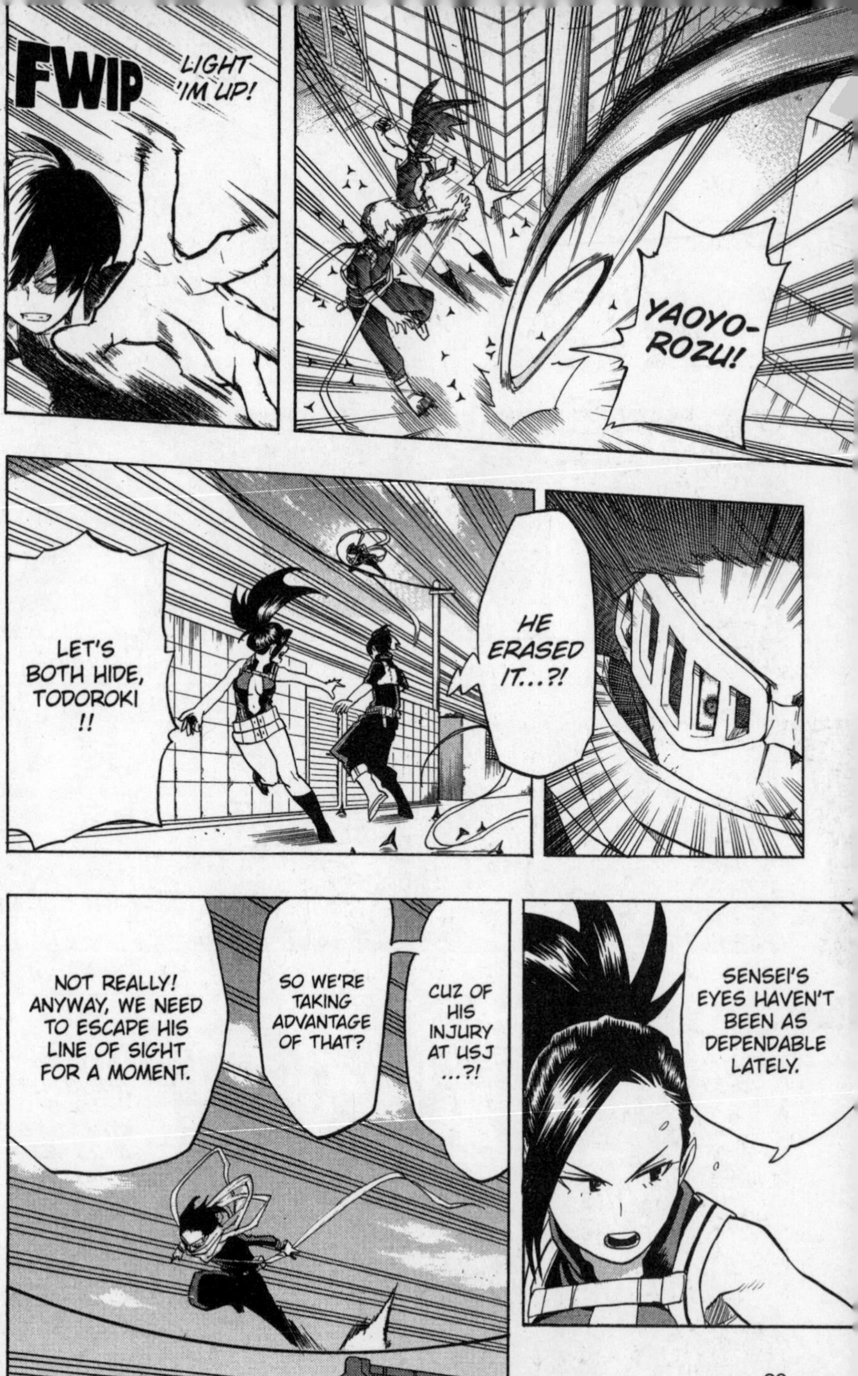
YAOYO-ROZU!
FWIP
LIGHT 'IM UP!
HE ERASED IT...?!
LET'S BOTH HIDE, TODOROKI !!
SENSEI'S EYES HAVEN'T BEEN AS DEPENDABLE LATELY.
CUZ OF HIS INJURY AT USJ ...?!
SO WE'RE TAKING ADVANTAGE OF THAT?
NOT REALLY! ANYWAY, WE NEED TO ESCAPE HIS LINE OF SIGHT FOR A MOMENT.

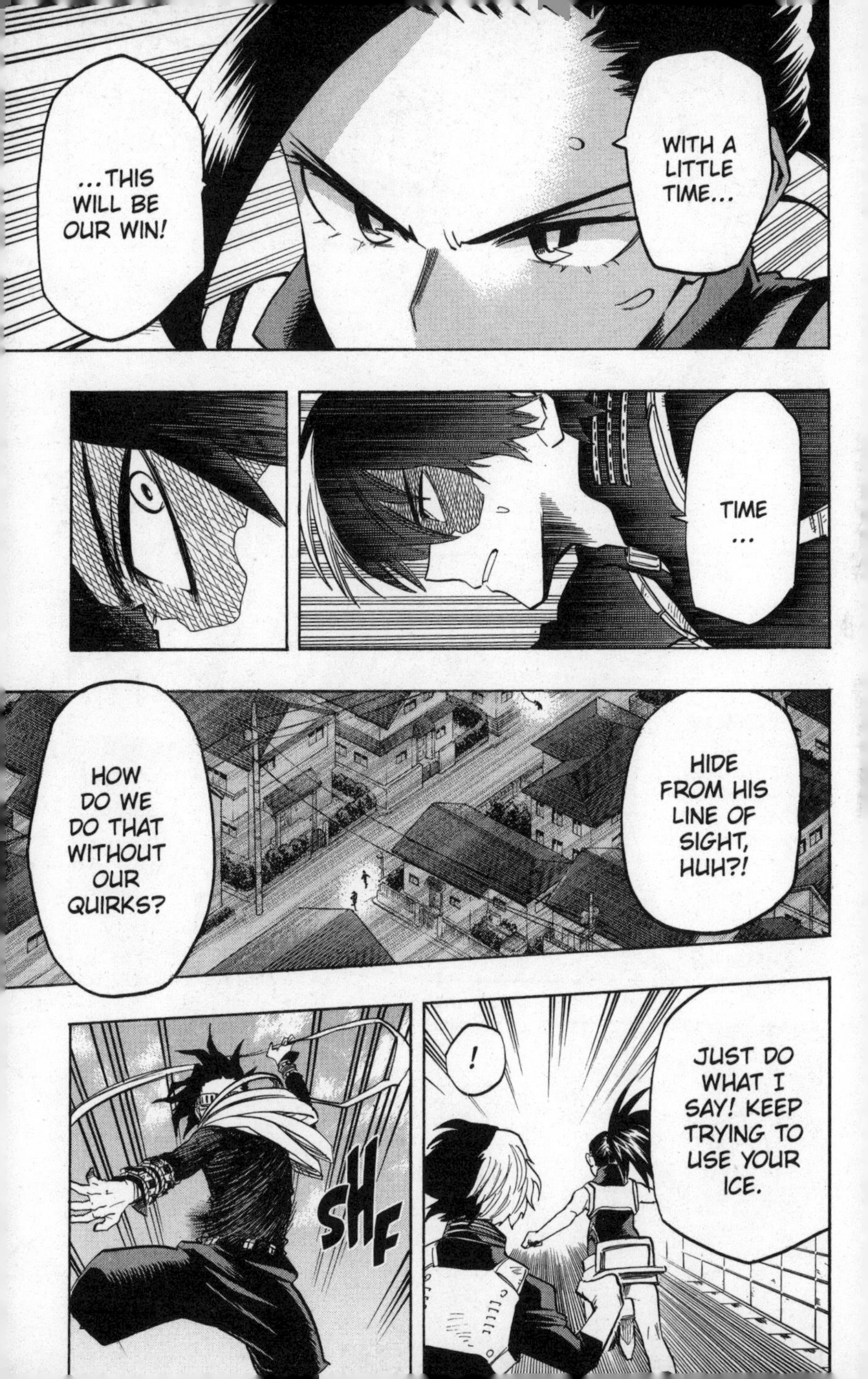
WITH A LITTLE TIME...
...THIS WILL BE OUR WIN!
TIME ...
HIDE FROM HIS LINE OF SIGHT, HUH?!
HOW DO WE DO THAT WITHOUT OUR QUIRKS?
JUST DO WHAT I SAY! KEEP TRYING TO USE YOUR ICE.
!
SHF

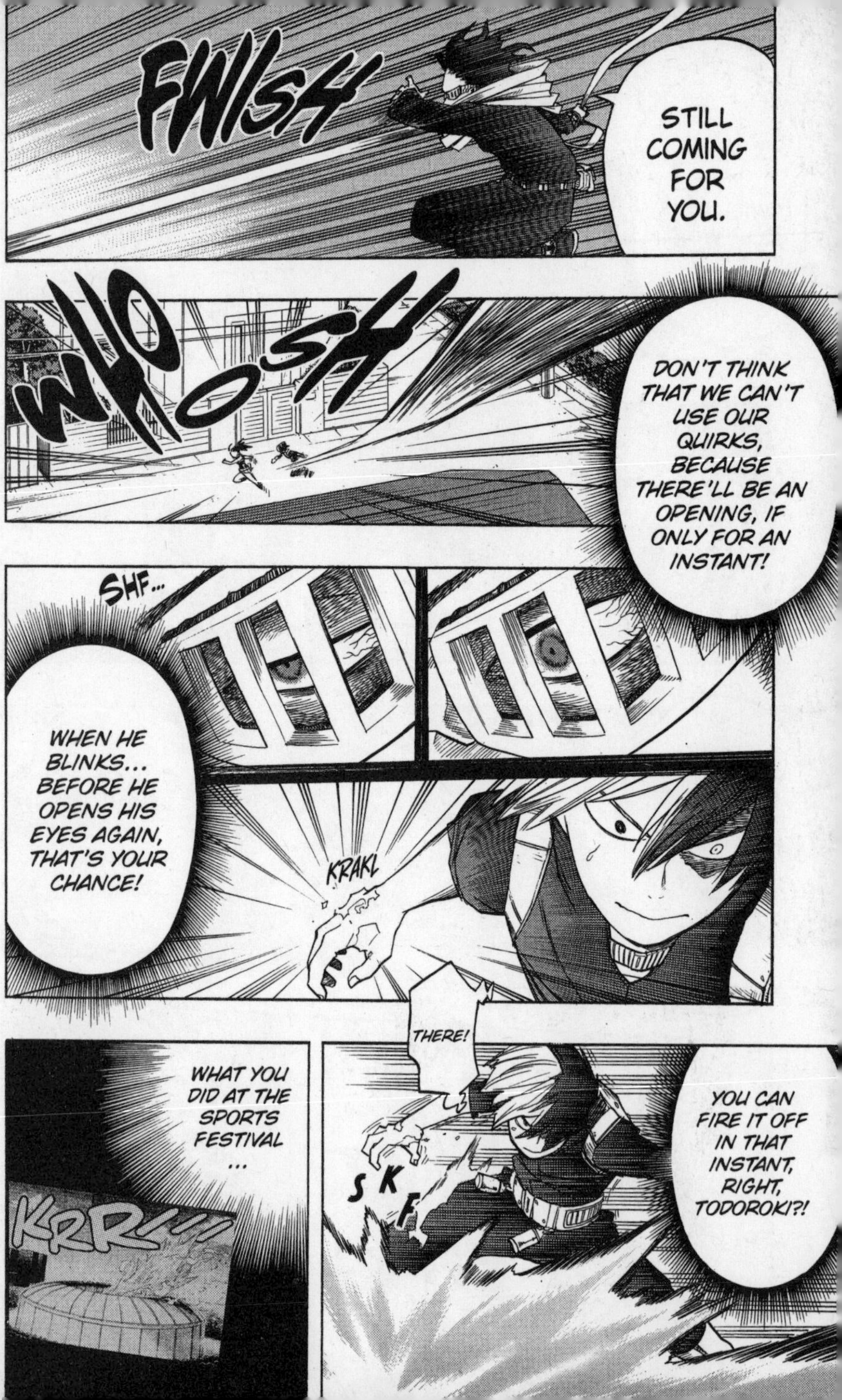
STILL COMING FOR YOU.
FWISH
DON'T THINK THAT WE CAN'T USE OUR QUIRKS, BECAUSE THERE'LL BE AN OPENING, IF ONLY FOR AN INSTANT!
WHOOSH
SHF...
WHEN HE BLINKS... BEFORE HE OPENS HIS EYES AGAIN, THAT'S YOUR CHANCE!
KRAKL
THERE!
YOU CAN FIRE IT OFF IN THAT INSTANT, RIGHT, TODOROKI?!
SKF
WHAT YOU DID AT THE SPORTS FESTIVAL ...
KRR

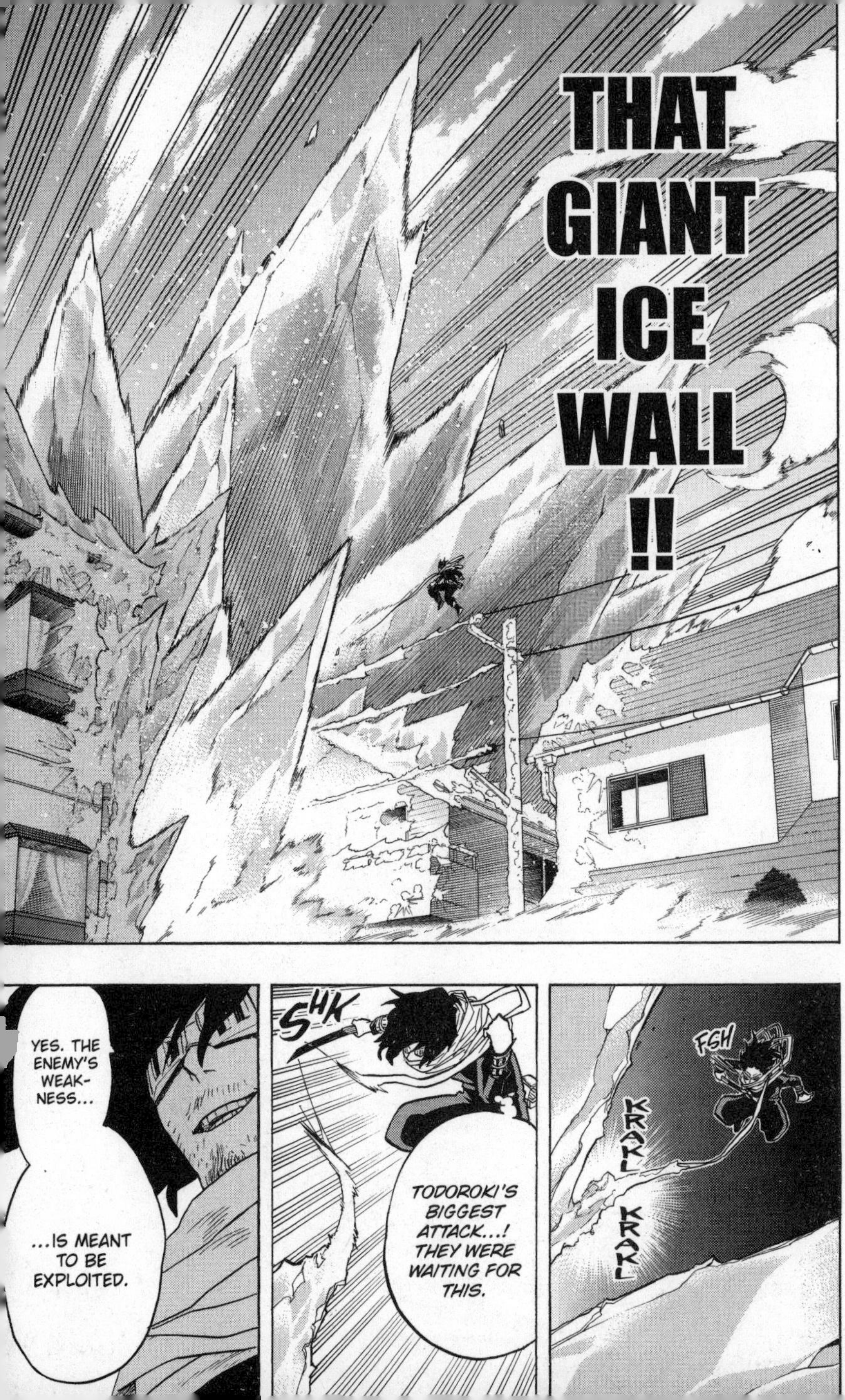
THAT GIANT ICE WALL !!
FSH
KRAKL
KRAKL
SHK
TODOROKI'S BIGGEST ATTACK...! THEY WERE WAITING FOR THIS.
YES. THE ENEMY'S WEAK-NESS...
...IS MEANT TO BE EXPLOITED.

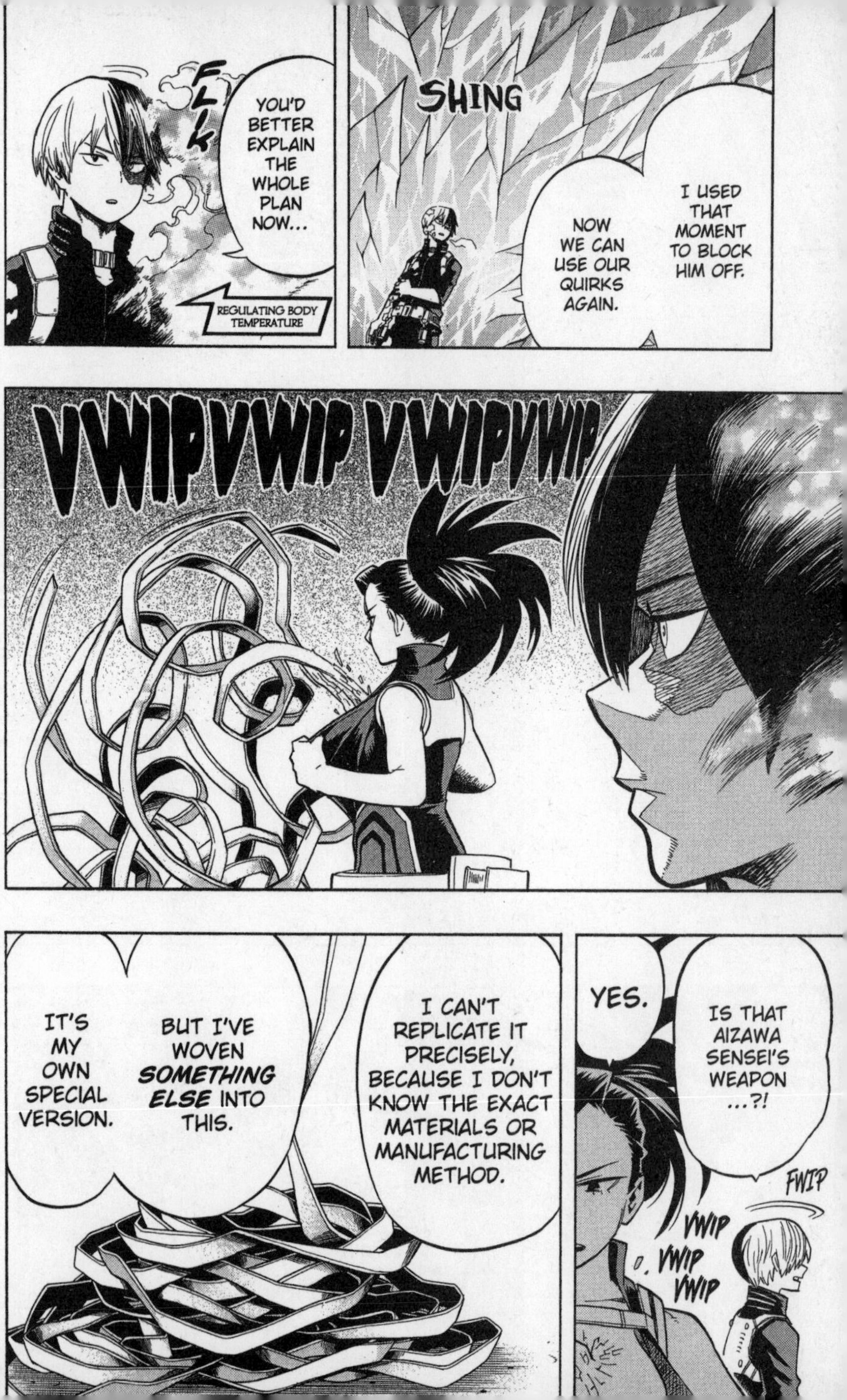
SHING
I USED THAT MOMENT TO BLOCK HIM OFF.
NOW WE CAN USE OUR QUIRKS AGAIN.
FLK
YOU'D BETTER EXPLAIN THE WHOLE PLAN NOW...
REGULATING BODY TEMPERATURE
VWIPVWIP VWIPVWIP
IS THAT AIZAWA SENSEI'S WEAPON ...?!
YES.
FWIP
VWIP VWIP VWIP
I CAN'T REPLICATE IT PRECISELY, BECAUSE I DON'T KNOW THE EXACT MATERIALS OR MANUFACTURING METHOD.
BUT I'VE WOVEN **SOMETHING ELSE** INTO THIS.
IT'S MY OWN SPECIAL VERSION.

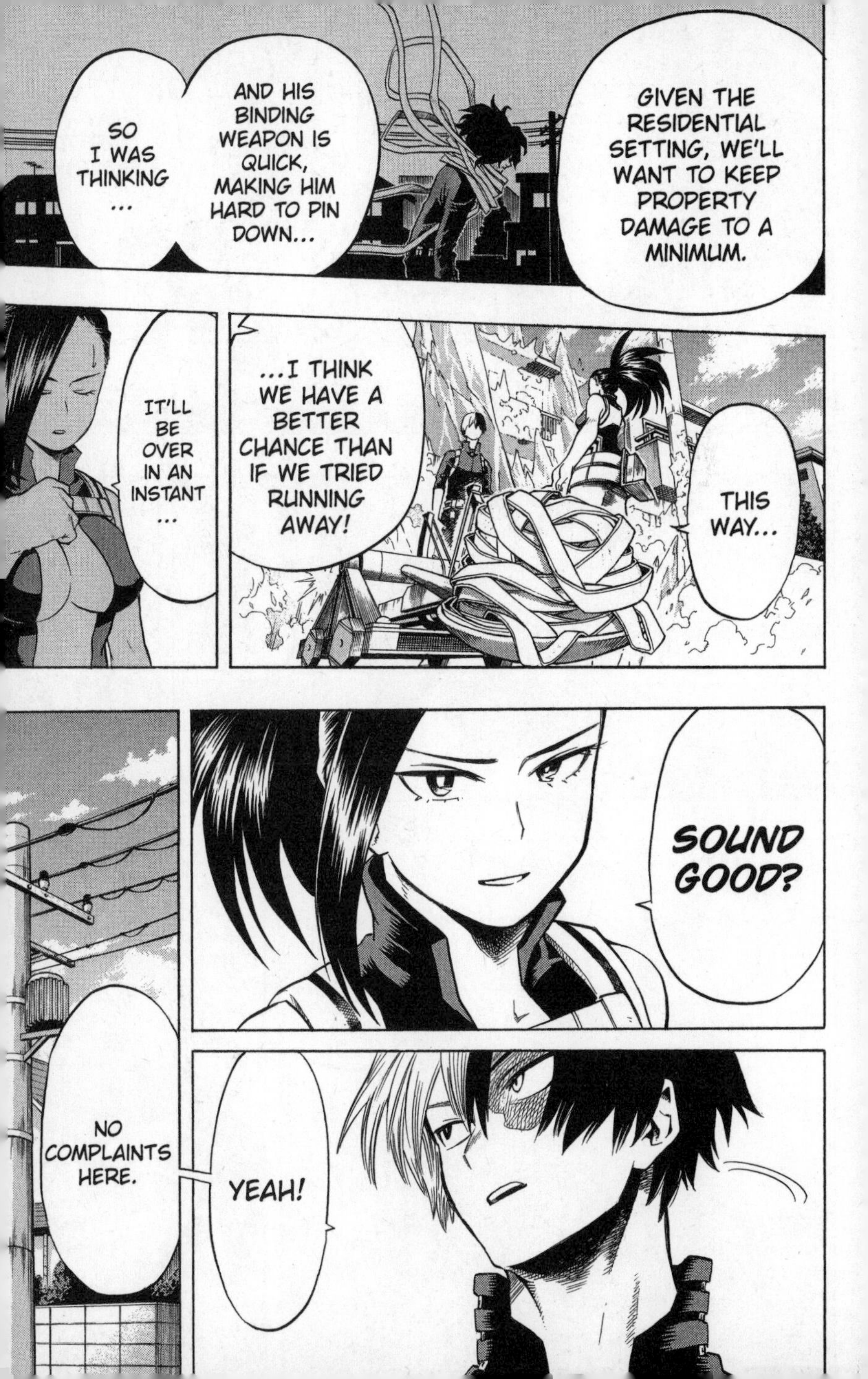
GIVEN THE RESIDENTIAL SETTING, WE'LL WANT TO KEEP PROPERTY DAMAGE TO A MINIMUM.
AND HIS BINDING WEAPON IS QUICK, MAKING HIM HARD TO PIN DOWN...
SO I WAS THINKING ...
THIS WAY...
...I THINK WE HAVE A BETTER CHANCE THAN IF WE TRIED RUNNING AWAY!
IT'LL BE OVER IN AN INSTANT ...
SOUND GOOD?
YEAH!
NO COMPLAINTS HERE.

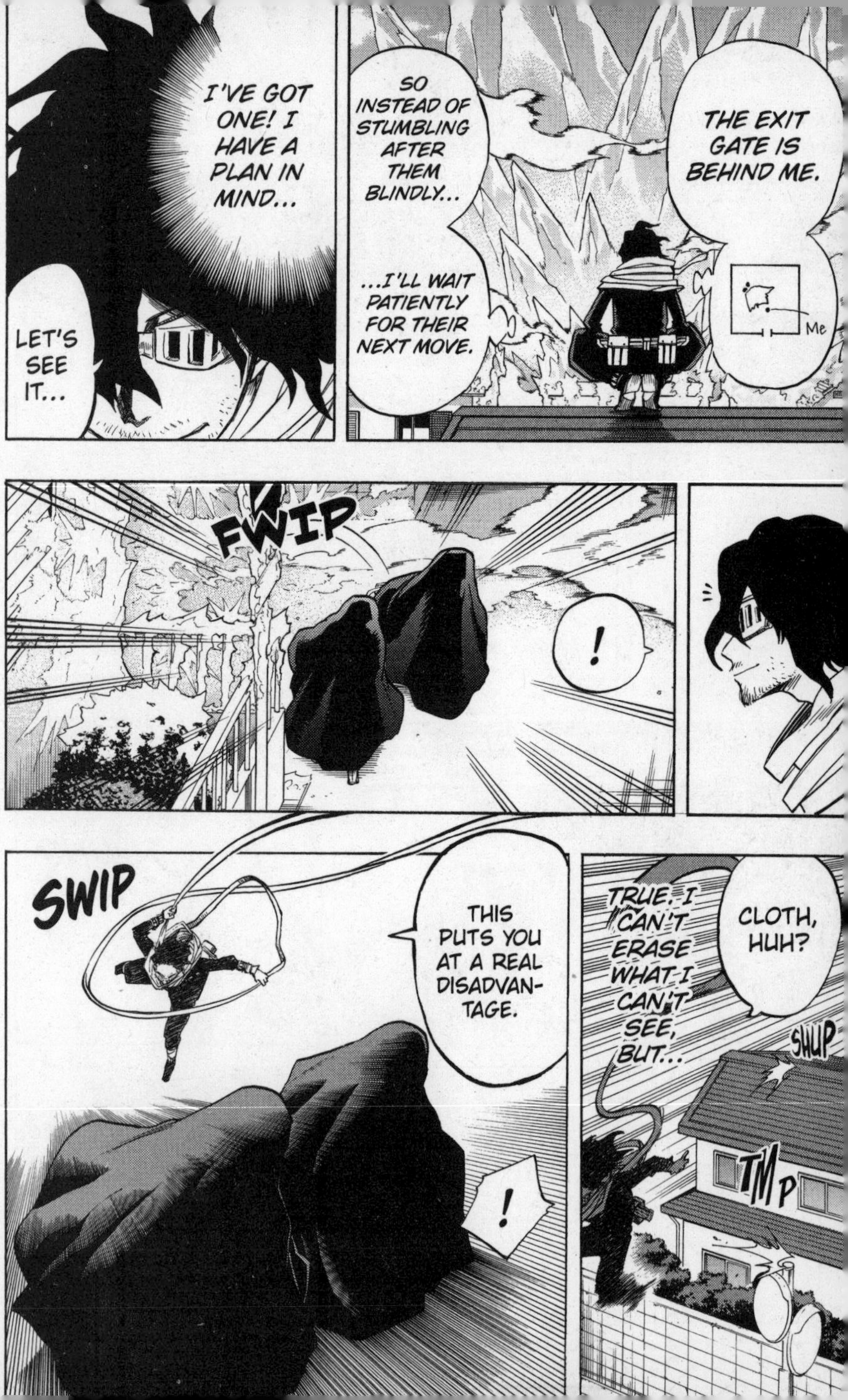
THE EXIT GATE IS BEHIND ME.
Me
SO INSTEAD OF STUMBLING AFTER THEM BLINDLY...
...I'LL WAIT PATIENTLY FOR THEIR NEXT MOVE.
I'VE GOT ONE! I HAVE A PLAN IN MIND...
LET'S SEE IT...
FWIP
!
CLOTH, HUH?
TRUE. I CAN'T ERASE WHAT I CAN'T SEE, BUT...
SHUP
TMP
THIS PUTS YOU AT A REAL DISADVANTAGE.
SWIP
!

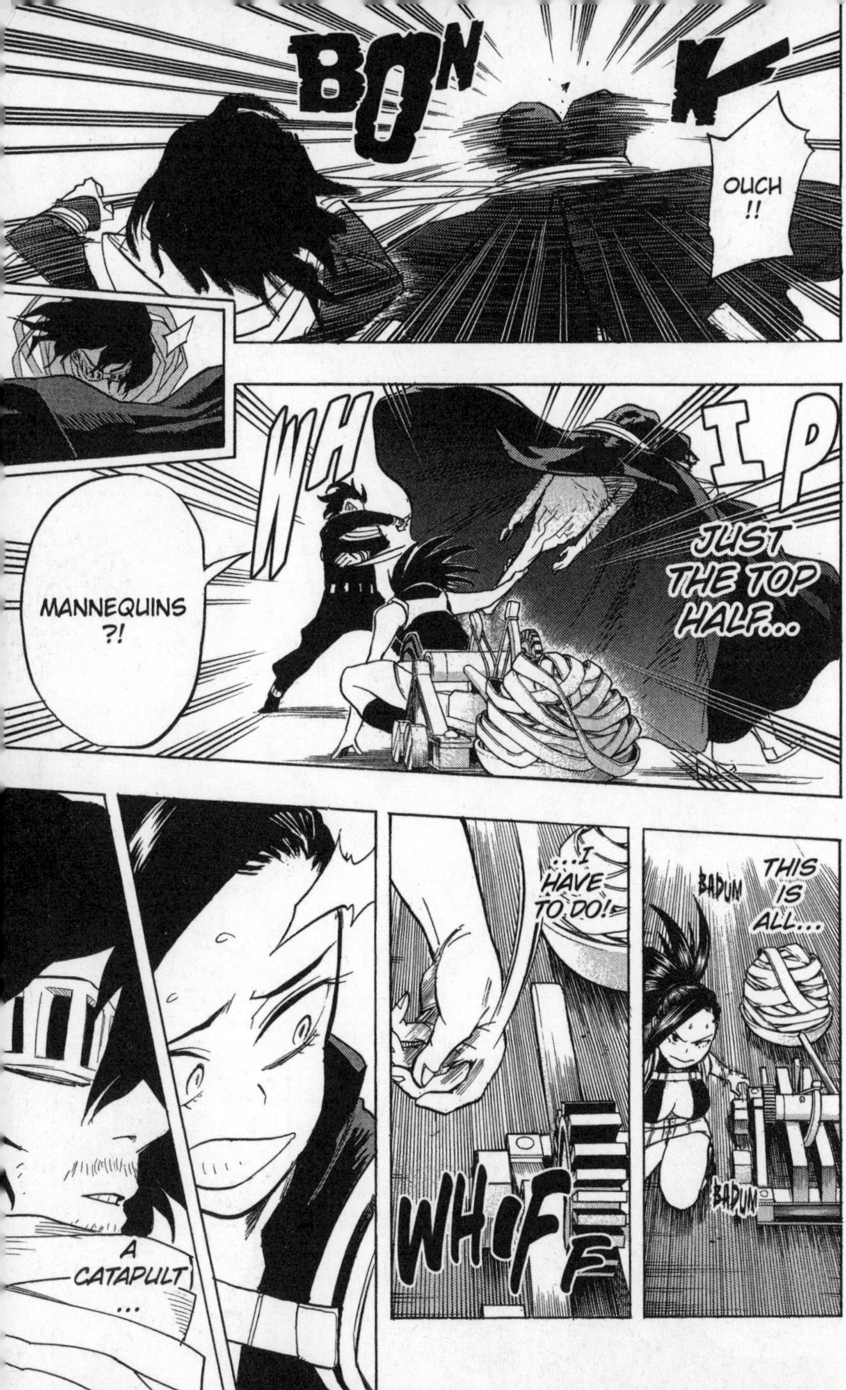

BONK
OUCH !!
WHIP
JUST THE TOP HALF...
MANNEQUINS ?!
THIS IS ALL...
BADUM
BADUM
...I HAVE TO DO!
WHIFF
A CATAPULT ...

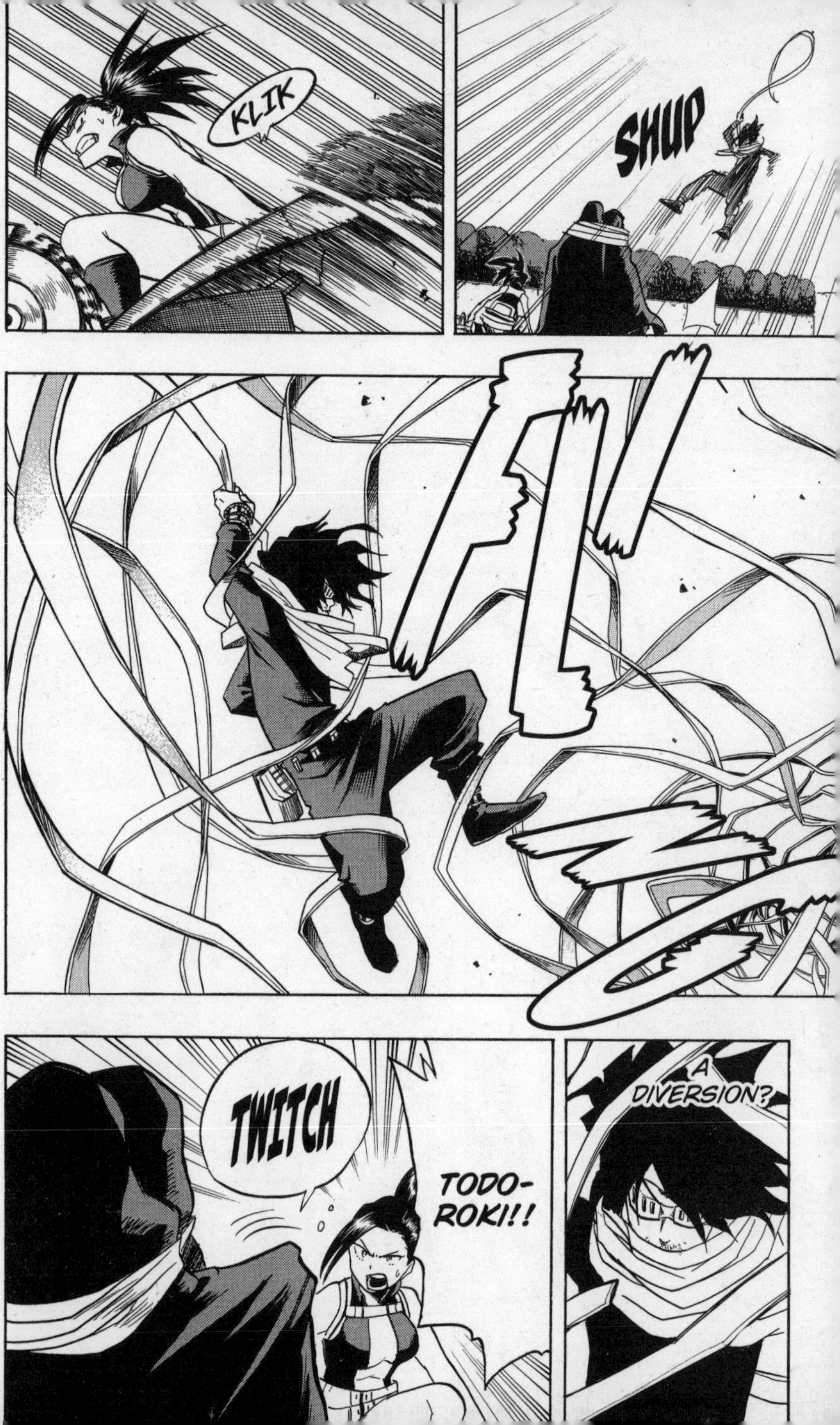
SHUP
KLIK
A DIVERSION?
TWITCH
TODO-ROKI!!

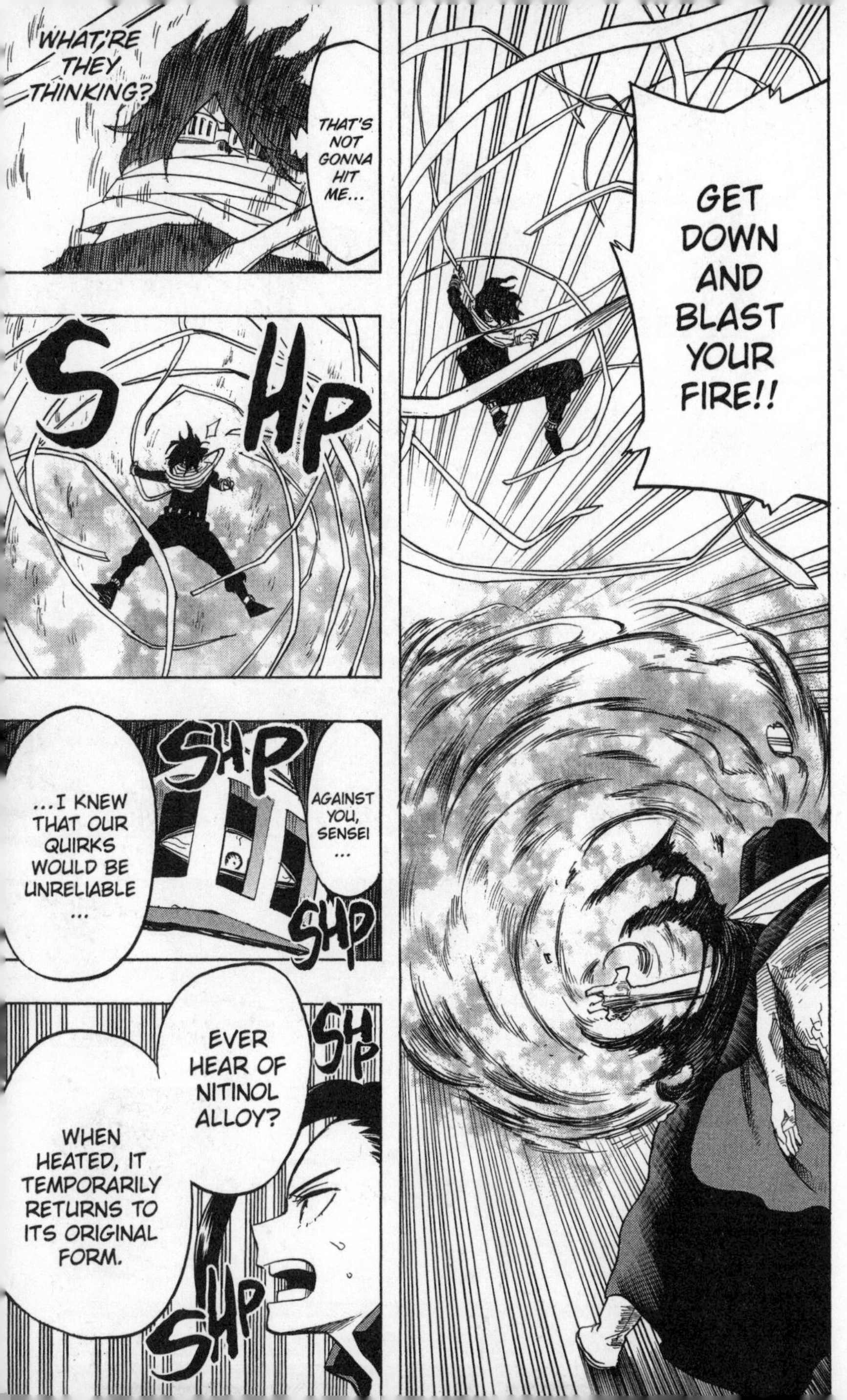
WHAT'RE THEY THINKING?
THAT'S NOT GONNA HIT ME...
S HP
SHP
AGAINST YOU, SENSEI ...
...I KNEW THAT OUR QUIRKS WOULD BE UNRELIABLE ...
SHP
SHP
EVER HEAR OF NITINOL ALLOY?
WHEN HEATED, IT TEMPORARILY RETURNS TO ITS ORIGINAL FORM.
SHP
GET DOWN AND BLAST YOUR FIRE!!

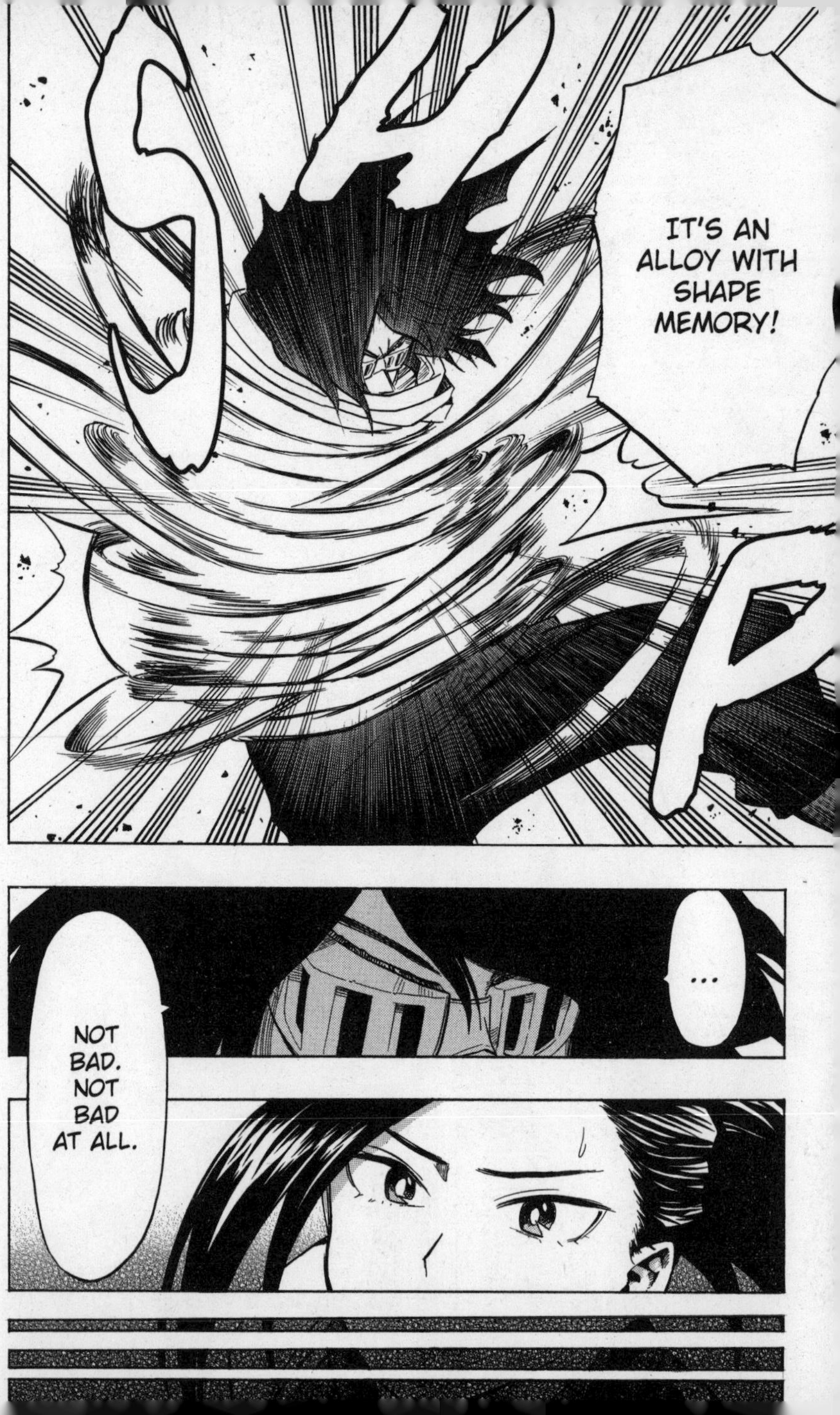
IT'S AN ALLOY WITH SHAPE MEMORY!
...
NOT BAD. NOT BAD AT ALL.

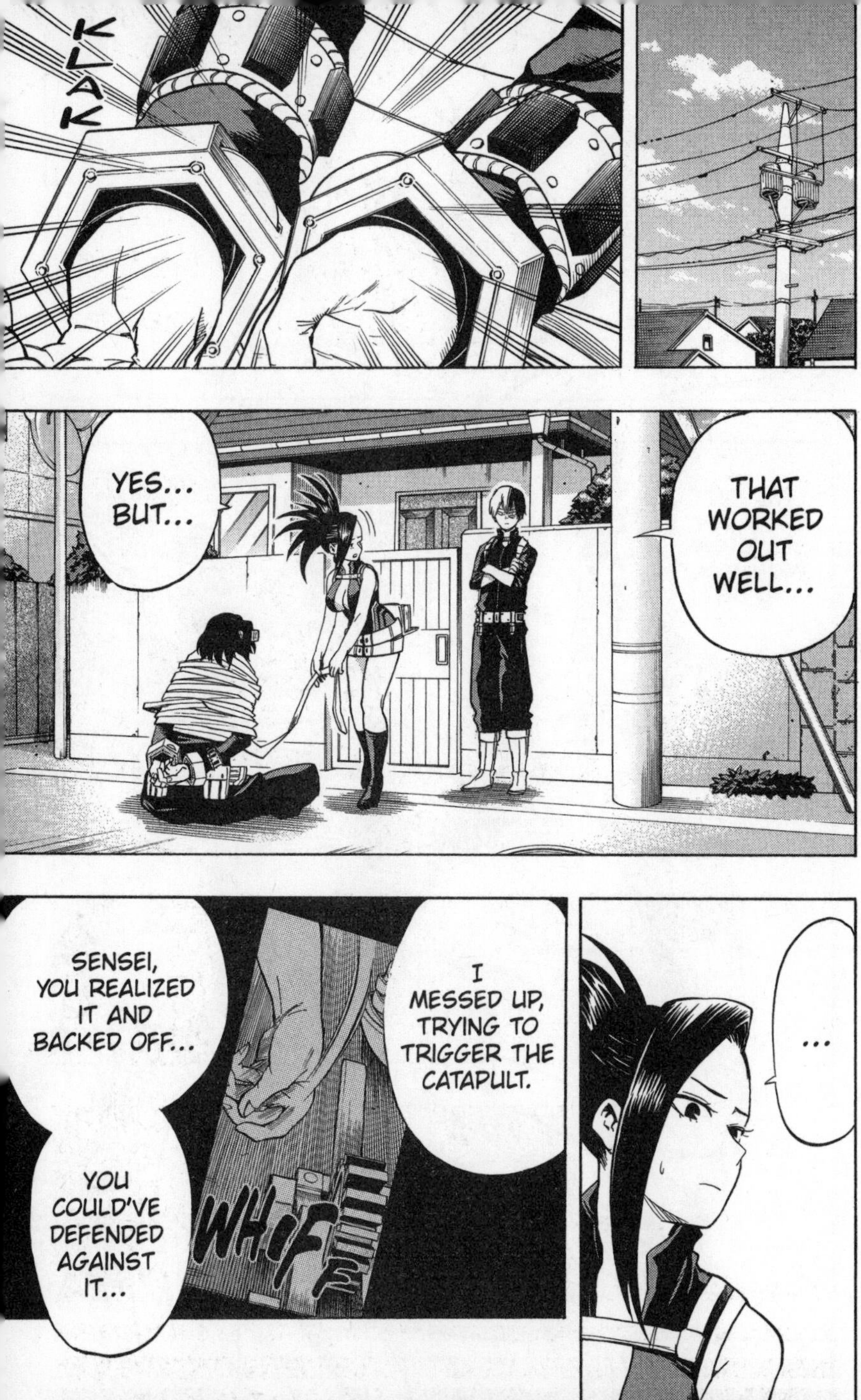
KLAK
THAT WORKED OUT WELL...
YES... BUT...
...
I MESSED UP, TRYING TO TRIGGER THE CATAPULT.
SENSEI, YOU REALIZED IT AND BACKED OFF...
YOU COULD'VE DEFENDED AGAINST IT...
WHIFF

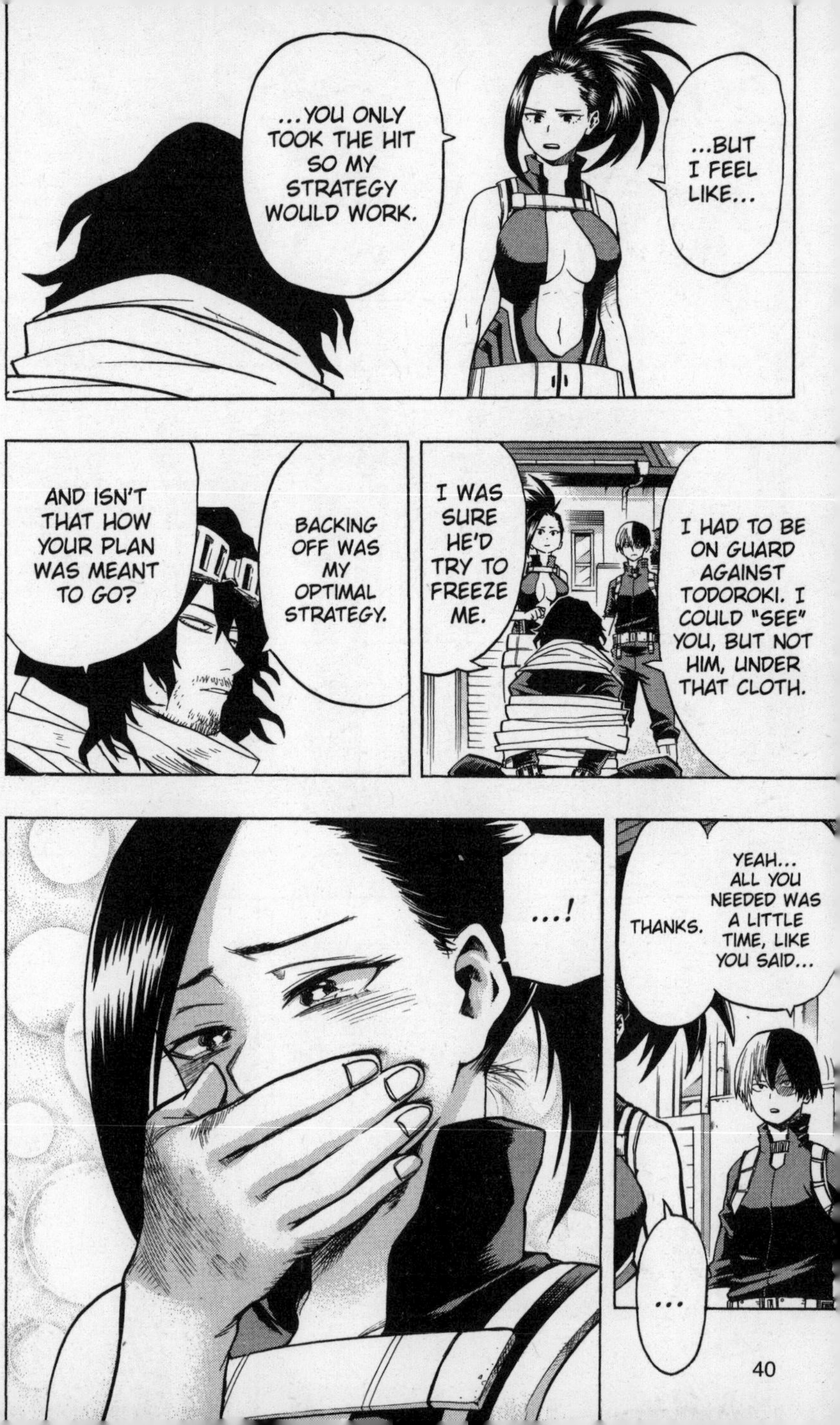
...BUT I FEEL LIKE...
...YOU ONLY TOOK THE HIT SO MY STRATEGY WOULD WORK.
I HAD TO BE ON GUARD AGAINST TODOROKI. I COULD "SEE" YOU, BUT NOT HIM, UNDER THAT CLOTH.
I WAS SURE HE'D TRY TO FREEZE ME.
BACKING OFF WAS MY OPTIMAL STRATEGY.
AND ISN'T THAT HOW YOUR PLAN WAS MEANT TO GO?
YEAH... ALL YOU NEEDED WAS A LITTLE TIME, LIKE YOU SAID...
THANKS.
...
...!

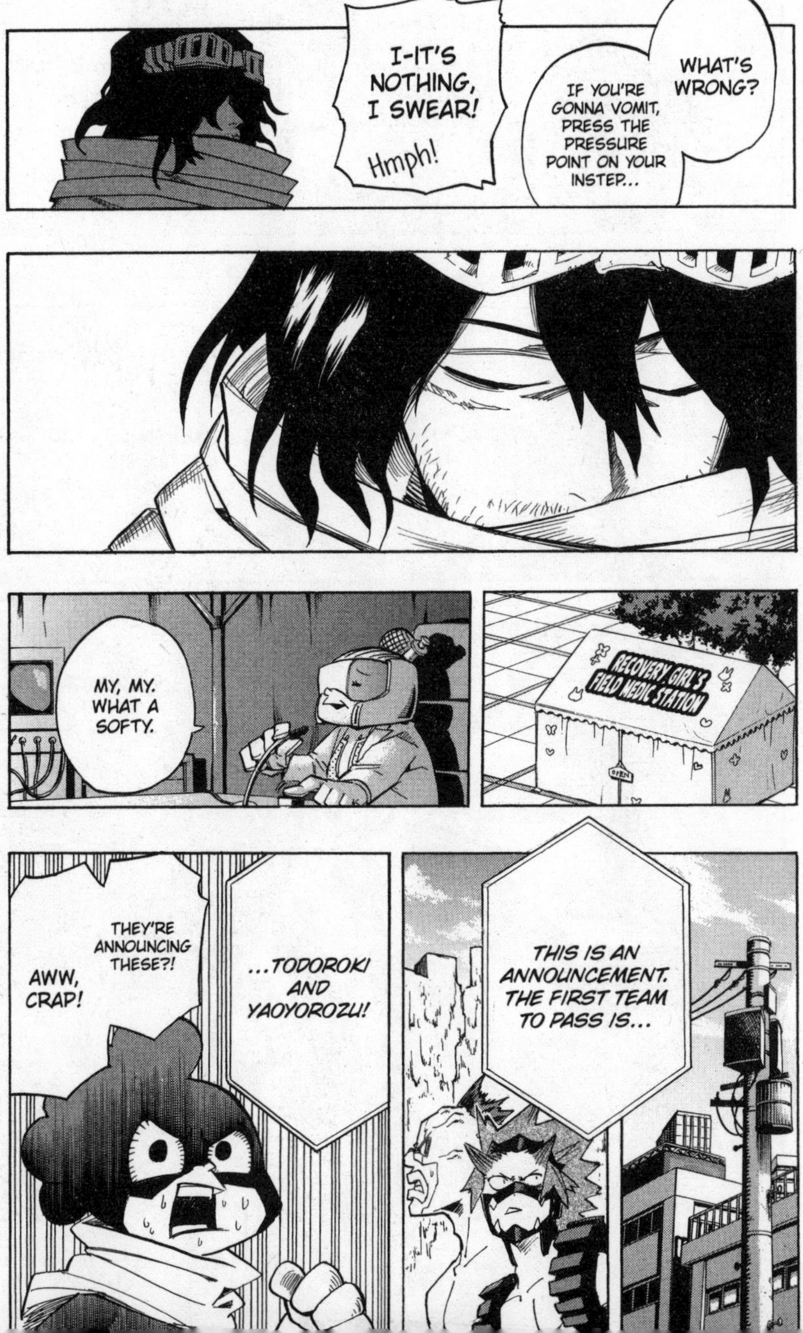
WHAT'S WRONG?
IF YOU'RE GONNA VOMIT, PRESS THE PRESSURE POINT ON YOUR INSTEP...
I-IT'S NOTHING, I SWEAR!
Hmph!
RECOVERY GIRL'S FIELD MEDIC STATION
MY, MY. WHAT A SOFTY.
THIS IS AN ANNOUNCEMENT. THE FIRST TEAM TO PASS IS...
...TODOROKI AND YAOYOROZU!
THEY'RE ANNOUNCING THESE?!
AWW, CRAP!

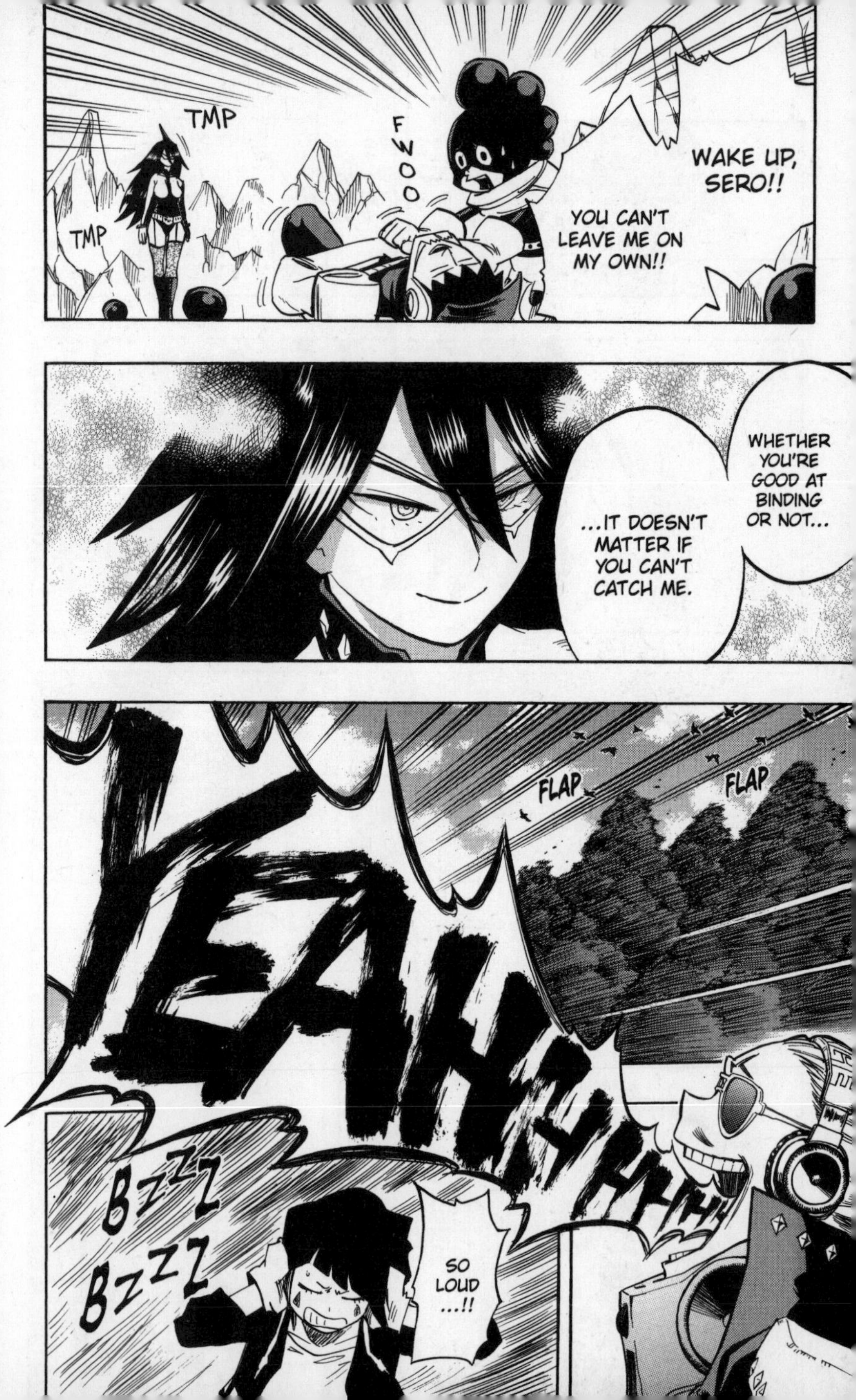
WAKE UP, SERO!!
YOU CAN'T LEAVE ME ON MY OWN!!
FWOOO
TMP
TMP
WHETHER YOU'RE GOOD AT BINDING OR NOT...
...IT DOESN'T MATTER IF YOU CAN'T CATCH ME.
FLAP
FLAP
YEAHHHHHHH
BZZZ
BZZZ
SO LOUD ...!!

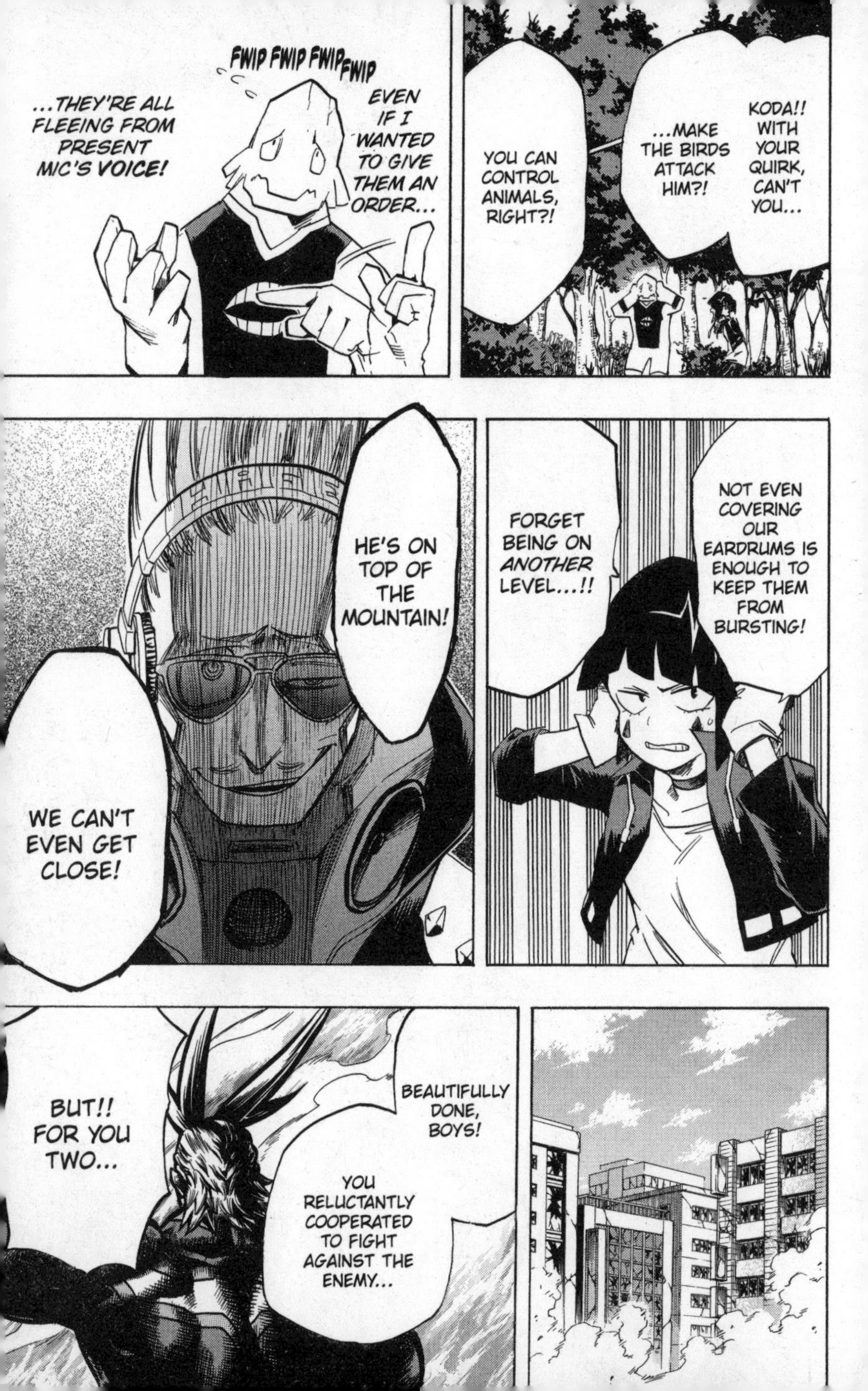
KODA!! WITH YOUR QUIRK, CAN'T YOU...
...MAKE THE BIRDS ATTACK HIM?!
YOU CAN CONTROL ANIMALS, RIGHT?!
FWIP FWIP FWIP FWIP
EVEN IF I WANTED TO GIVE THEM AN ORDER...
...THEY'RE ALL FLEEING FROM PRESENT MIC'S VOICE!
NOT EVEN COVERING OUR EARDRUMS IS ENOUGH TO KEEP THEM FROM BURSTING!
FORGET BEING ON ANOTHER LEVEL...!!
HE'S ON TOP OF THE MOUNTAIN!
WE CAN'T EVEN GET CLOSE!
BEAUTIFULLY DONE, BOYS!
YOU RELUCTANTLY COOPERATED TO FIGHT AGAINST THE ENEMY...
BUT!! FOR YOU TWO...

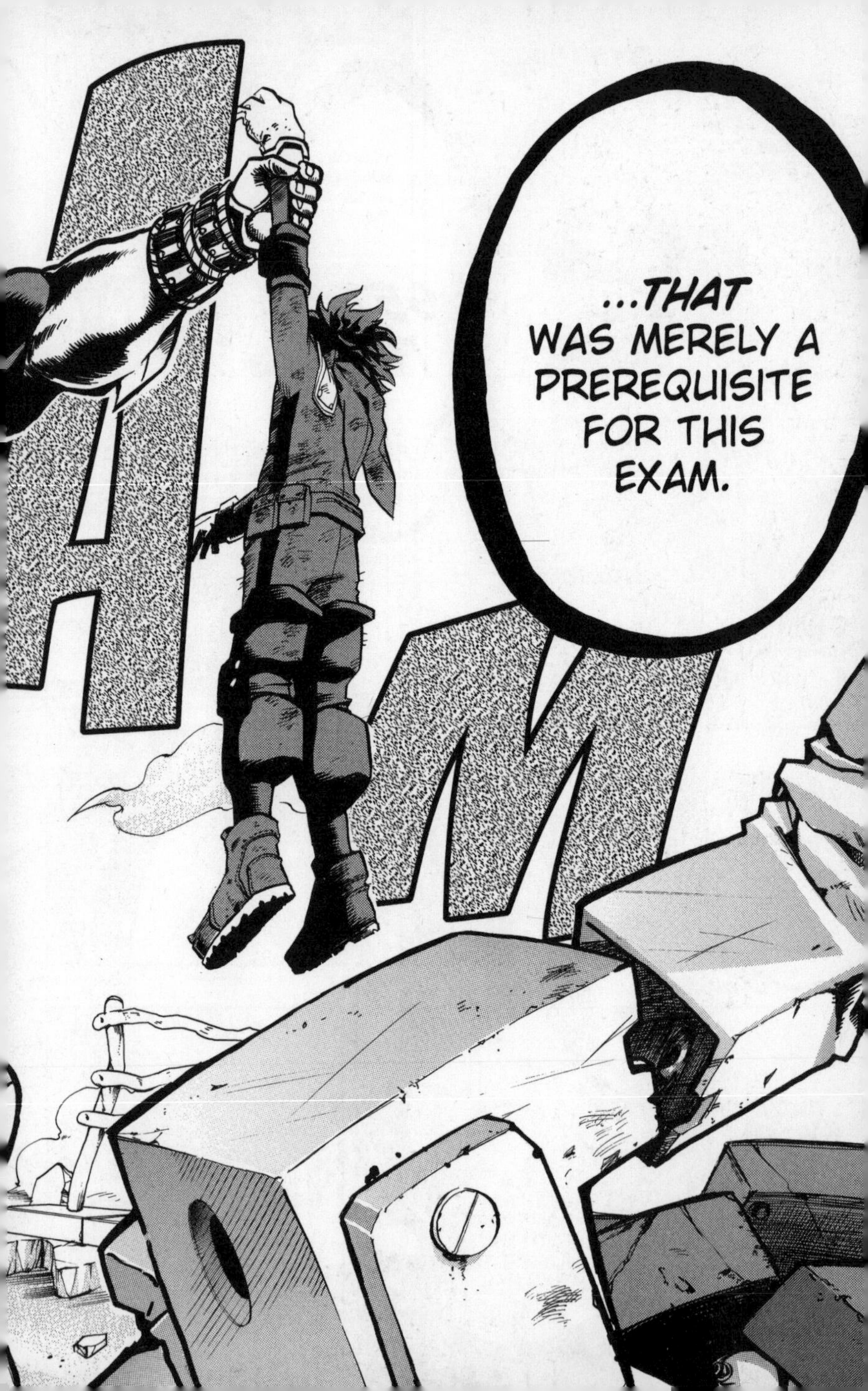
...THAT WAS MERELY A PREREQUISITE FOR THIS EXAM.

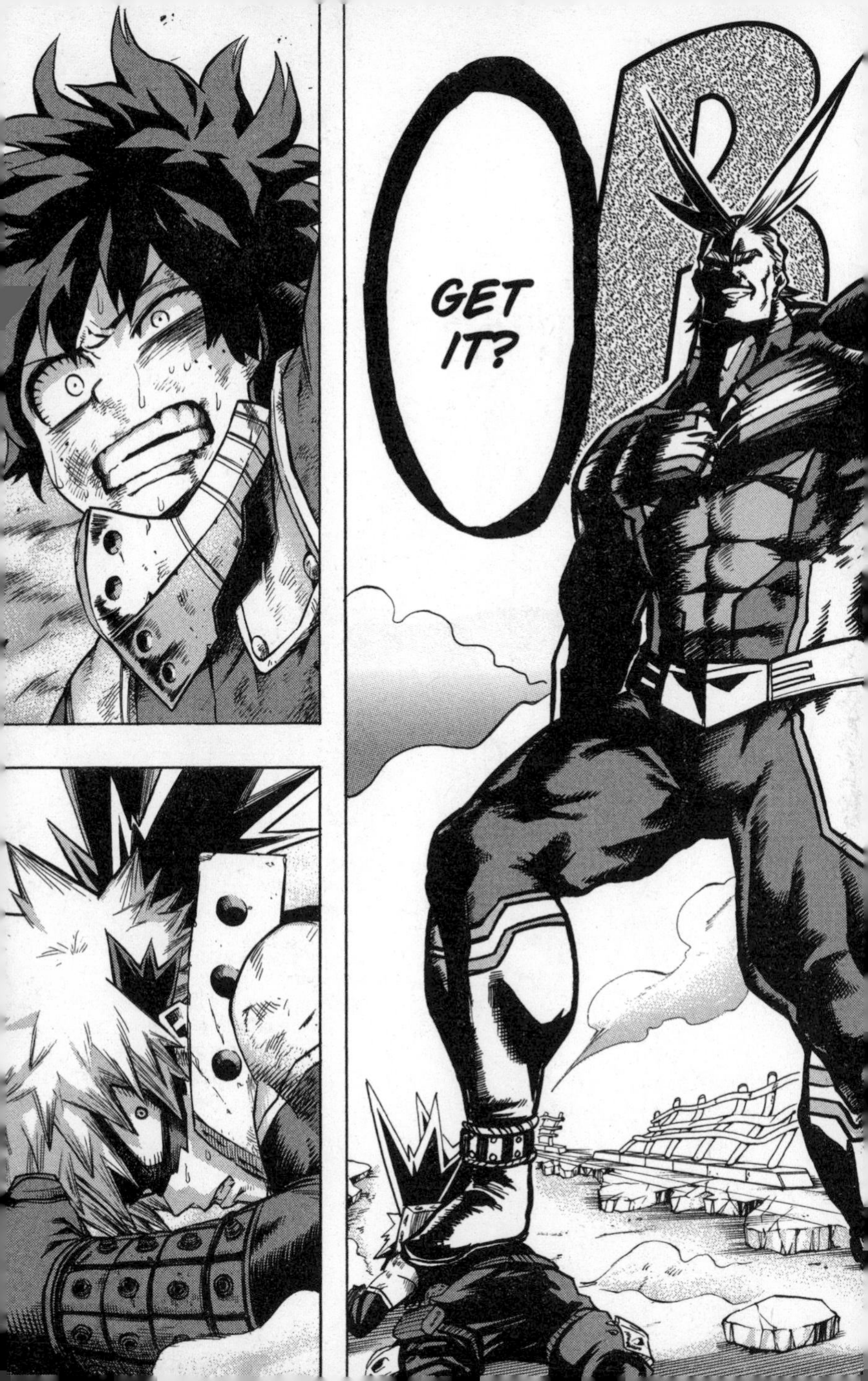
GET IT?

HERO

RECOVERY GIRL (?) (CHIYO SHUZENJI)

STREET CLOTHES

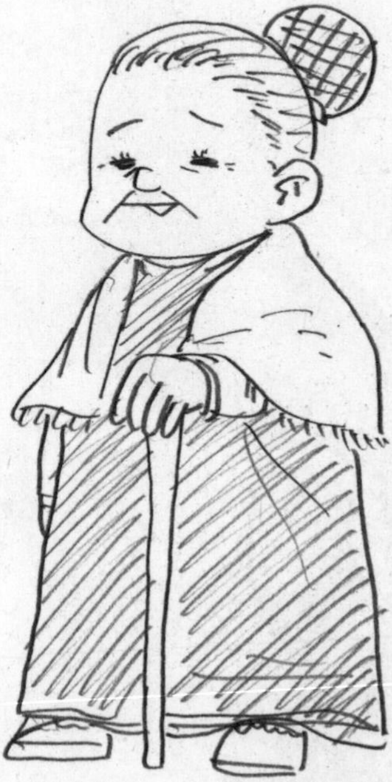

Birthday: 4/4
Height: 115 cm
Favorite Thing: Candy

BEHIND THE SCENES

I was shocked to realize that I hadn't done her profile yet. Basically, she's the backbone of U.A. She's been with the school for over forty years, and in practice, her voice is just as influential as the principal's.

Her Quirk is extraordinarily rare and valuable. As a result, she makes scheduled visits to hospitals in the area to provide healing services. She's got a busy life.

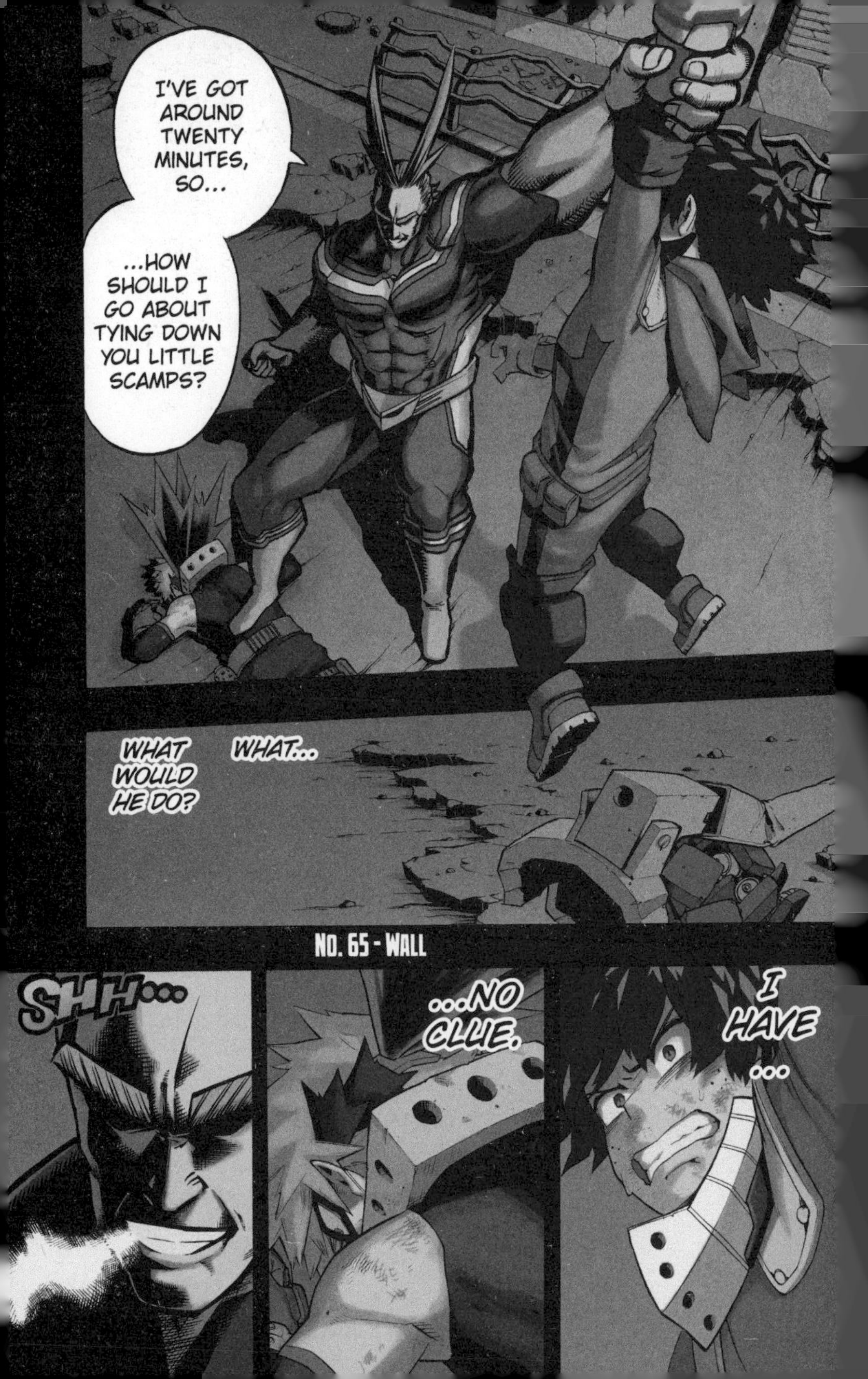
I'VE GOT AROUND TWENTY MINUTES, SO...
...HOW SHOULD I GO ABOUT TYING DOWN YOU LITTLE SCAMPS?
WHAT...
WHAT WOULD HE DO?
NO. 65 - WALL
I HAVE...
...NO CLUE.
SHH...

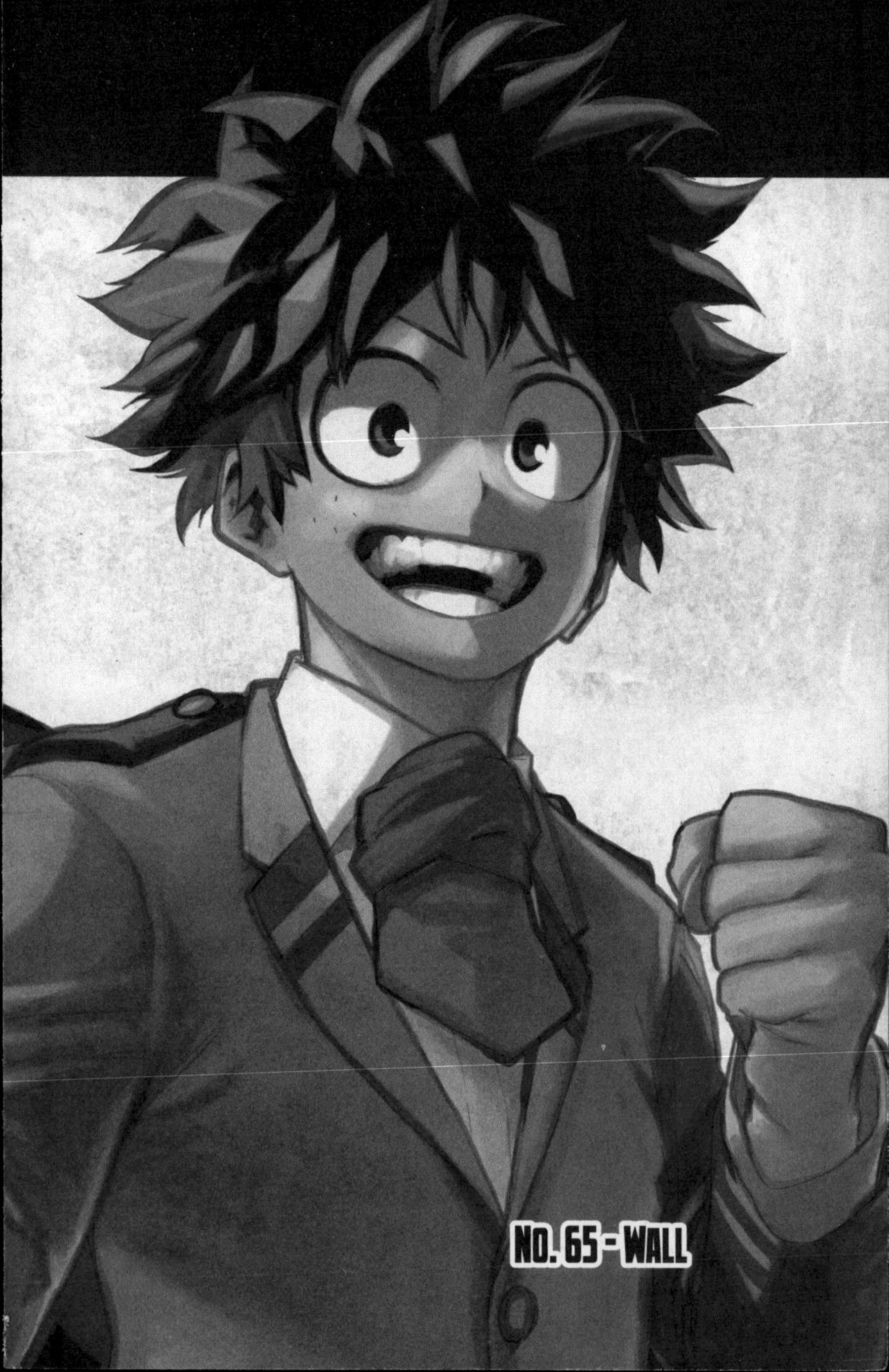
NO. 65 - WALL

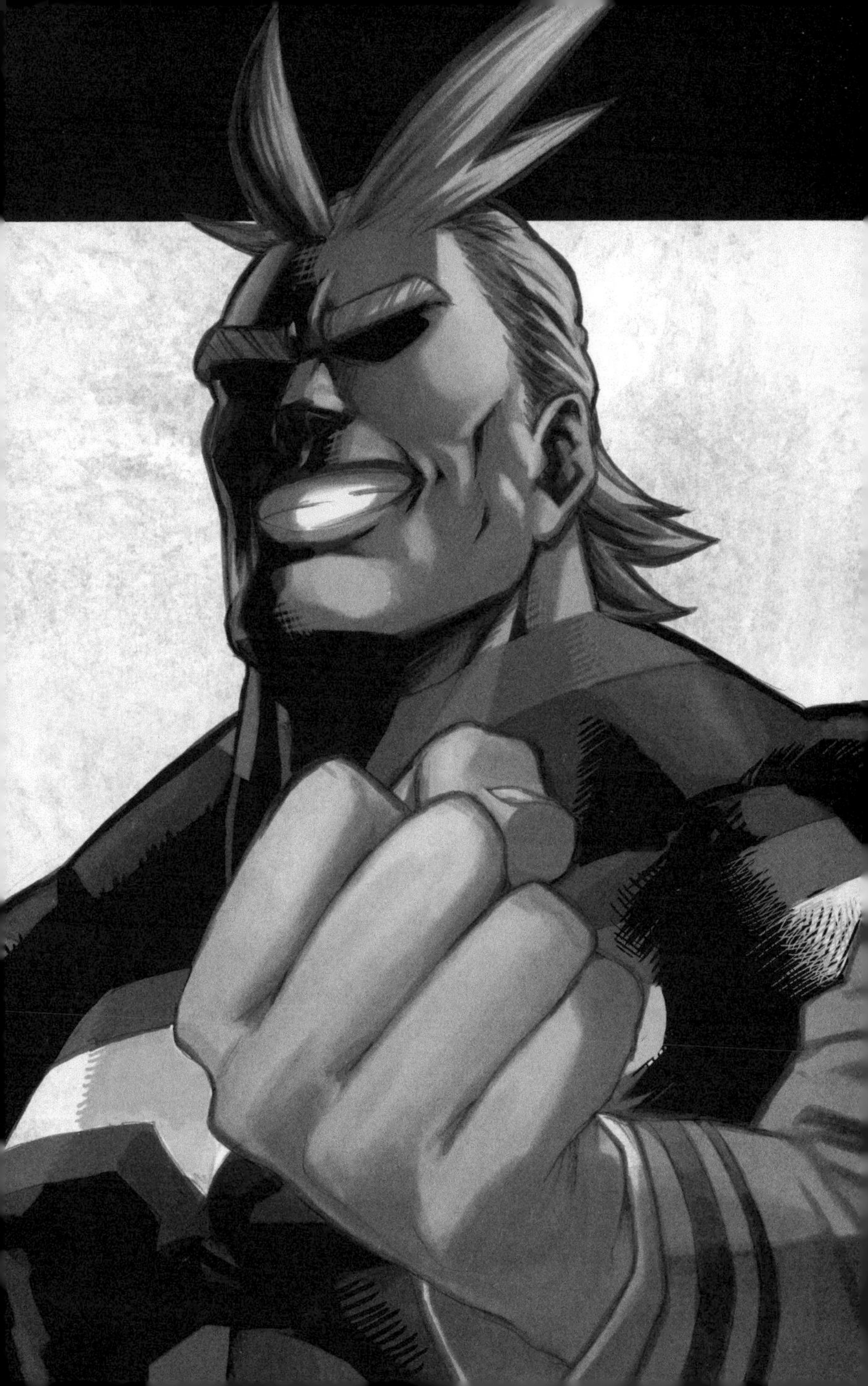

MY HERO ACADEMIA

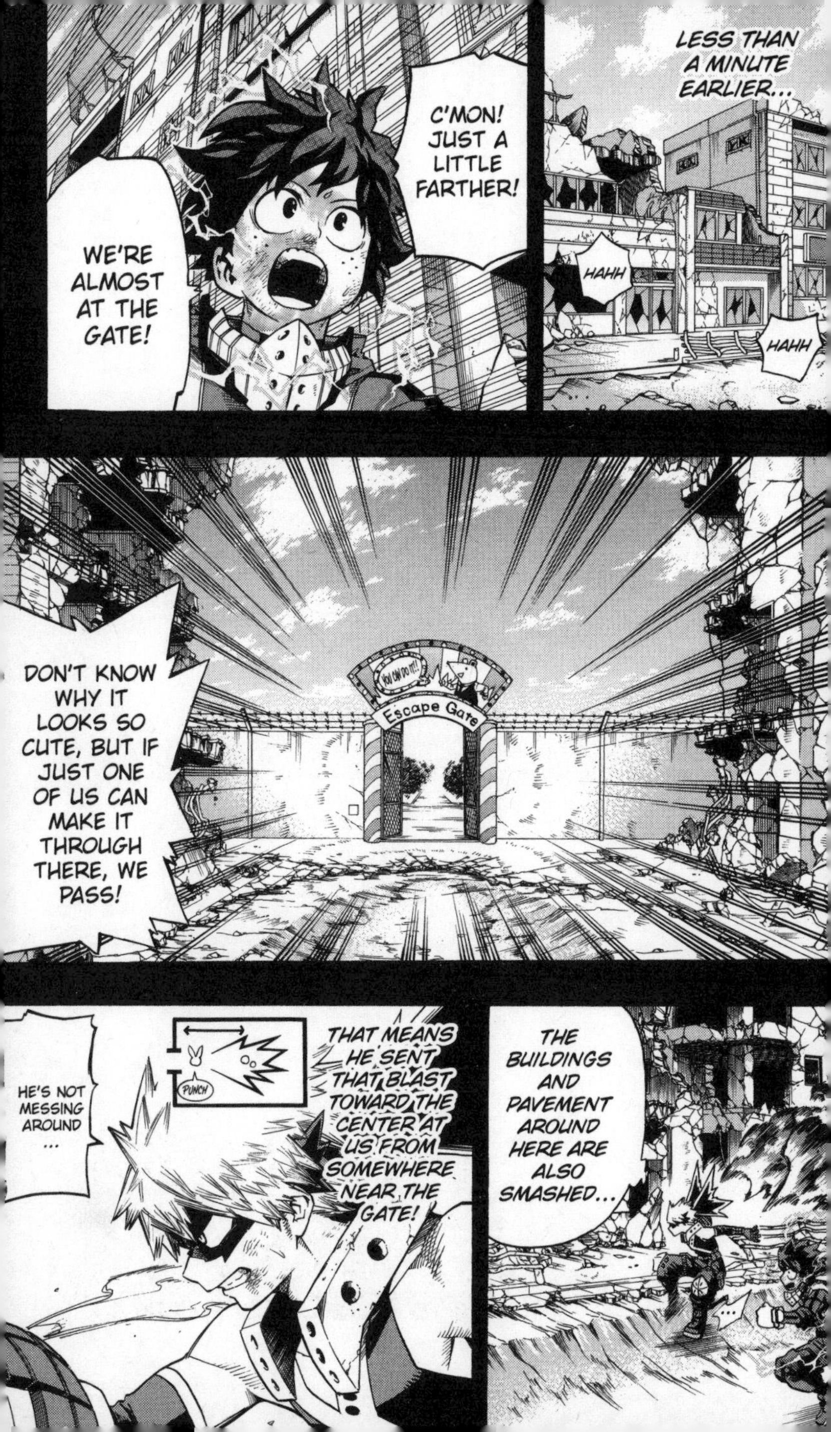
LESS THAN A MINUTE EARLIER...
HAHH
HAHH
C'MON! JUST A LITTLE FARTHER!
WE'RE ALMOST AT THE GATE!
YOU CAN DO IT!!
Escape Gate
DON'T KNOW WHY IT LOOKS SO CUTE, BUT IF JUST ONE OF US CAN MAKE IT THROUGH THERE, WE PASS!
THE BUILDINGS AND PAVEMENT AROUND HERE ARE ALSO SMASHED...
...
THAT MEANS HE SENT THAT BLAST TOWARD THE CENTER AT US FROM SOMEWHERE NEAR THE GATE!
PUNCH
HE'S NOT MESSING AROUND ...

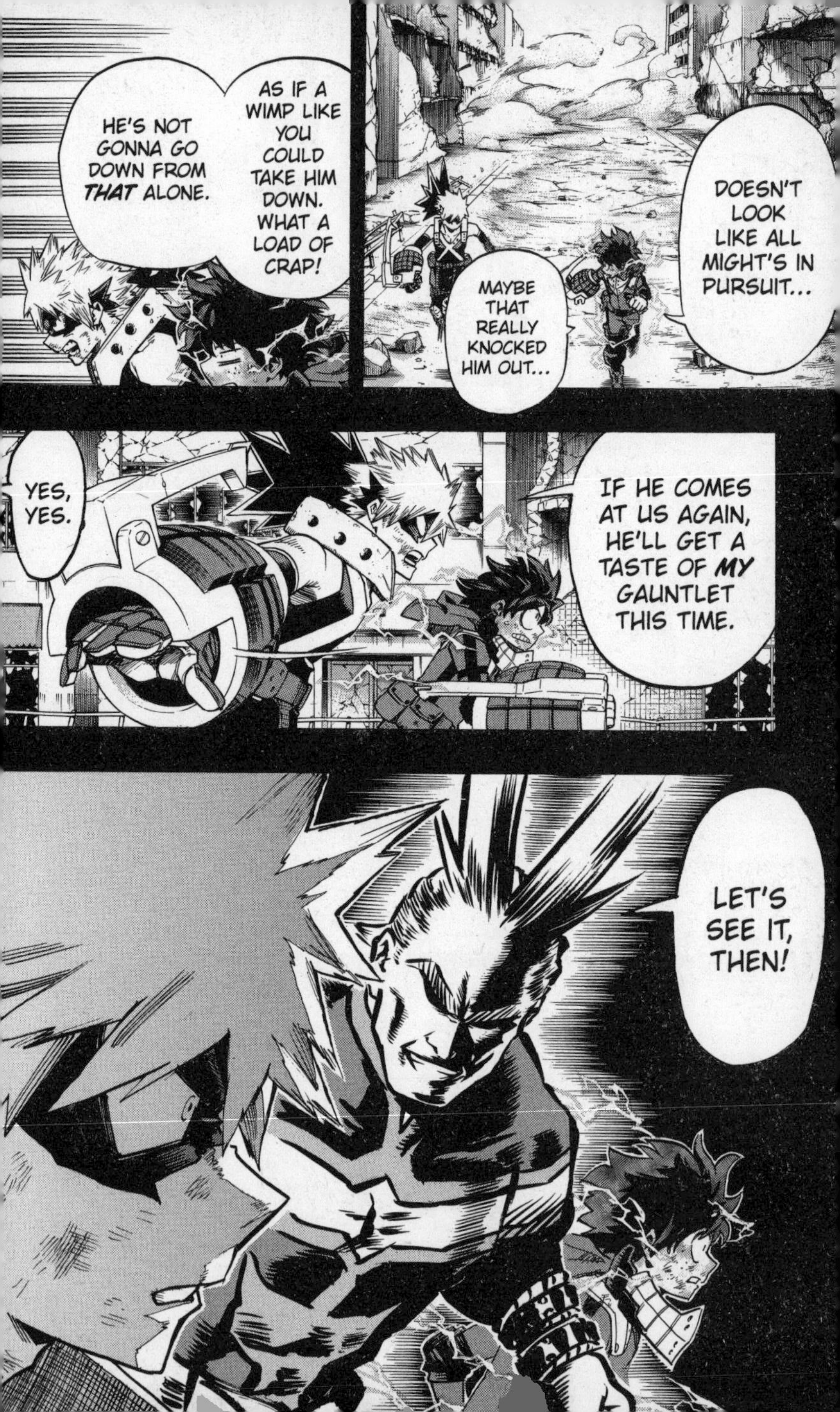
DOESN'T LOOK LIKE ALL MIGHT'S IN PURSUIT...
MAYBE THAT REALLY KNOCKED HIM OUT...
AS IF A WIMP LIKE YOU COULD TAKE HIM DOWN. WHAT A LOAD OF CRAP!
HE'S NOT GONNA GO DOWN FROM ***THAT*** ALONE.
IF HE COMES AT US AGAIN, HE'LL GET A TASTE OF ***MY*** GAUNTLET THIS TIME.
YES, YES.
LET'S SEE IT, THEN!

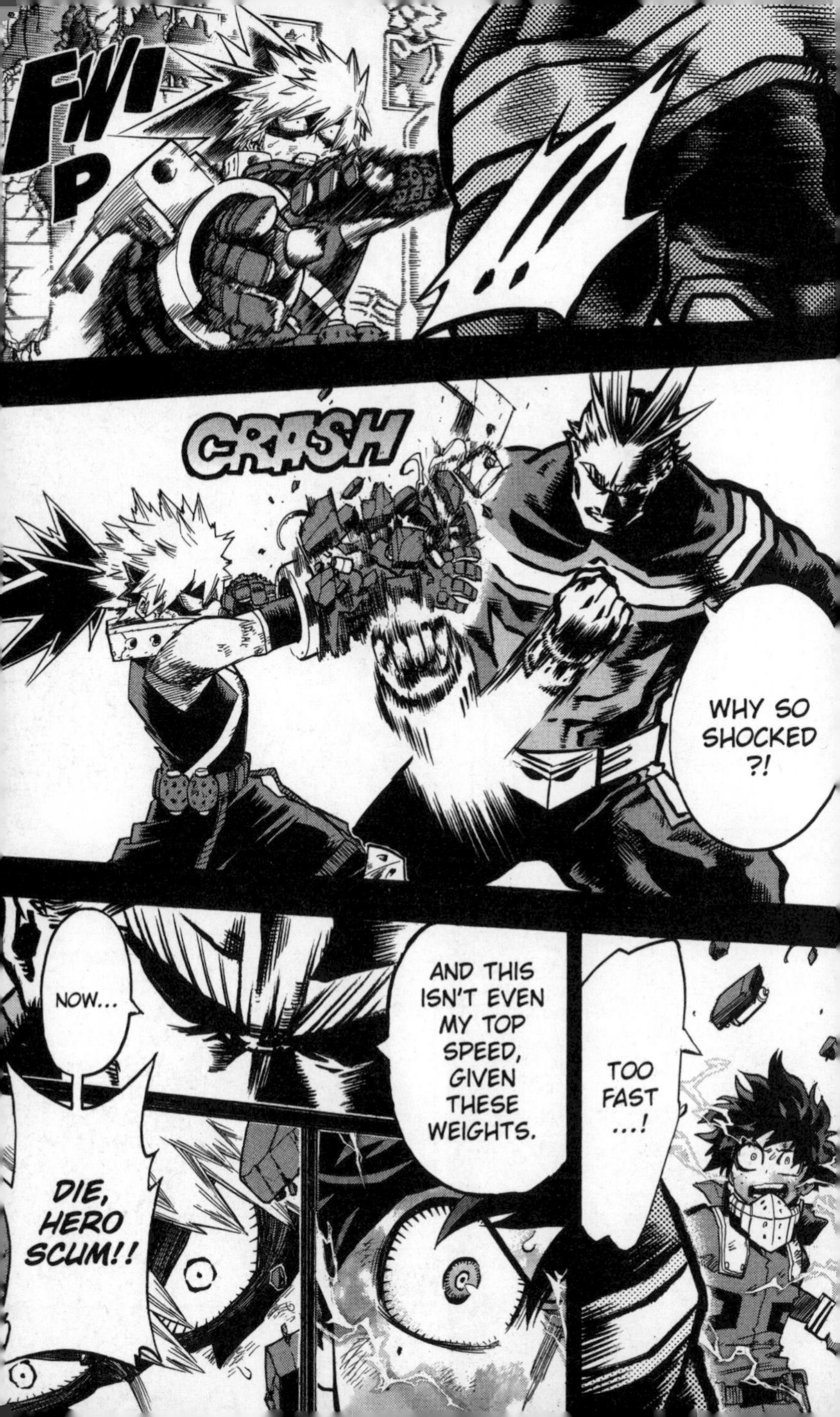
FWIP
CRASH
WHY SO SHOCKED?!
TOO FAST...!
AND THIS ISN'T EVEN MY TOP SPEED, GIVEN THESE WEIGHTS.
NOW...
DIE, HERO SCUM!!

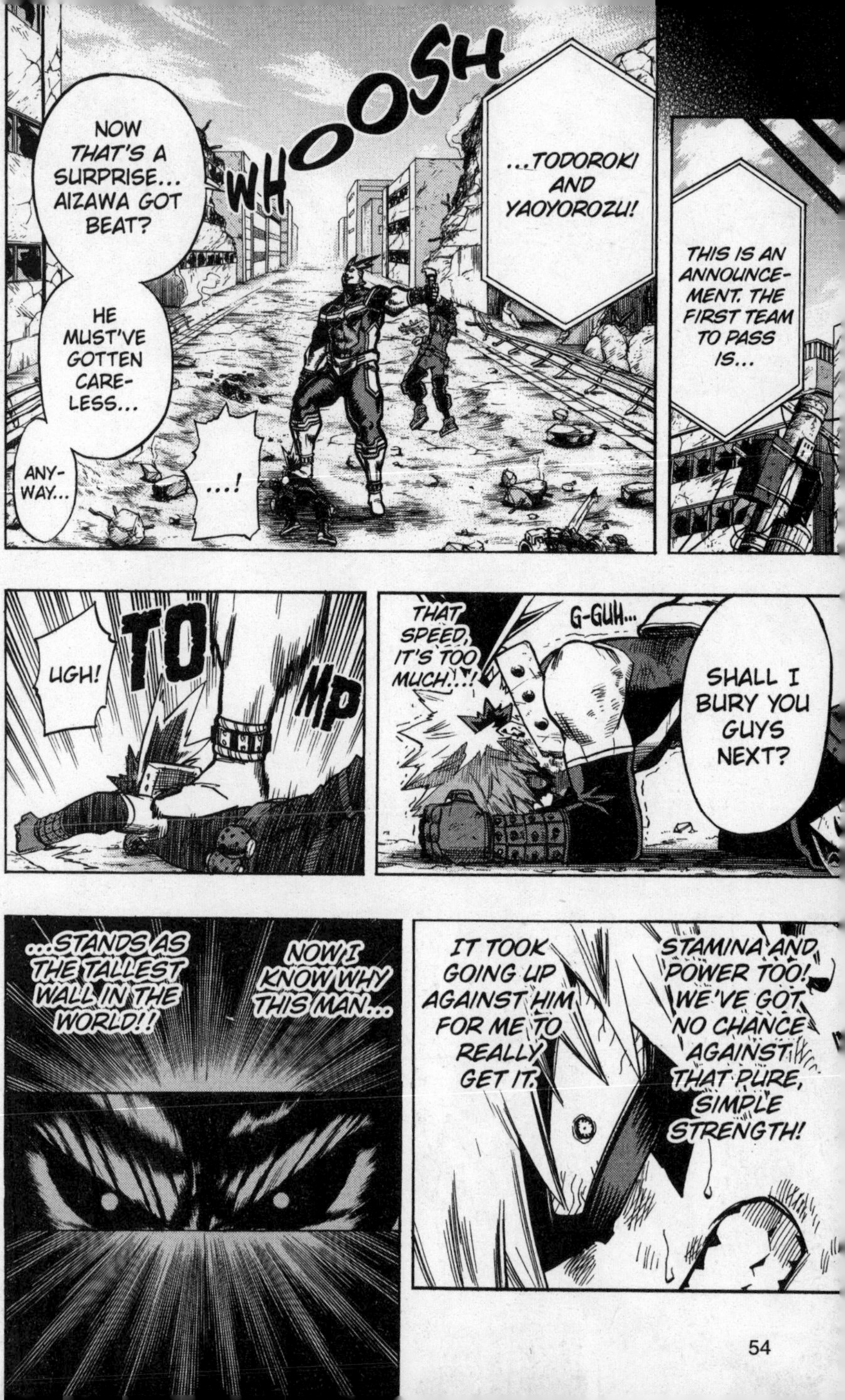
THIS IS AN ANNOUNCEMENT. THE FIRST TEAM TO PASS IS...
...TODOROKI AND YAOYOROZU!
WHOOSH
NOW THAT'S A SURPRISE... AIZAWA GOT BEAT?
HE MUST'VE GOTTEN CARELESS...
ANYWAY...
...!
SHALL I BURY YOU GUYS NEXT?
G-GUH...
THAT SPEED, IT'S TOO MUCH...!
TOMP
UGH!
STAMINA AND POWER TOO! WE'VE GOT NO CHANCE AGAINST THAT PURE, SIMPLE STRENGTH!
IT TOOK GOING UP AGAINST HIM FOR ME TO REALLY GET IT.
NOW I KNOW WHY THIS MAN...
...STANDS AS THE TALLEST WALL IN THE WORLD!!

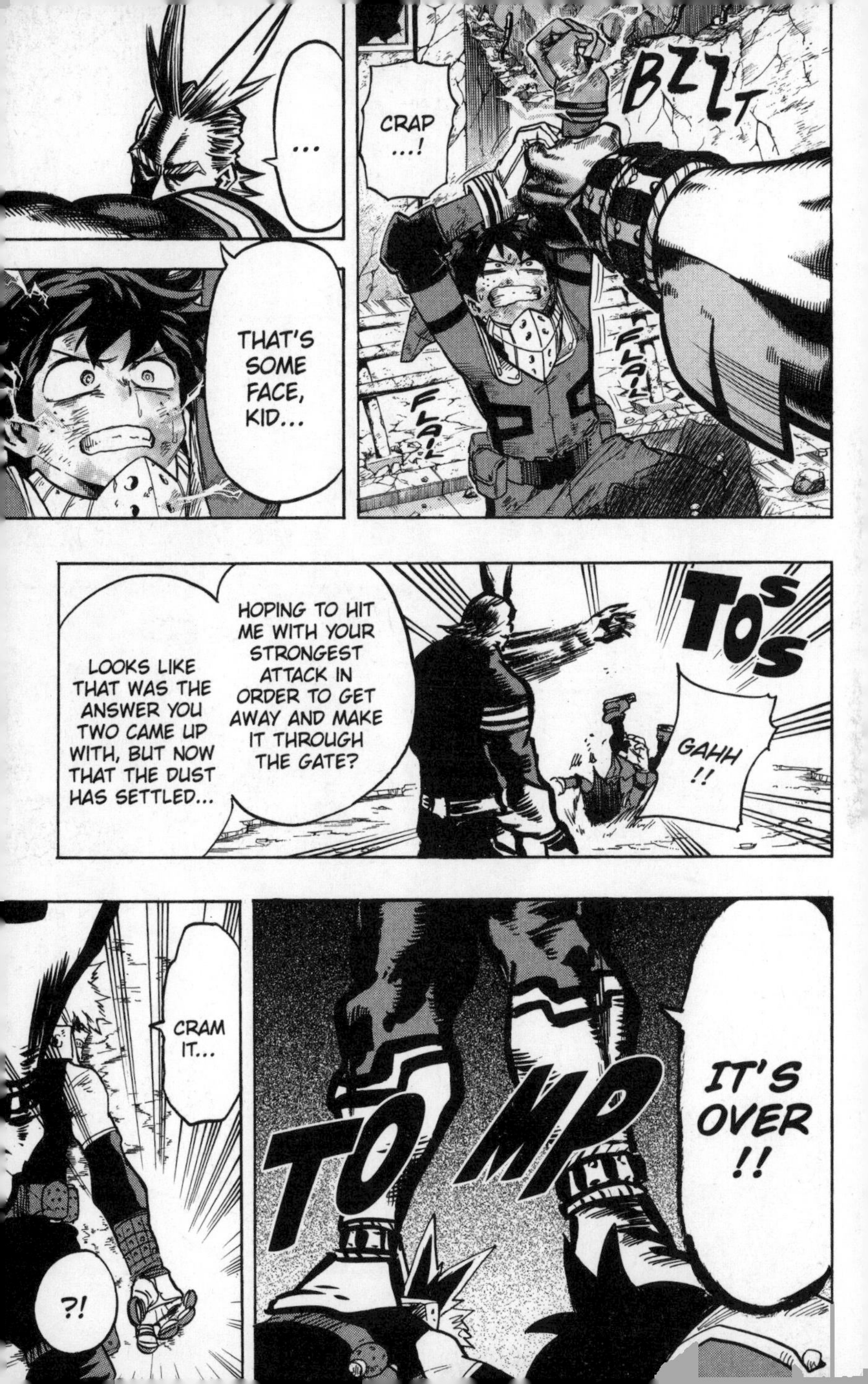
CRAP ...!
BZZT
FLAIL
FLAIL
...
THAT'S SOME FACE, KID...
TOS
GAHH !!
HOPING TO HIT ME WITH YOUR STRONGEST ATTACK IN ORDER TO GET AWAY AND MAKE IT THROUGH THE GATE?
LOOKS LIKE THAT WAS THE ANSWER YOU TWO CAME UP WITH, BUT NOW THAT THE DUST HAS SETTLED...
TOMP
IT'S OVER !!
CRAM IT...
?!

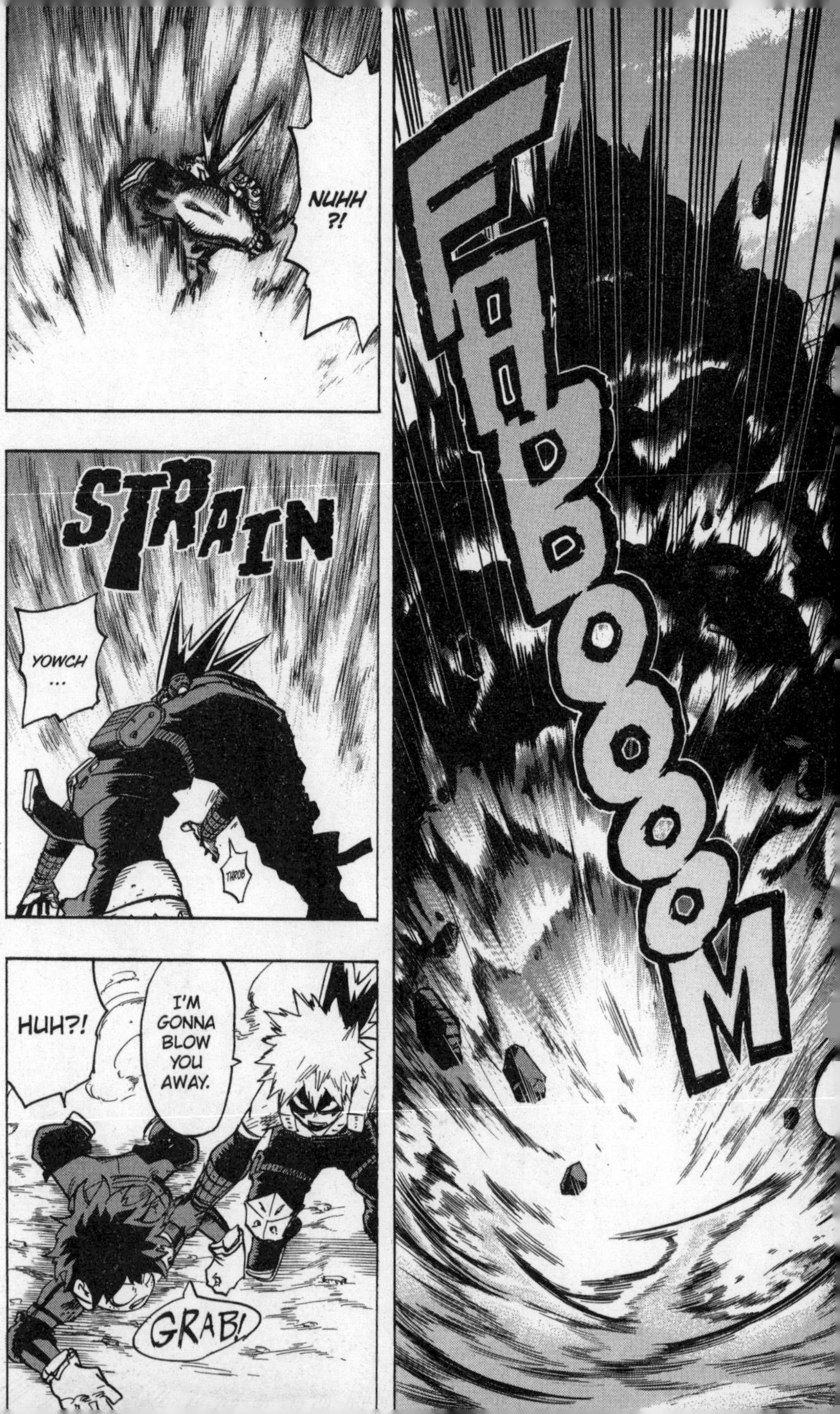
FDDDDOOOOOM
NUHH ?!
STRAIN
YOWCH ...
THROB
I'M GONNA BLOW YOU AWAY.
HUH?!
GRAB!

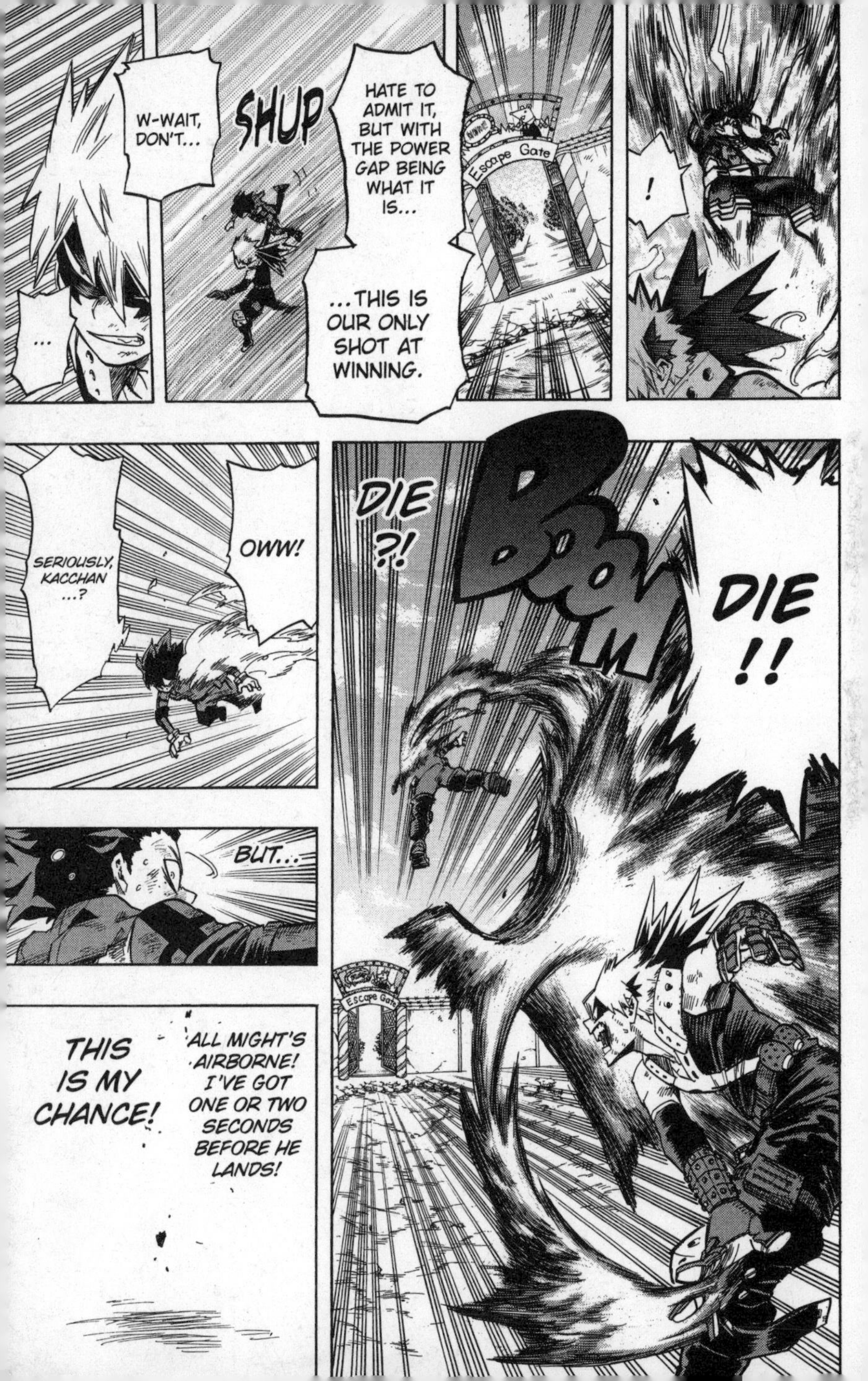
!
HATE TO ADMIT IT, BUT WITH THE POWER GAP BEING WHAT IT IS...
...THIS IS OUR ONLY SHOT AT WINNING.
Escape Gate
SHUP
W-WAIT, DON'T...
...
DIE !!
BOOM
DIE ?!
Escape Gate
OWW!
SERIOUSLY, KACCHAN ...?
BUT...
ALL MIGHT'S AIRBORNE! I'VE GOT ONE OR TWO SECONDS BEFORE HE LANDS!
THIS IS MY CHANCE!

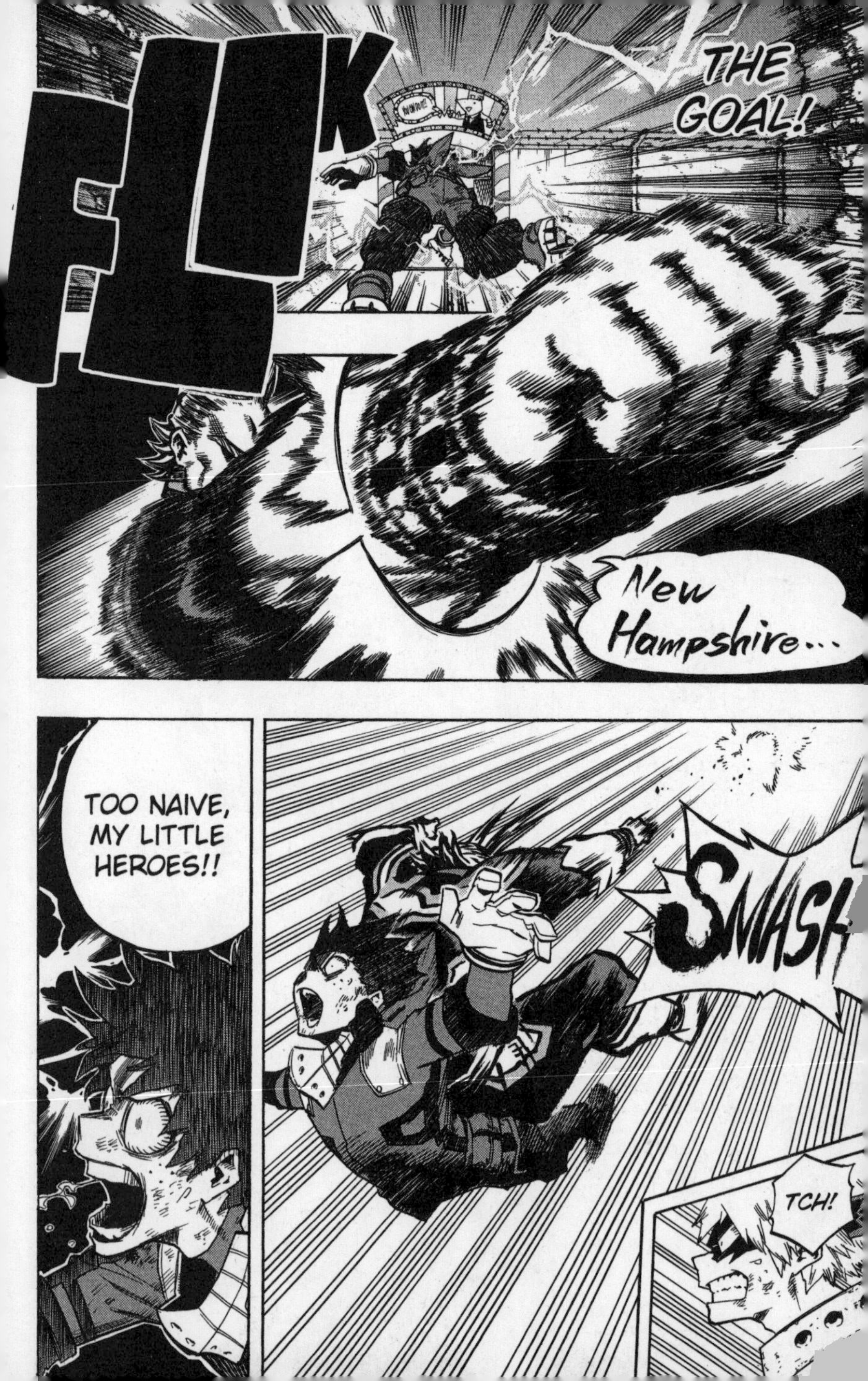
THE GOAL!
New Hampshire...
FLIK
SMASH
TCH!
TOO NAIVE, MY LITTLE HEROES!!

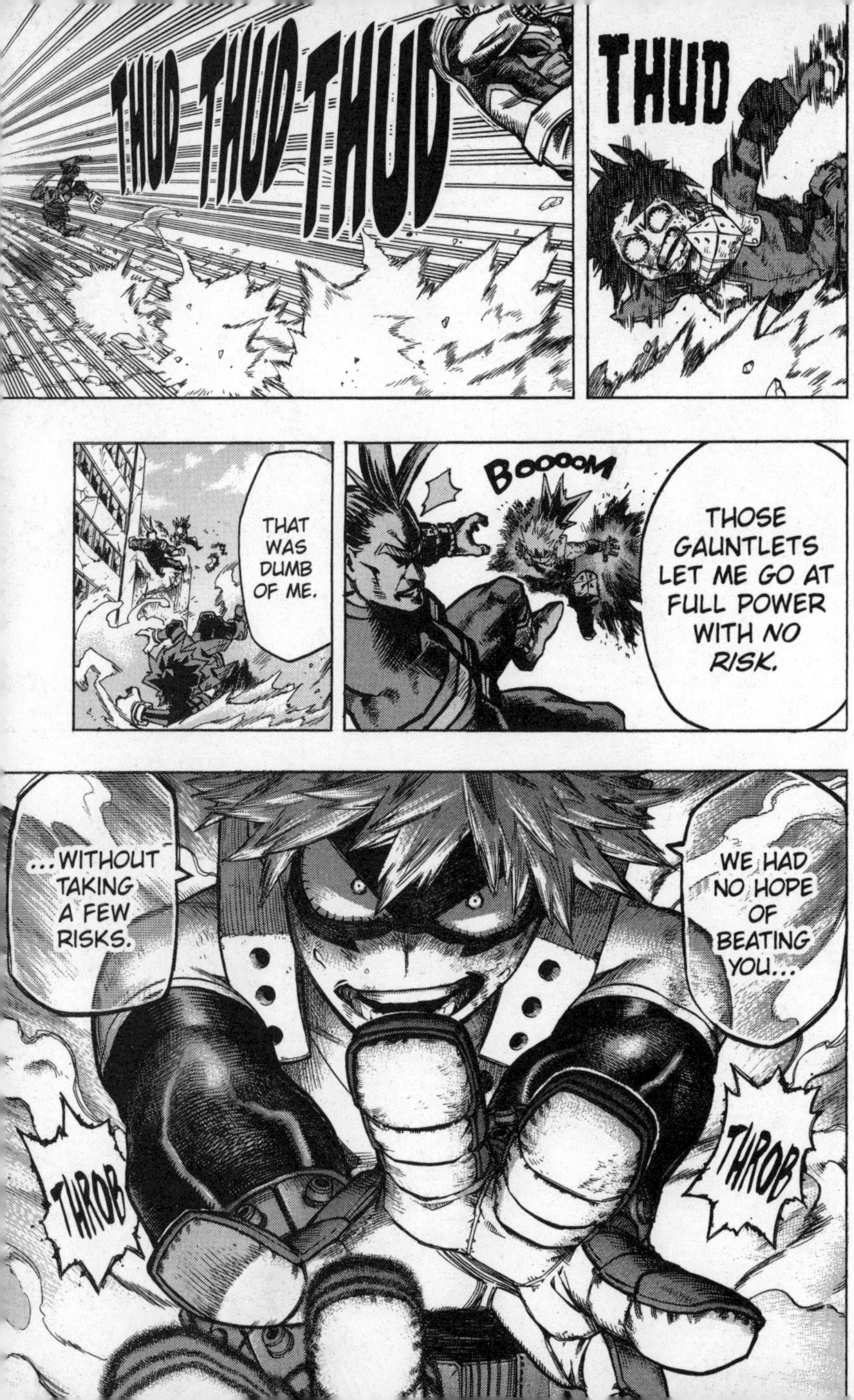
THUD
THUD THUD THUD
BOOOOM
THOSE GAUNTLETS LET ME GO AT FULL POWER WITH *NO RISK.*
THAT WAS DUMB OF ME.
WE HAD NO HOPE OF BEATING YOU...
...WITHOUT TAKING A FEW RISKS.
THROB
THROB

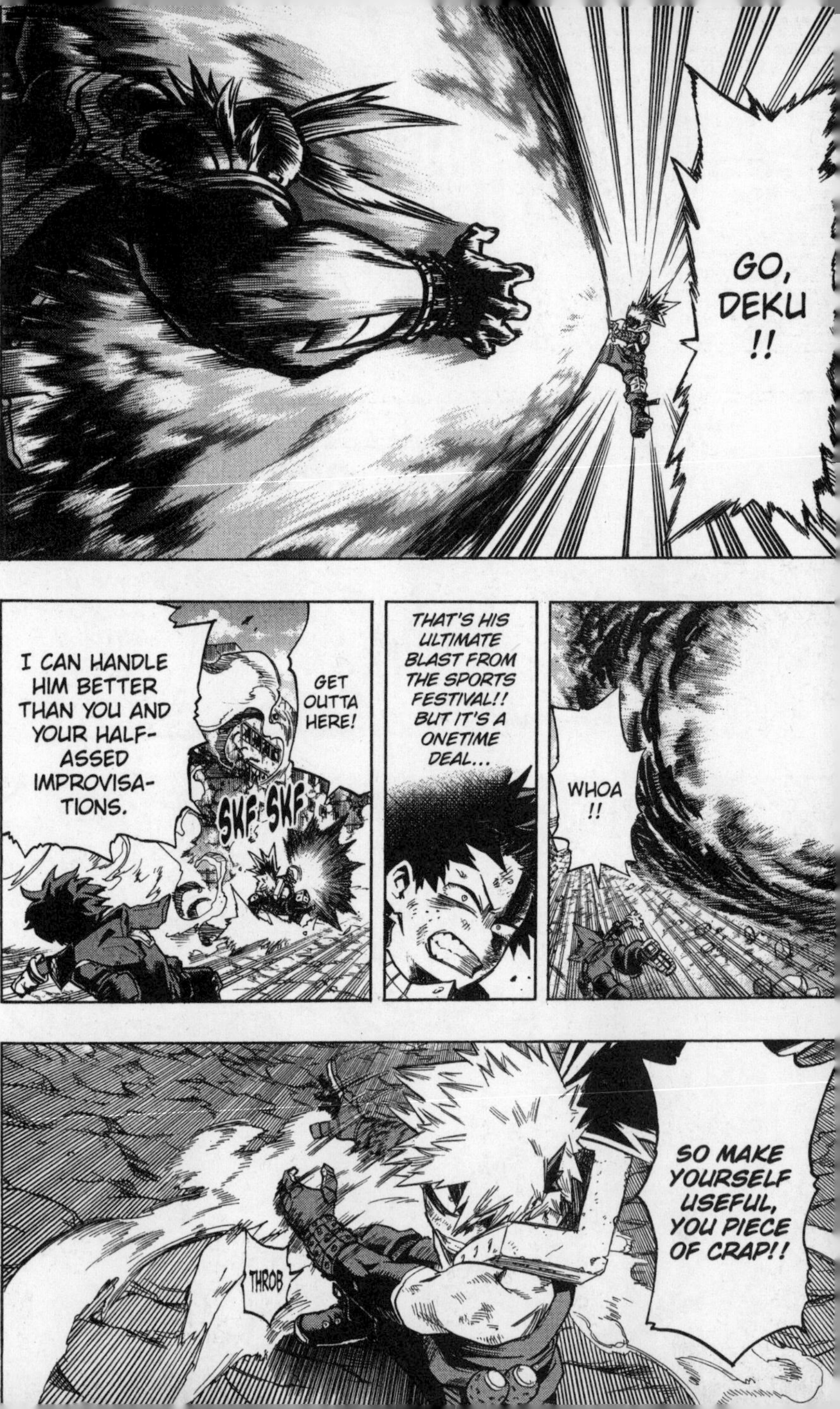
GO, DEKU !!
WHOA !!
THAT'S HIS ULTIMATE BLAST FROM THE SPORTS FESTIVAL!! BUT IT'S A ONETIME DEAL...
GET OUTTA HERE!
I CAN HANDLE HIM BETTER THAN YOU AND YOUR HALF-ASSED IMPROVISA-TIONS.
SKF SKF
SO MAKE YOURSELF USEFUL, YOU PIECE OF CRAP!!
THROB

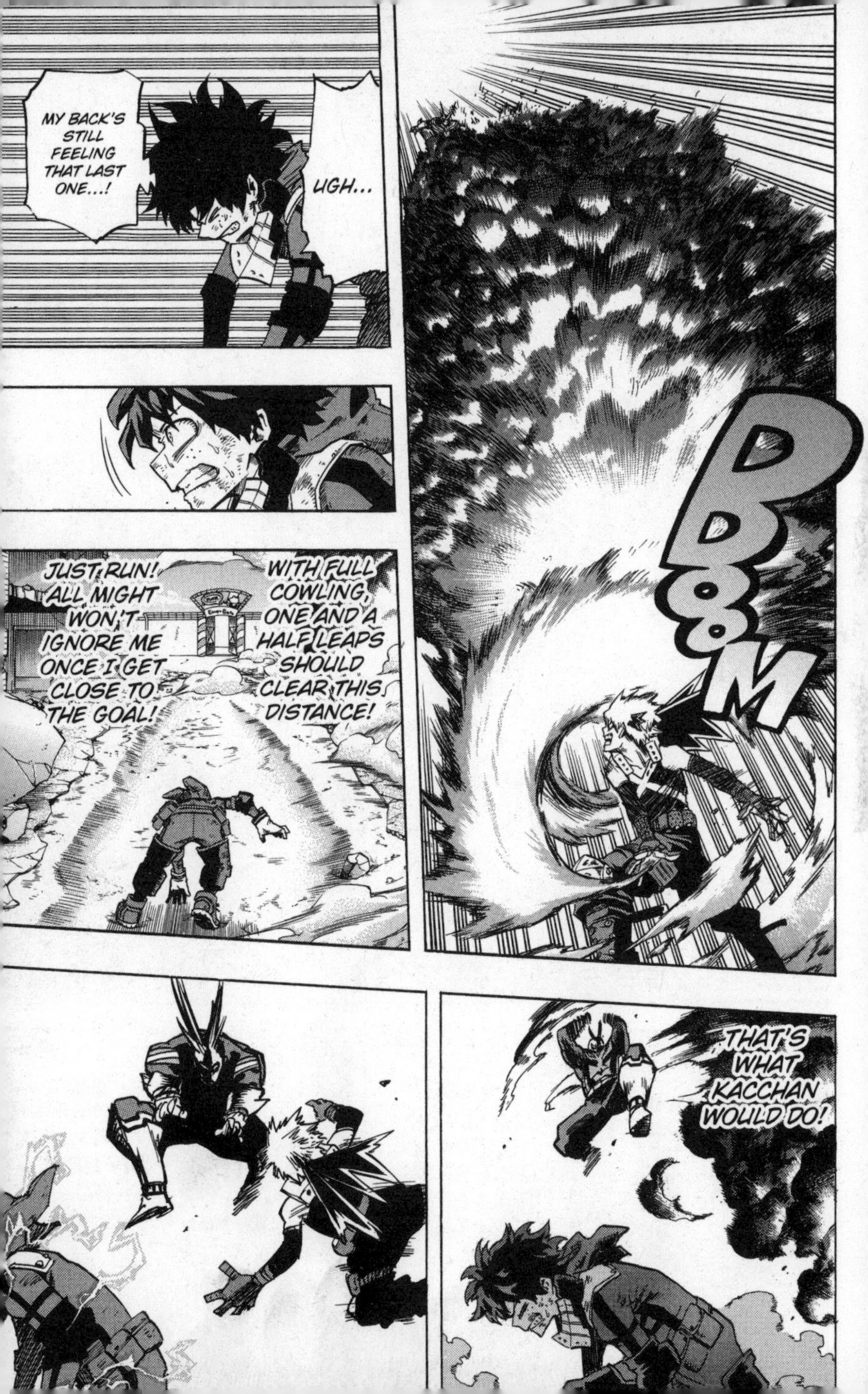
BOOM
UGH...
MY BACK'S STILL FEELING THAT LAST ONE...!
WITH FULL COWLING, ONE AND A HALF LEAPS SHOULD CLEAR THIS DISTANCE!
JUST RUN! ALL MIGHT WON'T IGNORE ME ONCE I GET CLOSE TO THE GOAL!
THAT'S WHAT KACCHAN WOULD DO!

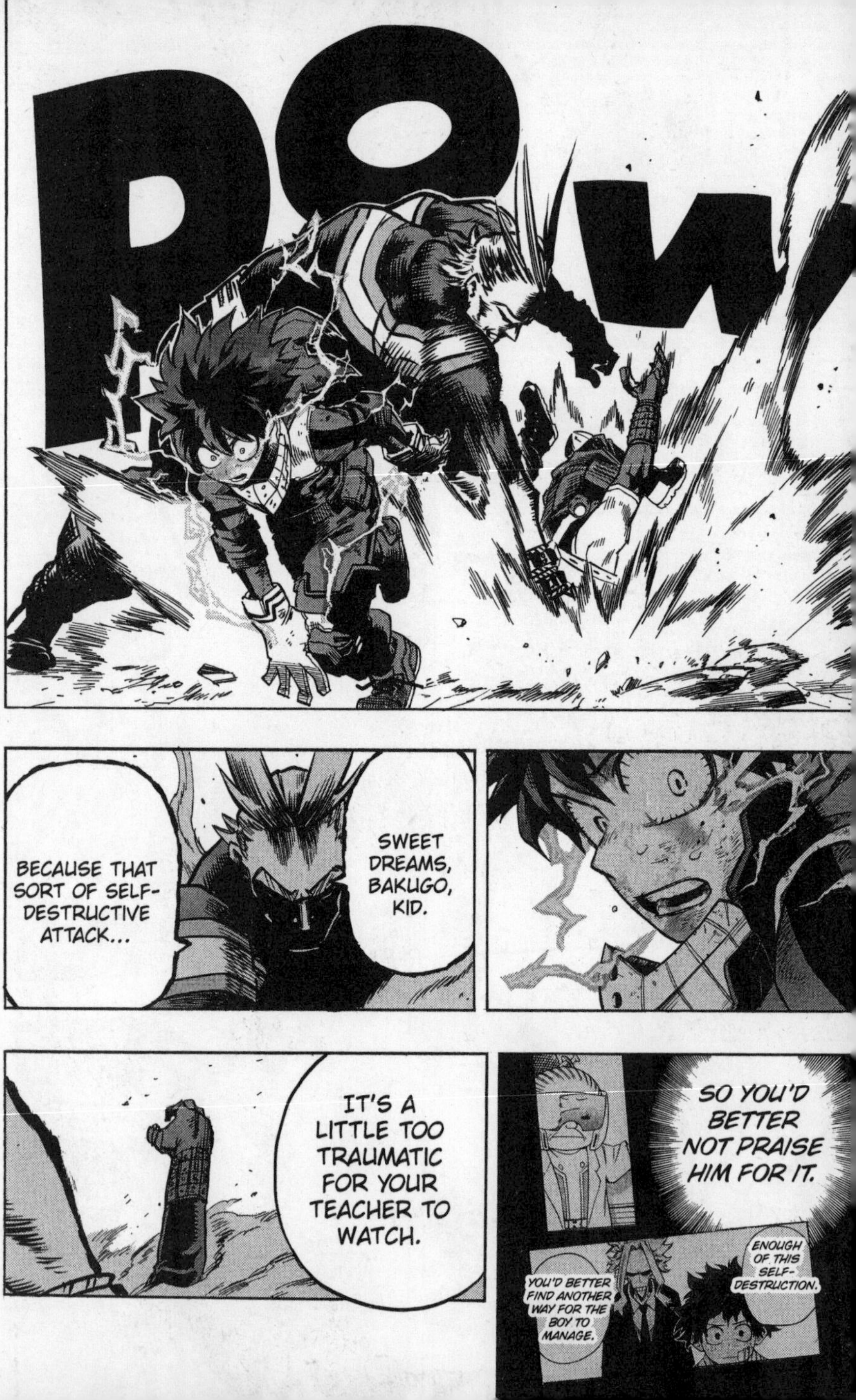
DOW
SWEET DREAMS, BAKUGO, KID.
BECAUSE THAT SORT OF SELF-DESTRUCTIVE ATTACK...
SO YOU'D BETTER NOT PRAISE HIM FOR IT.
ENOUGH OF THIS SELF-DESTRUCTION.
YOU'D BETTER FIND ANOTHER WAY FOR THE BOY TO MANAGE.
IT'S A LITTLE TOO TRAUMATIC FOR YOUR TEACHER TO WATCH.

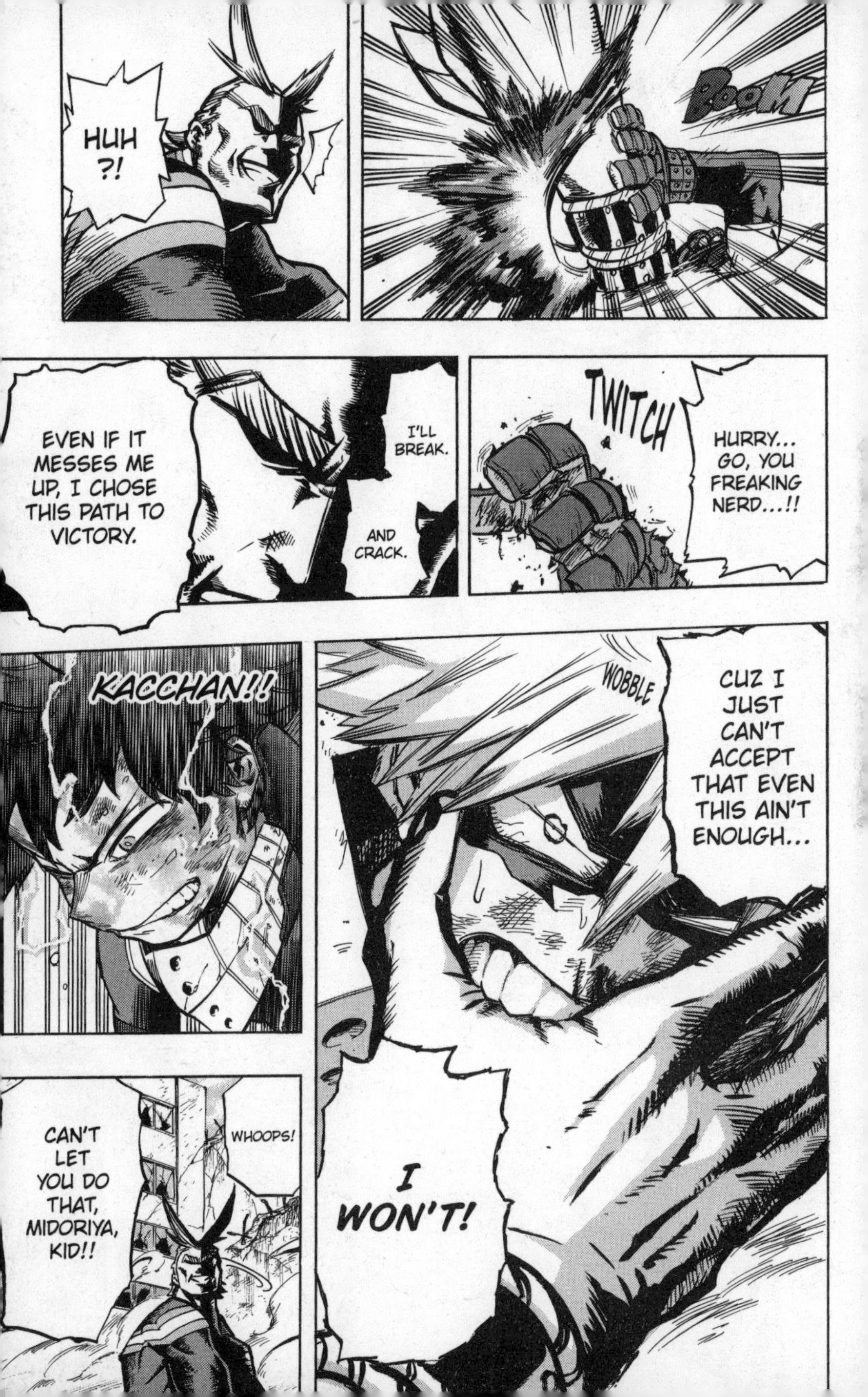
BOOM
HUH ?!
TWITCH
HURRY... GO, YOU FREAKING NERD...!!
I'LL BREAK.
AND CRACK.
EVEN IF IT MESSES ME UP, I CHOSE THIS PATH TO VICTORY.
WOBBLE
CUZ I JUST CAN'T ACCEPT THAT EVEN THIS AIN'T ENOUGH...
I WON'T!
KACCHAN!!
WHOOPS!
CAN'T LET YOU DO THAT, MIDORIYA, KID!!

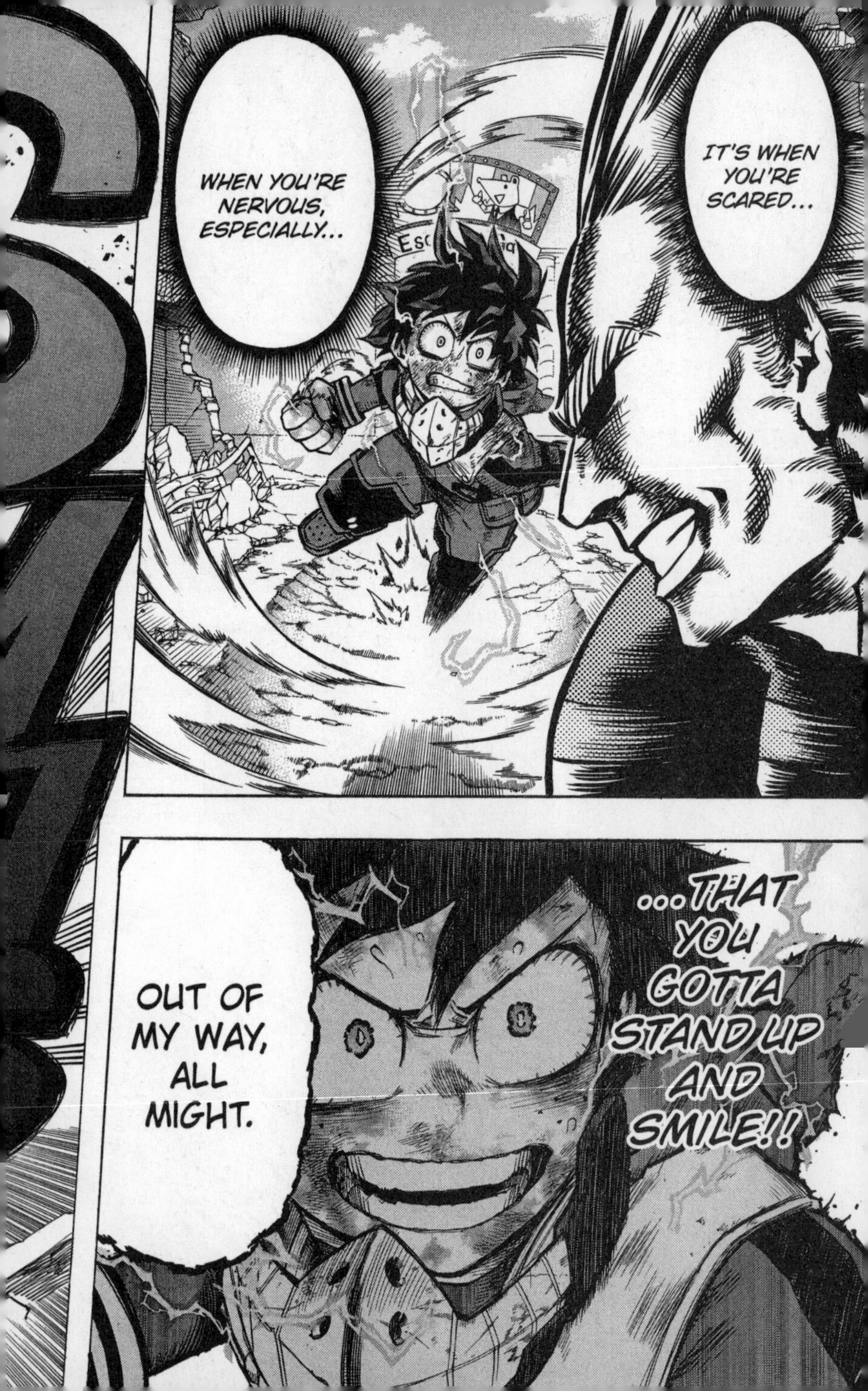
IT'S WHEN YOU'RE SCARED...
WHEN YOU'RE NERVOUS, ESPECIALLY...
...THAT YOU GOTTA STAND UP AND SMILE!!
OUT OF MY WAY, ALL MIGHT.

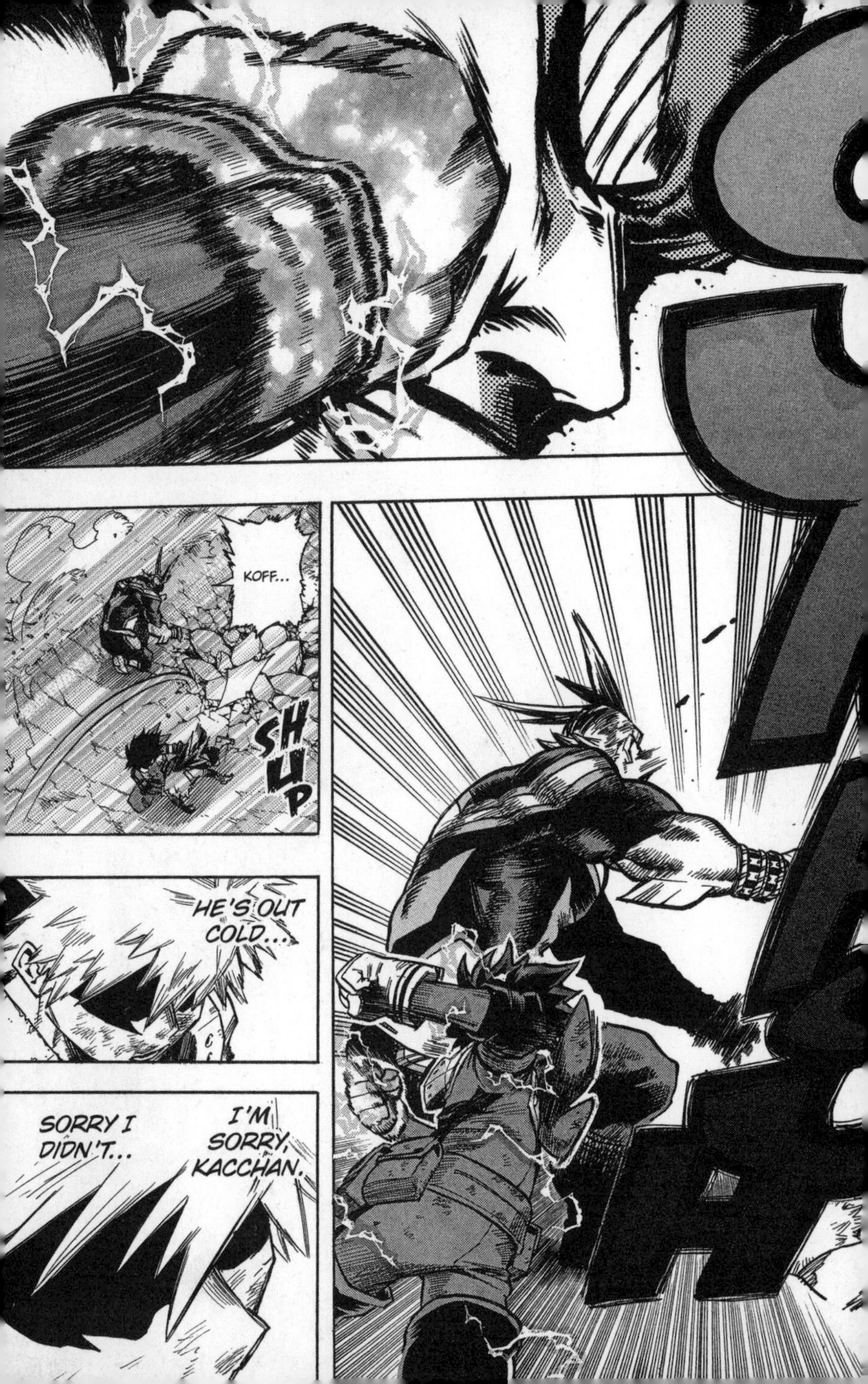
KOFF...
SHUP
HE'S OUT COLD...
I'M SORRY, KACCHAN.
SORRY I DIDN'T...

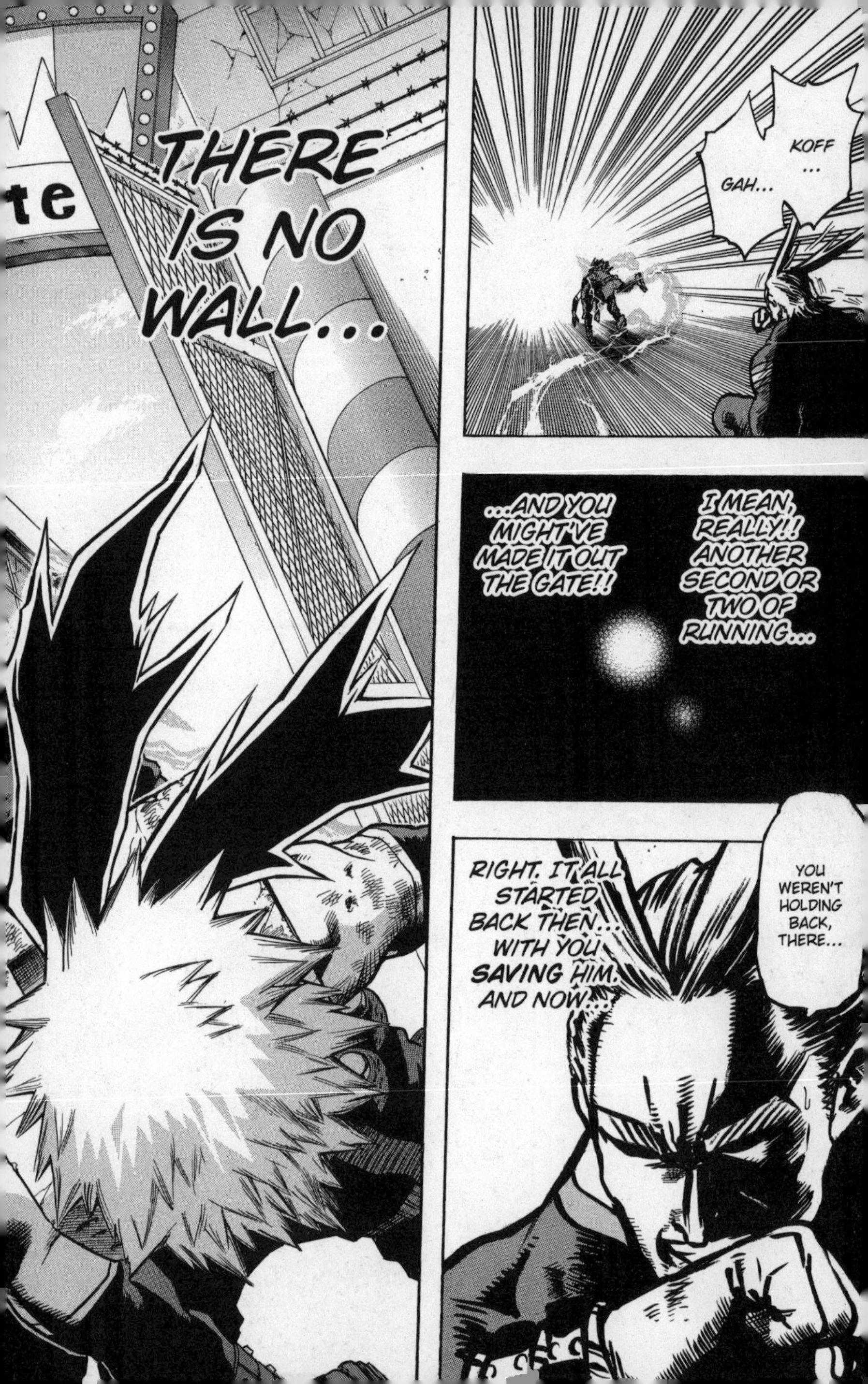
KOFF ... GAH...
I MEAN, REALLY!! ANOTHER SECOND OR TWO OF RUNNING...
...AND YOU MIGHT'VE MADE IT OUT THE GATE!!
YOU WEREN'T HOLDING BACK, THERE...
RIGHT. IT ALL STARTED BACK THEN... WITH YOU SAVING HIM. AND NOW...
THERE IS NO WALL...

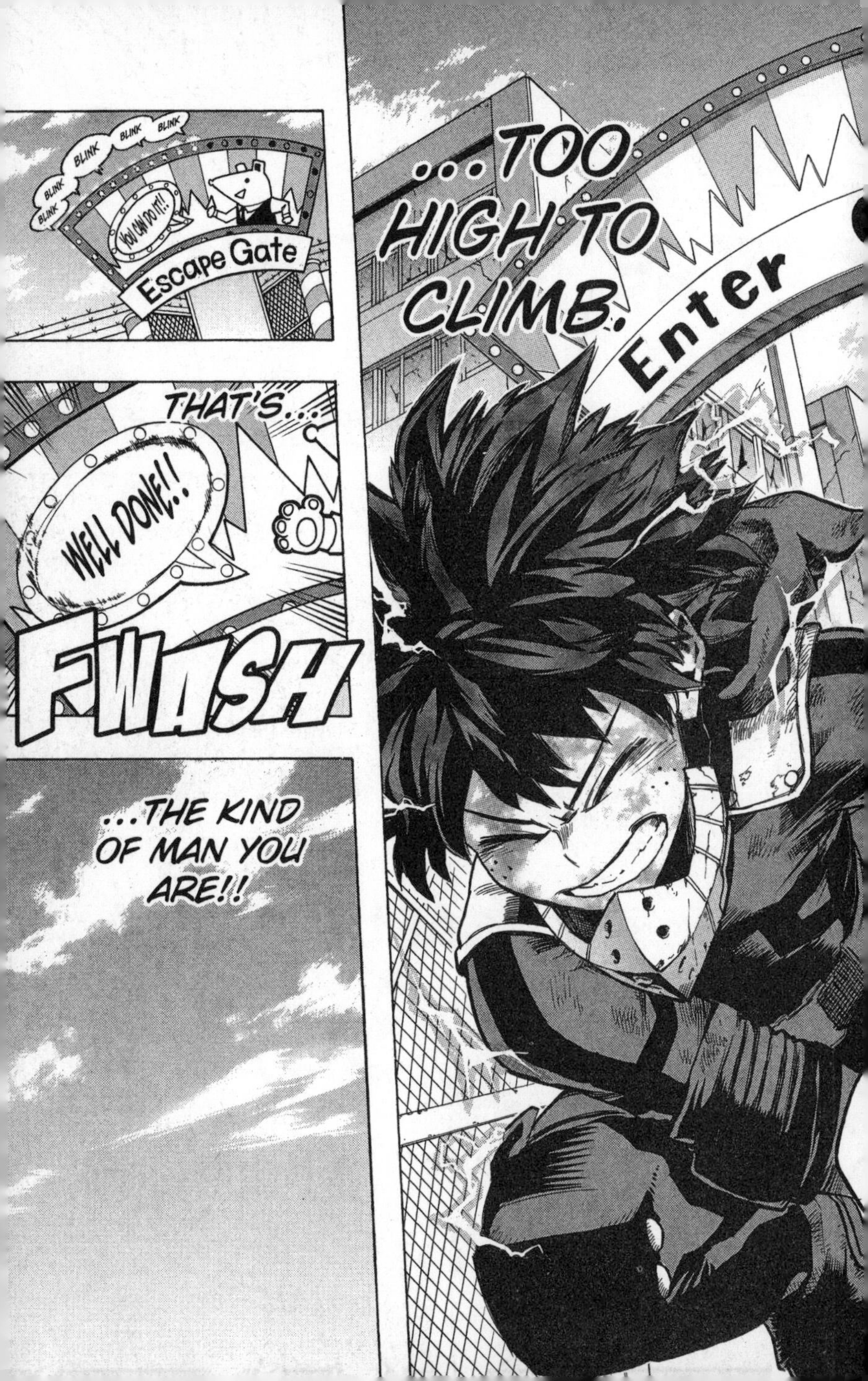
...TOO HIGH TO CLIMB.
Enter
BLINK
BLINK
BLINK
BLINK
BLINK
YOU CAN DO IT!!
Escape Gate
THAT'S...
WELL DONE!!
FWASH
...THE KIND OF MAN YOU ARE!!

THE COSTUME

MOMO YAOYOROZU'S COSTUME

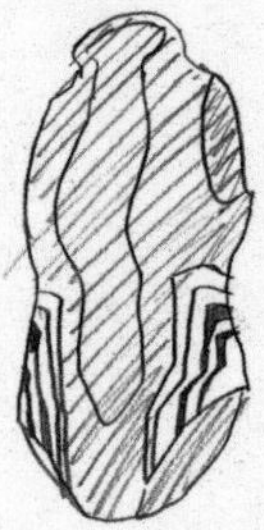

Yaoyoro Leotard
Exposes a lot of skin to allow her to use her Creation more easily. Her original Quirk specifications actually had even more skin showing, but that design was borderline illegal, so it was modified. The area exposed around her navel keeps expanding, somehow, thanks to the author's... inclinations.

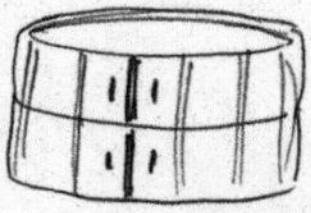

Yaoyoro Belt
Nice and thick, made to support the Yaoyoro Reference Books.

Yaoyoro Reference Books

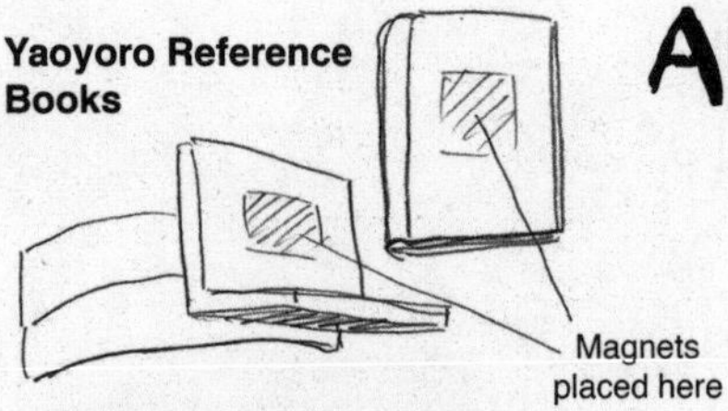
Magnets placed here

Contain information on the composition of items that could be useful during hero endeavors. Magnets are attached to the front and back of the books to ensure they won't accidentally flip open or fall off entirely.

ALL IN ALL: SEXY

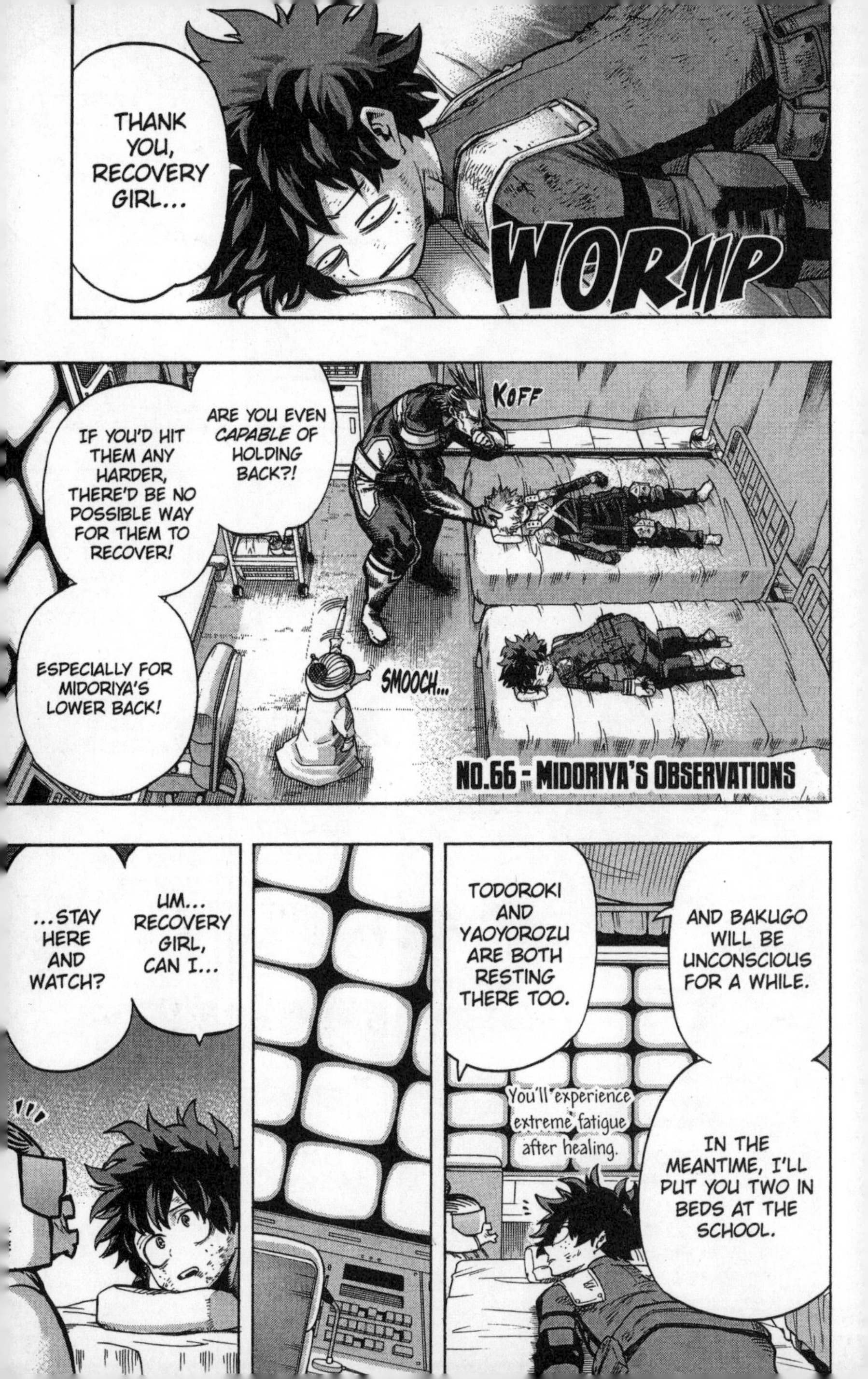
THANK YOU, RECOVERY GIRL...
WORMP
KOFF
ARE YOU EVEN CAPABLE OF HOLDING BACK?!
IF YOU'D HIT THEM ANY HARDER, THERE'D BE NO POSSIBLE WAY FOR THEM TO RECOVER!
SMOOCH...
ESPECIALLY FOR MIDORIYA'S LOWER BACK!
NO.66 - MIDORIYA'S OBSERVATIONS
AND BAKUGO WILL BE UNCONSCIOUS FOR A WHILE.
TODOROKI AND YAOYOROZU ARE BOTH RESTING THERE TOO.
IN THE MEANTIME, I'LL PUT YOU TWO IN BEDS AT THE SCHOOL.
You'll experience extreme fatigue after healing.
UM... RECOVERY GIRL, CAN I...
...STAY HERE AND WATCH?

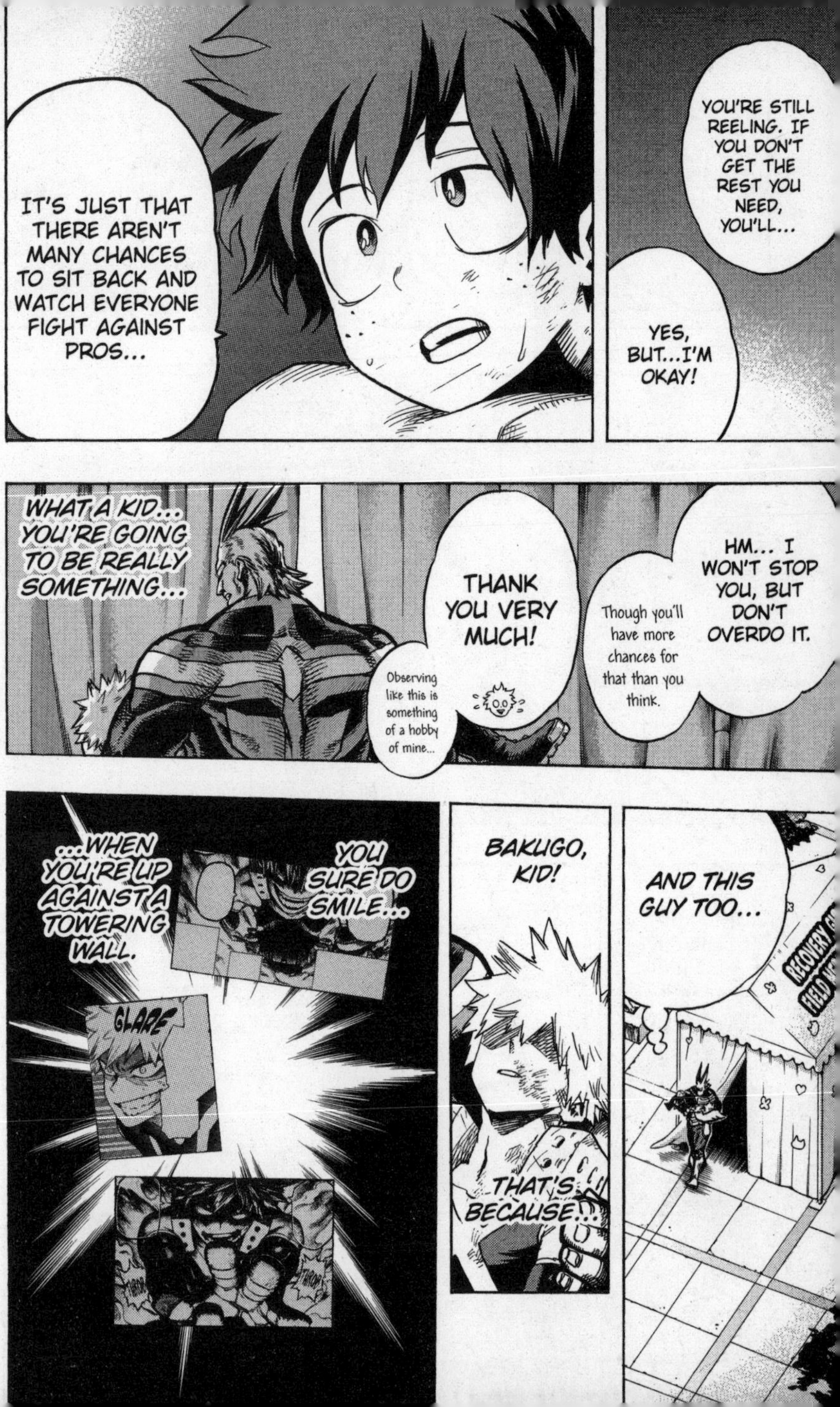
YOU'RE STILL REELING. IF YOU DON'T GET THE REST YOU NEED, YOU'LL...
YES, BUT...I'M OKAY!
IT'S JUST THAT THERE AREN'T MANY CHANCES TO SIT BACK AND WATCH EVERYONE FIGHT AGAINST PROS...
HM... I WON'T STOP YOU, BUT DON'T OVERDO IT.
Though you'll have more chances for that than you think.
THANK YOU VERY MUCH!
Observing like this is something of a hobby of mine...
WHAT A KID... YOU'RE GOING TO BE REALLY SOMETHING...
AND THIS GUY TOO...
BAKUGO, KID!
THAT'S BECAUSE...
YOU SURE DO SMILE...
...WHEN YOU'RE UP AGAINST A TOWERING WALL.
GLARE
THROB
THROB

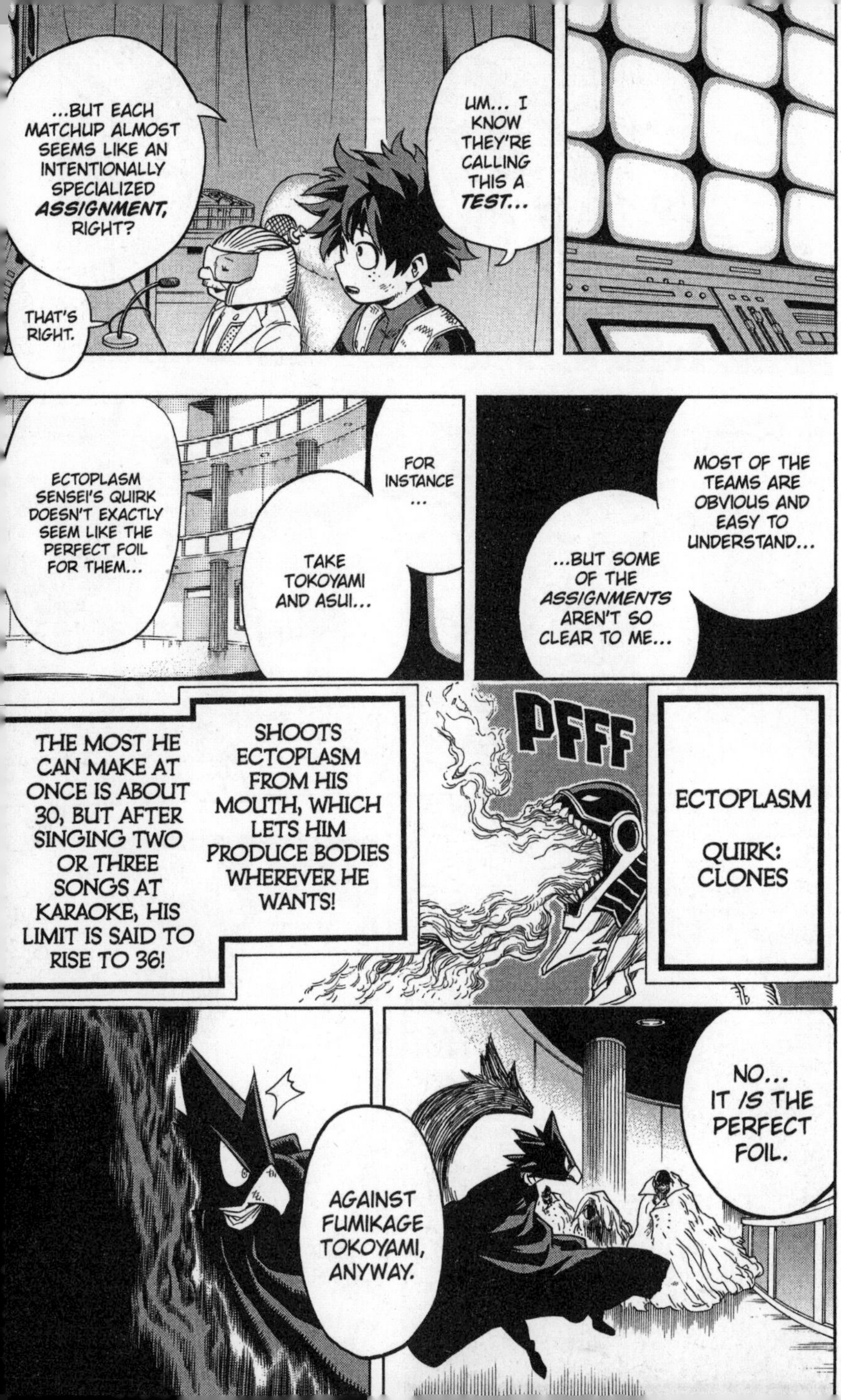
UM... I KNOW THEY'RE CALLING THIS A *TEST*...
...BUT EACH MATCHUP ALMOST SEEMS LIKE AN INTENTIONALLY SPECIALIZED ***ASSIGNMENT***, RIGHT?
THAT'S RIGHT.
MOST OF THE TEAMS ARE OBVIOUS AND EASY TO UNDERSTAND...
...BUT SOME OF THE *ASSIGNMENTS* AREN'T SO CLEAR TO ME...
FOR INSTANCE...
TAKE TOKOYAMI AND ASUI...
ECTOPLASM SENSEI'S QUIRK DOESN'T EXACTLY SEEM LIKE THE PERFECT FOIL FOR THEM...
ECTOPLASM
QUIRK: CLONES
PFFF
SHOOTS ECTOPLASM FROM HIS MOUTH, WHICH LETS HIM PRODUCE BODIES WHEREVER HE WANTS!
THE MOST HE CAN MAKE AT ONCE IS ABOUT 30, BUT AFTER SINGING TWO OR THREE SONGS AT KARAOKE, HIS LIMIT IS SAID TO RISE TO 36!
NO... IT *IS* THE PERFECT FOIL.
AGAINST FUMIKAGE TOKOYAMI, ANYWAY.

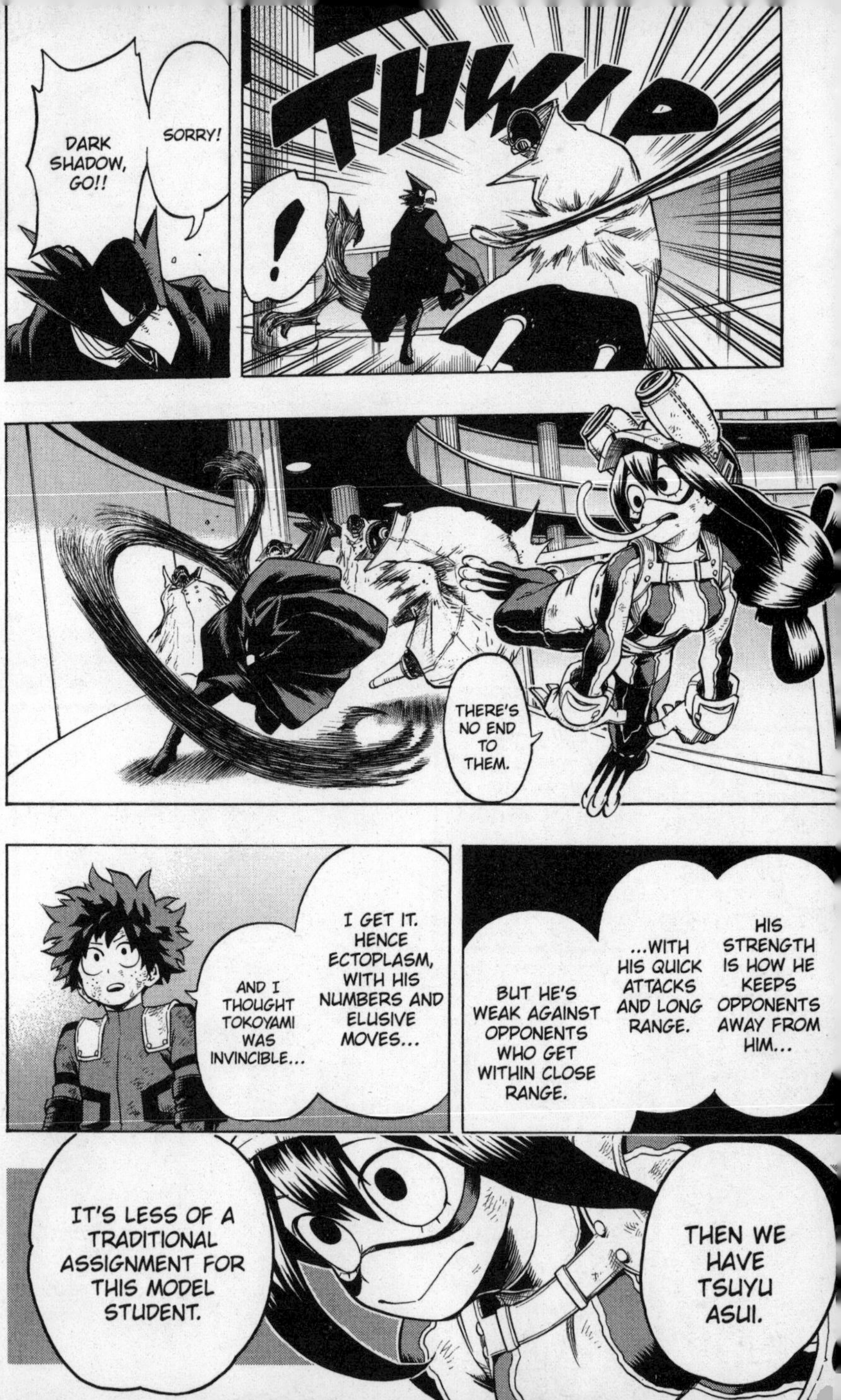
THWIP
!
SORRY!
DARK SHADOW, GO!!
THERE'S NO END TO THEM.
HIS STRENGTH IS HOW HE KEEPS OPPONENTS AWAY FROM HIM...
...WITH HIS QUICK ATTACKS AND LONG RANGE.
BUT HE'S WEAK AGAINST OPPONENTS WHO GET WITHIN CLOSE RANGE.
I GET IT. HENCE ECTOPLASM, WITH HIS NUMBERS AND ELUSIVE MOVES...
AND I THOUGHT TOKOYAMI WAS INVINCIBLE...
THEN WE HAVE TSUYU ASUI.
IT'S LESS OF A TRADITIONAL ASSIGNMENT FOR THIS MODEL STUDENT.

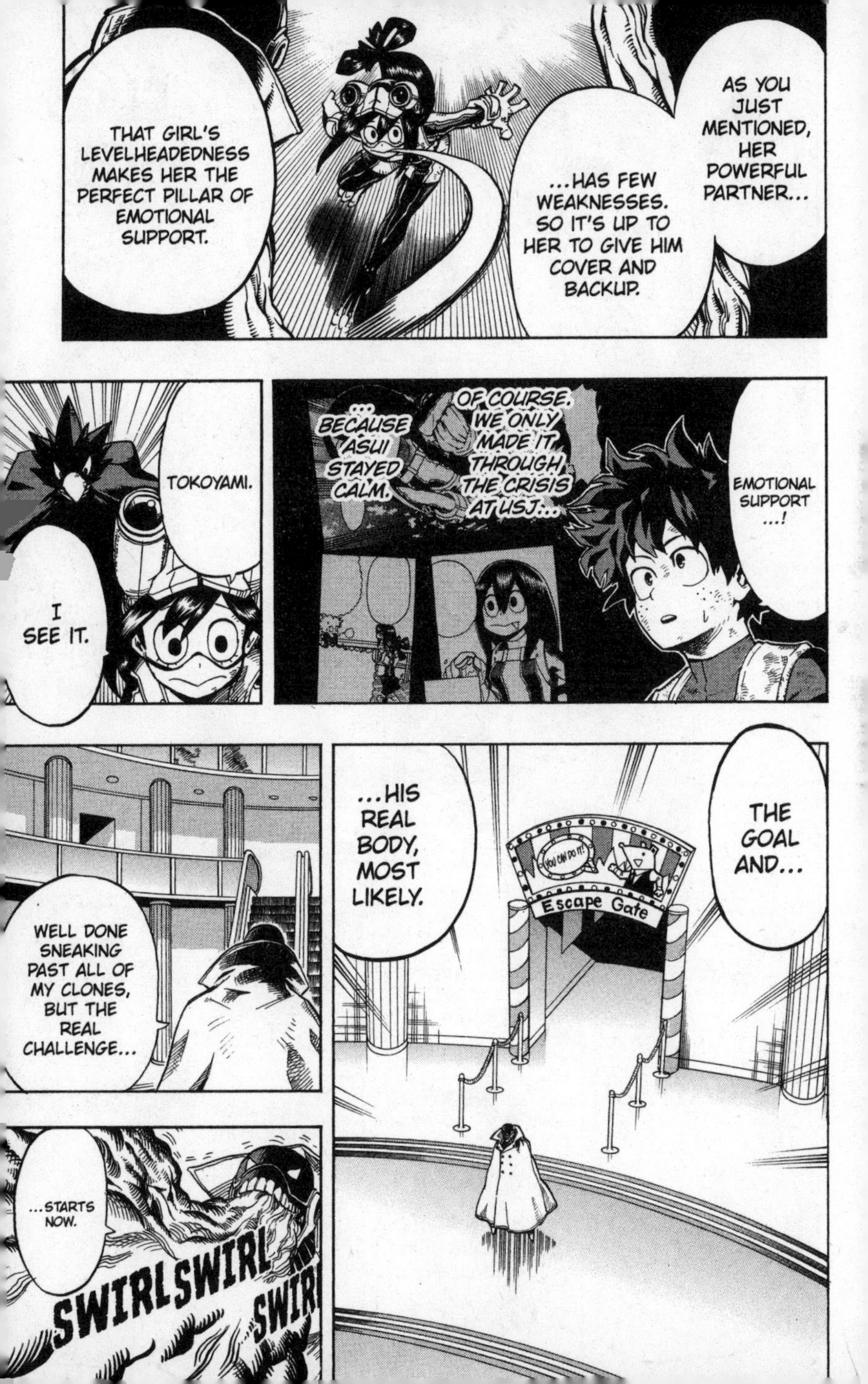
AS YOU JUST MENTIONED, HER POWERFUL PARTNER...
...HAS FEW WEAKNESSES. SO IT'S UP TO HER TO GIVE HIM COVER AND BACKUP.
THAT GIRL'S LEVELHEADEDNESS MAKES HER THE PERFECT PILLAR OF EMOTIONAL SUPPORT.
EMOTIONAL SUPPORT ...!
OF COURSE. WE ONLY MADE IT THROUGH THE CRISIS AT USJ...
...BECAUSE ASUI STAYED CALM.
TOKOYAMI.
I SEE IT.
THE GOAL AND...
...HIS REAL BODY, MOST LIKELY.
YOU CAN DO IT!
Escape Gate
WELL DONE SNEAKING PAST ALL OF MY CLONES, BUT THE REAL CHALLENGE...
...STARTS NOW.
SWIRL SWIRL
SWIR

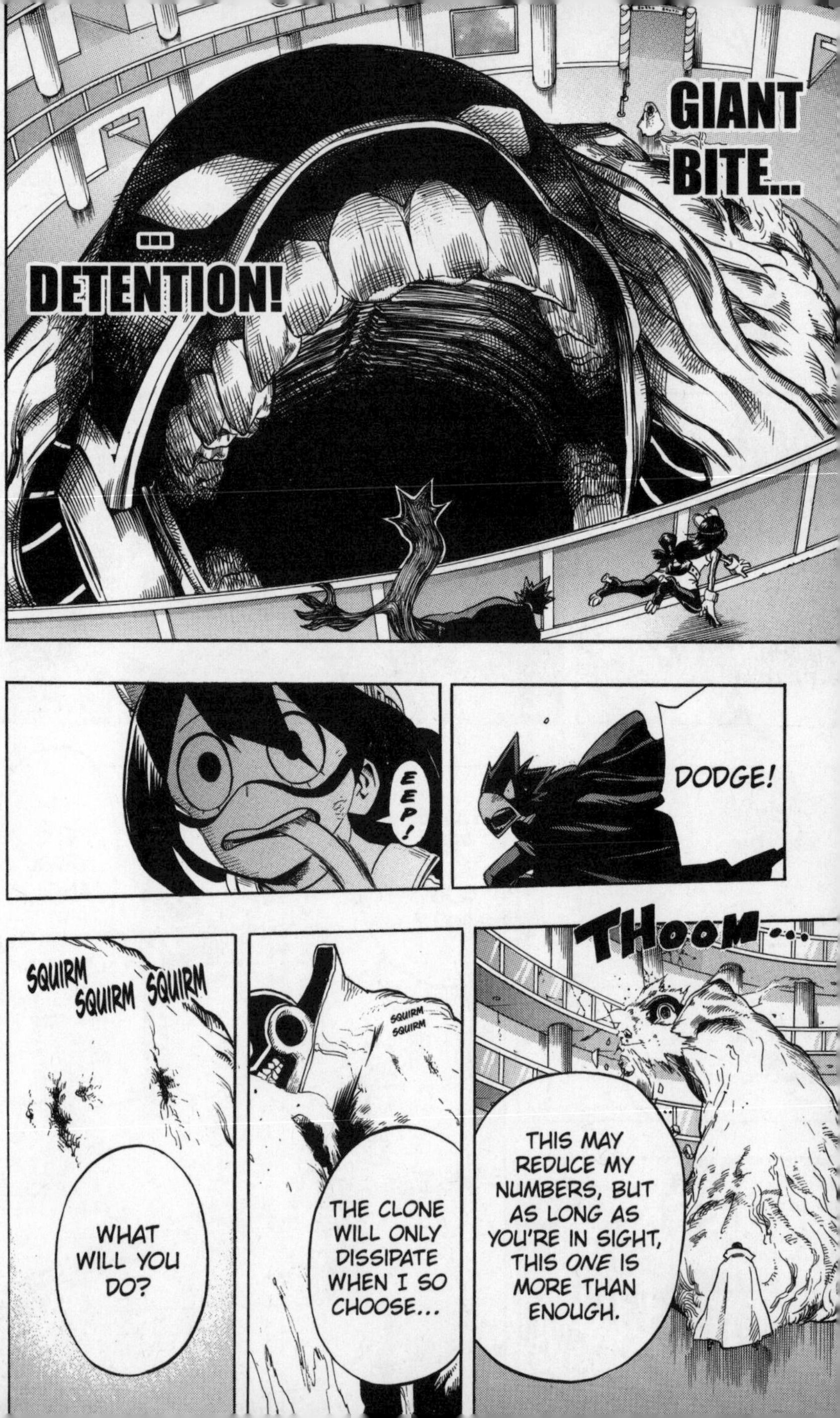
GIANT BITE...
... DETENTION!
DODGE!
EEP!
THOOM...
THIS MAY REDUCE MY NUMBERS, BUT AS LONG AS YOU'RE IN SIGHT, THIS *ONE* IS MORE THAN ENOUGH.
SQUIRM SQUIRM
THE CLONE WILL ONLY DISSIPATE WHEN I SO CHOOSE...
SQUIRM SQUIRM SQUIRM
WHAT WILL YOU DO?

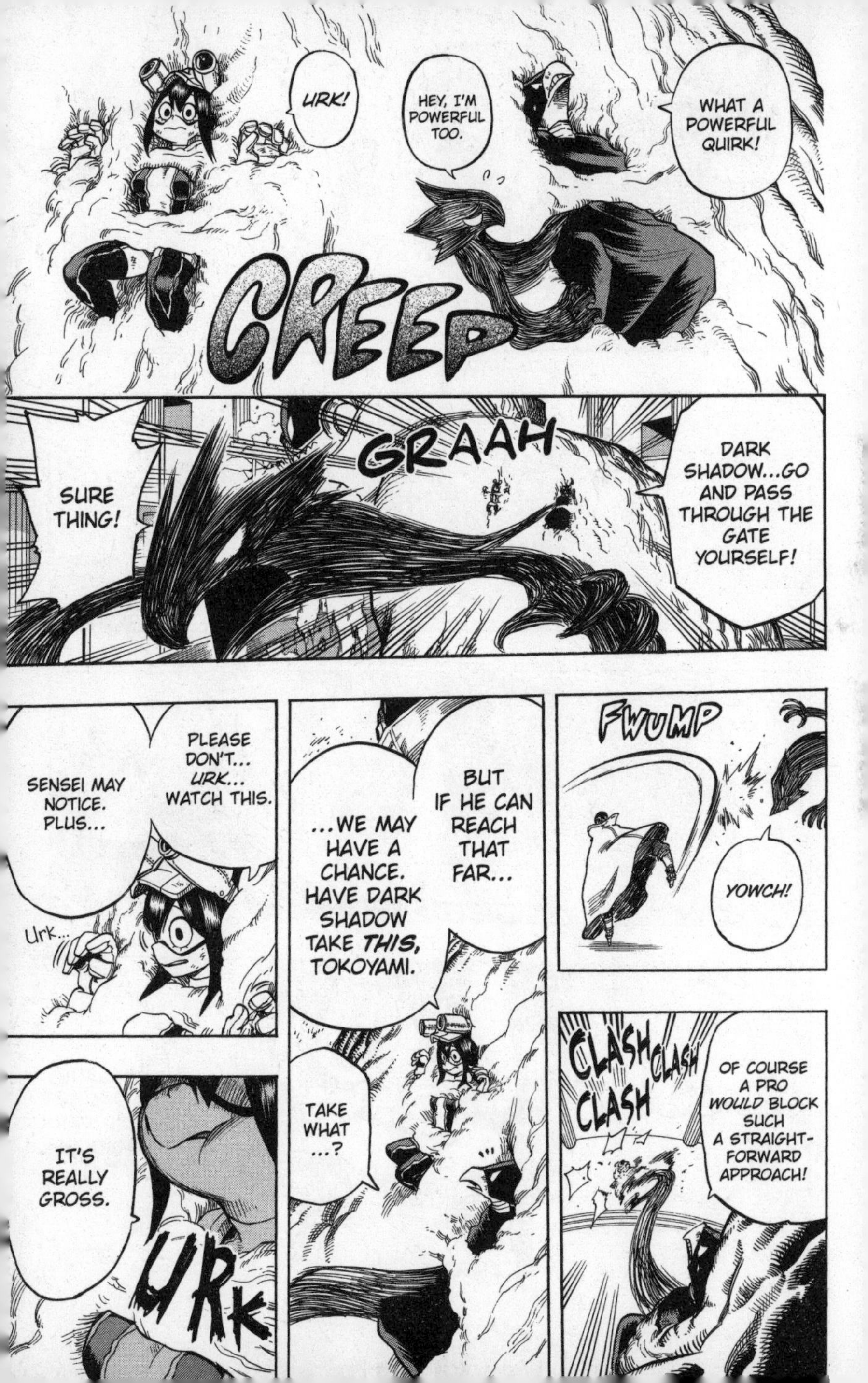
WHAT A POWERFUL QUIRK!
HEY, I'M POWERFUL TOO.
URK!
CREEP
DARK SHADOW...GO AND PASS THROUGH THE GATE YOURSELF!
GRAAH
SURE THING!
FWUMP
YOWCH!
CLASH CLASH CLASH
OF COURSE A PRO WOULD BLOCK SUCH A STRAIGHT-FORWARD APPROACH!
BUT IF HE CAN REACH THAT FAR...
...WE MAY HAVE A CHANCE. HAVE DARK SHADOW TAKE THIS, TOKOYAMI.
TAKE WHAT ...?
PLEASE DON'T... URK... WATCH THIS.
SENSEI MAY NOTICE. PLUS...
Urk...
IT'S REALLY GROSS.
URK

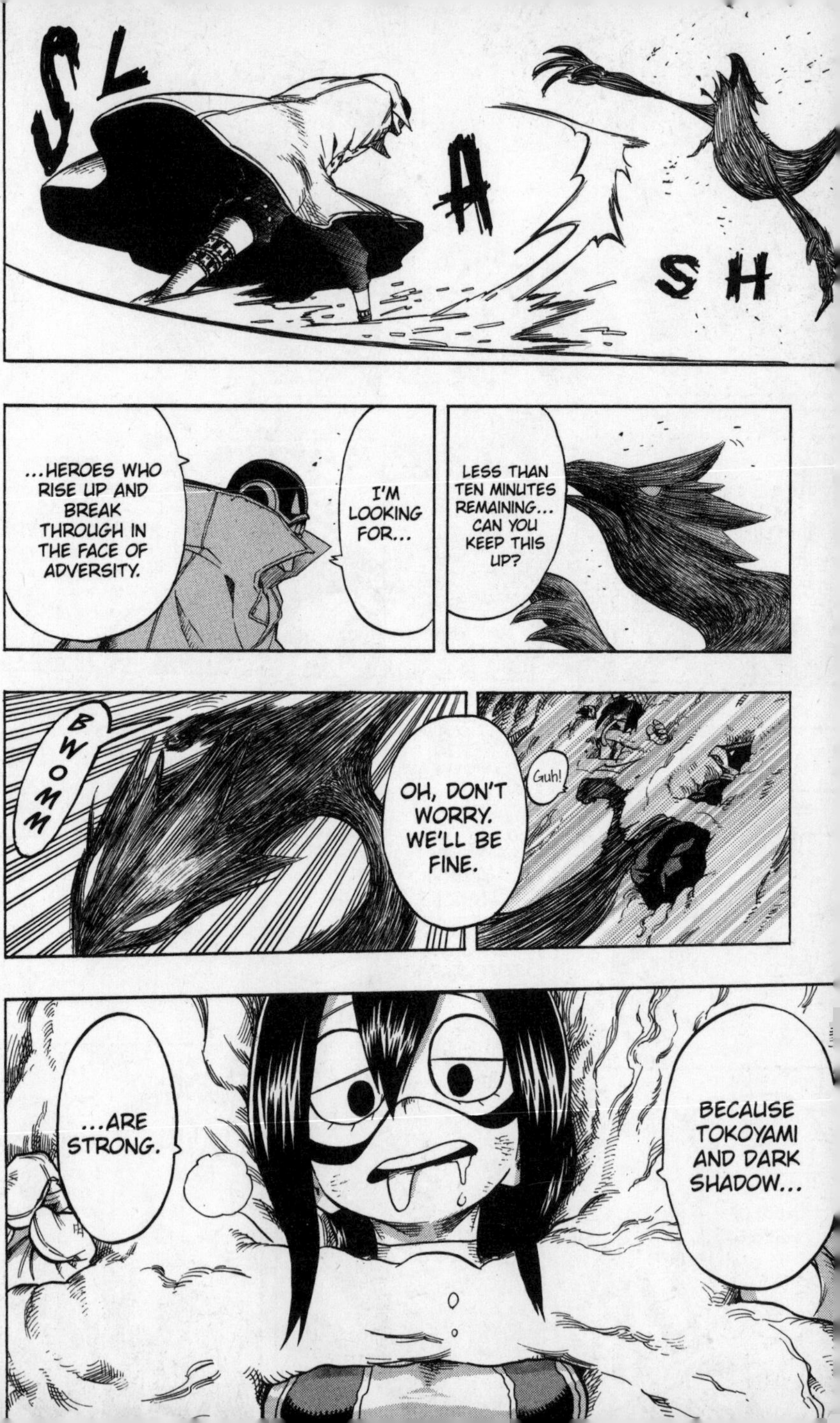
SLASH
LESS THAN TEN MINUTES REMAINING... CAN YOU KEEP THIS UP?
I'M LOOKING FOR...
...HEROES WHO RISE UP AND BREAK THROUGH IN THE FACE OF ADVERSITY.
Guh!
OH, DON'T WORRY. WE'LL BE FINE.
BWOMM
BECAUSE TOKOYAMI AND DARK SHADOW...
...ARE STRONG.

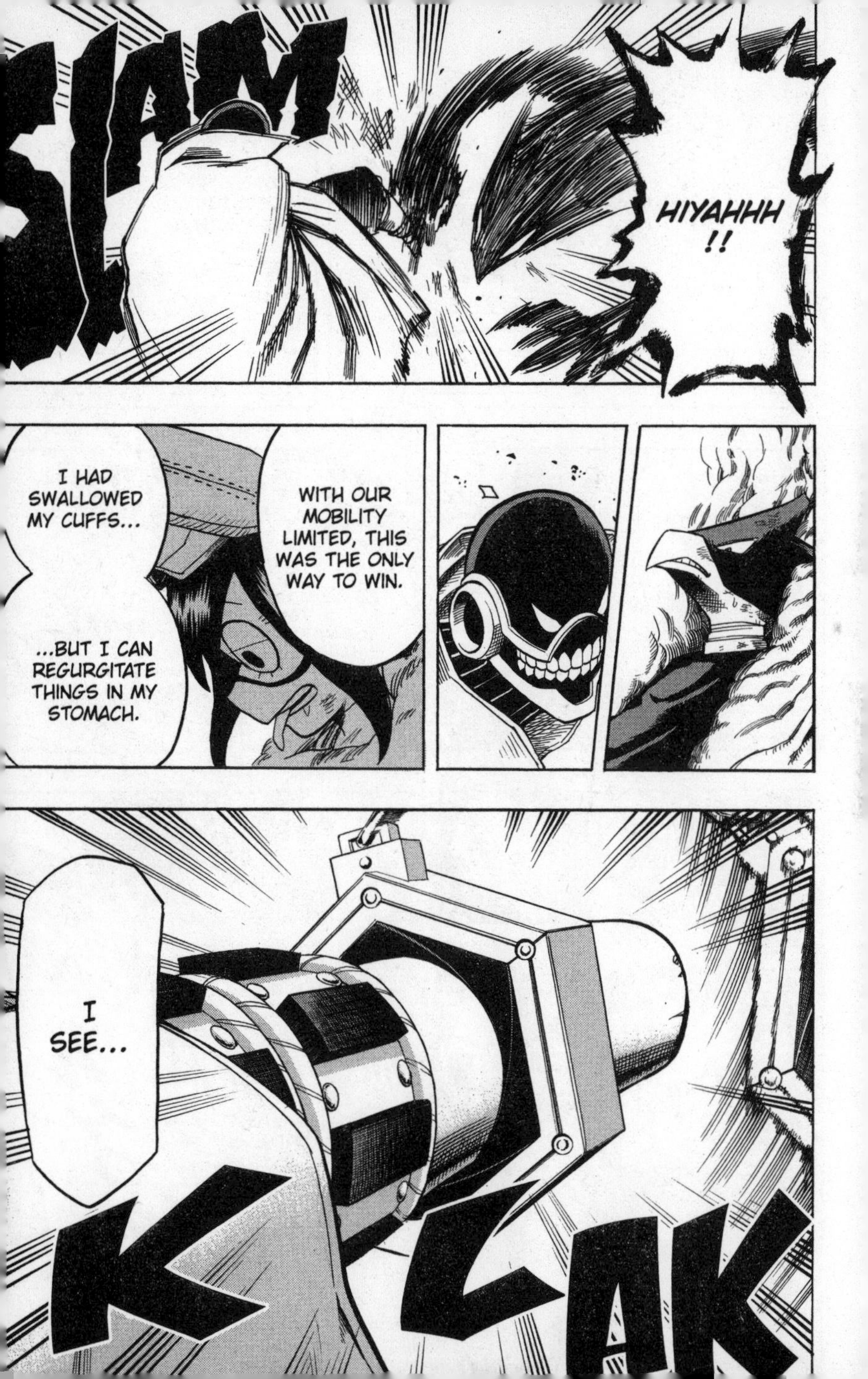
HIYAHHH !!
SLAM
WITH OUR MOBILITY LIMITED, THIS WAS THE ONLY WAY TO WIN.
I HAD SWALLOWED MY CUFFS...
...BUT I CAN REGURGITATE THINGS IN MY STOMACH.
I SEE...
KLAK

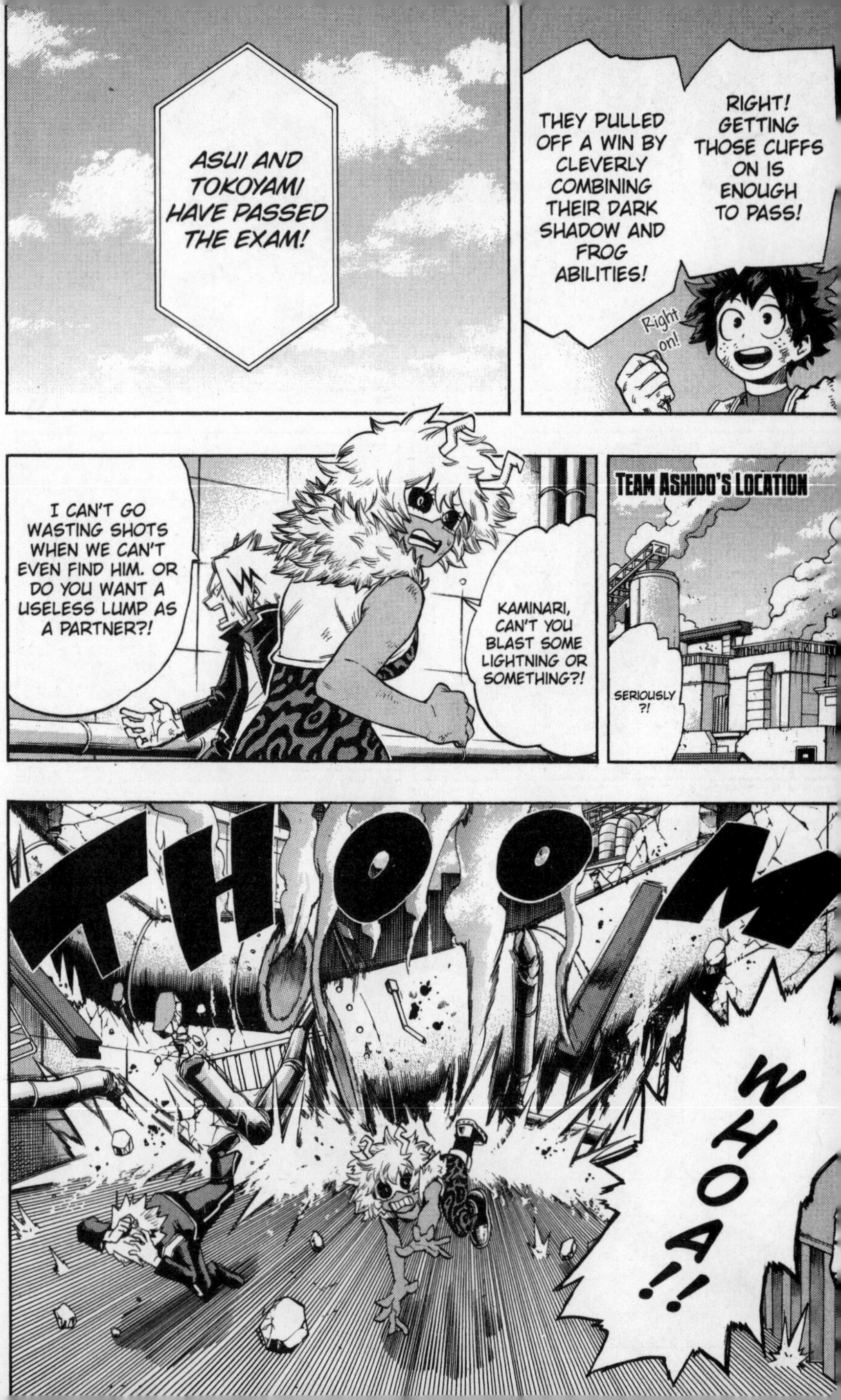
RIGHT! GETTING THOSE CUFFS ON IS ENOUGH TO PASS!
THEY PULLED OFF A WIN BY CLEVERLY COMBINING THEIR DARK SHADOW AND FROG ABILITIES!
Right on!
ASUI AND TOKOYAMI HAVE PASSED THE EXAM!
TEAM ASHIDO'S LOCATION
SERIOUSLY ?!
KAMINARI, CAN'T YOU BLAST SOME LIGHTNING OR SOMETHING?!
I CAN'T GO WASTING SHOTS WHEN WE CAN'T EVEN FIND HIM. OR DO YOU WANT A USELESS LUMP AS A PARTNER?!
WHOA!!
THOOM

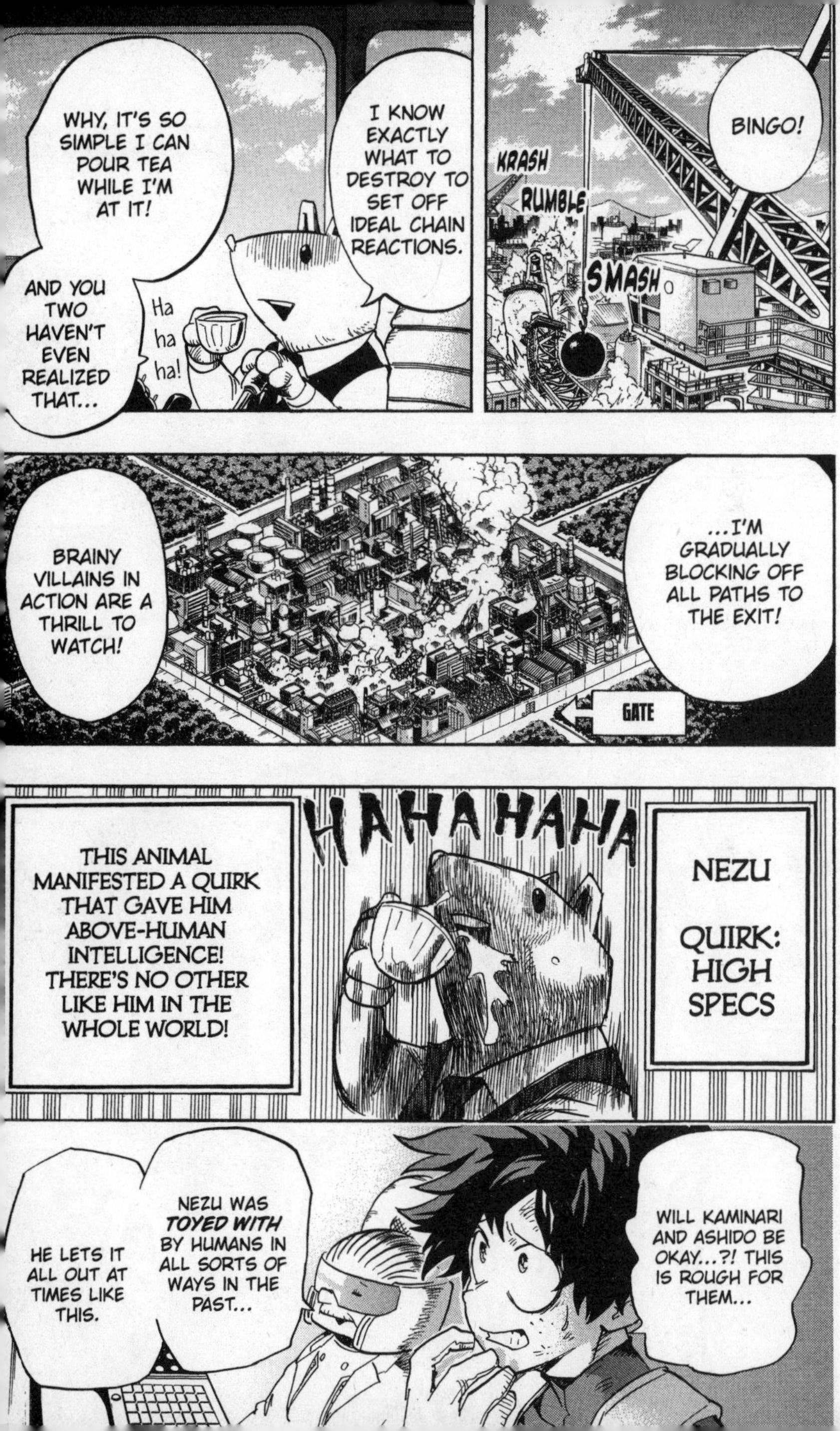
BINGO!
KRASH
RUMBLE
SMASH
I KNOW EXACTLY WHAT TO DESTROY TO SET OFF IDEAL CHAIN REACTIONS.
WHY, IT'S SO SIMPLE I CAN POUR TEA WHILE I'M AT IT!
Ha ha ha!
AND YOU TWO HAVEN'T EVEN REALIZED THAT...
...I'M GRADUALLY BLOCKING OFF ALL PATHS TO THE EXIT!
GATE
BRAINY VILLAINS IN ACTION ARE A THRILL TO WATCH!
NEZU
QUIRK: HIGH SPECS
HAHAHAHA
THIS ANIMAL MANIFESTED A QUIRK THAT GAVE HIM ABOVE-HUMAN INTELLIGENCE! THERE'S NO OTHER LIKE HIM IN THE WHOLE WORLD!
WILL KAMINARI AND ASHIDO BE OKAY...?! THIS IS ROUGH FOR THEM...
NEZU WAS TOYED WITH BY HUMANS IN ALL SORTS OF WAYS IN THE PAST...
HE LETS IT ALL OUT AT TIMES LIKE THIS.

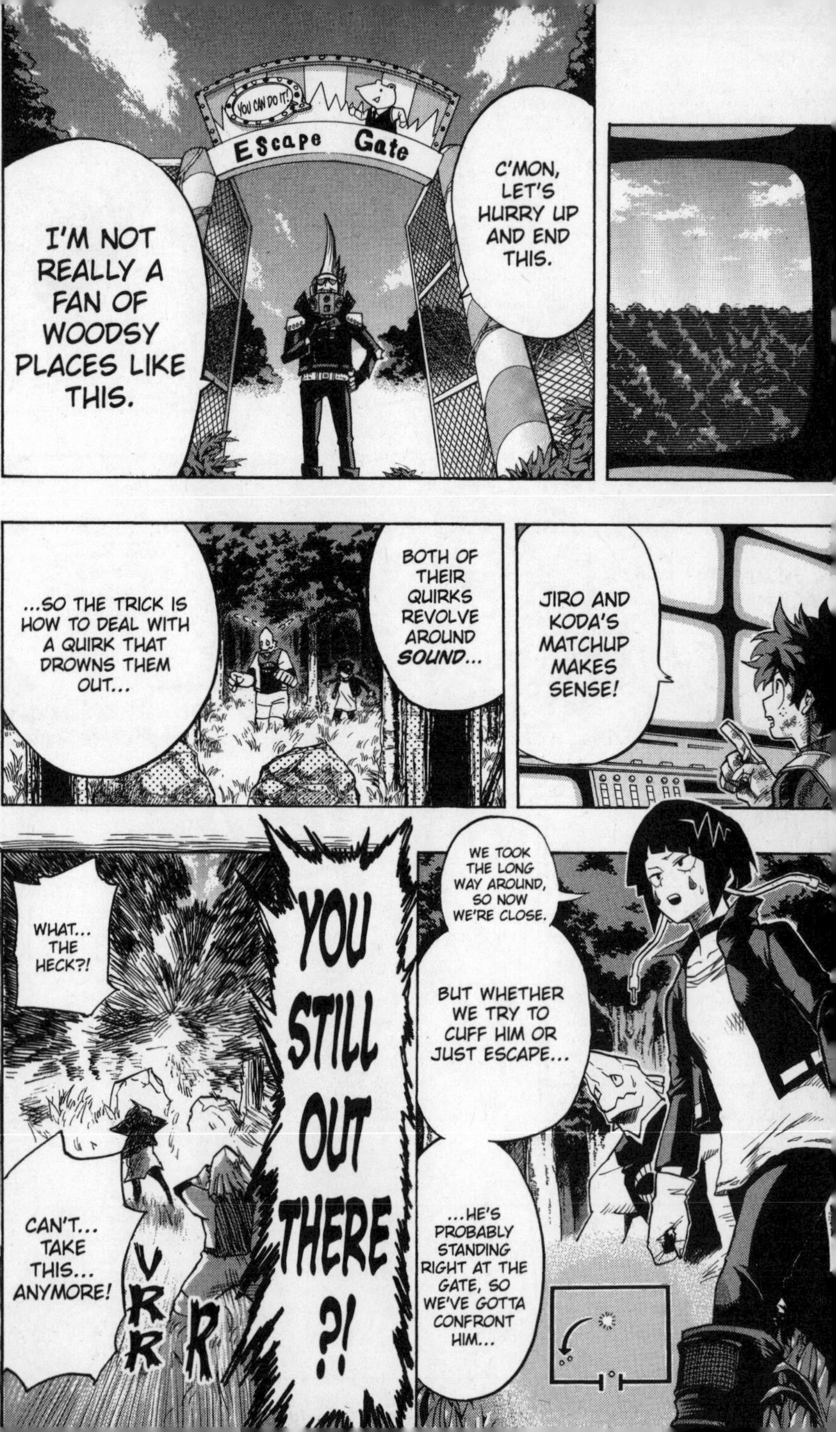
YOU CAN DO IT!
EScape Gate
C'MON, LET'S HURRY UP AND END THIS.
I'M NOT REALLY A FAN OF WOODSY PLACES LIKE THIS.
JIRO AND KODA'S MATCHUP MAKES SENSE!
BOTH OF THEIR QUIRKS REVOLVE AROUND *SOUND*...
...SO THE TRICK IS HOW TO DEAL WITH A QUIRK THAT DROWNS THEM OUT...
WE TOOK THE LONG WAY AROUND, SO NOW WE'RE CLOSE.
BUT WHETHER WE TRY TO CUFF HIM OR JUST ESCAPE...
...HE'S PROBABLY STANDING RIGHT AT THE GATE, SO WE'VE GOTTA CONFRONT HIM...
YOU STILL OUT THERE?!
WHAT... THE HECK?!
CAN'T... TAKE THIS... ANYMORE!
VRR
R

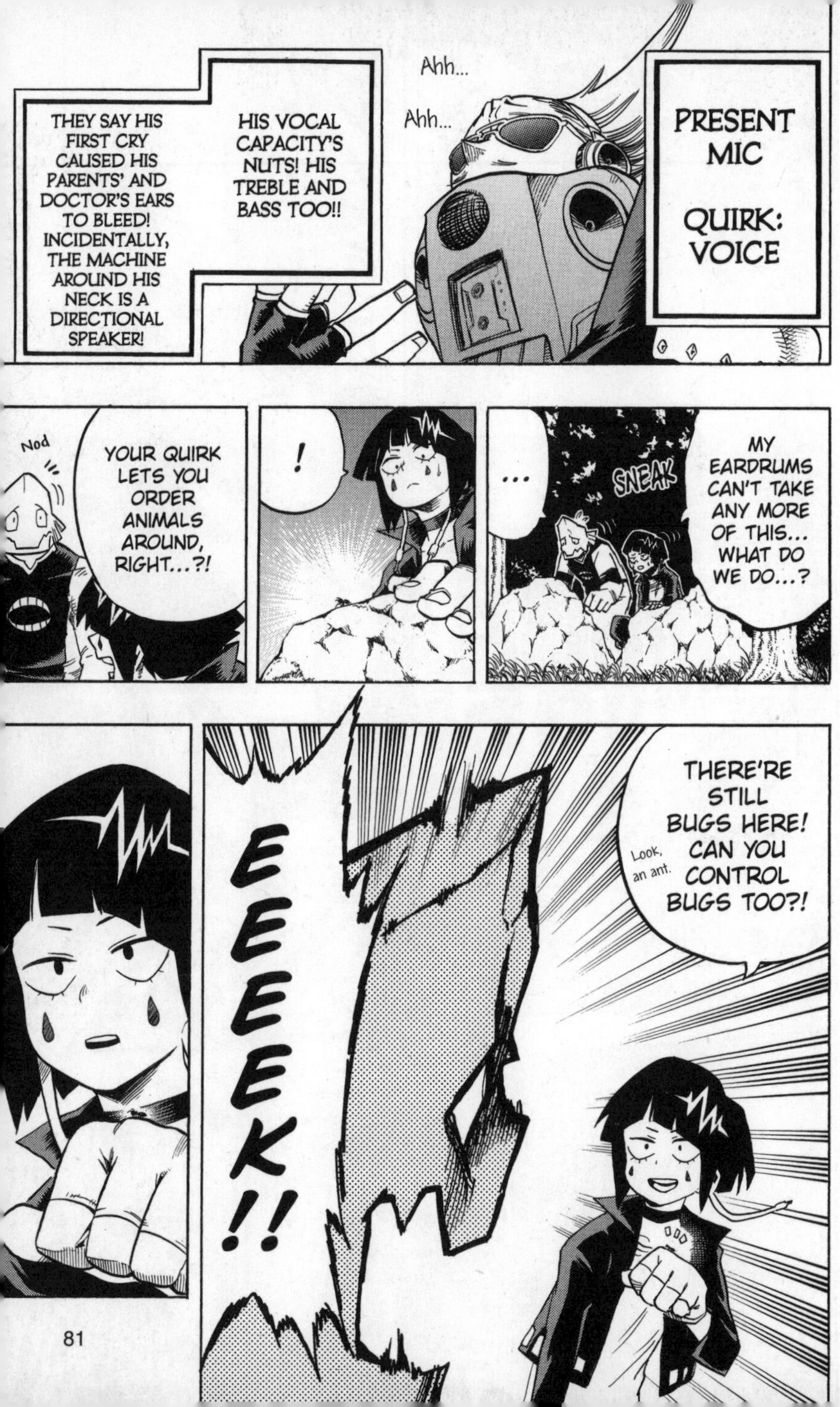
PRESENT MIC
QUIRK: VOICE
Ahh...
Ahh...
HIS VOCAL CAPACITY'S NUTS! HIS TREBLE AND BASS TOO!!
THEY SAY HIS FIRST CRY CAUSED HIS PARENTS' AND DOCTOR'S EARS TO BLEED! INCIDENTALLY, THE MACHINE AROUND HIS NECK IS A DIRECTIONAL SPEAKER!
MY EARDRUMS CAN'T TAKE ANY MORE OF THIS... WHAT DO WE DO...?
SNEAK
...
!
YOUR QUIRK LETS YOU ORDER ANIMALS AROUND, RIGHT...?!
Nod
THERE'RE STILL BUGS HERE! CAN YOU CONTROL BUGS TOO?!
Look, an ant.
EEEEK!!

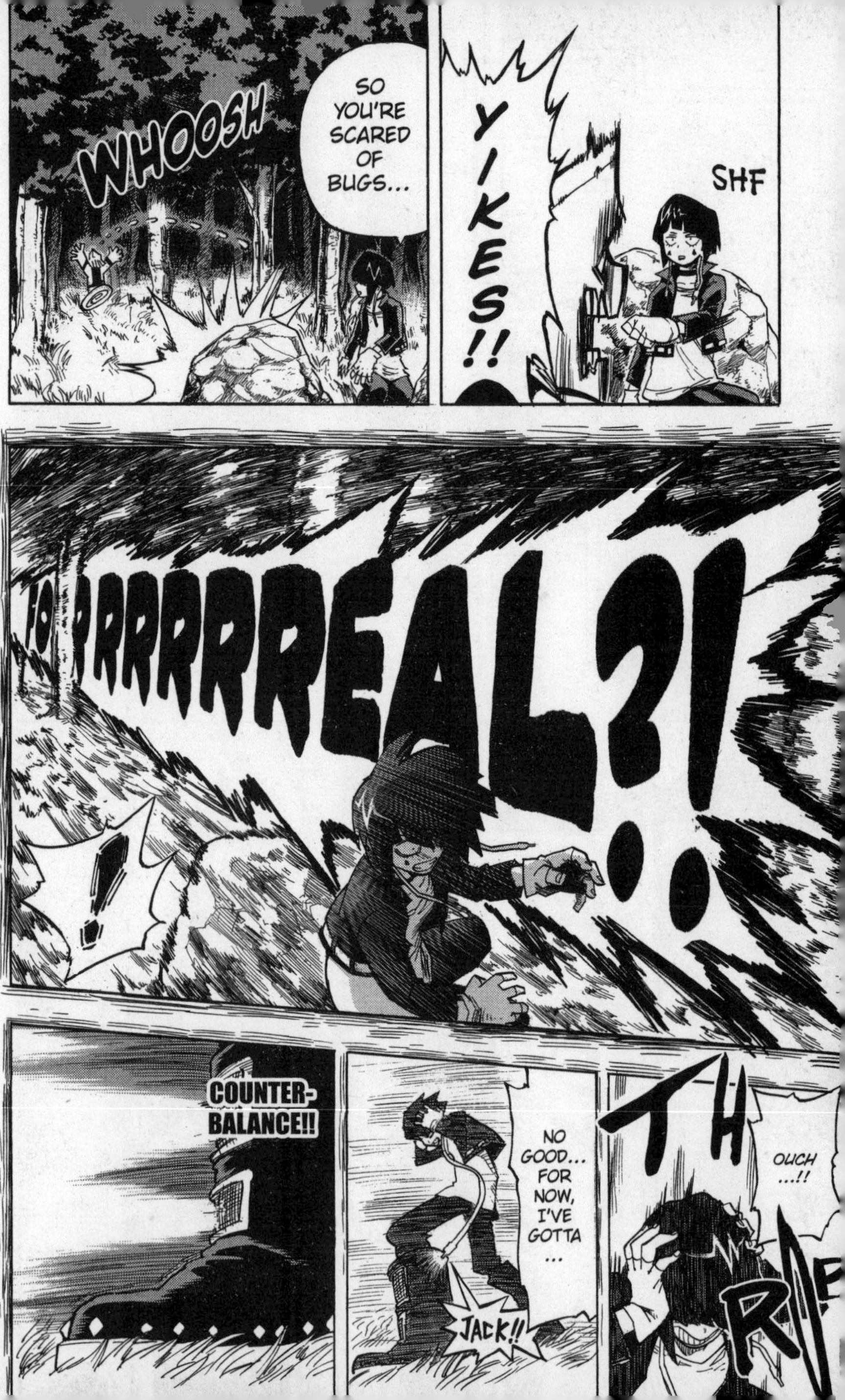
SHF
YIKES!!
SO YOU'RE SCARED OF BUGS...
WHOOSH
FORRRRRREAL?!
!
OUCH ...!!
TH
RIP
NO GOOD... FOR NOW, I'VE GOTTA ...
JACK!!
COUNTER-BALANCE!!

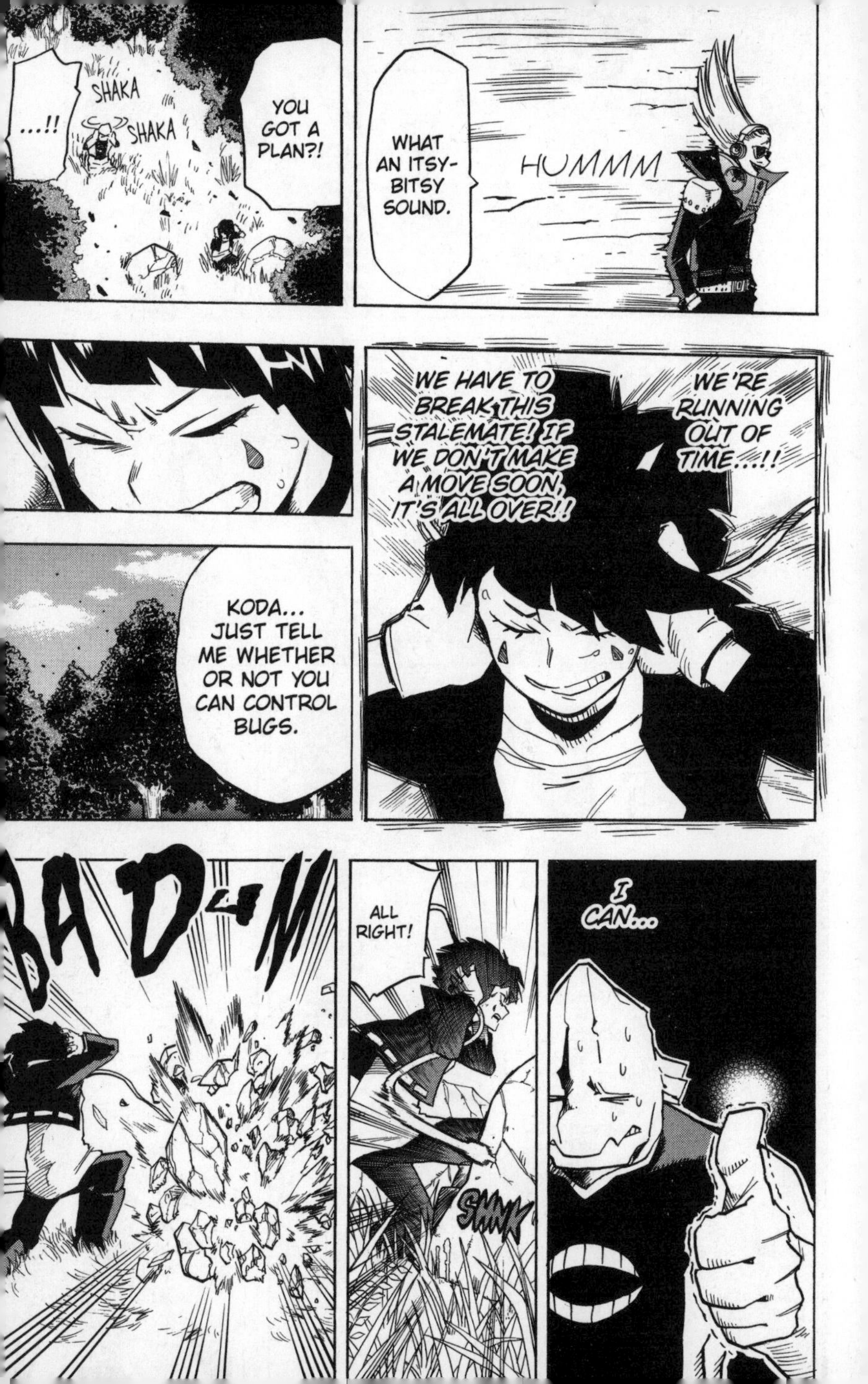
WHAT AN ITSY-BITSY SOUND.
HUMMMM
YOU GOT A PLAN?!
SHAKA
SHAKA
...!!
WE'RE RUNNING OUT OF TIME...!!
WE HAVE TO BREAK THIS STALEMATE! IF WE DON'T MAKE A MOVE SOON, IT'S ALL OVER!!
KODA... JUST TELL ME WHETHER OR NOT YOU CAN CONTROL BUGS.
I CAN...
ALL RIGHT!
SHNK
BAD-M

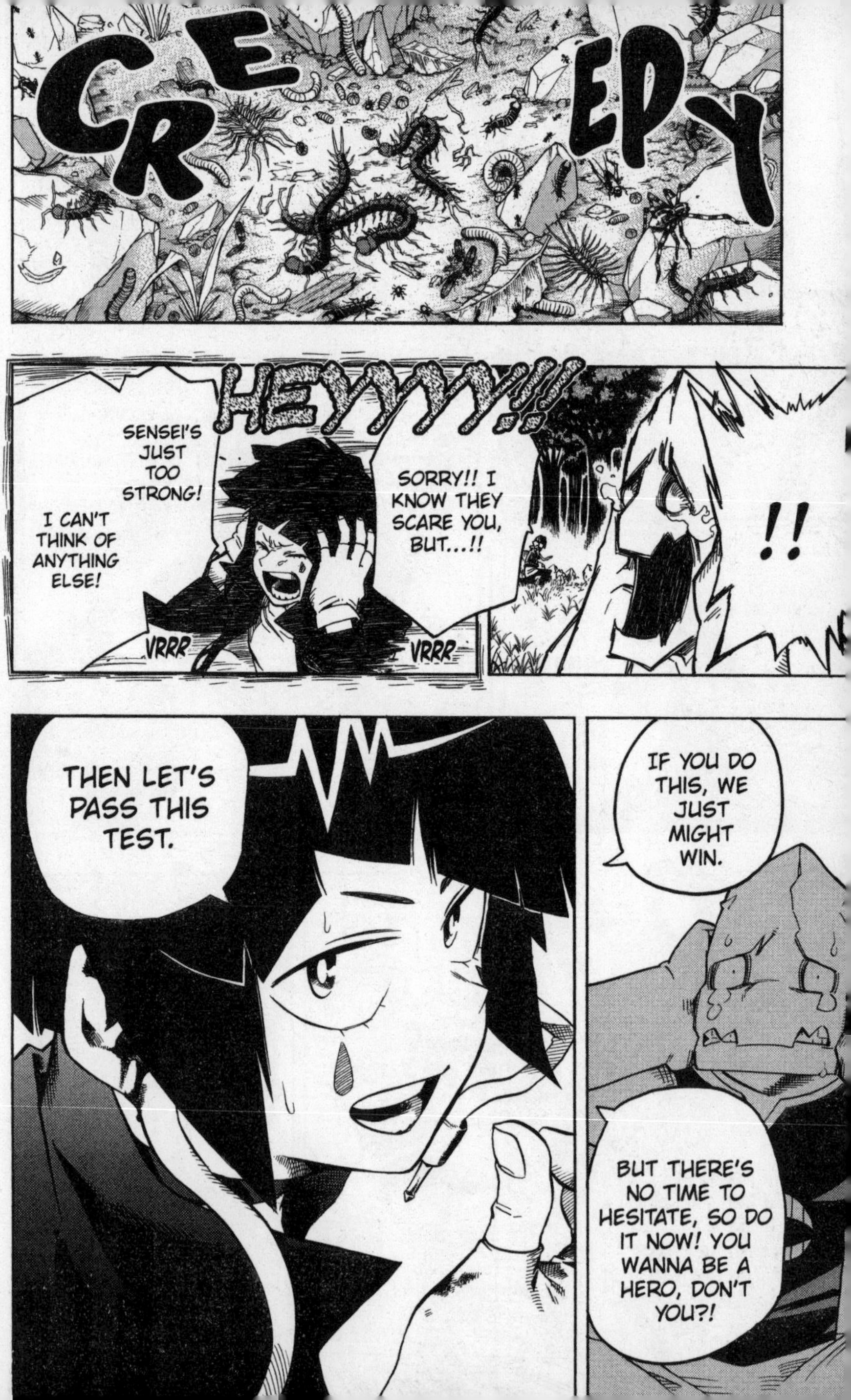
CREEPY
!!
HEYYY!!!
SORRY!! I KNOW THEY SCARE YOU, BUT...!!
SENSEI'S JUST TOO STRONG!
I CAN'T THINK OF ANYTHING ELSE!
VRRR
VRRR
IF YOU DO THIS, WE JUST MIGHT WIN.
BUT THERE'S NO TIME TO HESITATE, SO DO IT NOW! YOU WANNA BE A HERO, DON'T YOU?!
THEN LET'S PASS THIS TEST.

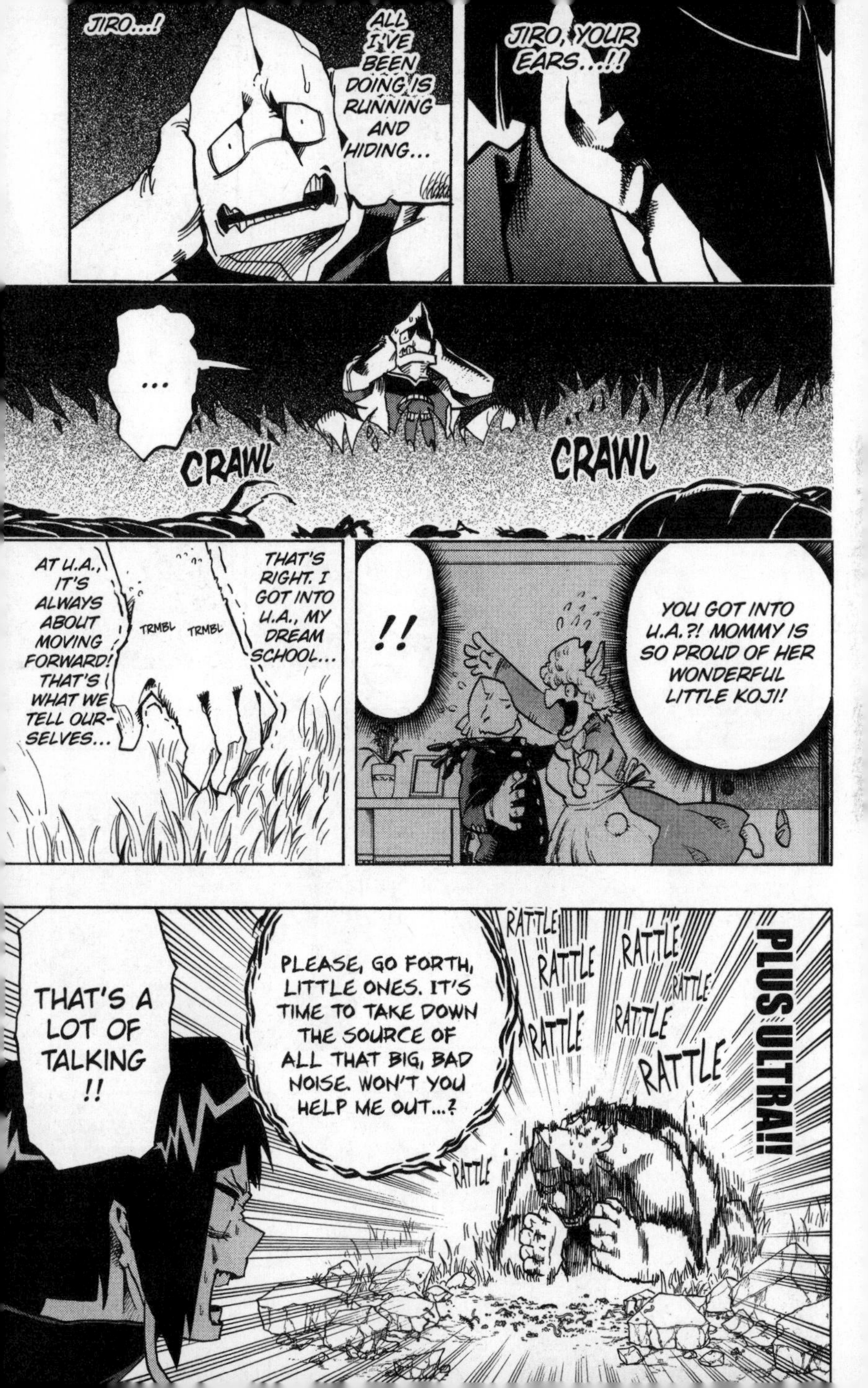
JIRO, YOUR EARS...!!
ALL I'VE BEEN DOING IS RUNNING AND HIDING...
JIRO...!
...
CRAWL
CRAWL
YOU GOT INTO U.A.?! MOMMY IS SO PROUD OF HER WONDERFUL LITTLE KOJI!
!!
THAT'S RIGHT. I GOT INTO U.A., MY DREAM SCHOOL...
TRMBL
TRMBL
AT U.A., IT'S ALWAYS ABOUT MOVING FORWARD! THAT'S WHAT WE TELL OUR-SELVES...
PLUS ULTRA!!
RATTLE
RATTLE
RATTLE
RATTLE
RATTLE
RATTLE
RATTLE
RATTLE
PLEASE, GO FORTH, LITTLE ONES. IT'S TIME TO TAKE DOWN THE SOURCE OF ALL THAT BIG, BAD NOISE. WON'T YOU HELP ME OUT...?
THAT'S A LOT OF TALKING !!

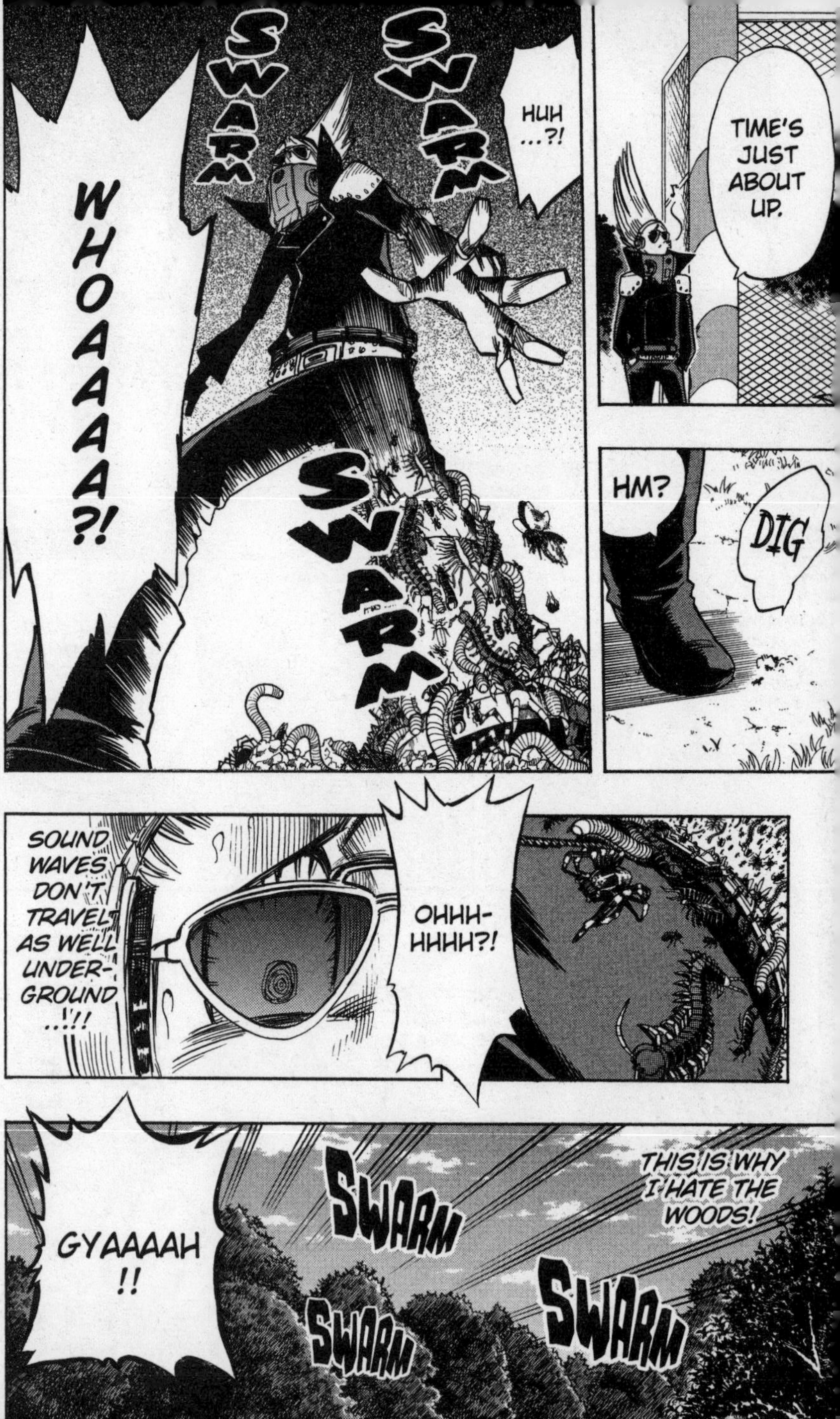
TIME'S JUST ABOUT UP.
HM?
DIG
HUH ...?!
SWARM
SWARM
WHOAAAAAA?!
SWARM
OHHH-HHHH?!
SOUND WAVES DON'T TRAVEL AS WELL UNDER-GROUND ...!?!
THIS IS WHY I HATE THE WOODS!
SWARM
SWARM
GYAAAAH !!
SWARM

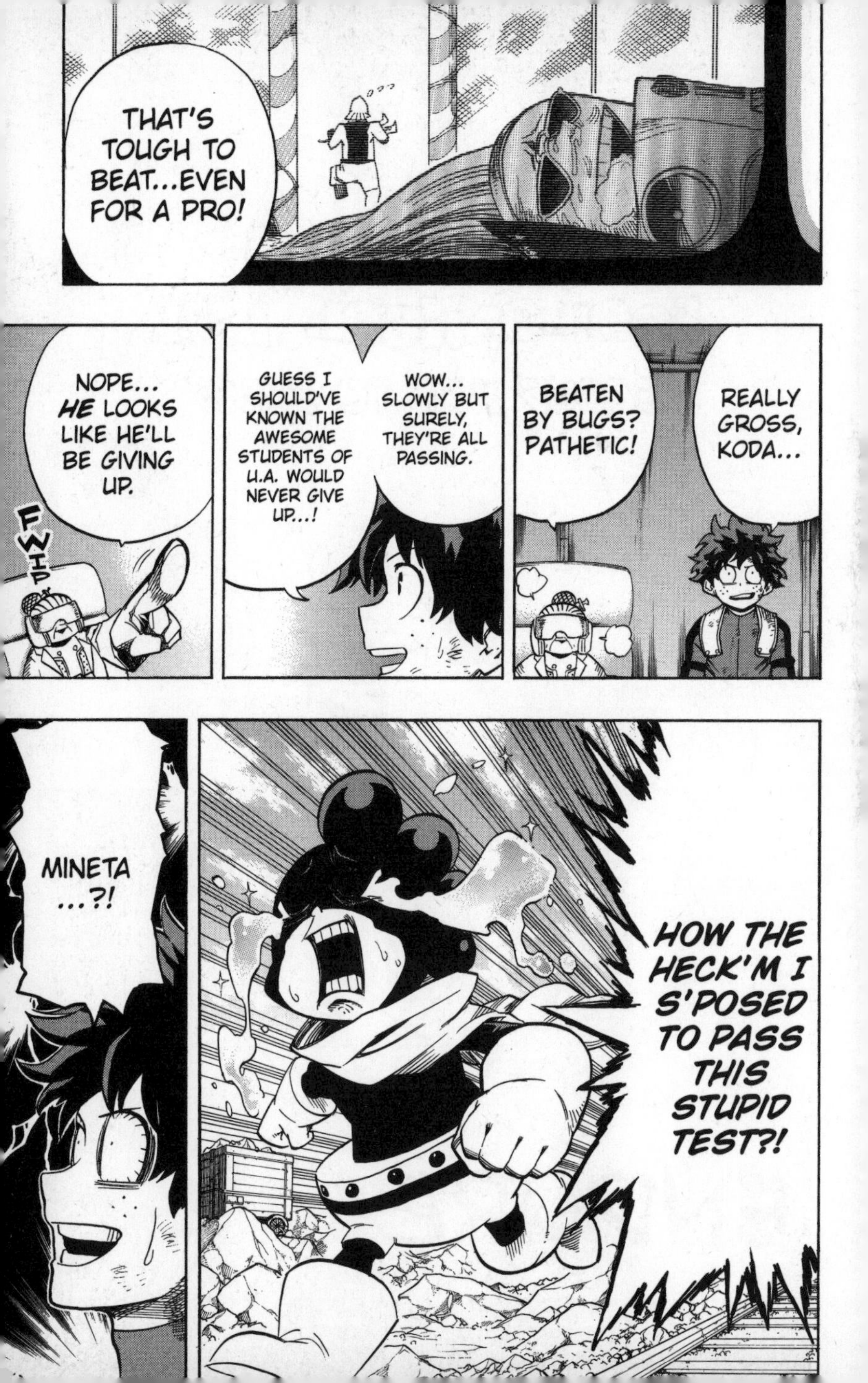
THAT'S TOUGH TO BEAT...EVEN FOR A PRO!
REALLY GROSS, KODA...
BEATEN BY BUGS? PATHETIC!
WOW... SLOWLY BUT SURELY, THEY'RE ALL PASSING.
GUESS I SHOULD'VE KNOWN THE AWESOME STUDENTS OF U.A. WOULD NEVER GIVE UP...!
NOPE... ***HE*** LOOKS LIKE HE'LL BE GIVING UP.
FWIP
HOW THE HECK'M I S'POSED TO PASS THIS STUPID TEST?!
MINETA ...?!

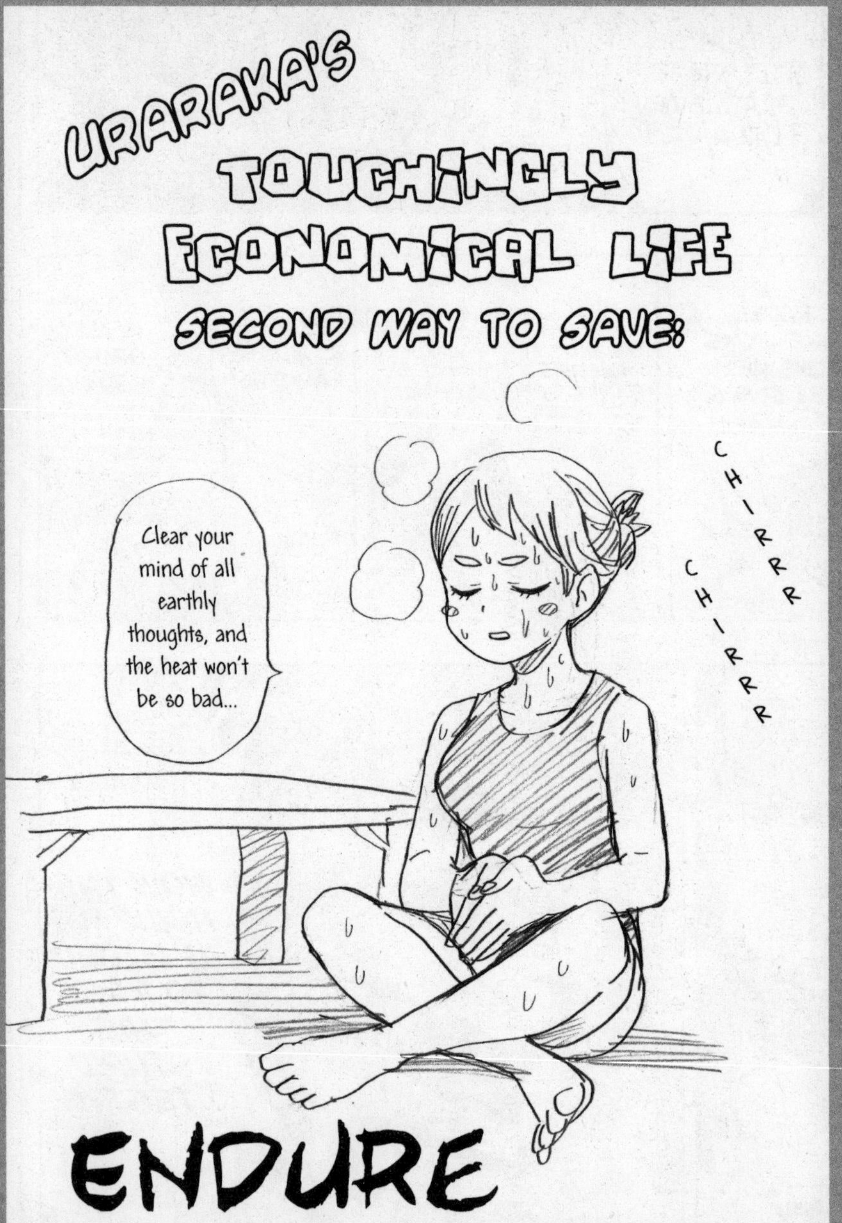
URARAKA'S
TOUCHINGLY ECONOMICAL LIFE
SECOND WAY TO SAVE:
Clear your mind of all earthly thoughts, and the heat won't be so bad...
CHIRRR CHIRRR
ENDURE

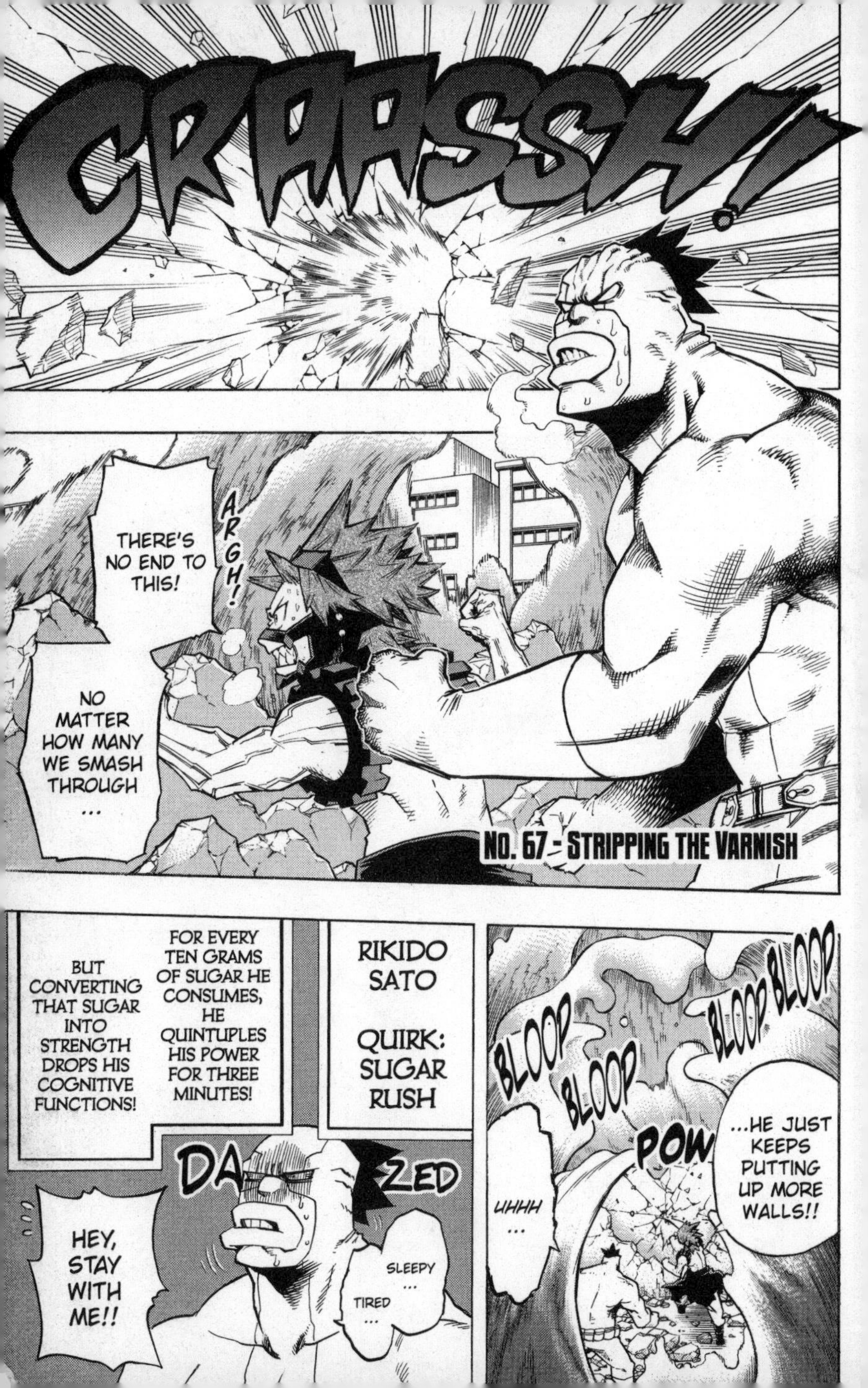
CRAASH!
ARGH!
THERE'S NO END TO THIS!
NO MATTER HOW MANY WE SMASH THROUGH...
No. 67 - Stripping the Varnish
BLOOP BLOOP
BLOOP
BLOOP
POW
...HE JUST KEEPS PUTTING UP MORE WALLS!!
UHHH...
RIKIDO SATO
QUIRK: SUGAR RUSH
FOR EVERY TEN GRAMS OF SUGAR HE CONSUMES, HE QUINTUPLES HIS POWER FOR THREE MINUTES!
BUT CONVERTING THAT SUGAR INTO STRENGTH DROPS HIS COGNITIVE FUNCTIONS!
DAZED
SLEEPY...
TIRED...
HEY, STAY WITH ME!!

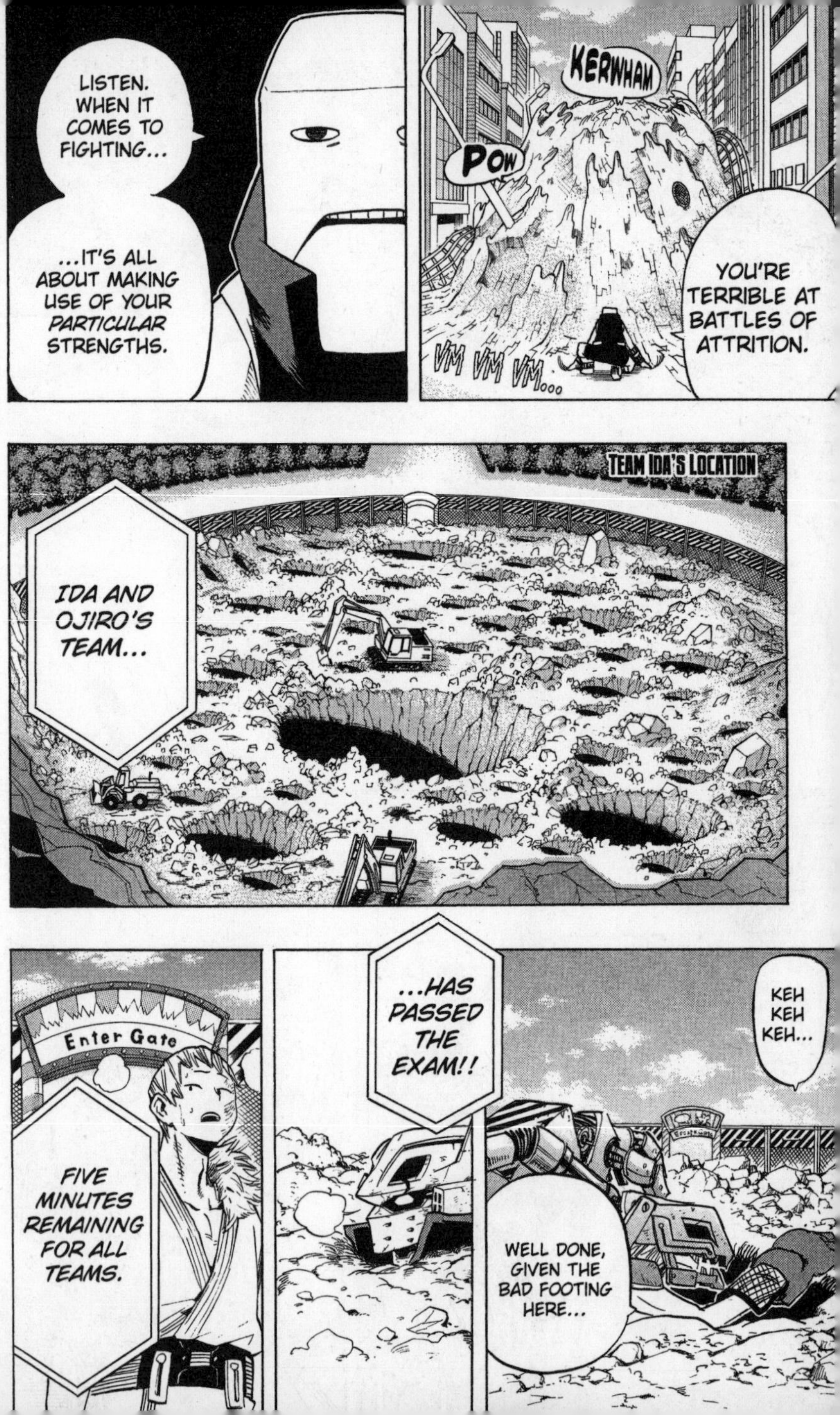
KERWHAM
POW
VM VM VM...
YOU'RE TERRIBLE AT BATTLES OF ATTRITION.
LISTEN. WHEN IT COMES TO FIGHTING...
...IT'S ALL ABOUT MAKING USE OF YOUR *PARTICULAR* STRENGTHS.
TEAM IDA'S LOCATION
IDA AND OJIRO'S TEAM...
...HAS PASSED THE EXAM!!
KEH KEH KEH...
WELL DONE, GIVEN THE BAD FOOTING HERE...
Enter Gate
FIVE MINUTES REMAINING FOR ALL TEAMS.

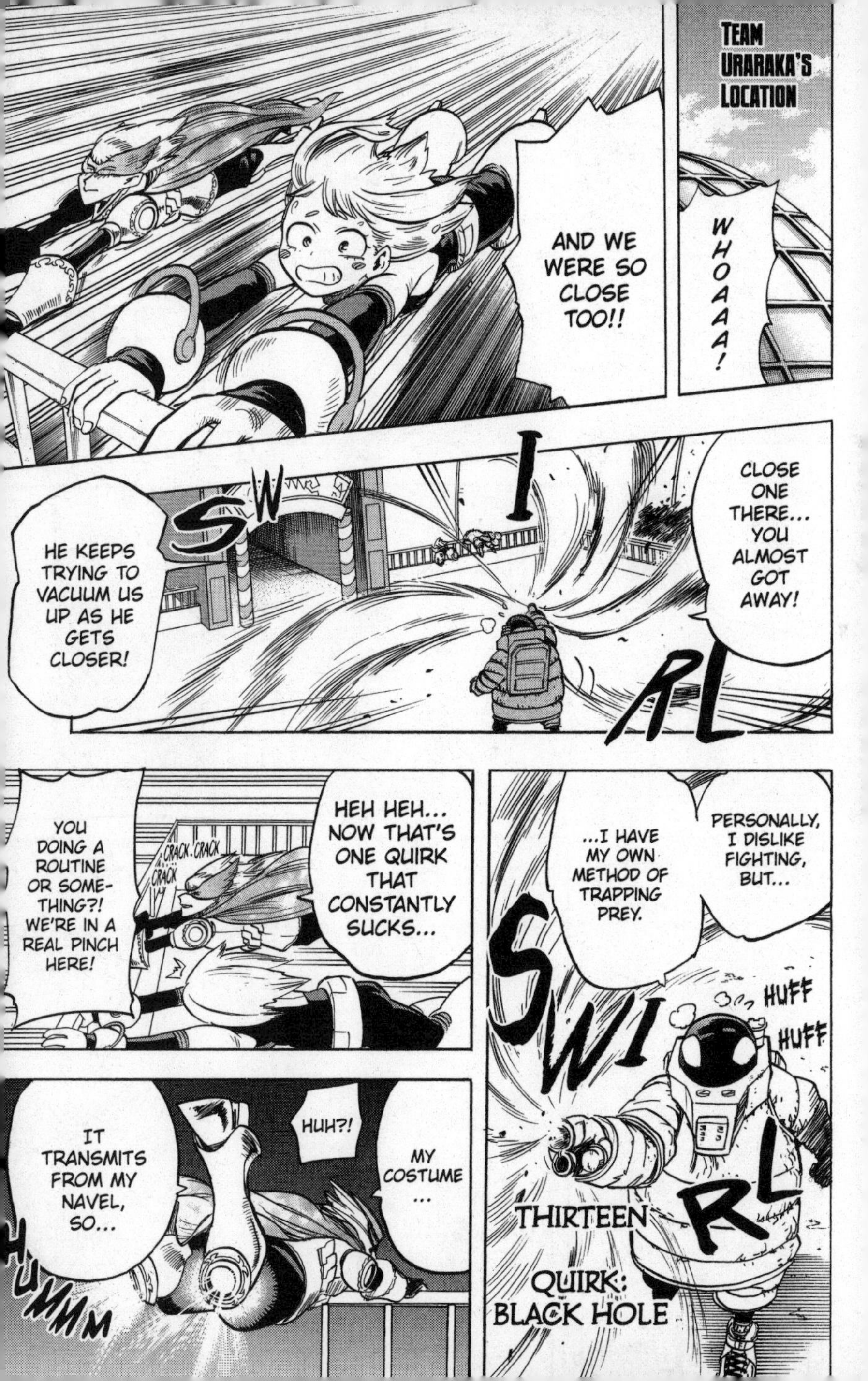
TEAM URARAKA'S LOCATION
WHOAAAA!
AND WE WERE SO CLOSE TOO!!
CLOSE ONE THERE... YOU ALMOST GOT AWAY!
SWIRL
HE KEEPS TRYING TO VACUUM US UP AS HE GETS CLOSER!
PERSONALLY, I DISLIKE FIGHTING, BUT...
...I HAVE MY OWN METHOD OF TRAPPING PREY.
HUFF HUFF
SWIRL
THIRTEEN
QUIRK: BLACK HOLE
HEH HEH... NOW THAT'S ONE QUIRK THAT CONSTANTLY SUCKS...
CRACK CRACK CRACK
YOU DOING A ROUTINE OR SOME-THING?! WE'RE IN A REAL PINCH HERE!
HUH?!
MY COSTUME ...
IT TRANSMITS FROM MY NAVEL, SO...
HUMMMM

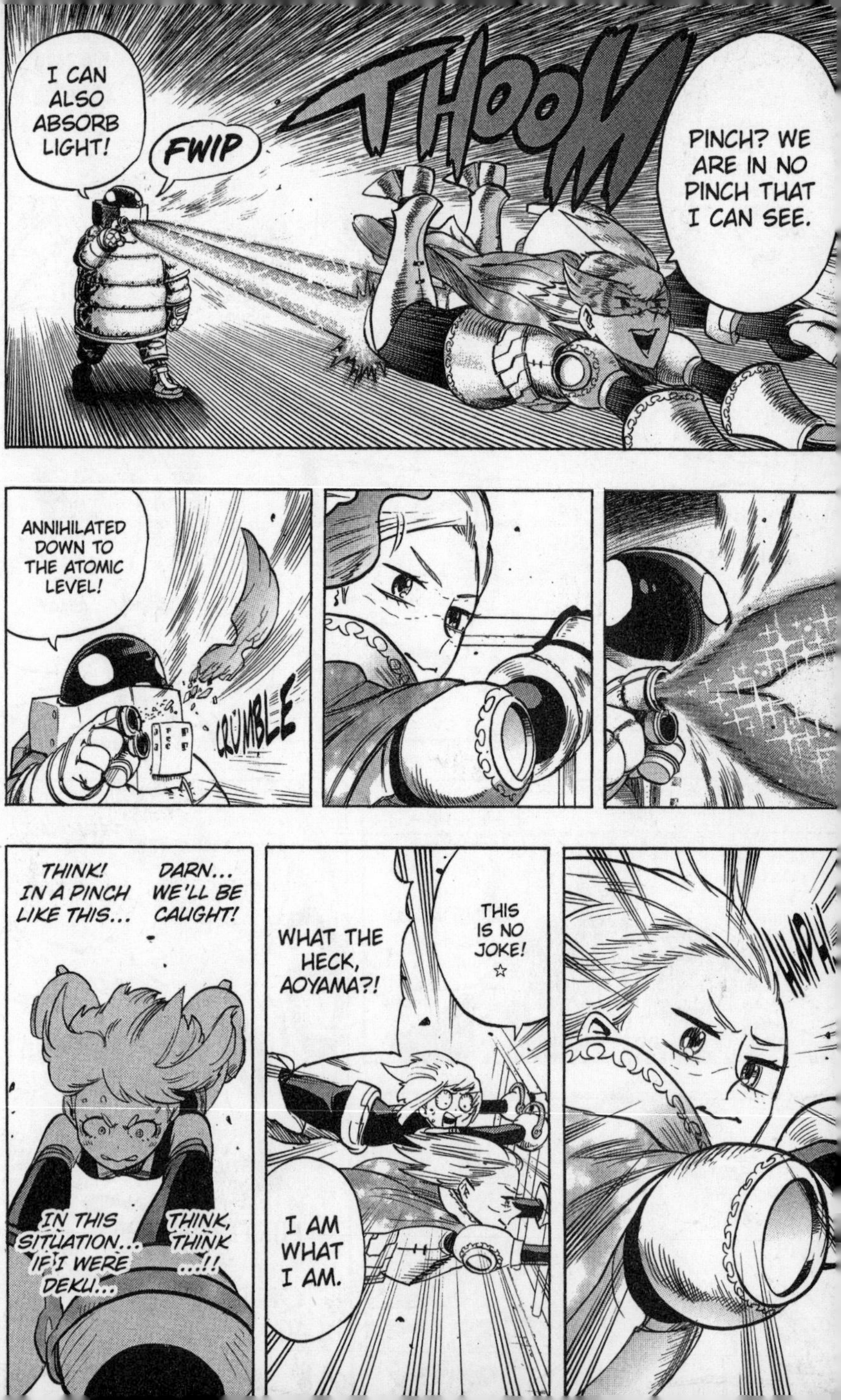
PINCH? WE ARE IN NO PINCH THAT I CAN SEE.
THOOM
I CAN ALSO ABSORB LIGHT!
FWIP
ANNIHILATED DOWN TO THE ATOMIC LEVEL!
CRUMBLE
HMPH
THIS IS NO JOKE! ☆
WHAT THE HECK, AOYAMA?!
I AM WHAT I AM.
DARN... WE'LL BE CAUGHT!
THINK! IN A PINCH LIKE THIS...
THINK, THINK ...!!
IN THIS SITUATION... IF I WERE DEKU...

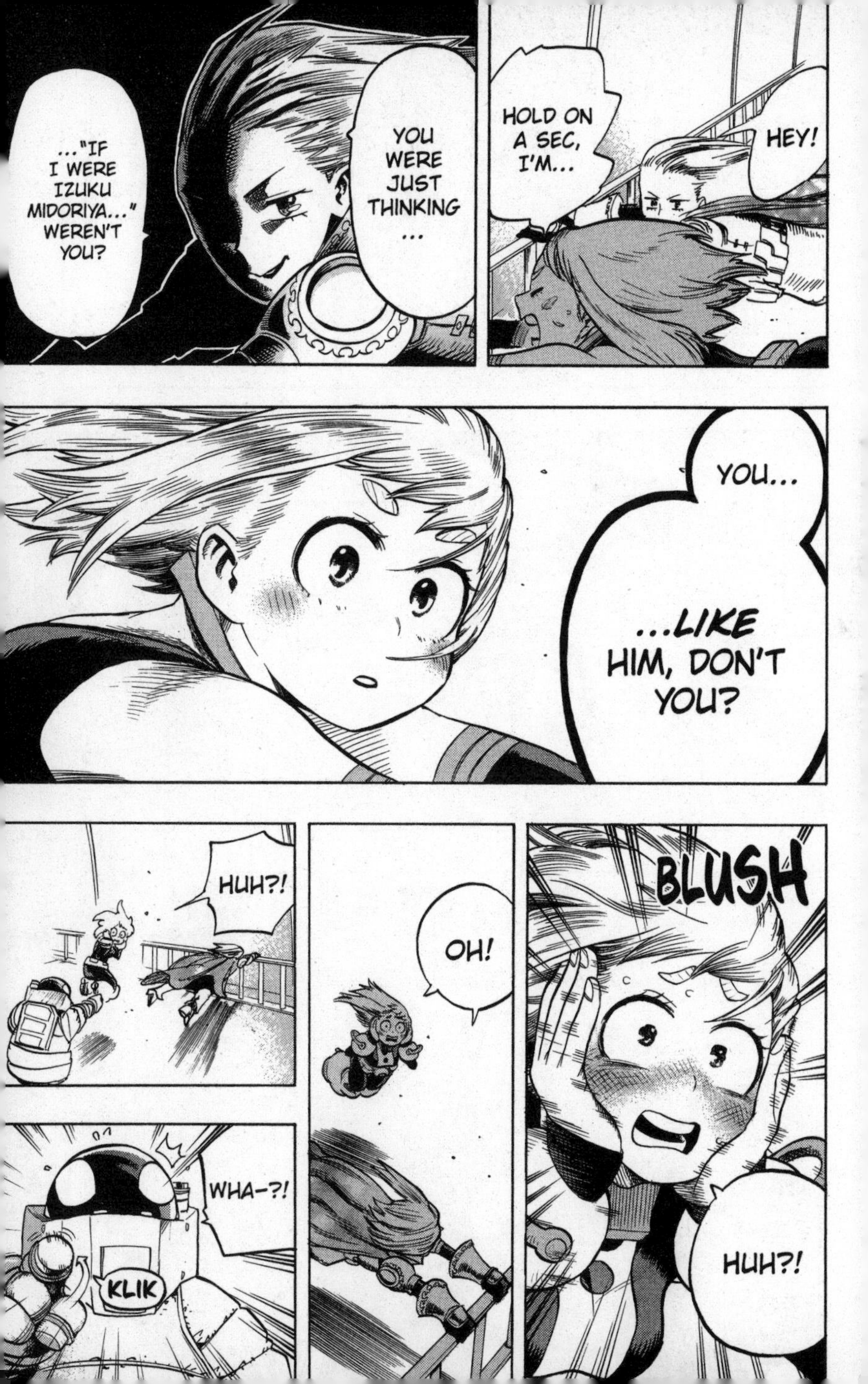
HEY!
HOLD ON A SEC, I'M...
YOU WERE JUST THINKING ...
..."IF I WERE IZUKU MIDORIYA..." WEREN'T YOU?
YOU...
...LIKE HIM, DON'T YOU?
BLUSH
HUH?!
OH!
HUH?!
WHA-?!
KLIK

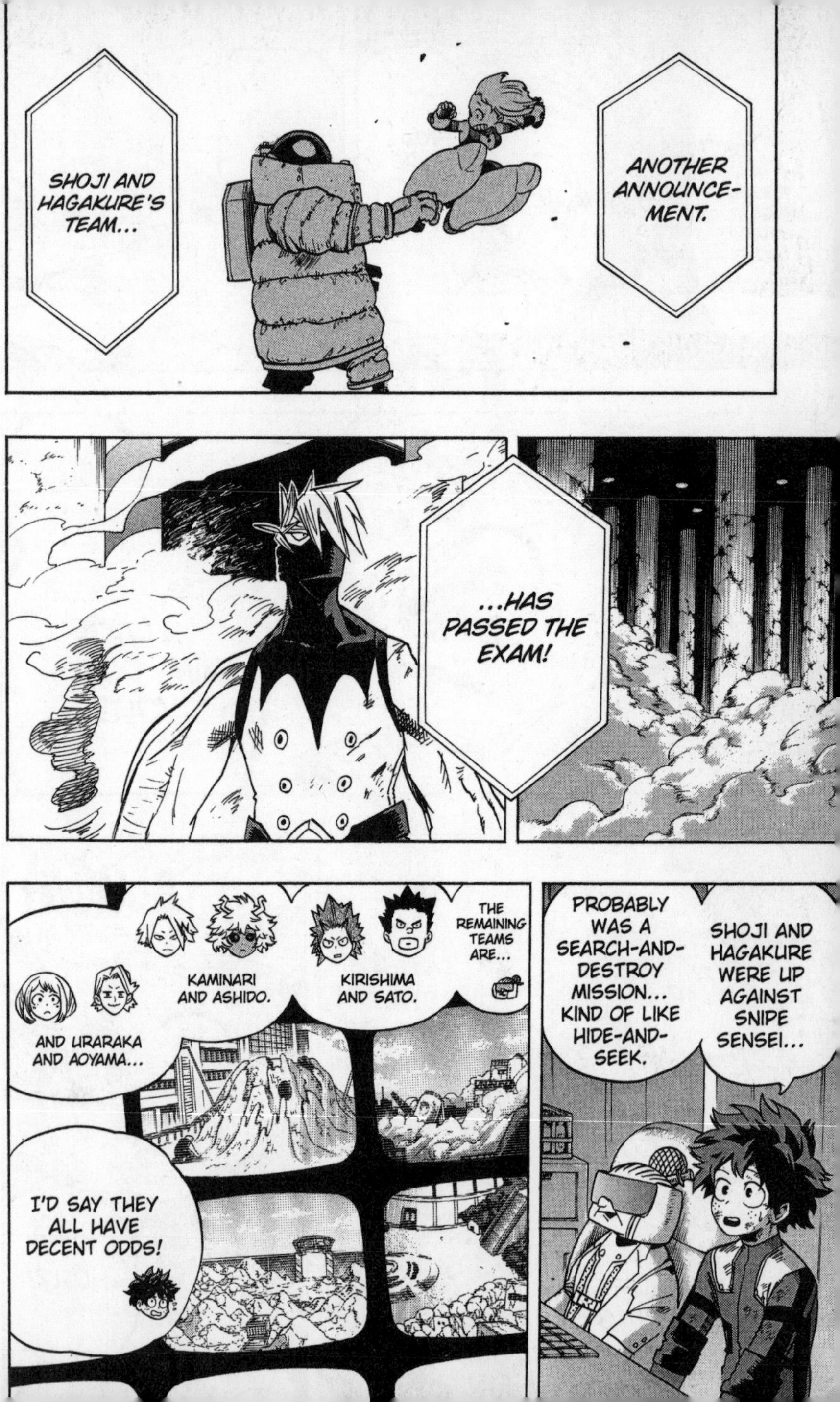
ANOTHER ANNOUNCEMENT.
SHOJI AND HAGAKURE'S TEAM...
...HAS PASSED THE EXAM!
SHOJI AND HAGAKURE WERE UP AGAINST SNIPE SENSEI...
PROBABLY WAS A SEARCH-AND-DESTROY MISSION... KIND OF LIKE HIDE-AND-SEEK.
THE REMAINING TEAMS ARE...
KIRISHIMA AND SATO.
KAMINARI AND ASHIDO.
AND URARAKA AND AOYAMA...
I'D SAY THEY ALL HAVE DECENT ODDS!

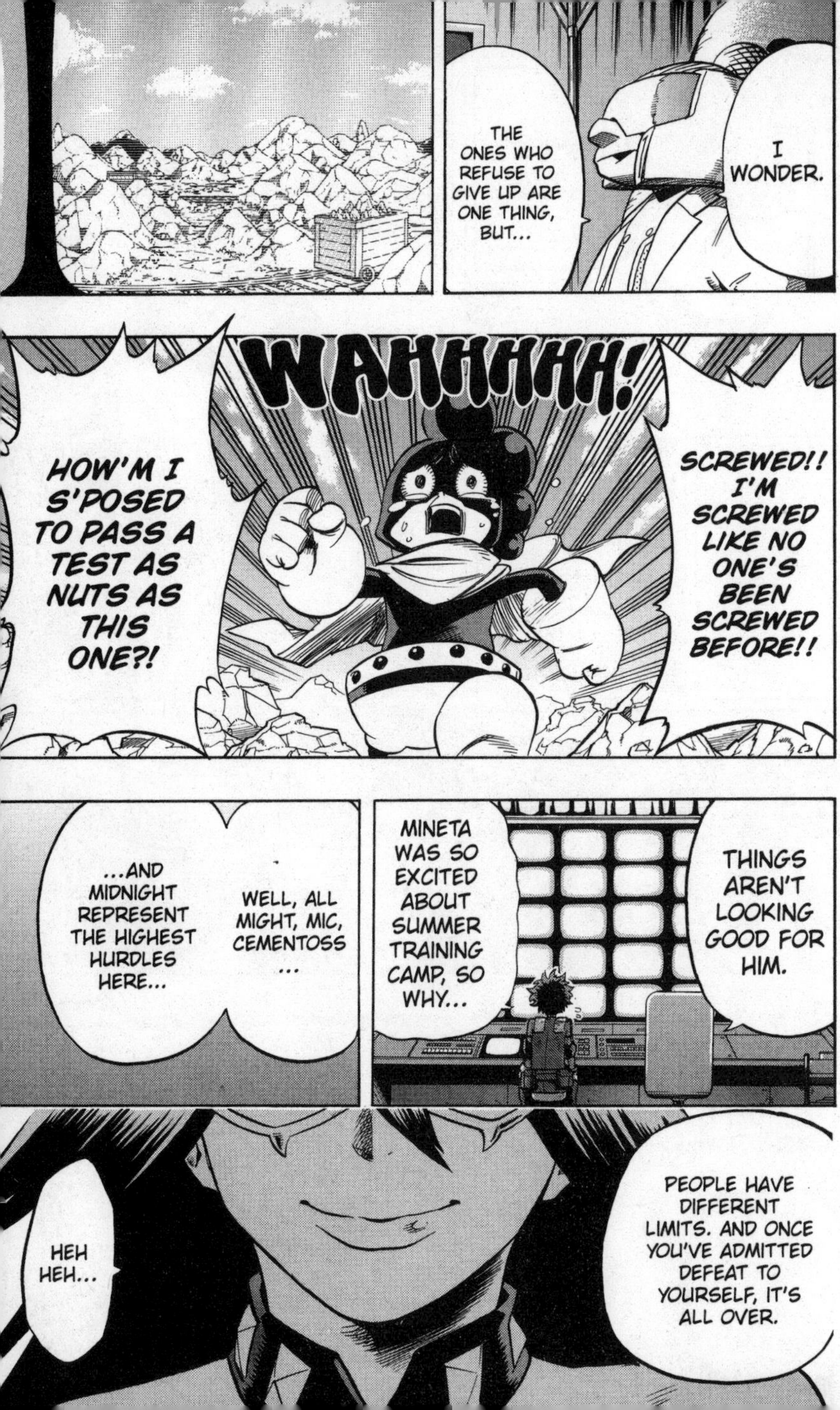
THE ONES WHO REFUSE TO GIVE UP ARE ONE THING, BUT...
I WONDER.
WAHHHHHH!
SCREWED!! I'M SCREWED LIKE NO ONE'S BEEN SCREWED BEFORE!!
HOW'M I S'POSED TO PASS A TEST AS NUTS AS THIS ONE?!
THINGS AREN'T LOOKING GOOD FOR HIM.
MINETA WAS SO EXCITED ABOUT SUMMER TRAINING CAMP, SO WHY...
WELL, ALL MIGHT, MIC, CEMENTOSS...
...AND MIDNIGHT REPRESENT THE HIGHEST HURDLES HERE...
PEOPLE HAVE DIFFERENT LIMITS. AND ONCE YOU'VE ADMITTED DEFEAT TO YOURSELF, IT'S ALL OVER.
HEH HEH...

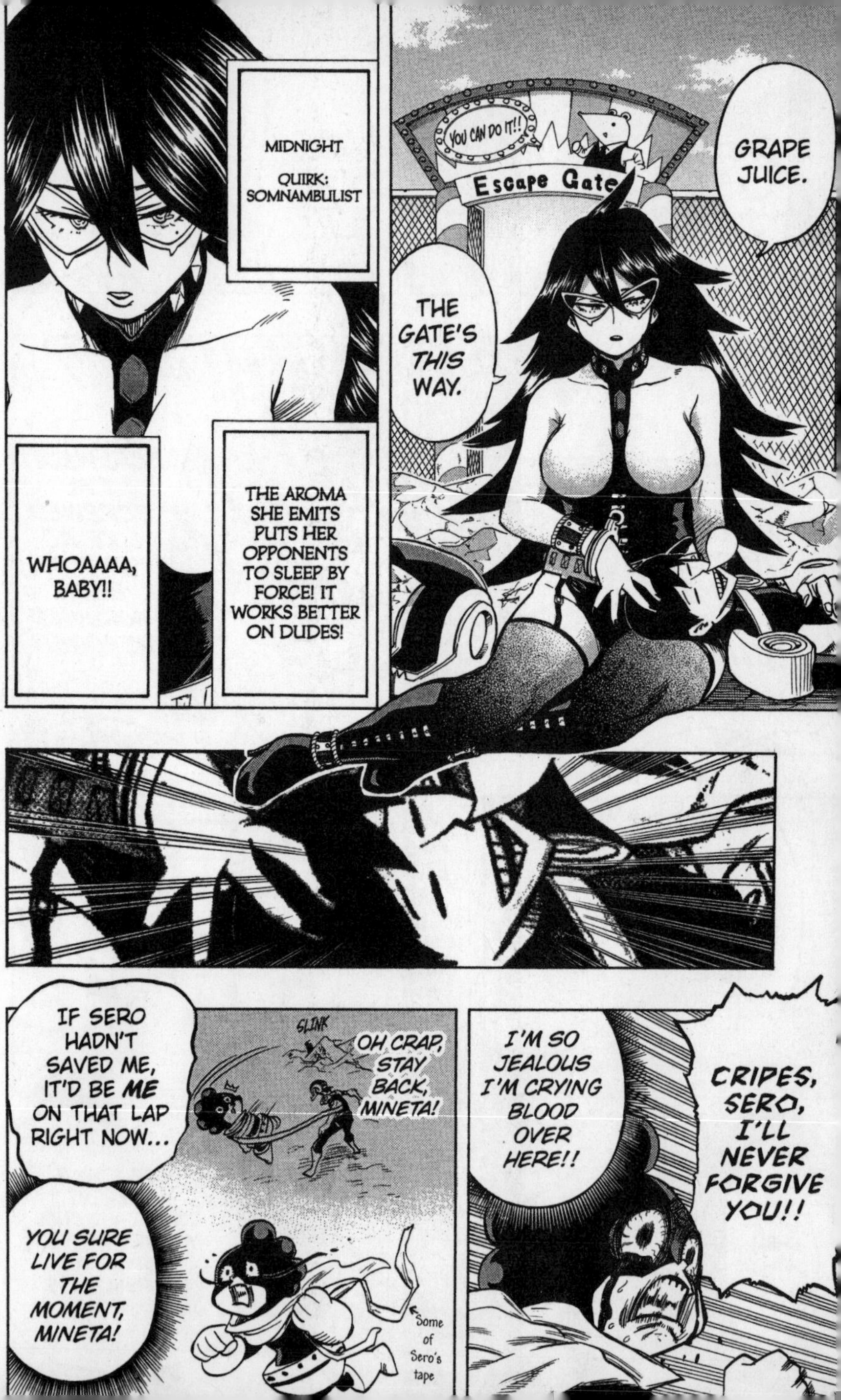
YOU CAN DO IT!!
Escape Gate
GRAPE JUICE.
THE GATE'S THIS WAY.
MIDNIGHT
QUIRK: SOMNAMBULIST
THE AROMA SHE EMITS PUTS HER OPPONENTS TO SLEEP BY FORCE! IT WORKS BETTER ON DUDES!
WHOAAAA, BABY!!
CRIPES, SERO, I'LL NEVER FORGIVE YOU!!
I'M SO JEALOUS I'M CRYING BLOOD OVER HERE!!
SLINK
OH CRAP, STAY BACK, MINETA!
IF SERO HADN'T SAVED ME, IT'D BE ME ON THAT LAP RIGHT NOW...
YOU SURE LIVE FOR THE MOMENT, MINETA!
Some of Sero's tape

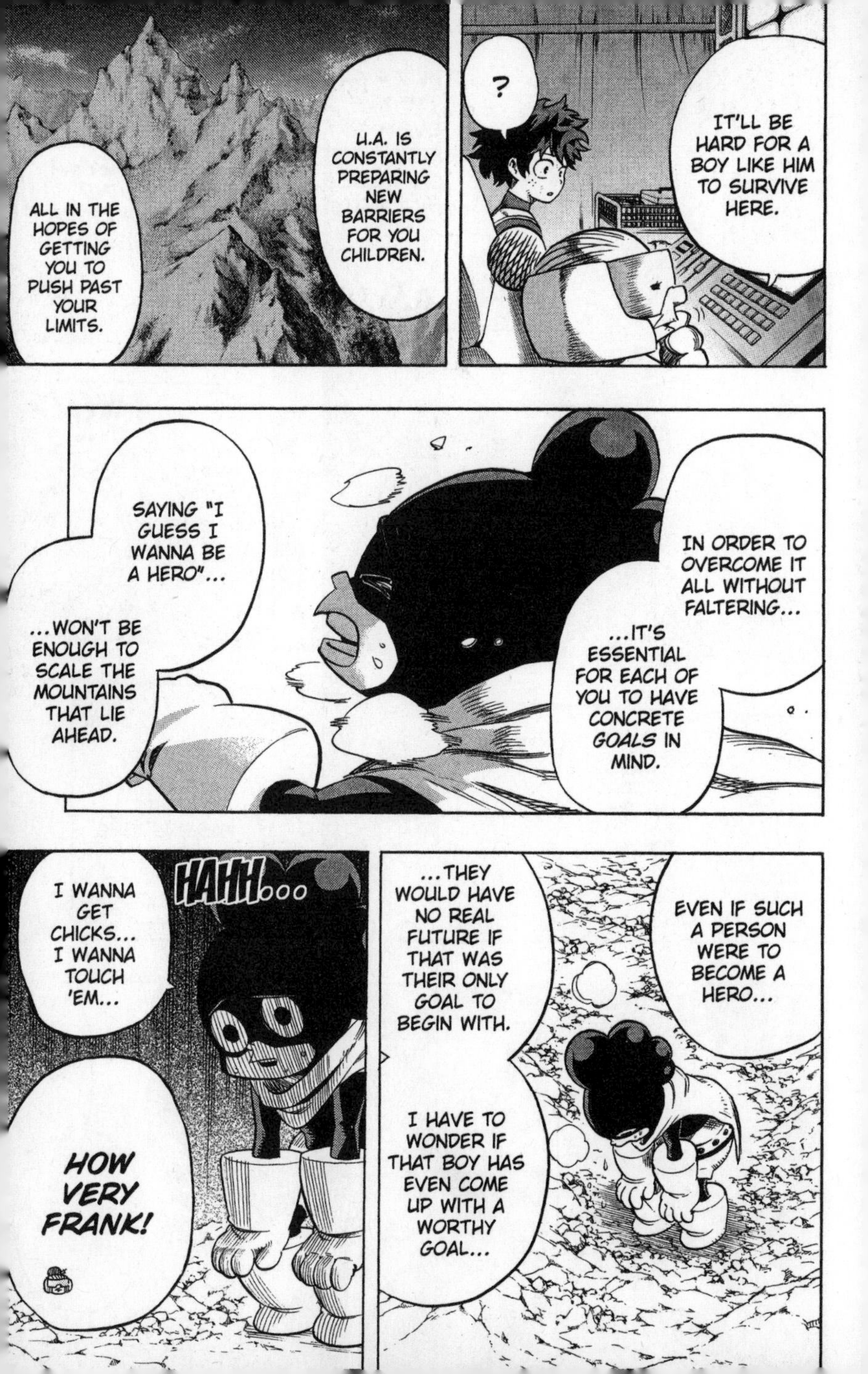
IT'LL BE HARD FOR A BOY LIKE HIM TO SURVIVE HERE.
?
U.A. IS CONSTANTLY PREPARING NEW BARRIERS FOR YOU CHILDREN.
ALL IN THE HOPES OF GETTING YOU TO PUSH PAST YOUR LIMITS.
IN ORDER TO OVERCOME IT ALL WITHOUT FALTERING...
...IT'S ESSENTIAL FOR EACH OF YOU TO HAVE CONCRETE GOALS IN MIND.
SAYING "I GUESS I WANNA BE A HERO"...
...WON'T BE ENOUGH TO SCALE THE MOUNTAINS THAT LIE AHEAD.
EVEN IF SUCH A PERSON WERE TO BECOME A HERO...
...THEY WOULD HAVE NO REAL FUTURE IF THAT WAS THEIR ONLY GOAL TO BEGIN WITH.
I HAVE TO WONDER IF THAT BOY HAS EVEN COME UP WITH A WORTHY GOAL...
HAHH...
I WANNA GET CHICKS... I WANNA TOUCH 'EM...
HOW VERY FRANK!

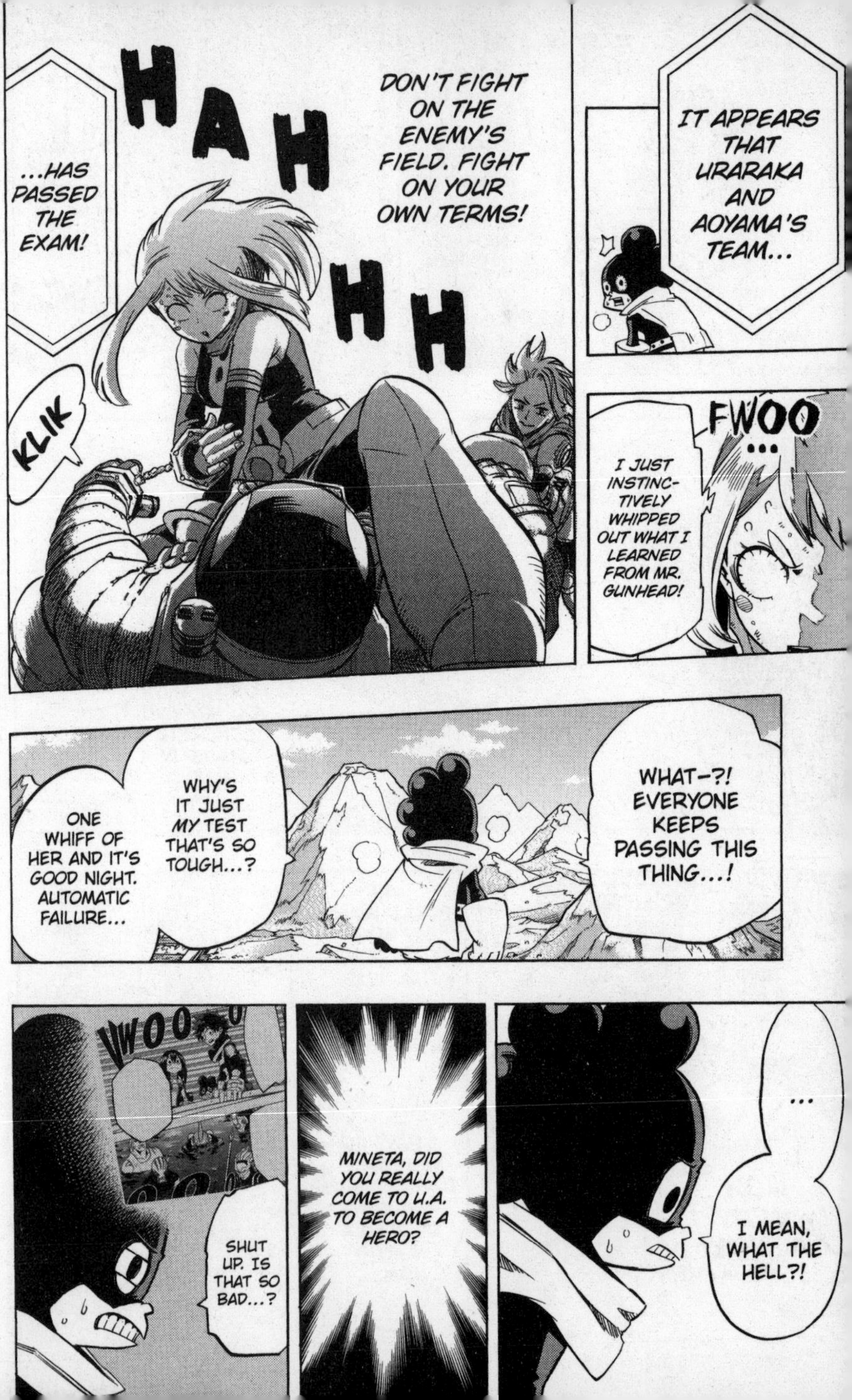
IT APPEARS THAT URARAKA AND AOYAMA'S TEAM...
FWOO...
I JUST INSTINCTIVELY WHIPPED OUT WHAT I LEARNED FROM MR. GUNHEAD!
...HAS PASSED THE EXAM!
HAHHHH
DON'T FIGHT ON THE ENEMY'S FIELD. FIGHT ON YOUR OWN TERMS!
KLIK
WHAT-?! EVERYONE KEEPS PASSING THIS THING...!
WHY'S IT JUST MY TEST THAT'S SO TOUGH...?
ONE WHIFF OF HER AND IT'S GOOD NIGHT. AUTOMATIC FAILURE...
...
I MEAN, WHAT THE HELL?!
MINETA, DID YOU REALLY COME TO U.A. TO BECOME A HERO?
VWOOO
SHUT UP. IS THAT SO BAD...?

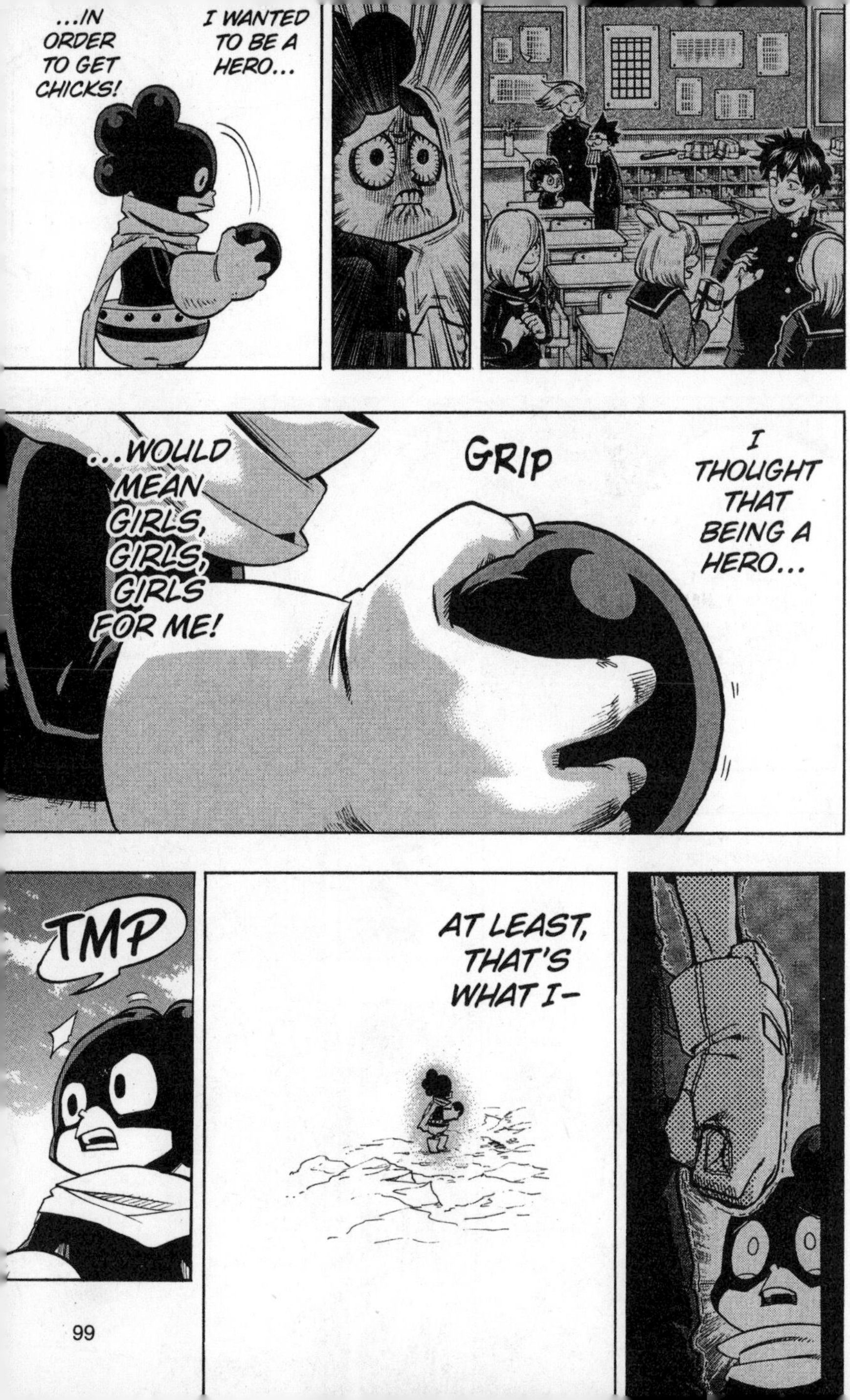
I WANTED TO BE A HERO...
...IN ORDER TO GET CHICKS!
I THOUGHT THAT BEING A HERO...
GRIP
...WOULD MEAN GIRLS, GIRLS, GIRLS FOR ME!
AT LEAST, THAT'S WHAT I-
TMP

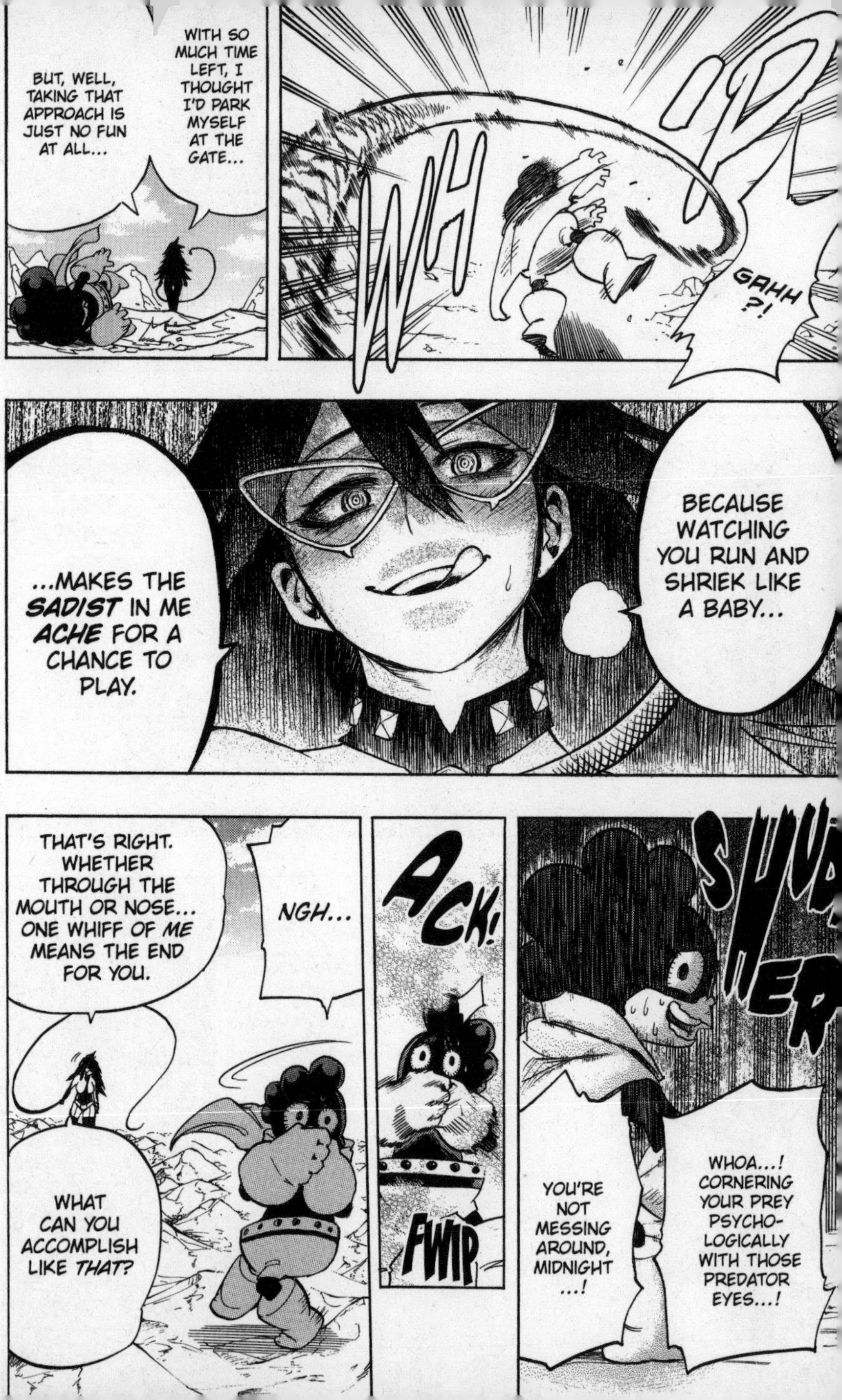
GAHH ?!
WITH SO MUCH TIME LEFT, I THOUGHT I'D PARK MYSELF AT THE GATE...
BUT, WELL, TAKING THAT APPROACH IS JUST NO FUN AT ALL...
BECAUSE WATCHING YOU RUN AND SHRIEK LIKE A BABY...
...MAKES THE *SADIST* IN ME *ACHE* FOR A CHANCE TO PLAY.
WHOA...! CORNERING YOUR PREY PSYCHO-LOGICALLY WITH THOSE PREDATOR EYES...!
YOU'RE NOT MESSING AROUND, MIDNIGHT...!
ACK!
FWIP
NGH...
THAT'S RIGHT. WHETHER THROUGH THE MOUTH OR NOSE... ONE WHIFF OF *ME* MEANS THE END FOR YOU.
WHAT CAN YOU ACCOMPLISH LIKE *THAT*?

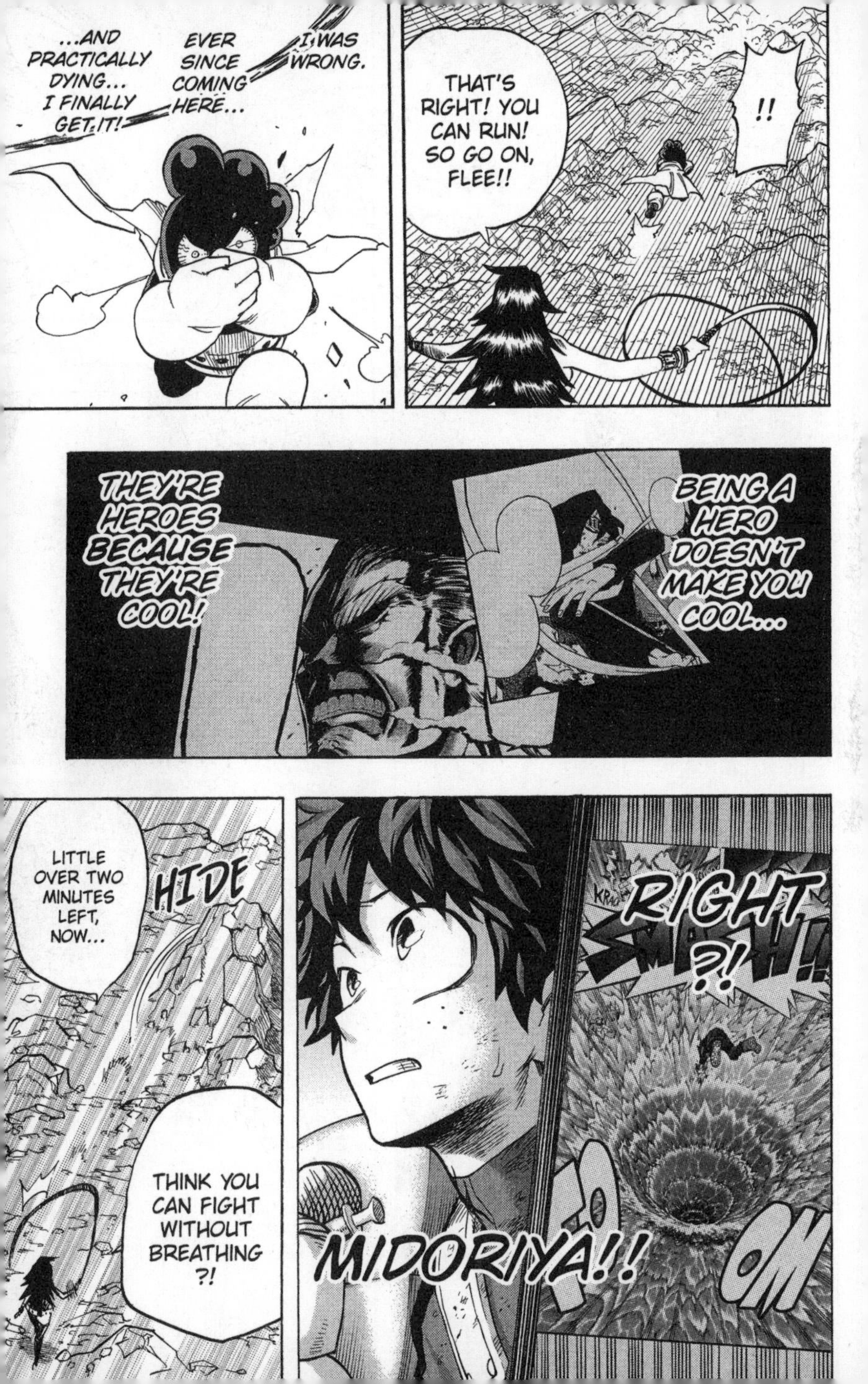
THAT'S RIGHT! YOU CAN RUN! SO GO ON, FLEE!!
!!
I WAS WRONG.
EVER SINCE COMING HERE...
...AND PRACTICALLY DYING... I FINALLY GET IT!
BEING A HERO DOESN'T MAKE YOU COOL...
THEY'RE HEROES BECAUSE THEY'RE COOL!
RIGHT SMASH!!
?!
MIDORIYA!!
LITTLE OVER TWO MINUTES LEFT, NOW...
HIDE
THINK YOU CAN FIGHT WITHOUT BREATHING ?!

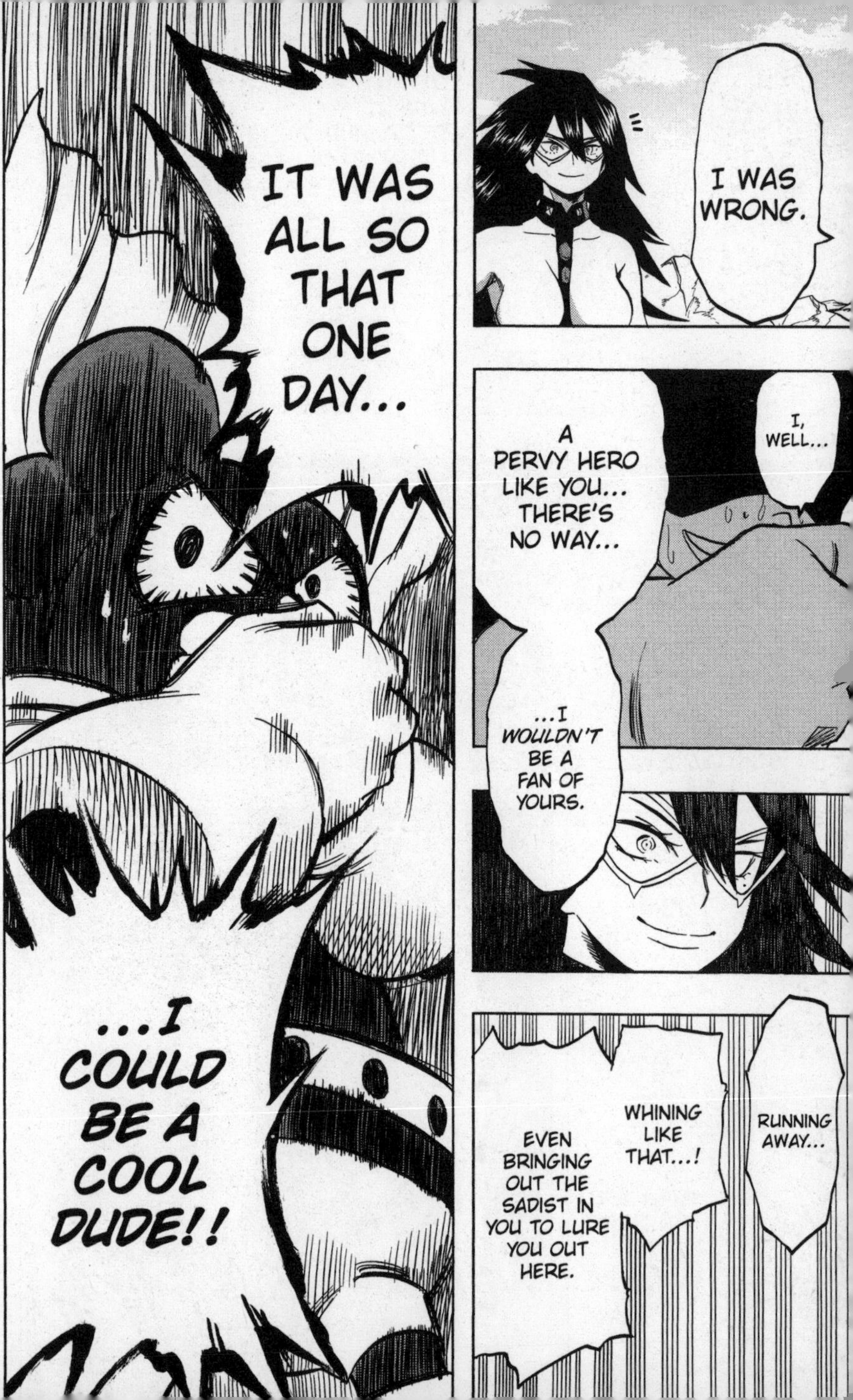
I WAS WRONG.
I, WELL...
A PERVY HERO LIKE YOU... THERE'S NO WAY...
...I *WOULDN'T* BE A FAN OF YOURS.
RUNNING AWAY...
WHINING LIKE THAT...!
EVEN BRINGING OUT THE SADIST IN YOU TO LURE YOU OUT HERE.
IT WAS ALL SO THAT ONE DAY...
...I COULD BE A COOL DUDE!!

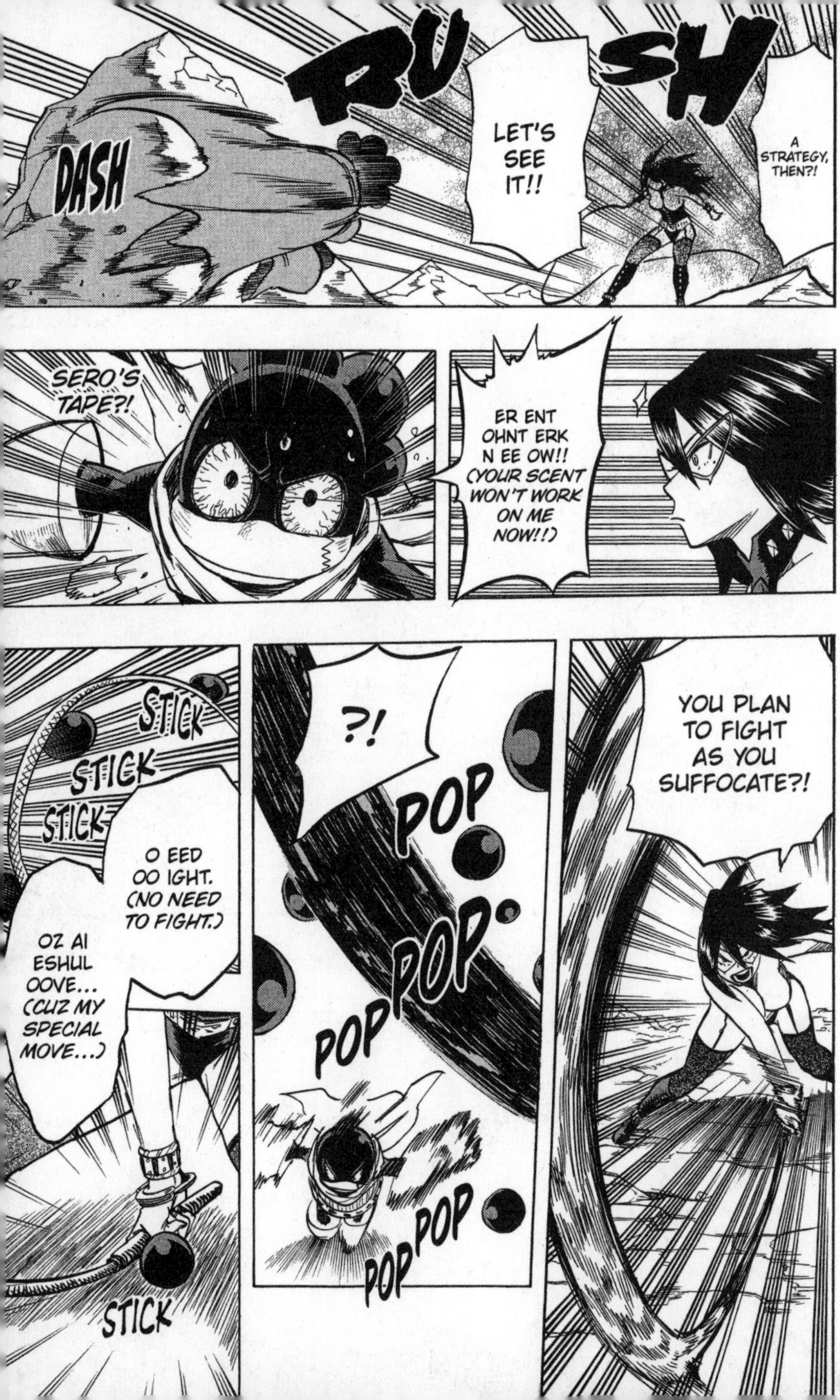
RUSH
A STRATEGY, THEN?!
LET'S SEE IT!!
DASH
ER ENT OHNT ERK N EE OW!! (YOUR SCENT WON'T WORK ON ME NOW!!)
SERO'S TAPE?!
YOU PLAN TO FIGHT AS YOU SUFFOCATE?!
?!
POP
POP
POP
POP POP
STICK
STICK
STICK
O EED OO IGHT. (NO NEED TO FIGHT.)
OZ AI ESHUL OOVE... (CUZ MY SPECIAL MOVE...)
STICK

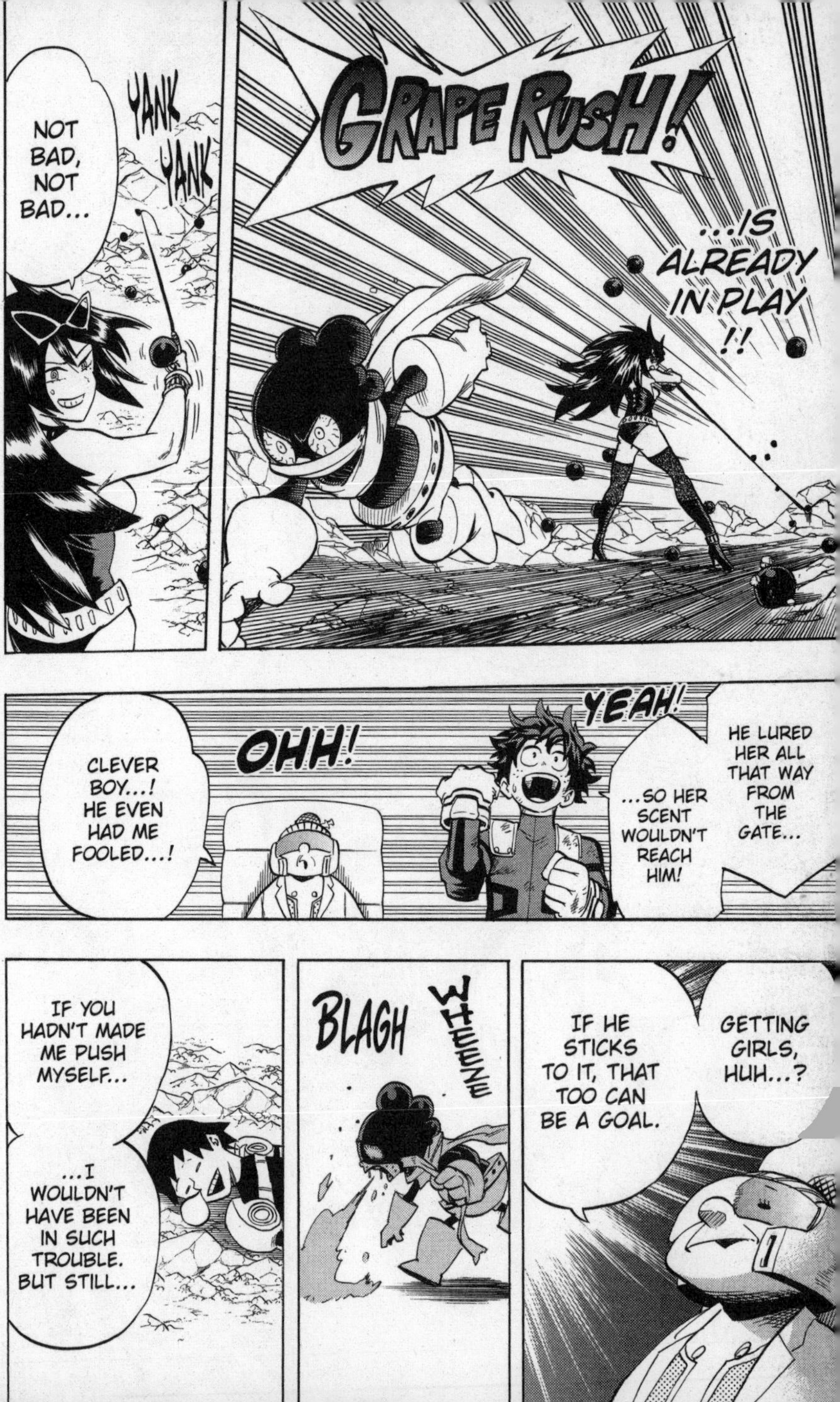

...IS ALREADY IN PLAY !!
GRAPE RUSH!
YANK YANK
NOT BAD, NOT BAD...
HE LURED HER ALL THAT WAY FROM THE GATE...
...SO HER SCENT WOULDN'T REACH HIM!
YEAH!
OHH!
CLEVER BOY...! HE EVEN HAD ME FOOLED...!
GETTING GIRLS, HUH...?
IF HE STICKS TO IT, THAT TOO CAN BE A GOAL.
WHEEZE
BLAGH
IF YOU HADN'T MADE ME PUSH MYSELF...
...I WOULDN'T HAVE BEEN IN SUCH TROUBLE. BUT STILL...

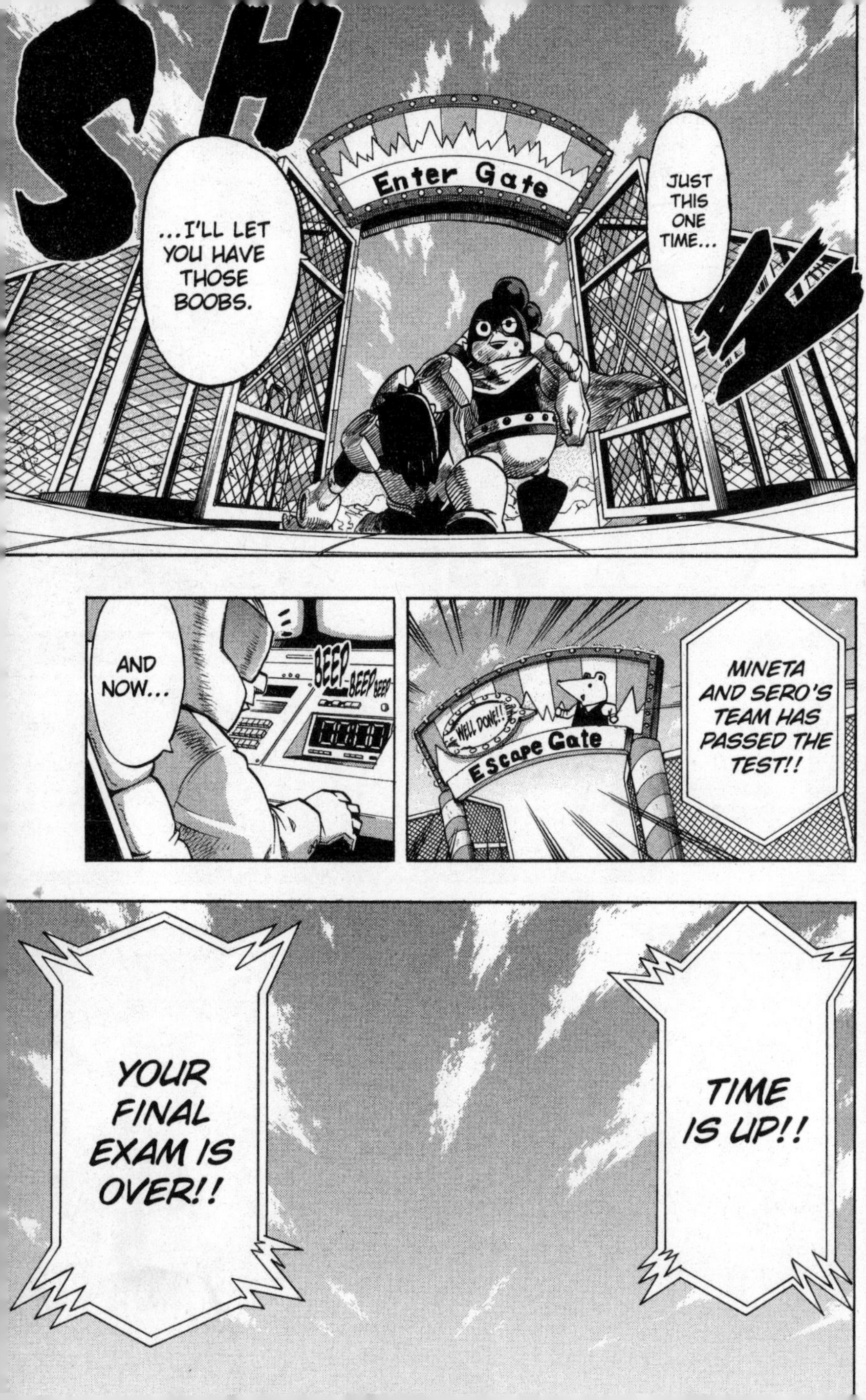
SHAH
Enter Gate
JUST THIS ONE TIME...
...I'LL LET YOU HAVE THOSE BOOBS.
MINETA AND SERO'S TEAM HAS PASSED THE TEST!!
WELL DONE!!
EScape Gate
BEEP BEEP BEEP
AND NOW...
TIME IS UP!!
YOUR FINAL EXAM IS OVER!!

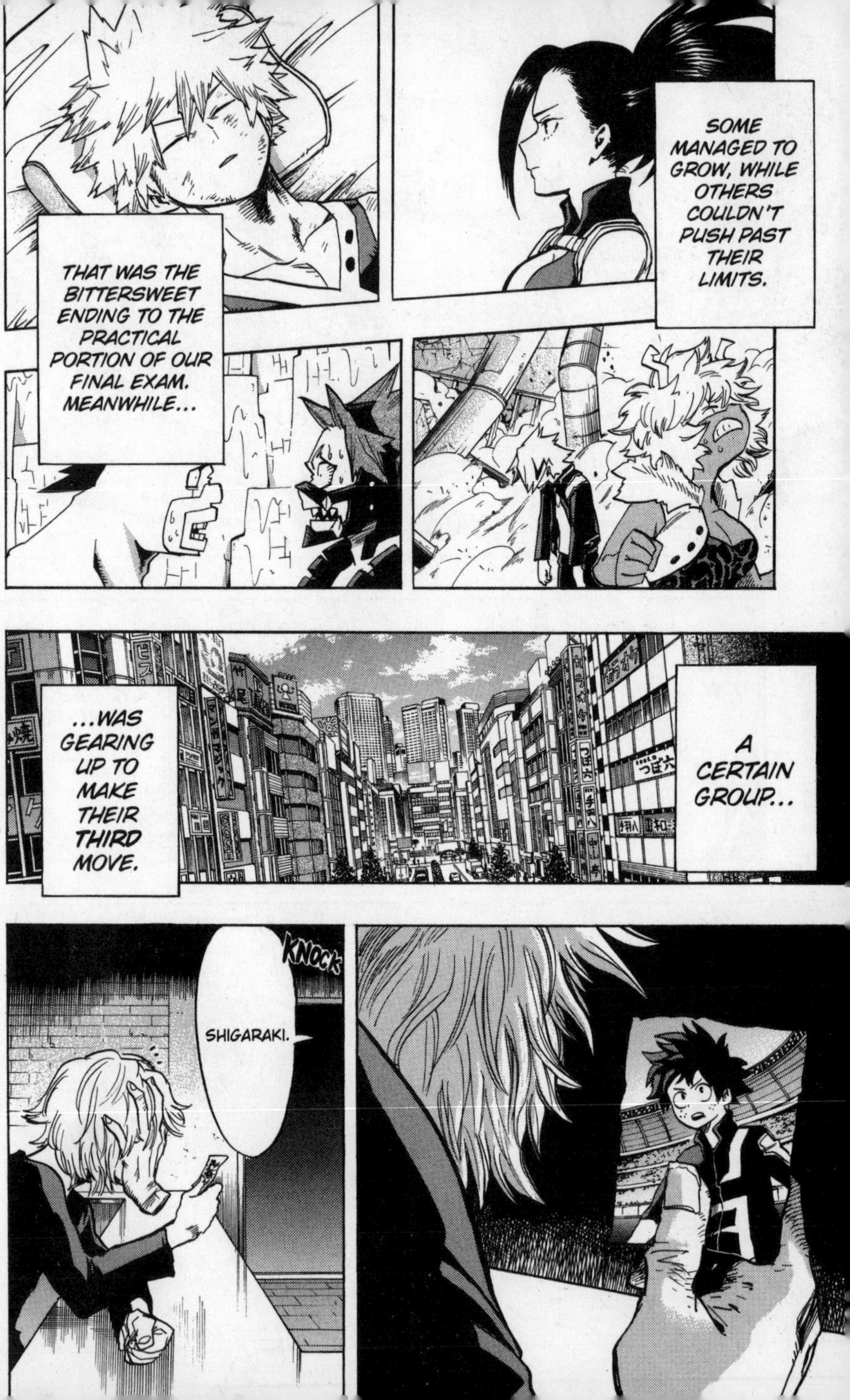
SOME MANAGED TO GROW, WHILE OTHERS COULDN'T PUSH PAST THEIR LIMITS.
THAT WAS THE BITTERSWEET ENDING TO THE PRACTICAL PORTION OF OUR FINAL EXAM. MEANWHILE...
A CERTAIN GROUP...
...WAS GEARING UP TO MAKE THEIR THIRD MOVE.
KNOCK
SHIGARAKI.

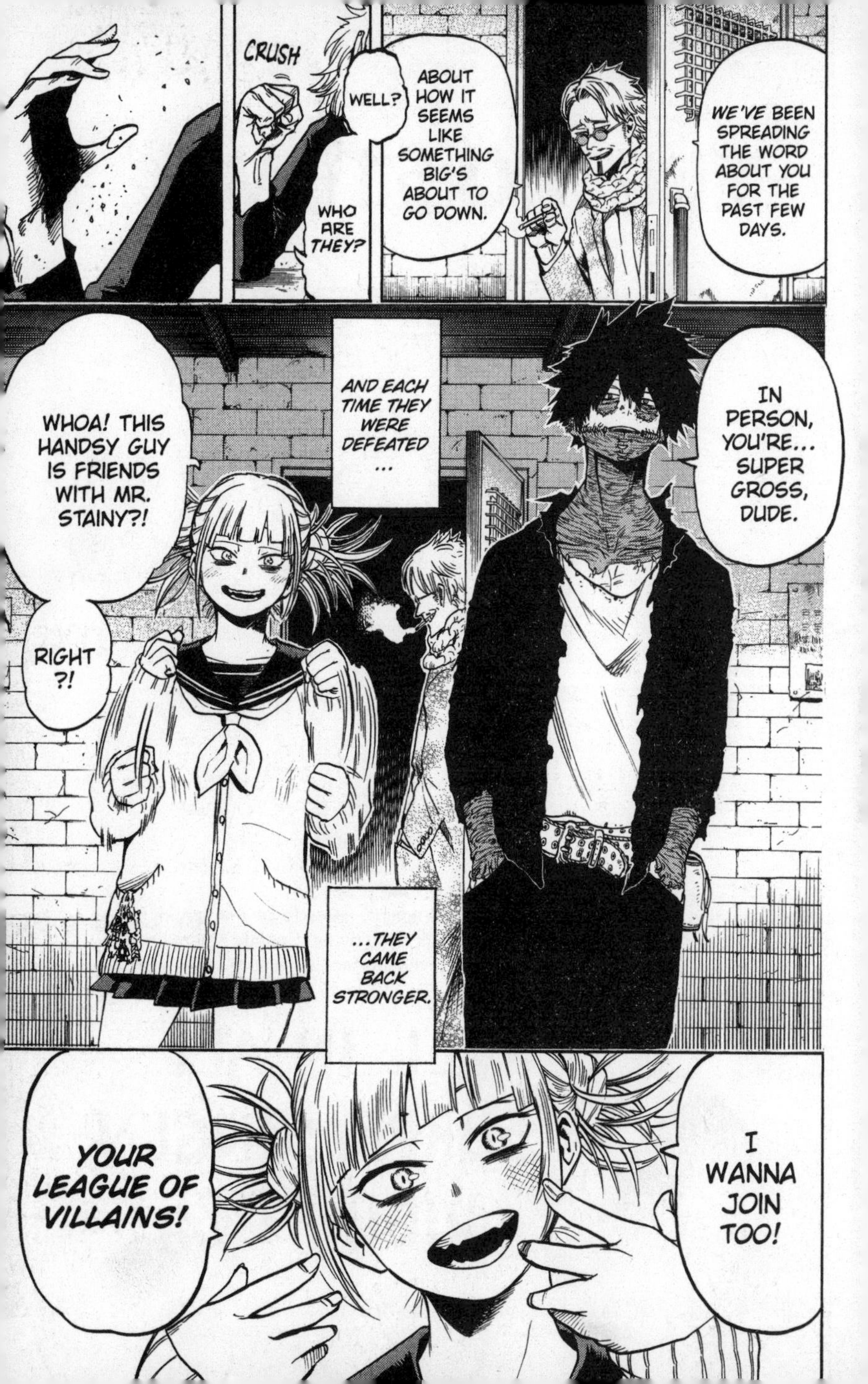
WE'VE BEEN SPREADING THE WORD ABOUT YOU FOR THE PAST FEW DAYS.
ABOUT HOW IT SEEMS LIKE SOMETHING BIG'S ABOUT TO GO DOWN.
WELL?
WHO ARE THEY?
CRUSH
IN PERSON, YOU'RE... SUPER GROSS, DUDE.
AND EACH TIME THEY WERE DEFEATED ...
WHOA! THIS HANDSY GUY IS FRIENDS WITH MR. STAINY?!
RIGHT ?!
...THEY CAME BACK STRONGER.
I WANNA JOIN TOO!
YOUR LEAGUE OF VILLAINS!

THE COSTUME

YUGA AOYAMA'S COSTUME

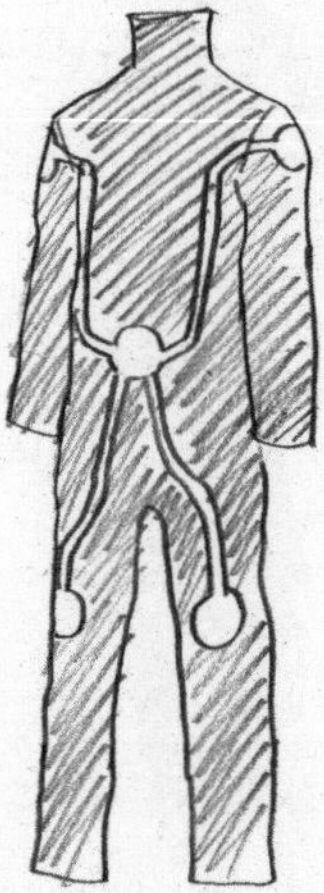

Sparkly Innerwear
Redirects the energy shot out of his navel. For some reason or another, it's remarkably high-tech.

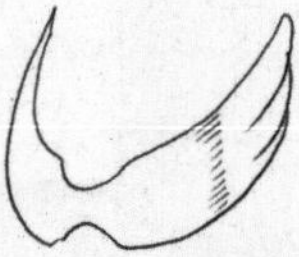

Sparkly Glasses
Keeps him from being blinded by his own light.

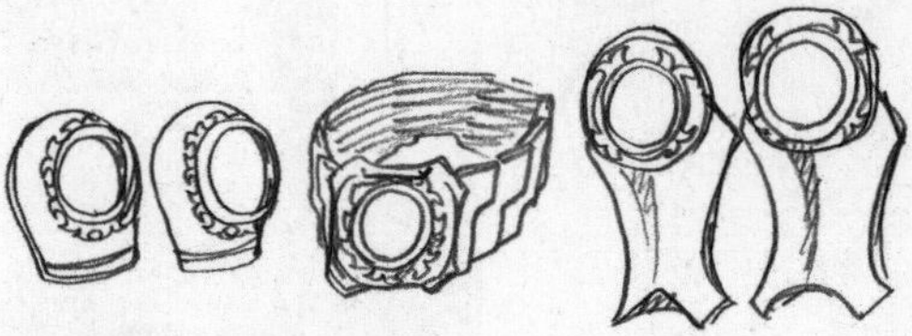

Sparkly Effusion Set
These five sparkly items focus the sparkly beams redirected by the Sparkly Innerwear in order to make them extra sparkly.

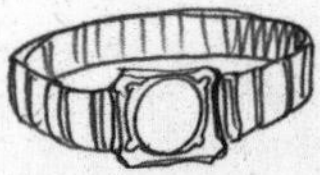

Lightweight Sparkly Belt
Aoyama's always had this belt, which he wears under his clothes in everyday life.

ALL IN ALL: SURPRISINGLY HIGH-TECH

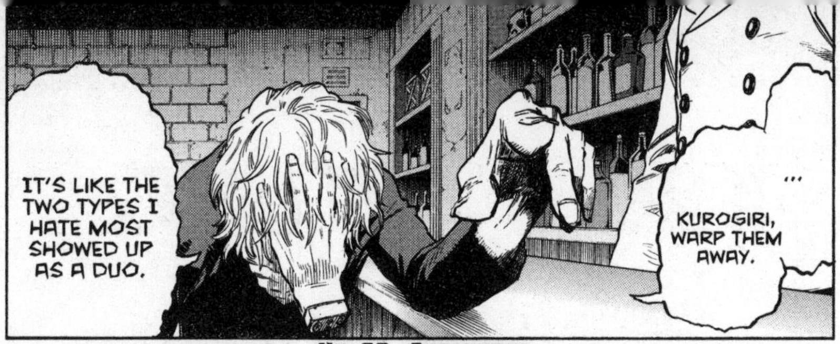
IT'S LIKE THE TWO TYPES I HATE MOST SHOWED UP AS A DUO.
...
KUROGIRI, WARP THEM AWAY.

NO. 68 - ENCOUNTER

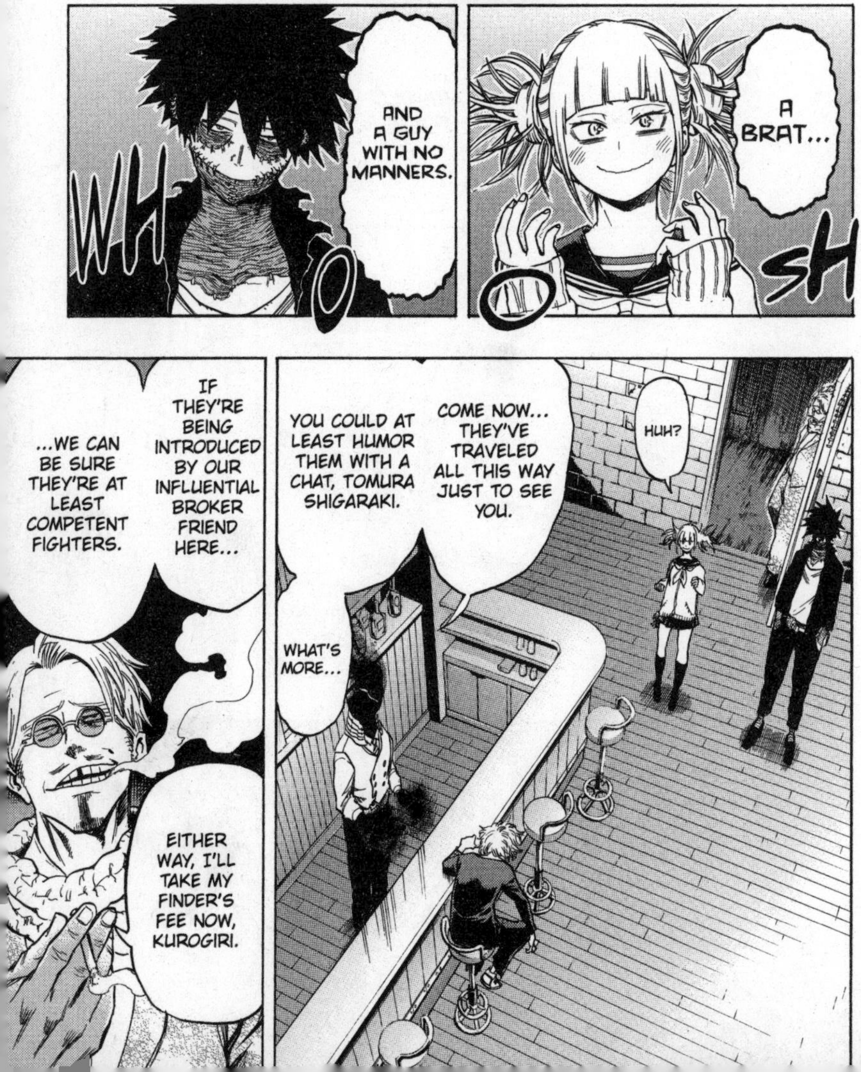
A BRAT...
SH
AND A GUY WITH NO MANNERS.
WH
HUH?
COME NOW... THEY'VE TRAVELED ALL THIS WAY JUST TO SEE YOU.
YOU COULD AT LEAST HUMOR THEM WITH A CHAT, TOMURA SHIGARAKI.
WHAT'S MORE...
IF THEY'RE BEING INTRODUCED BY OUR INFLUENTIAL BROKER FRIEND HERE...
...WE CAN BE SURE THEY'RE AT LEAST COMPETENT FIGHTERS.
EITHER WAY, I'LL TAKE MY FINDER'S FEE NOW, KUROGIRI.

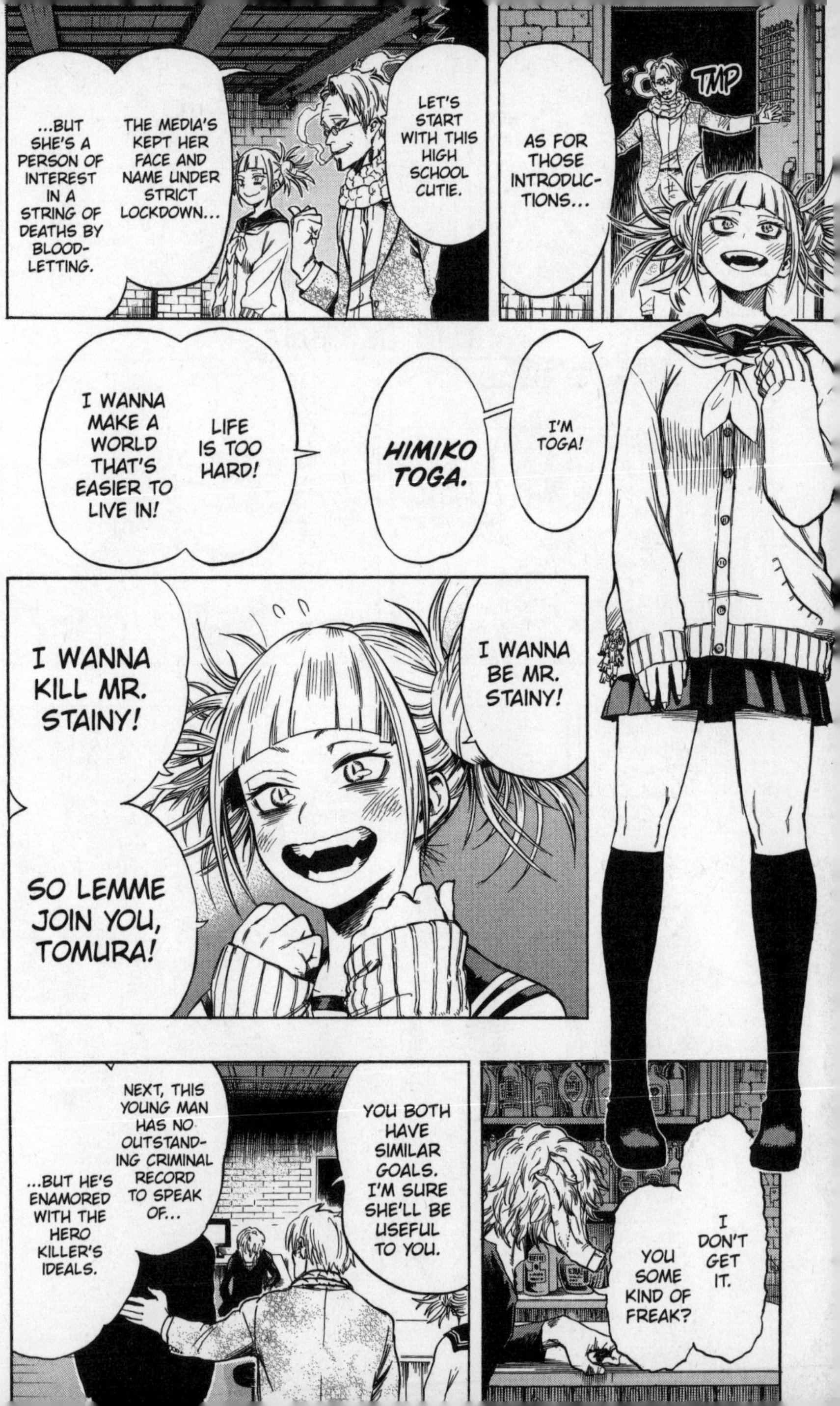
TMP
AS FOR THOSE INTRODUCTIONS...
LET'S START WITH THIS HIGH SCHOOL CUTIE.
THE MEDIA'S KEPT HER FACE AND NAME UNDER STRICT LOCKDOWN...
...BUT SHE'S A PERSON OF INTEREST IN A STRING OF DEATHS BY BLOODLETTING.
I'M TOGA!
HIMIKO TOGA.
LIFE IS TOO HARD!
I WANNA MAKE A WORLD THAT'S EASIER TO LIVE IN!
I WANNA BE MR. STAINY!
I WANNA KILL MR. STAINY!
SO LEMME JOIN YOU, TOMURA!
I DON'T GET IT.
YOU SOME KIND OF FREAK?
YOU BOTH HAVE SIMILAR GOALS. I'M SURE SHE'LL BE USEFUL TO YOU.
NEXT, THIS YOUNG MAN HAS NO OUTSTANDING CRIMINAL RECORD TO SPEAK OF...
...BUT HE'S ENAMORED WITH THE HERO KILLER'S IDEALS.

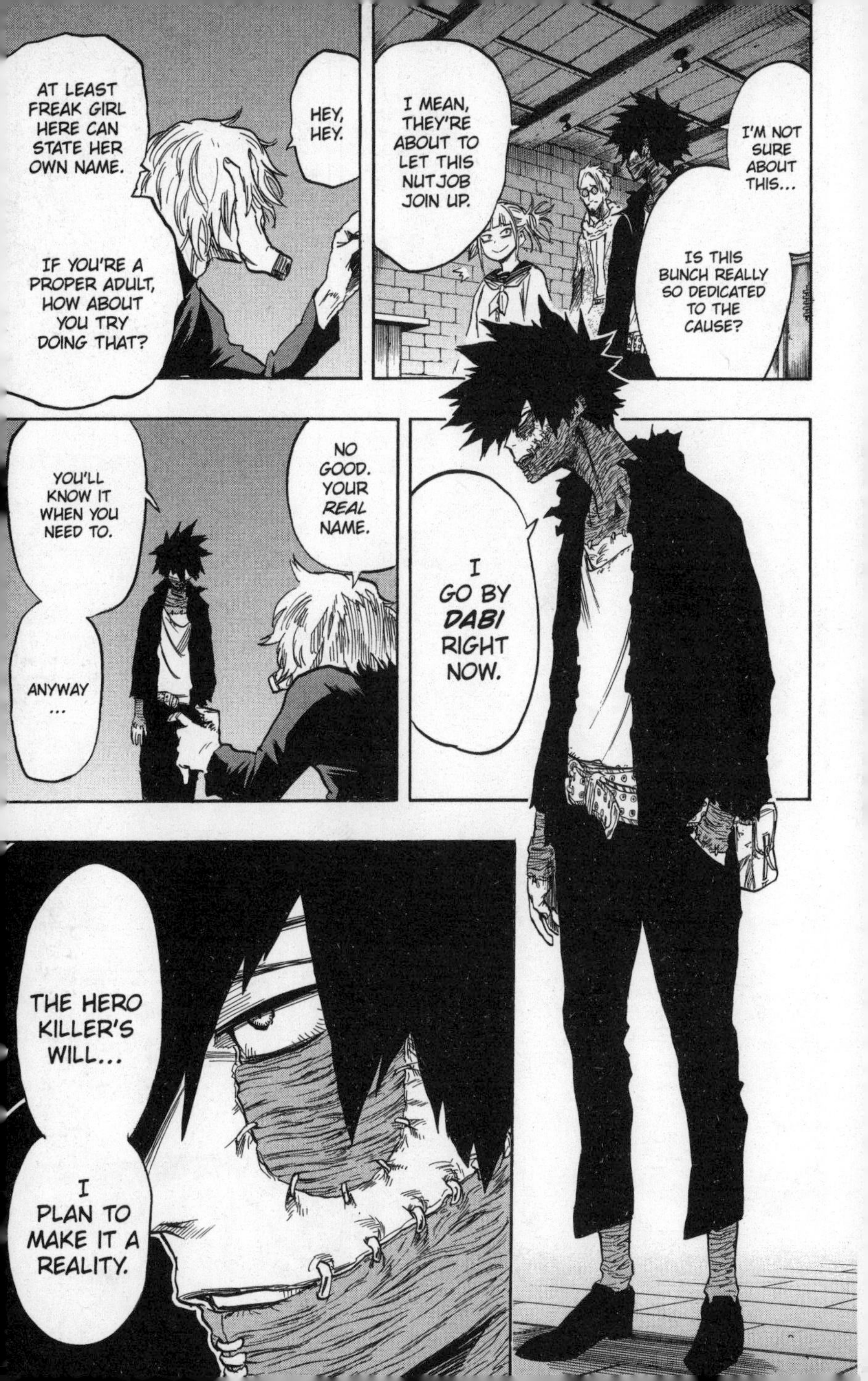

I'M NOT SURE ABOUT THIS...
IS THIS BUNCH REALLY SO DEDICATED TO THE CAUSE?
I MEAN, THEY'RE ABOUT TO LET THIS NUTJOB JOIN UP.
HEY, HEY.
AT LEAST FREAK GIRL HERE CAN STATE HER OWN NAME.
IF YOU'RE A PROPER ADULT, HOW ABOUT YOU TRY DOING THAT?
I GO BY DABI RIGHT NOW.
NO GOOD. YOUR REAL NAME.
YOU'LL KNOW IT WHEN YOU NEED TO.
ANYWAY...
THE HERO KILLER'S WILL...
I PLAN TO MAKE IT A REALITY.

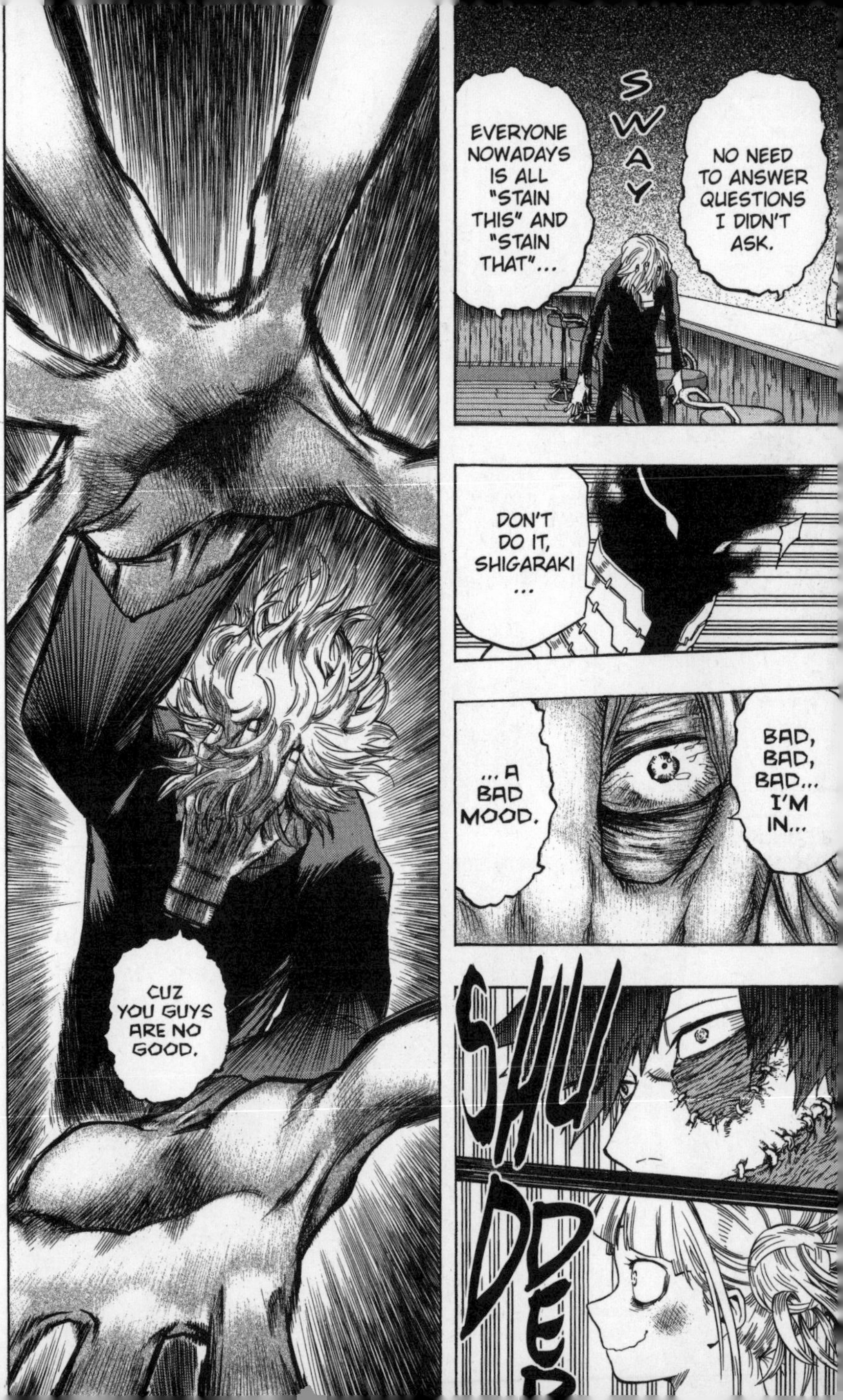
NO NEED TO ANSWER QUESTIONS I DIDN'T ASK.
SWAY
EVERYONE NOWADAYS IS ALL "STAIN THIS" AND "STAIN THAT"...
DON'T DO IT, SHIGARAKI ...
BAD, BAD, BAD... I'M IN...
... A BAD MOOD.
SHUDDE
CUZ YOU GUYS ARE NO GOOD.

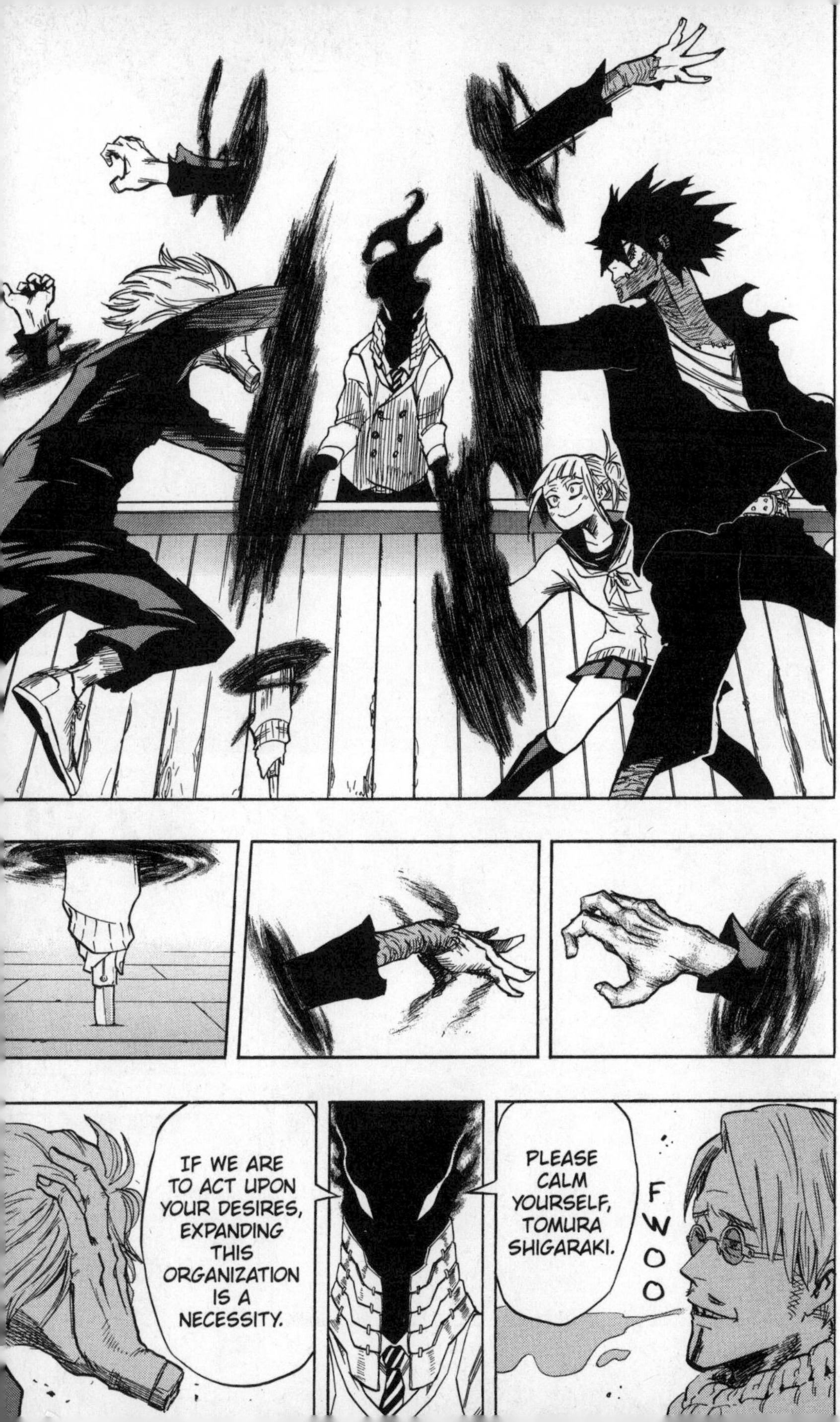

PLEASE CALM YOURSELF, TOMURA SHIGARAKI.
FWOO
IF WE ARE TO ACT UPON YOUR DESIRES, EXPANDING THIS ORGANIZATION IS A NECESSITY.

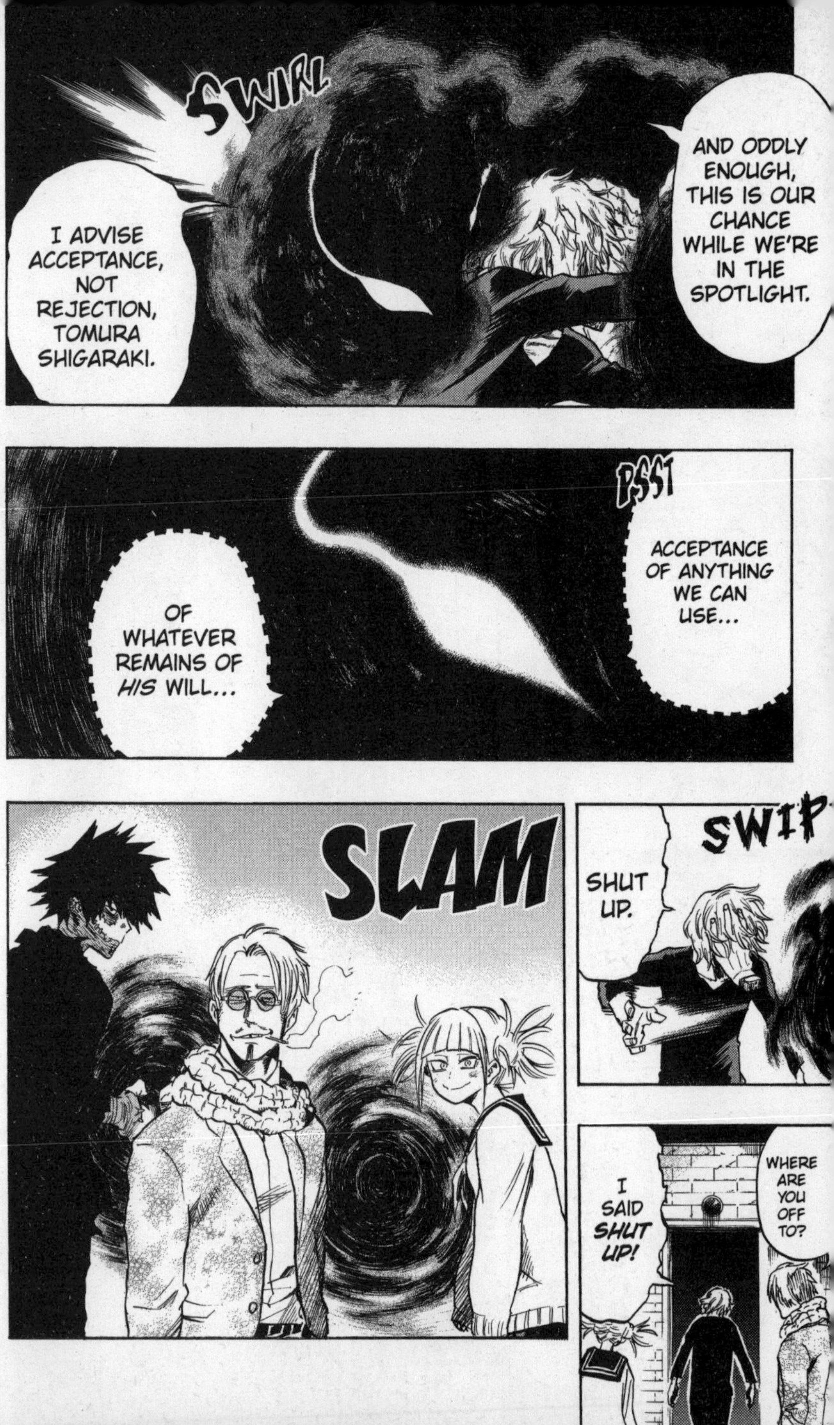
AND ODDLY ENOUGH, THIS IS OUR CHANCE WHILE WE'RE IN THE SPOTLIGHT.
SWIRL
I ADVISE ACCEPTANCE, NOT REJECTION, TOMURA SHIGARAKI.
PSST
ACCEPTANCE OF ANYTHING WE CAN USE...
OF WHATEVER REMAINS OF *HIS* WILL...
SWIP
SHUT UP.
WHERE ARE YOU OFF TO?
I SAID *SHUT UP!*
SLAM

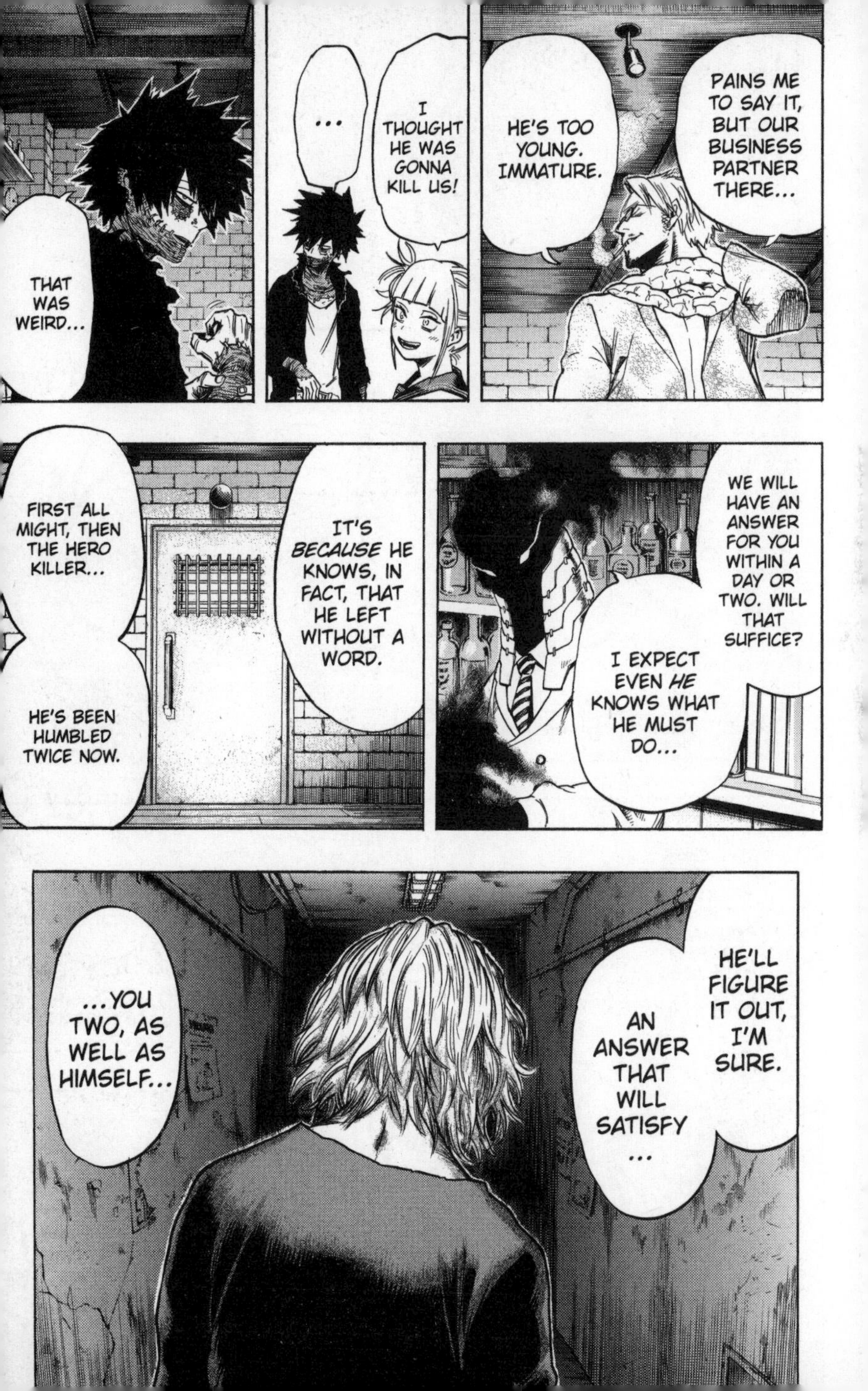
PAINS ME TO SAY IT, BUT OUR BUSINESS PARTNER THERE...
HE'S TOO YOUNG. IMMATURE.
I THOUGHT HE WAS GONNA KILL US!
...
THAT WAS WEIRD...
WE WILL HAVE AN ANSWER FOR YOU WITHIN A DAY OR TWO. WILL THAT SUFFICE?
I EXPECT EVEN *HE* KNOWS WHAT HE MUST DO...
IT'S *BECAUSE* HE KNOWS, IN FACT, THAT HE LEFT WITHOUT A WORD.
FIRST ALL MIGHT, THEN THE HERO KILLER...
HE'S BEEN HUMBLED TWICE NOW.
HE'LL FIGURE IT OUT, I'M SURE.
AN ANSWER THAT WILL SATISFY...
...YOU TWO, AS WELL AS HIMSELF...

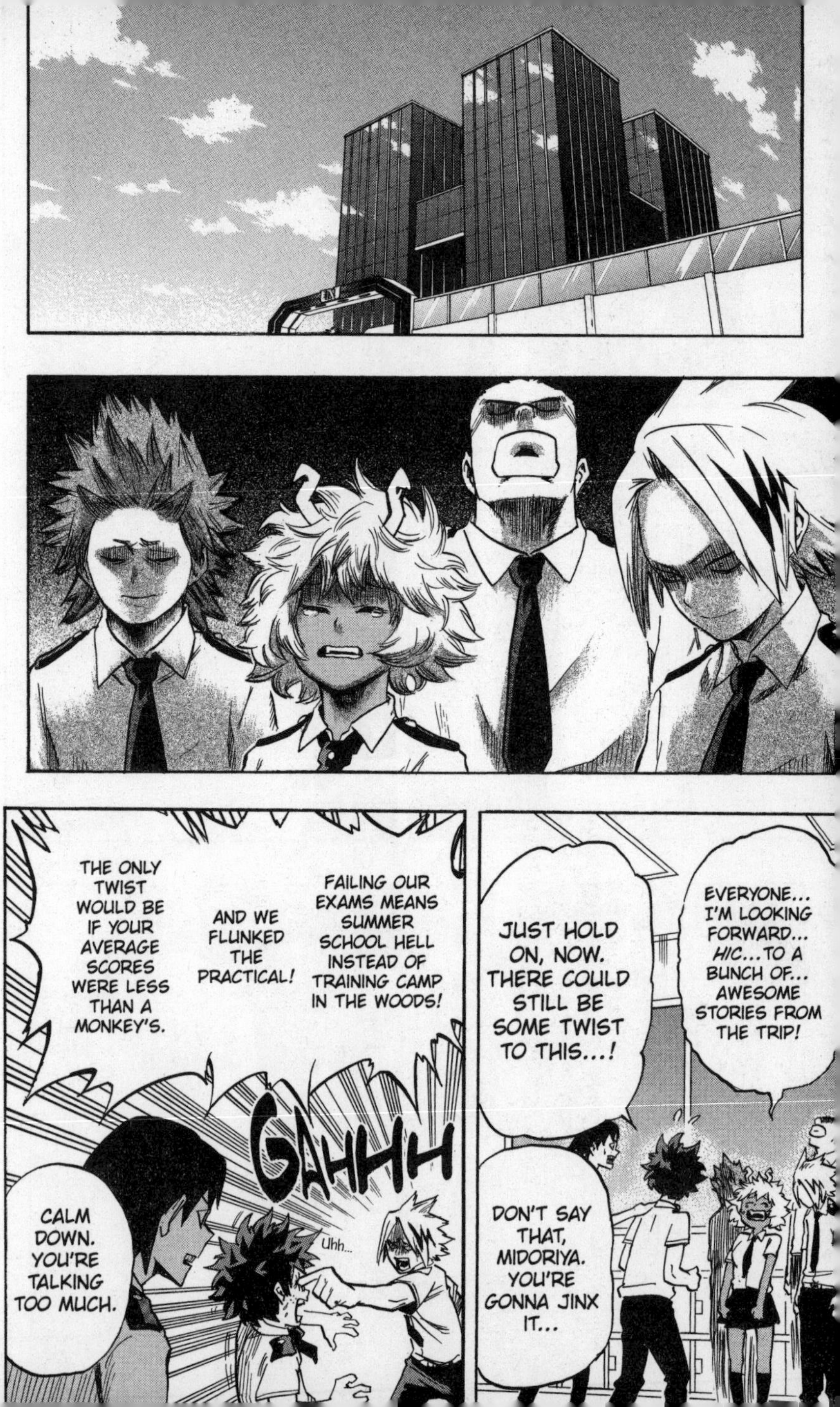
EVERYONE… I'M LOOKING FORWARD… *HIC*…TO A BUNCH OF… AWESOME STORIES FROM THE TRIP!
JUST HOLD ON, NOW. THERE COULD STILL BE SOME TWIST TO THIS…!
DON'T SAY THAT, MIDORIYA. YOU'RE GONNA JINX IT…
FAILING OUR EXAMS MEANS SUMMER SCHOOL HELL INSTEAD OF TRAINING CAMP IN THE WOODS!
AND WE FLUNKED THE PRACTICAL!
THE ONLY TWIST WOULD BE IF YOUR AVERAGE SCORES WERE LESS THAN A MONKEY'S.
GAHHH
Uhh…
CALM DOWN. YOU'RE TALKING TOO MUCH.

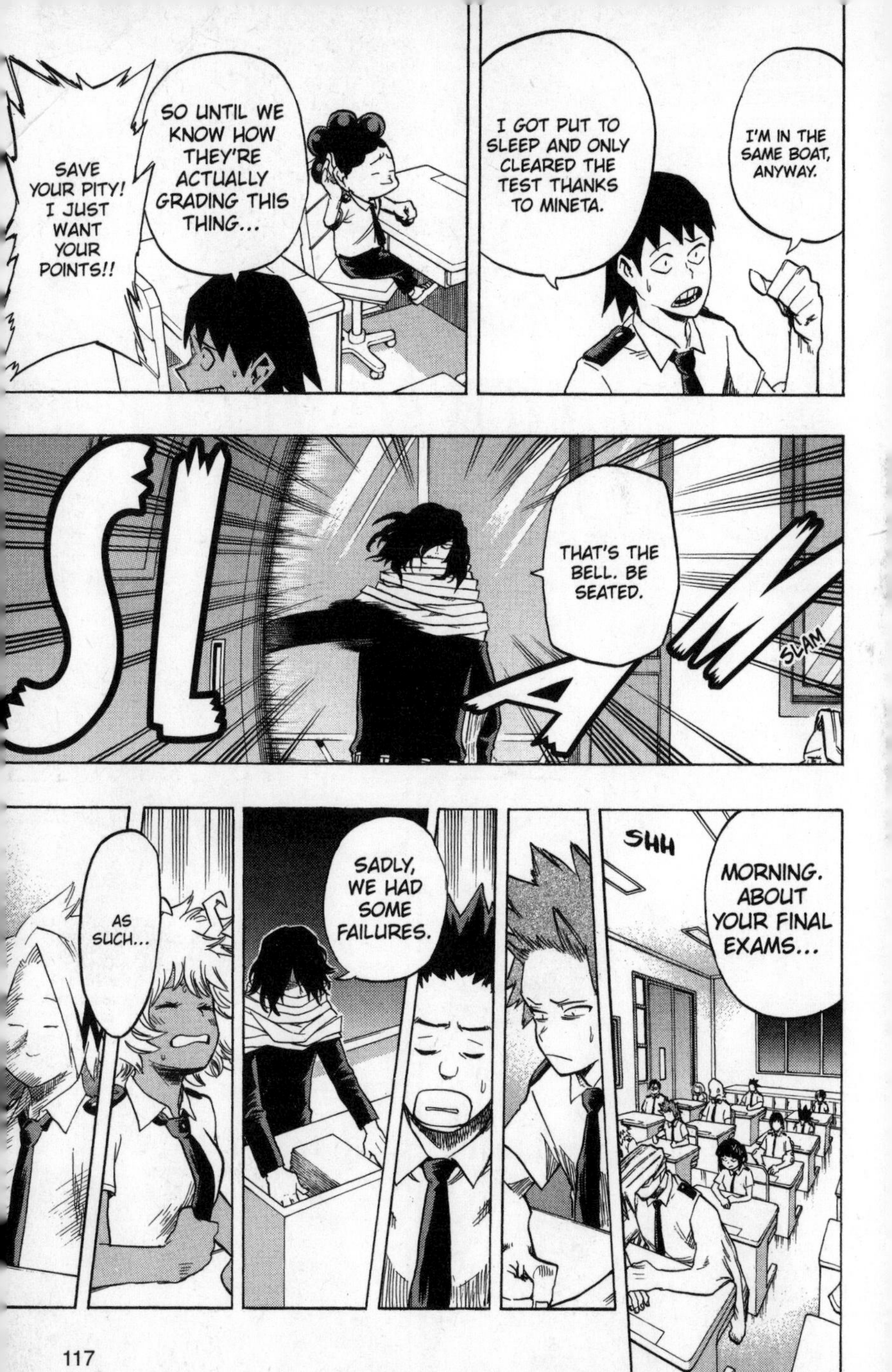
I'M IN THE SAME BOAT, ANYWAY.
I GOT PUT TO SLEEP AND ONLY CLEARED THE TEST THANKS TO MINETA.
SO UNTIL WE KNOW HOW THEY'RE ACTUALLY GRADING THIS THING...
SAVE YOUR PITY! I JUST WANT YOUR POINTS!!
THAT'S THE BELL. BE SEATED.
SLAM
MORNING. ABOUT YOUR FINAL EXAMS...
SHH
SADLY, WE HAD SOME FAILURES.
AS SUCH...

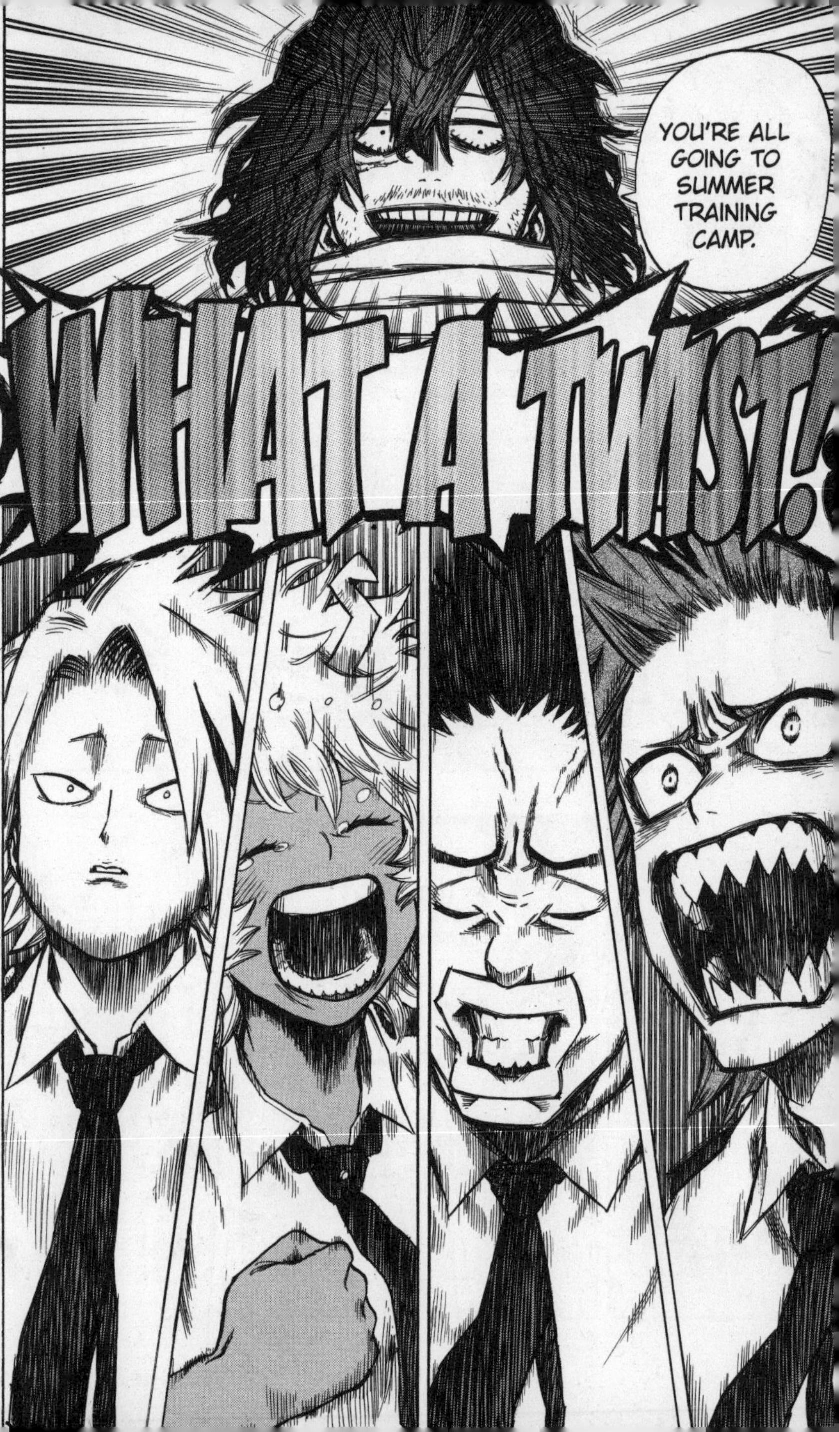
YOU'RE ALL GOING TO SUMMER TRAINING CAMP.
WHAT A TWIST!!

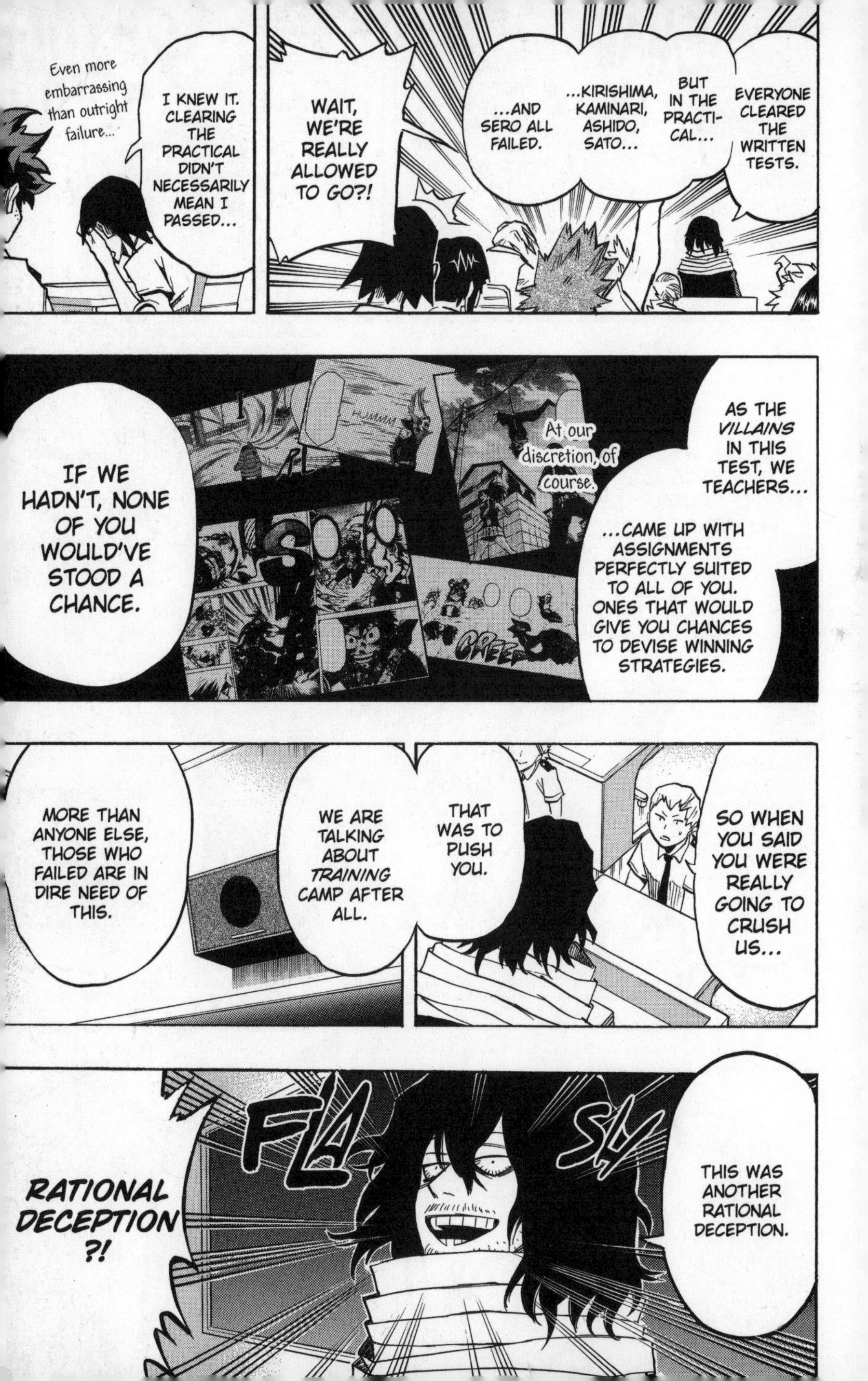
EVERYONE CLEARED THE WRITTEN TESTS.
BUT IN THE PRACTI-CAL...
...KIRISHIMA, KAMINARI, ASHIDO, SATO...
...AND SERO ALL FAILED.
WAIT, WE'RE REALLY ALLOWED TO GO?!
I KNEW IT. CLEARING THE PRACTICAL DIDN'T NECESSARILY MEAN I PASSED...
Even more embarrassing than outright failure...
AS THE *VILLAINS* IN THIS TEST, WE TEACHERS...
At our discretion, of course.
...CAME UP WITH ASSIGNMENTS PERFECTLY SUITED TO ALL OF YOU. ONES THAT WOULD GIVE YOU CHANCES TO DEVISE WINNING STRATEGIES.
IF WE HADN'T, NONE OF YOU WOULD'VE STOOD A CHANCE.
SO WHEN YOU SAID YOU WERE REALLY GOING TO CRUSH US...
THAT WAS TO PUSH YOU.
WE ARE TALKING ABOUT *TRAINING* CAMP AFTER ALL.
MORE THAN ANYONE ELSE, THOSE WHO FAILED ARE IN DIRE NEED OF THIS.
THIS WAS ANOTHER RATIONAL DECEPTION.
FLASHY
RATIONAL DECEPTION?!

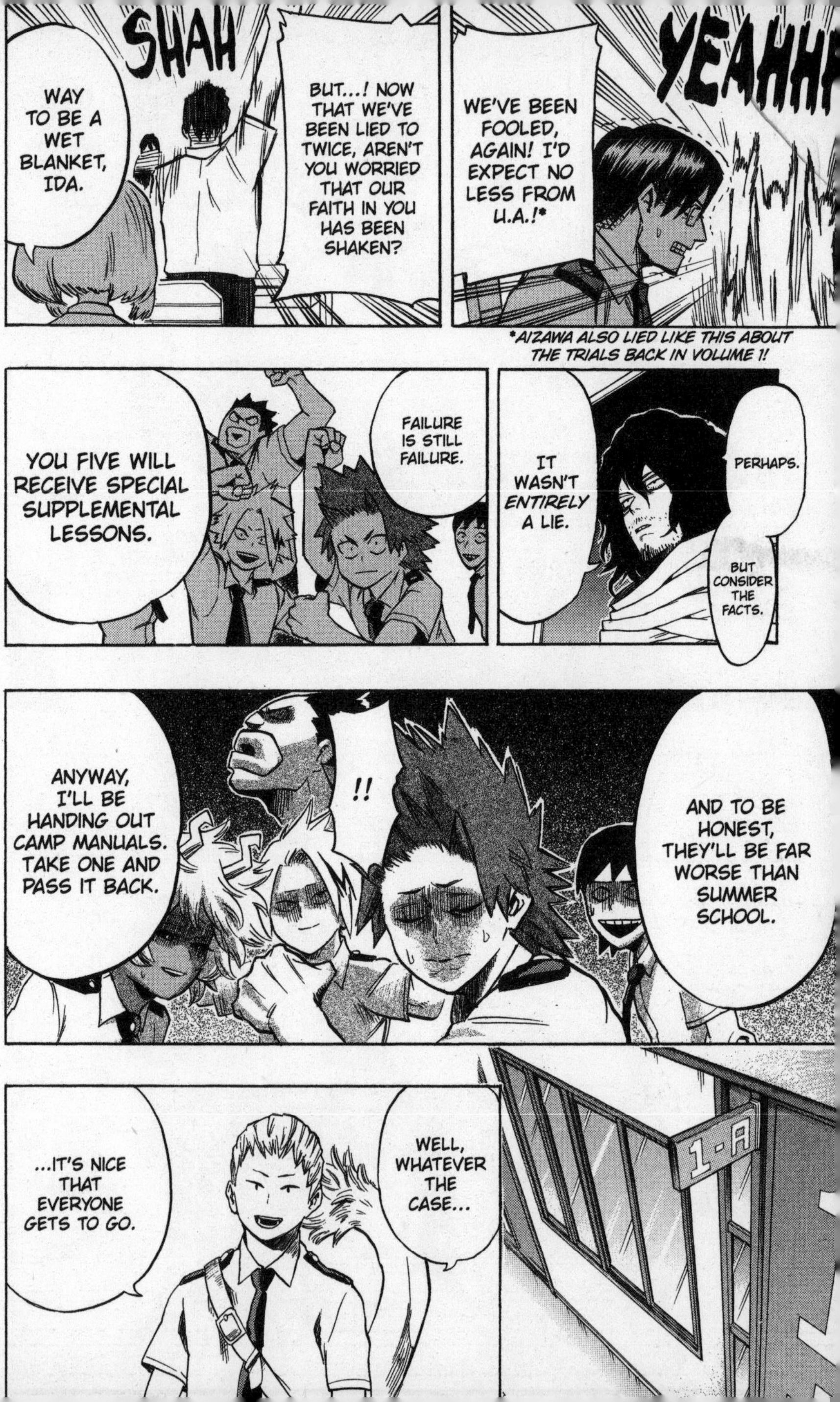
YEAHHH
WE'VE BEEN FOOLED, AGAIN! I'D EXPECT NO LESS FROM U.A.!*
BUT...! NOW THAT WE'VE BEEN LIED TO TWICE, AREN'T YOU WORRIED THAT OUR FAITH IN YOU HAS BEEN SHAKEN?
SHAH
WAY TO BE A WET BLANKET, IDA.
*AIZAWA ALSO LIED LIKE THIS ABOUT THE TRIALS BACK IN VOLUME 1!
PERHAPS.
IT WASN'T *ENTIRELY* A LIE.
BUT CONSIDER THE FACTS.
FAILURE IS STILL FAILURE.
YOU FIVE WILL RECEIVE SPECIAL SUPPLEMENTAL LESSONS.
AND TO BE HONEST, THEY'LL BE FAR WORSE THAN SUMMER SCHOOL.
!!
ANYWAY, I'LL BE HANDING OUT CAMP MANUALS. TAKE ONE AND PASS IT BACK.
1-A
WELL, WHATEVER THE CASE...
...IT'S NICE THAT EVERYONE GETS TO GO.

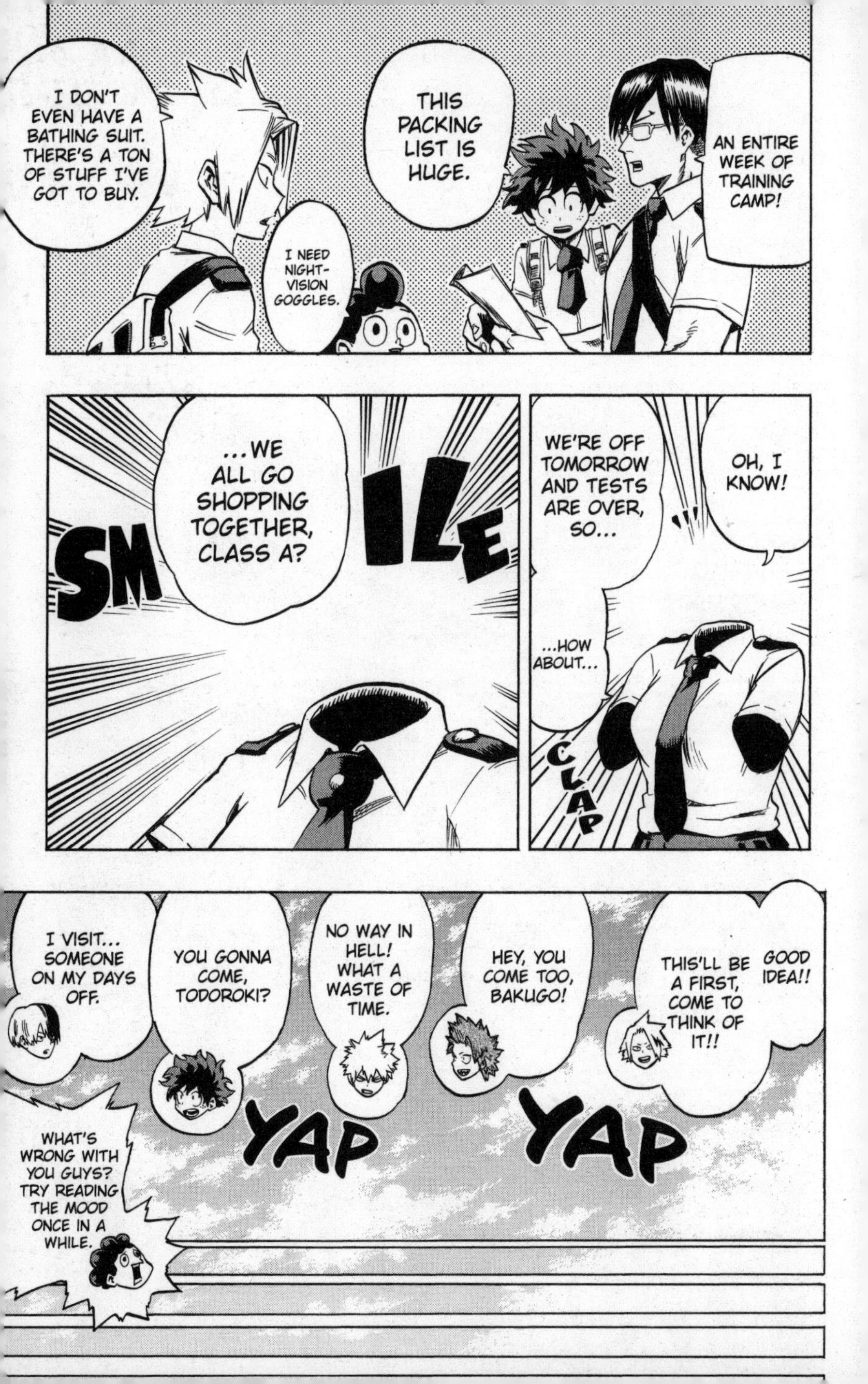
AN ENTIRE WEEK OF TRAINING CAMP!
THIS PACKING LIST IS HUGE.
I DON'T EVEN HAVE A BATHING SUIT. THERE'S A TON OF STUFF I'VE GOT TO BUY.
I NEED NIGHT-VISION GOGGLES.
OH, I KNOW!
WE'RE OFF TOMORROW AND TESTS ARE OVER, SO...
...HOW ABOUT...
CLAP
SMILE
...WE ALL GO SHOPPING TOGETHER, CLASS A?
GOOD IDEA!!
THIS'LL BE A FIRST, COME TO THINK OF IT!!
HEY, YOU COME TOO, BAKUGO!
NO WAY IN HELL! WHAT A WASTE OF TIME.
YOU GONNA COME, TODOROKI?
I VISIT... SOMEONE ON MY DAYS OFF.
YAP YAP
WHAT'S WRONG WITH YOU GUYS? TRY READING THE MOOD ONCE IN A WHILE.

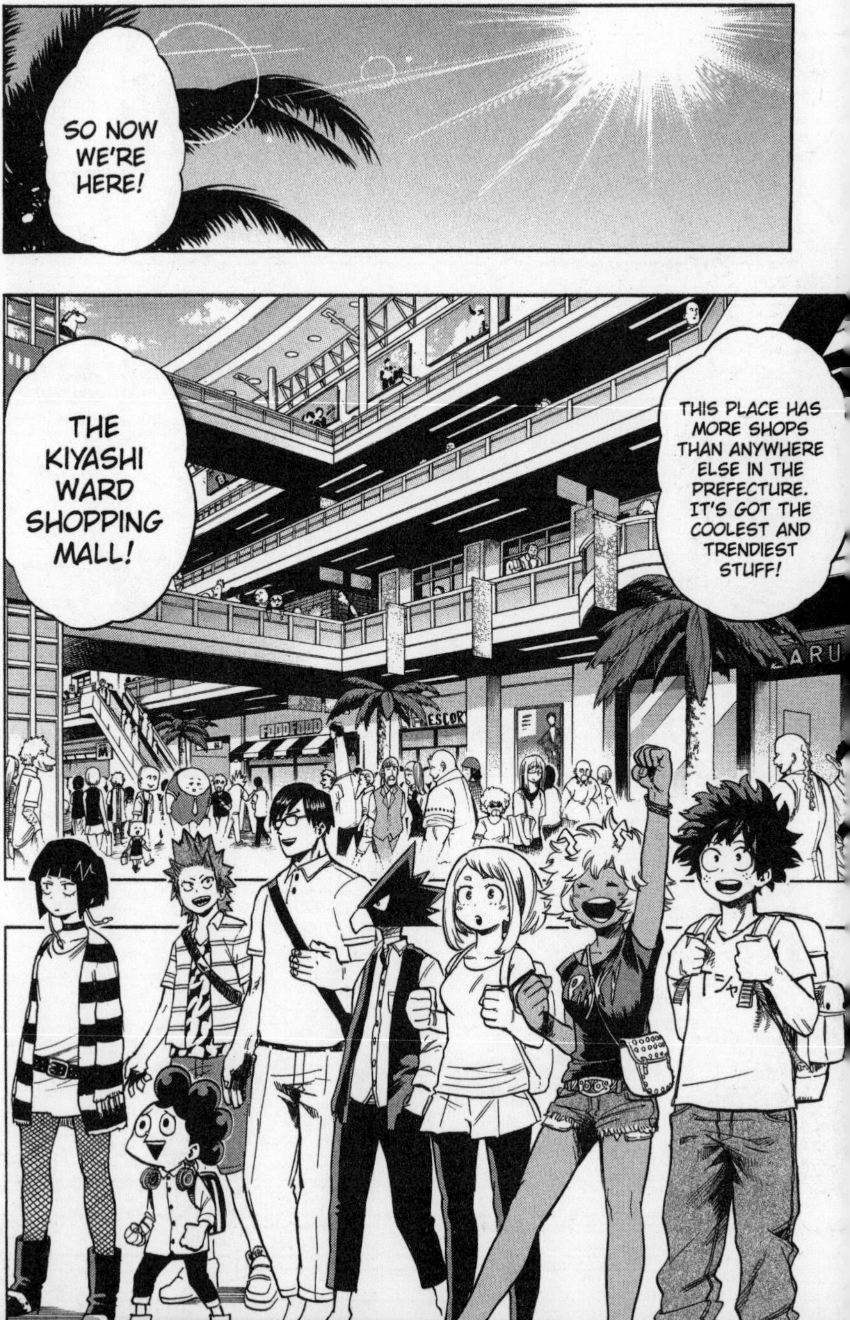
SO NOW WE'RE HERE!
THIS PLACE HAS MORE SHOPS THAN ANYWHERE ELSE IN THE PREFECTURE. IT'S GOT THE COOLEST AND TRENDIEST STUFF!
THE KIYASHI WARD SHOPPING MALL!

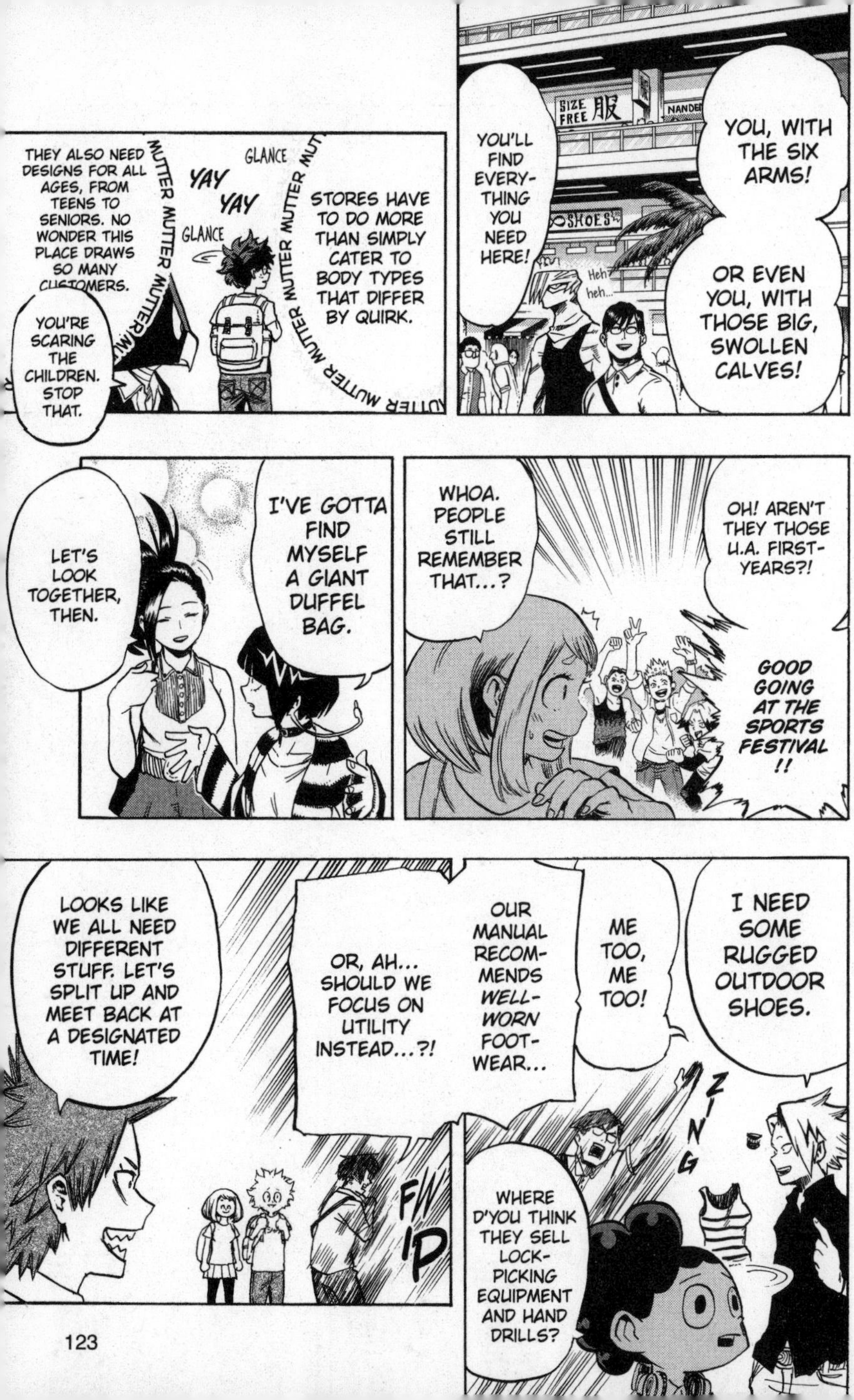
SIZE FREE 服
NANDE
SHOES
YOU, WITH THE SIX ARMS!
OR EVEN YOU, WITH THOSE BIG, SWOLLEN CALVES!
YOU'LL FIND EVERYTHING YOU NEED HERE!
Heh heh...
STORES HAVE TO DO MORE THAN SIMPLY CATER TO BODY TYPES THAT DIFFER BY QUIRK.
GLANCE
YAY
YAY
GLANCE
MUTTER MUTTER MUTTER MUTTER MUTTER MUTTER MUTTER MUTTER
THEY ALSO NEED DESIGNS FOR ALL AGES, FROM TEENS TO SENIORS. NO WONDER THIS PLACE DRAWS SO MANY CUSTOMERS.
YOU'RE SCARING THE CHILDREN. STOP THAT.
OH! AREN'T THEY THOSE U.A. FIRST-YEARS?!
GOOD GOING AT THE SPORTS FESTIVAL!!
WHOA. PEOPLE STILL REMEMBER THAT...?
I'VE GOTTA FIND MYSELF A GIANT DUFFEL BAG.
LET'S LOOK TOGETHER, THEN.
I NEED SOME RUGGED OUTDOOR SHOES.
ME TOO, ME TOO!
OUR MANUAL RECOMMENDS WELL-WORN FOOTWEAR...
ZING
WHERE D'YOU THINK THEY SELL LOCK-PICKING EQUIPMENT AND HAND DRILLS?
OR, AH... SHOULD WE FOCUS ON UTILITY INSTEAD...?!
LOOKS LIKE WE ALL NEED DIFFERENT STUFF. LET'S SPLIT UP AND MEET BACK AT A DESIGNATED TIME!
FWIP

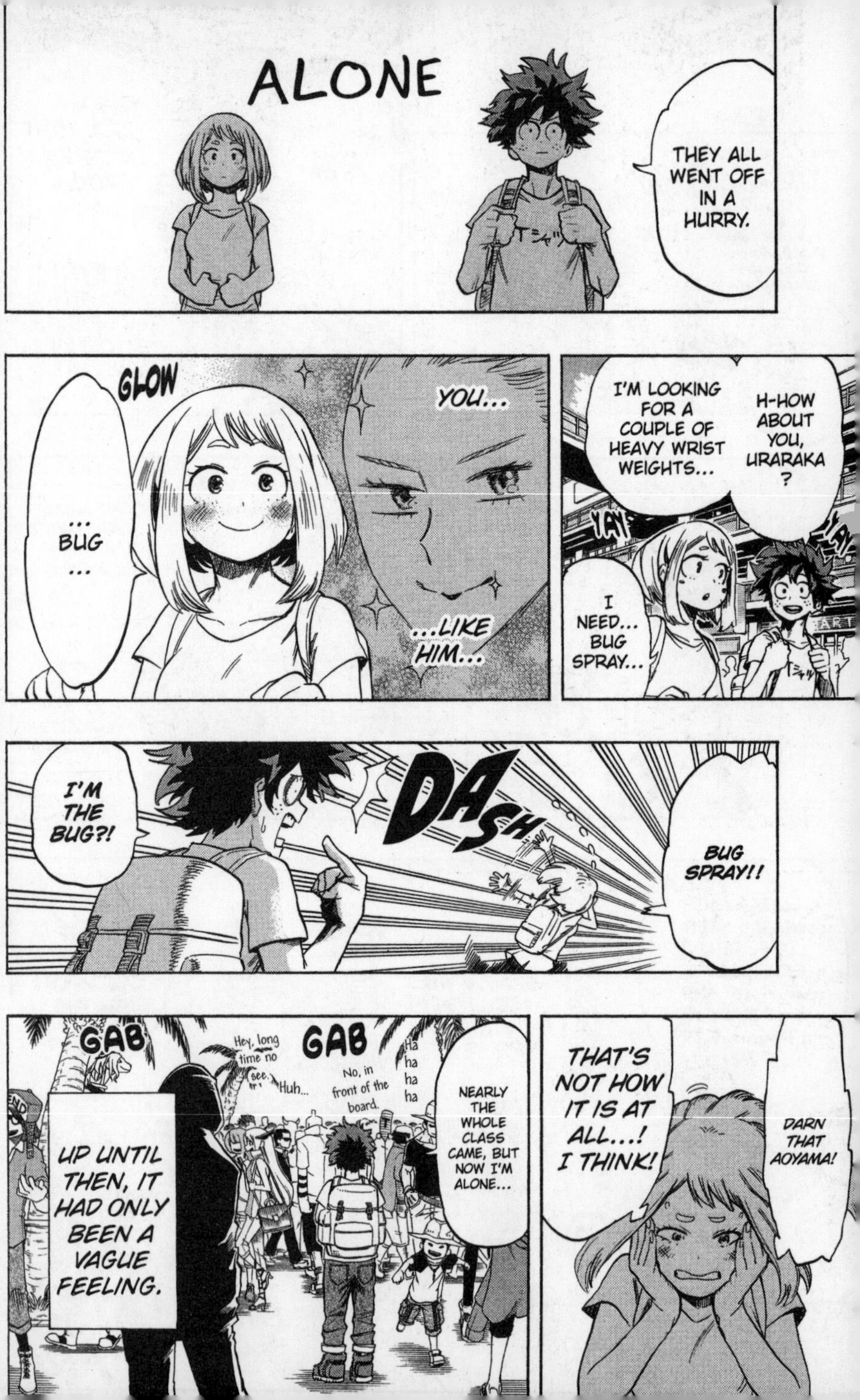
THEY ALL WENT OFF IN A HURRY.
ALONE
I'M LOOKING FOR A COUPLE OF HEAVY WRIST WEIGHTS...
H-HOW ABOUT YOU, URARAKA?
YAY
YAY
I NEED... BUG SPRAY...
YOU...
...LIKE HIM...
GLOW
... BUG ...
BUG SPRAY!!
DASH
I'M THE BUG?!
DARN THAT AOYAMA!
THAT'S NOT HOW IT IS AT ALL...! I THINK!
NEARLY THE WHOLE CLASS CAME, BUT NOW I'M ALONE...
GAB
Ha ha ha ha
No, in front of the board.
Huh...
Hey, long time no see.
GAB
UP UNTIL THEN, IT HAD ONLY BEEN A VAGUE FEELING.

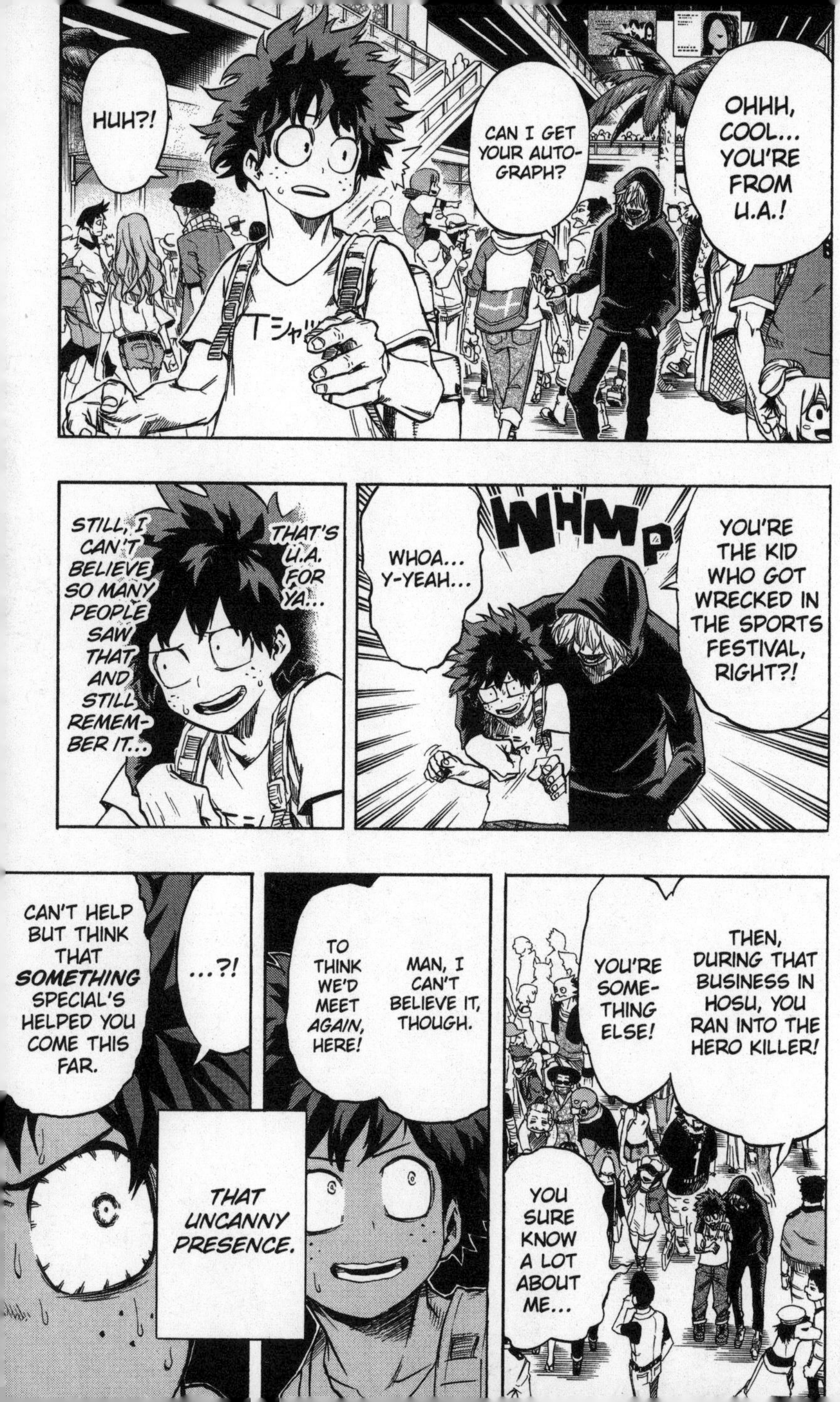
OHHH, COOL... YOU'RE FROM U.A.!
CAN I GET YOUR AUTO-GRAPH?
HUH?!
YOU'RE THE KID WHO GOT WRECKED IN THE SPORTS FESTIVAL, RIGHT?!
WHMP
WHOA... Y-YEAH...
THAT'S U.A. FOR YA...
STILL, I CAN'T BELIEVE SO MANY PEOPLE SAW THAT AND STILL REMEMBER IT...
THEN, DURING THAT BUSINESS IN HOSU, YOU RAN INTO THE HERO KILLER!
YOU'RE SOME-THING ELSE!
YOU SURE KNOW A LOT ABOUT ME...
MAN, I CAN'T BELIEVE IT, THOUGH.
TO THINK WE'D MEET AGAIN, HERE!
THAT UNCANNY PRESENCE.
...?!
CAN'T HELP BUT THINK THAT SOMETHING SPECIAL'S HELPED YOU COME THIS FAR.

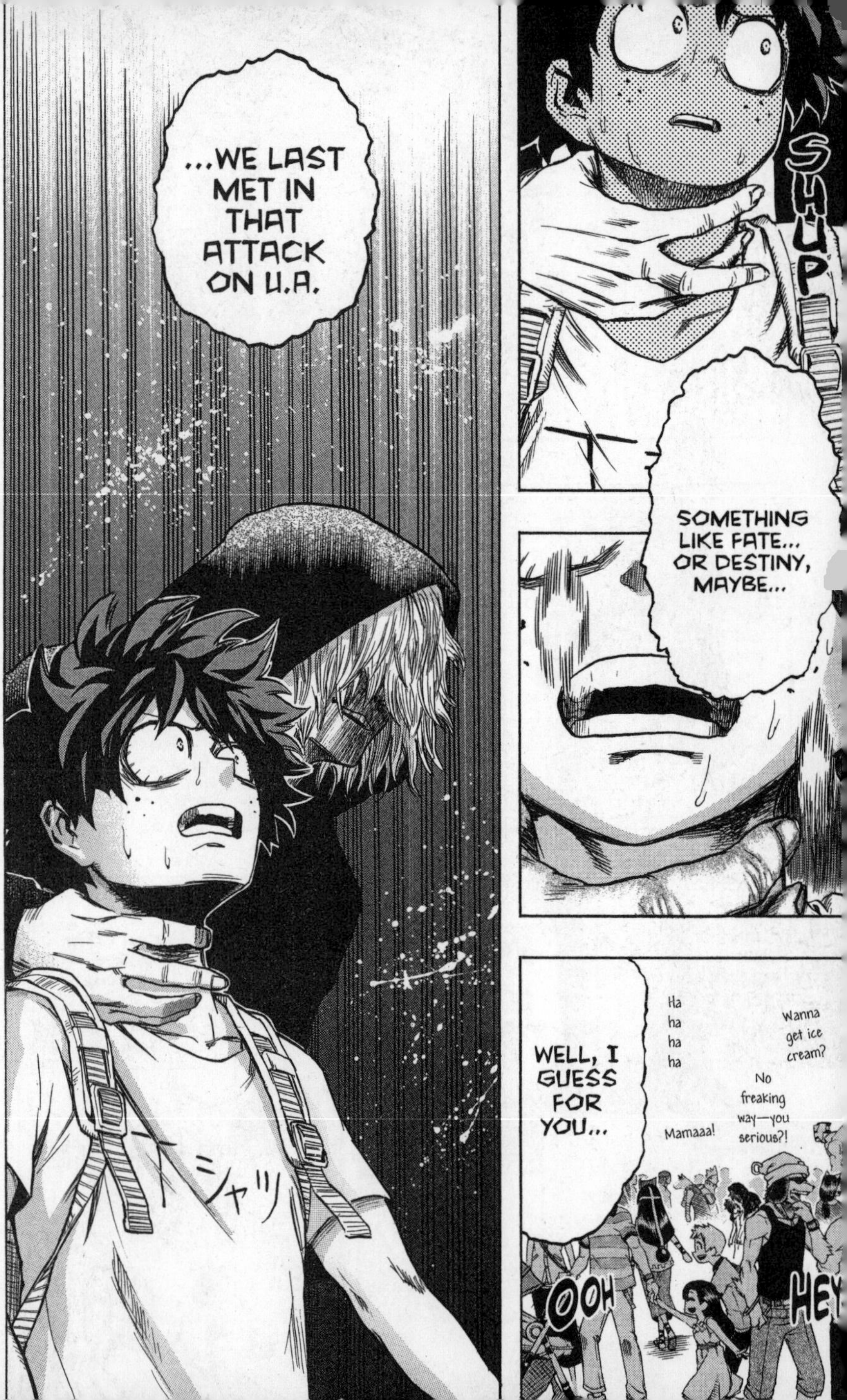
SHUP
SOMETHING LIKE FATE... OR DESTINY, MAYBE...
Wanna get ice cream?
Ha ha ha ha
WELL, I GUESS FOR YOU...
No freaking way—you serious?!
Mamaaa!
HEY
OOH
...WE LAST MET IN THAT ATTACK ON U.A.
シャツ

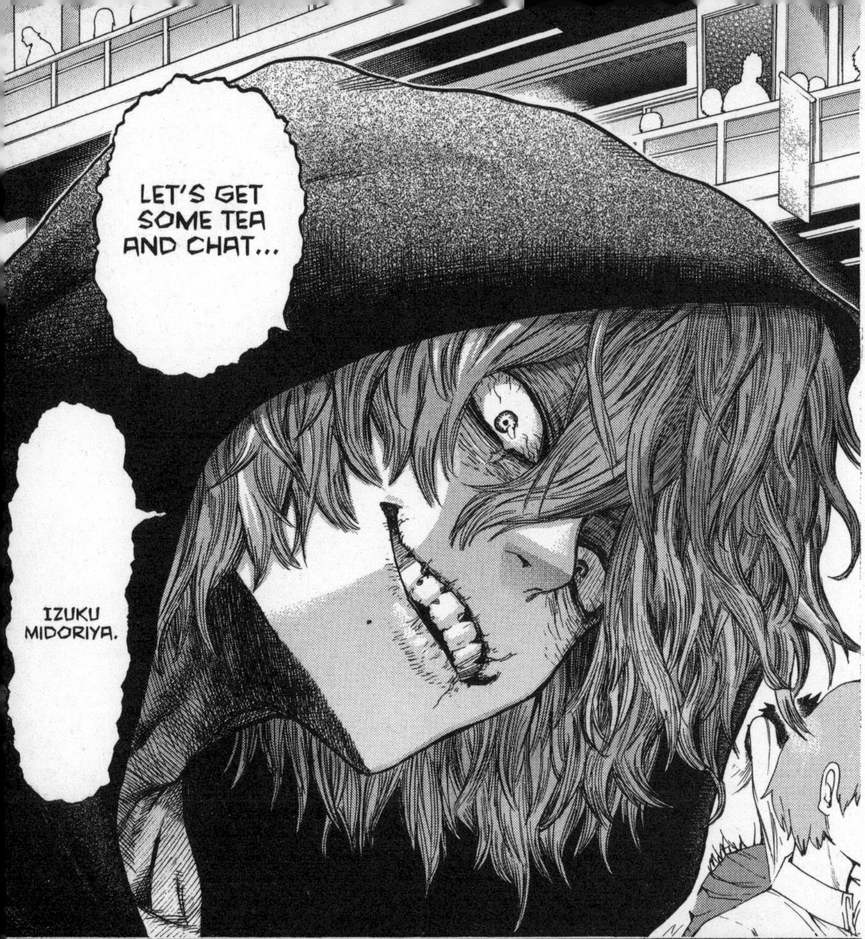
LET'S GET SOME TEA AND CHAT...
IZUKU MIDORIYA.

No. 68 - Encounter

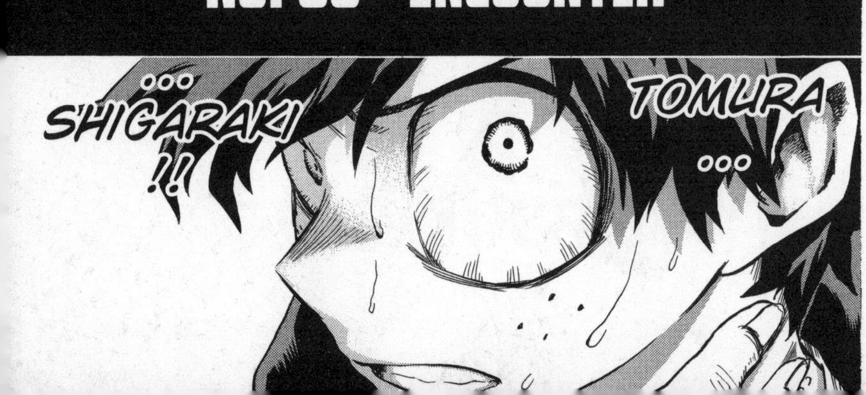
TOMURA ...
... SHIGARAKI !!

THE COSTUME

MINORU MINETA'S COSTUME

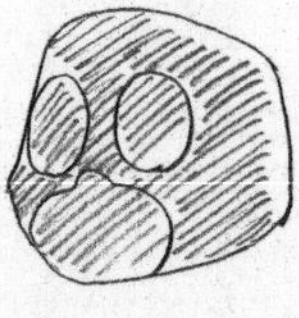

Grape Face Mask
Cool!

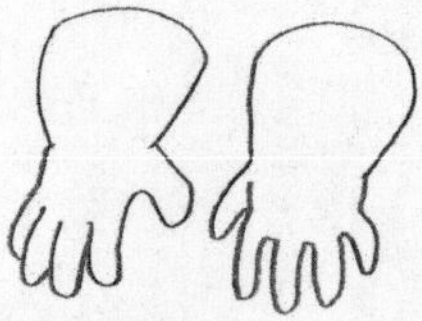

Pop-Off Gloves
Incorporates a special material developed from a sample of Mineta's scalp so that his orbs don't stick to them (just the palms and fingertips).

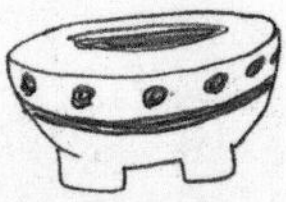

Grape Pants
The round parts—which seem decorative—are modeled on Mineta's hair and are appropriately sticky. While they're not nearly as sticky as the real things, they still get the job done when he wants to attach small objects to carry around.

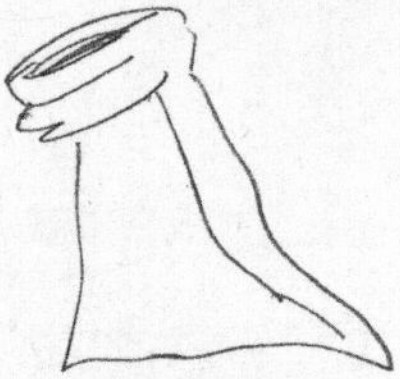

Minoru Cape
Mineta's always been obsessed with the idea of wearing a cape, but the development team took it upon themselves to shorten it. This was to avoid having his plucked-off hair balls stick to it.

ALL IN ALL: THAT POOR CAPE...

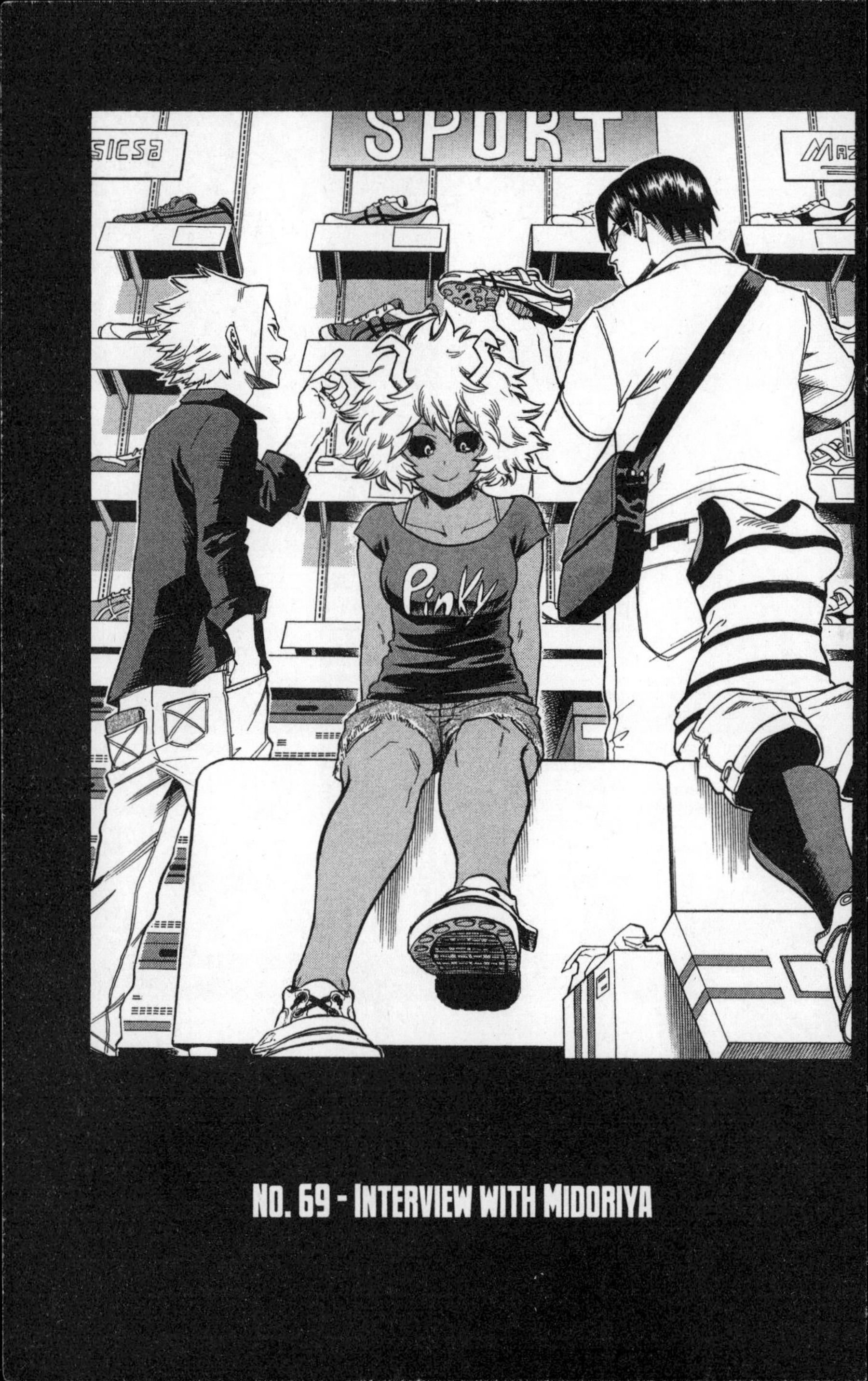
SPORT
Pinky

No. 69 - Interview with Midoriya

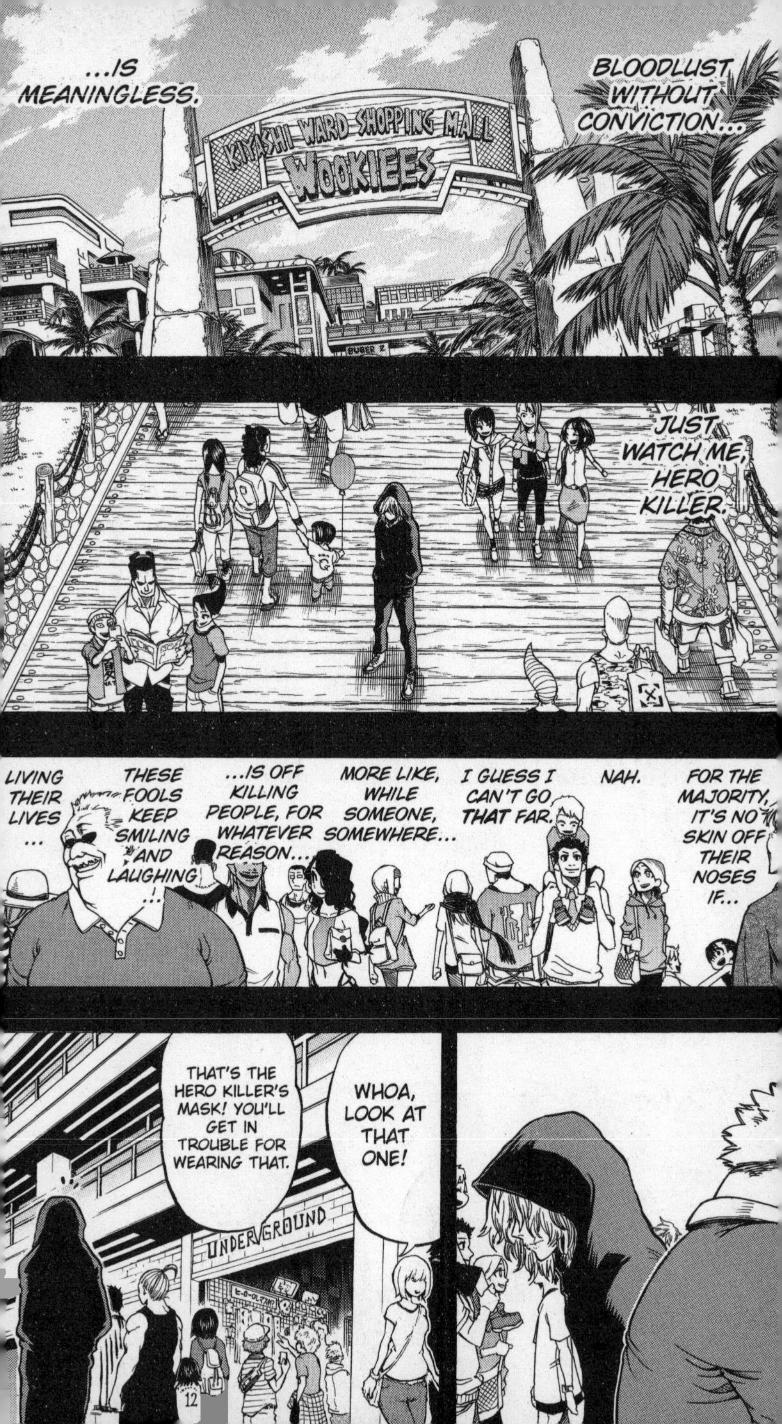
BLOODLUST WITHOUT CONVICTION...
...IS MEANINGLESS.
KIYASHI WARD SHOPPING MALL
WOOKIEES
JUST WATCH ME, HERO KILLER.
FOR THE MAJORITY, IT'S NO SKIN OFF THEIR NOSES IF...
NAH.
I GUESS I CAN'T GO THAT FAR.
MORE LIKE, WHILE SOMEONE, SOMEWHERE...
...IS OFF KILLING PEOPLE, FOR WHATEVER REASON...
THESE FOOLS KEEP SMILING AND LAUGHING...
LIVING THEIR LIVES...
WHOA, LOOK AT THAT ONE!
THAT'S THE HERO KILLER'S MASK! YOU'LL GET IN TROUBLE FOR WEARING THAT.
UNDERGROUND

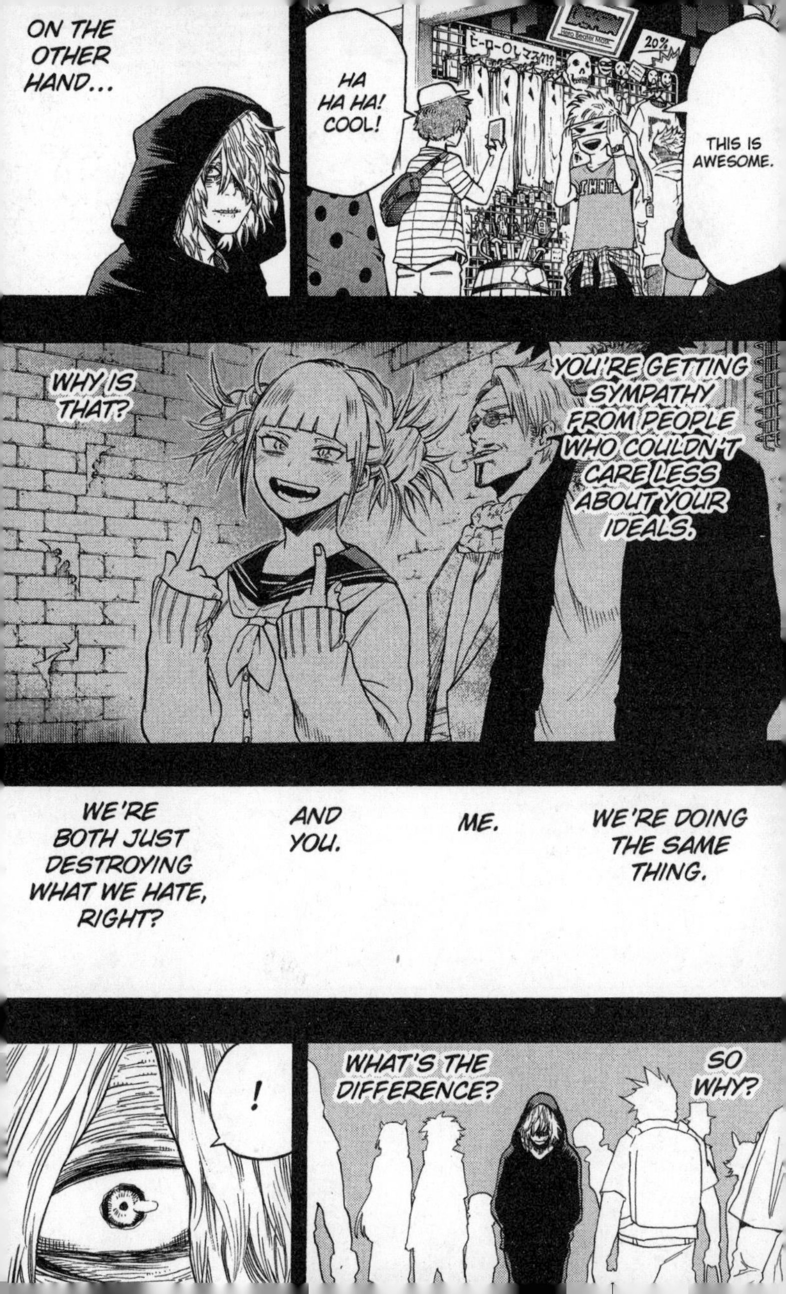
THIS IS AWESOME.
HA HA HA! COOL!
ON THE OTHER HAND...
YOU'RE GETTING SYMPATHY FROM PEOPLE WHO COULDN'T CARE LESS ABOUT YOUR IDEALS.
WHY IS THAT?
WE'RE DOING THE SAME THING.
ME.
AND YOU.
WE'RE BOTH JUST DESTROYING WHAT WE HATE, RIGHT?
SO WHY?
WHAT'S THE DIFFERENCE?
!

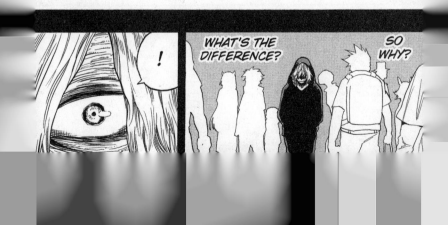

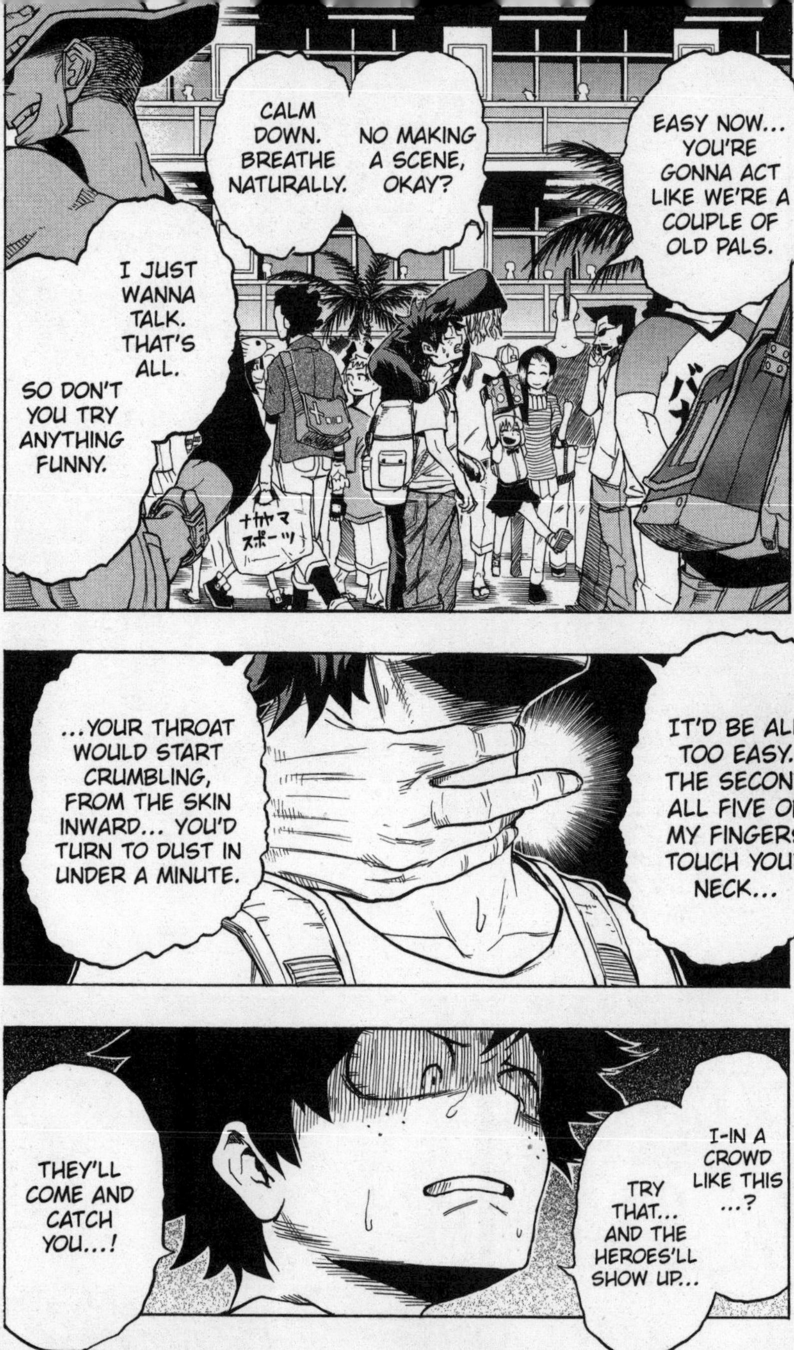
EASY NOW... YOU'RE GONNA ACT LIKE WE'RE A COUPLE OF OLD PALS.
NO MAKING A SCENE, OKAY?
CALM DOWN. BREATHE NATURALLY.
I JUST WANNA TALK. THAT'S ALL.
SO DON'T YOU TRY ANYTHING FUNNY.
ナカヤマ スポーツ
IT'D BE ALL TOO EASY. THE SECOND ALL FIVE OF MY FINGERS TOUCH YOUR NECK...
...YOUR THROAT WOULD START CRUMBLING, FROM THE SKIN INWARD... YOU'D TURN TO DUST IN UNDER A MINUTE.
I-IN A CROWD LIKE THIS ...?
TRY THAT... AND THE HEROES'LL SHOW UP...
THEY'LL COME AND CATCH YOU...!

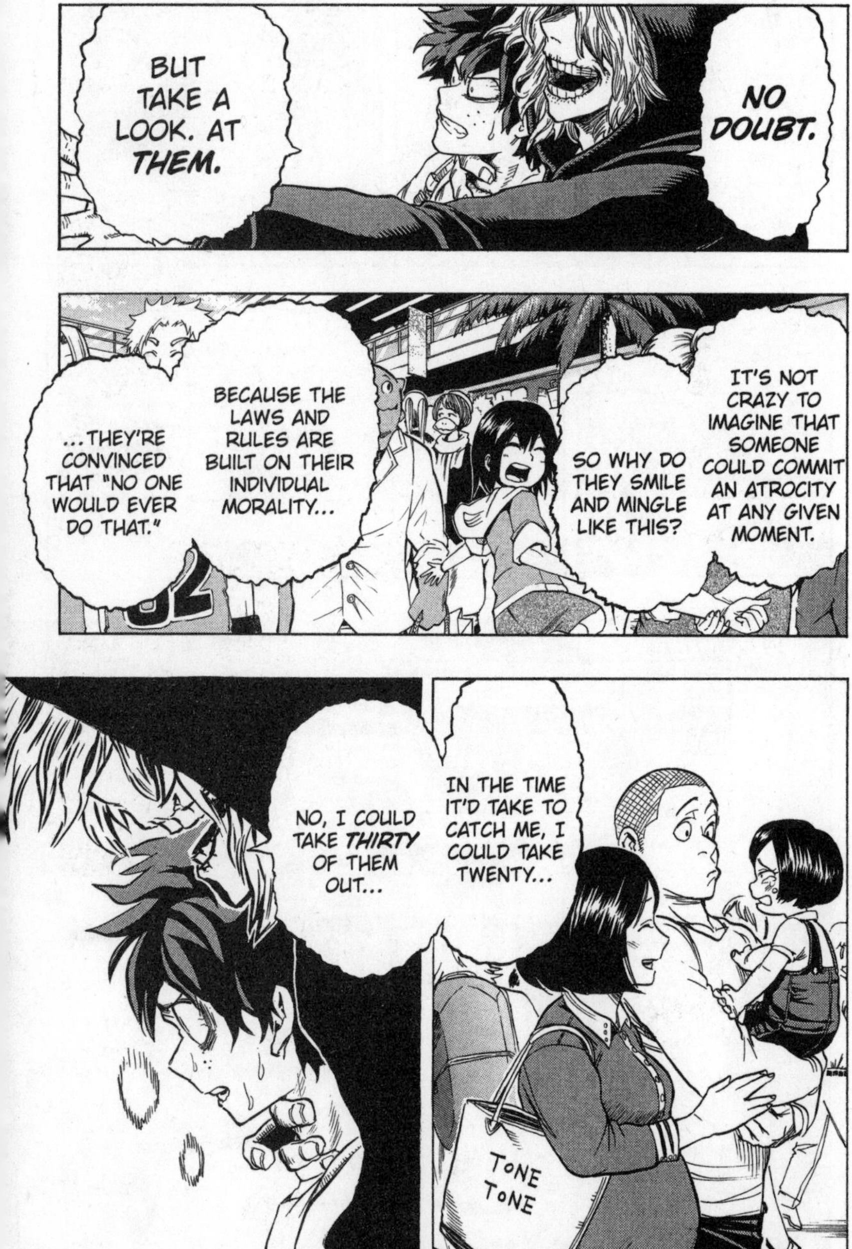
NO DOUBT.
BUT TAKE A LOOK. AT THEM.
IT'S NOT CRAZY TO IMAGINE THAT SOMEONE COULD COMMIT AN ATROCITY AT ANY GIVEN MOMENT.
SO WHY DO THEY SMILE AND MINGLE LIKE THIS?
BECAUSE THE LAWS AND RULES ARE BUILT ON THEIR INDIVIDUAL MORALITY...
...THEY'RE CONVINCED THAT "NO ONE WOULD EVER DO THAT."
IN THE TIME IT'D TAKE TO CATCH ME, I COULD TAKE TWENTY...
NO, I COULD TAKE THIRTY OF THEM OUT...
TONE TONE

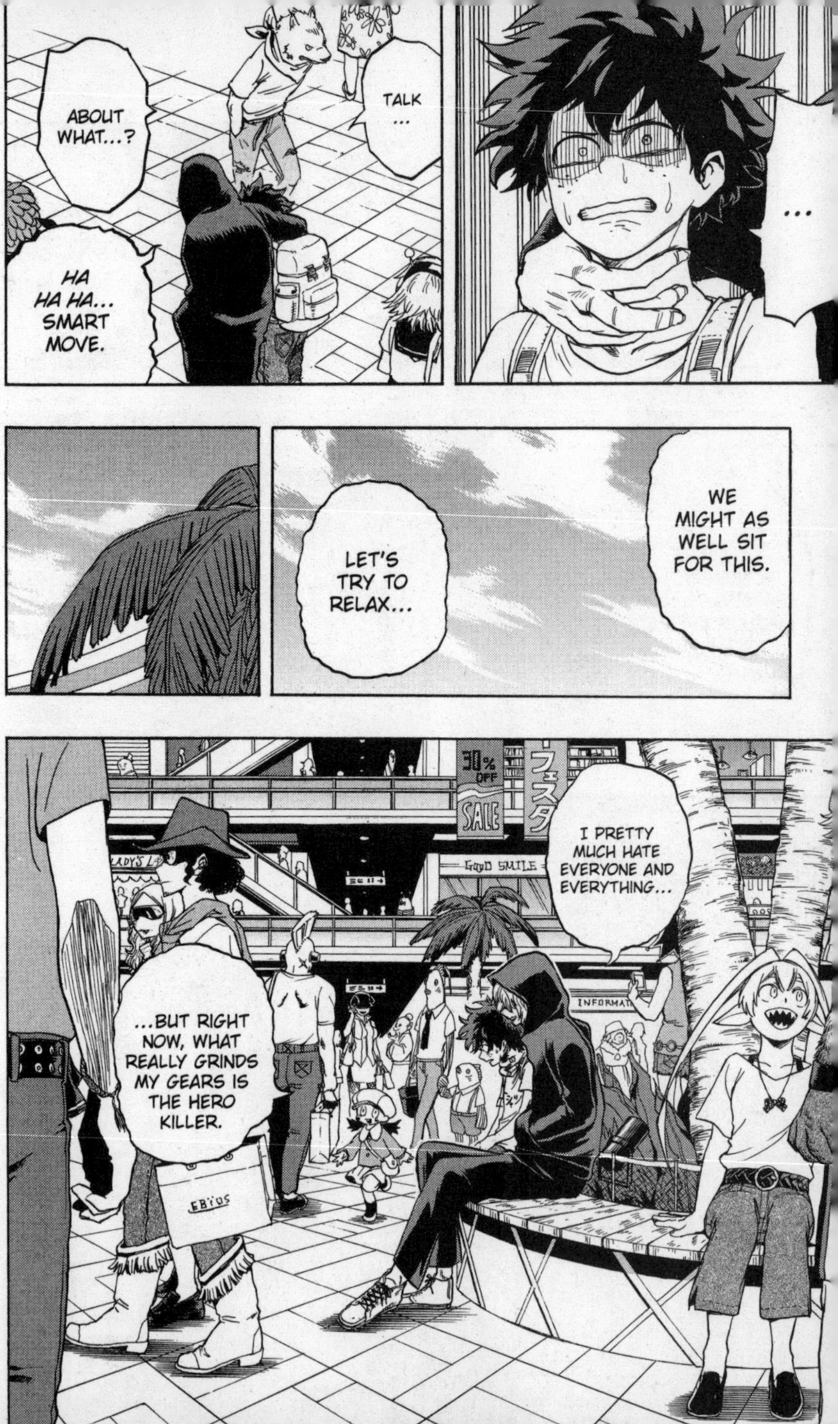
...
TALK ...
ABOUT WHAT...?
HA HA HA... SMART MOVE.
WE MIGHT AS WELL SIT FOR THIS.
LET'S TRY TO RELAX...
30% OFF
SALE
フェスタ
GOOD SMILE
I PRETTY MUCH HATE EVERYONE AND EVERYTHING...
...BUT RIGHT NOW, WHAT REALLY GRINDS MY GEARS IS THE HERO KILLER.

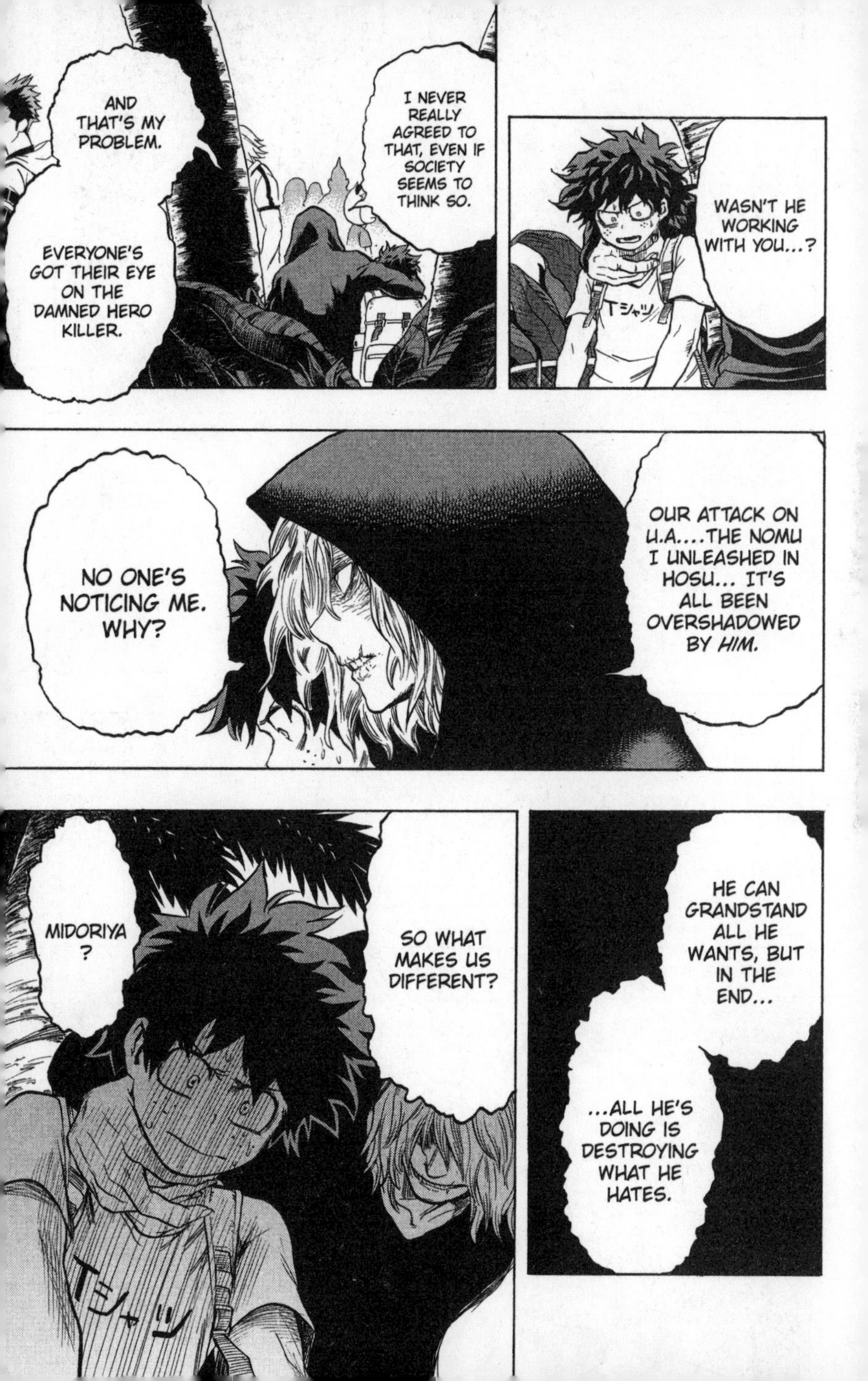
WASN'T HE WORKING WITH YOU...?
Tシャツ
I NEVER REALLY AGREED TO THAT, EVEN IF SOCIETY SEEMS TO THINK SO.
AND THAT'S MY PROBLEM.
EVERYONE'S GOT THEIR EYE ON THE DAMNED HERO KILLER.
OUR ATTACK ON U.A.... THE NOMU I UNLEASHED IN HOSU... IT'S ALL BEEN OVERSHADOWED BY *HIM*.
NO ONE'S NOTICING ME. WHY?
HE CAN GRANDSTAND ALL HE WANTS, BUT IN THE END...
...ALL HE'S DOING IS DESTROYING WHAT HE HATES.
SO WHAT MAKES US DIFFERENT?
MIDORIYA?
Tシャツ

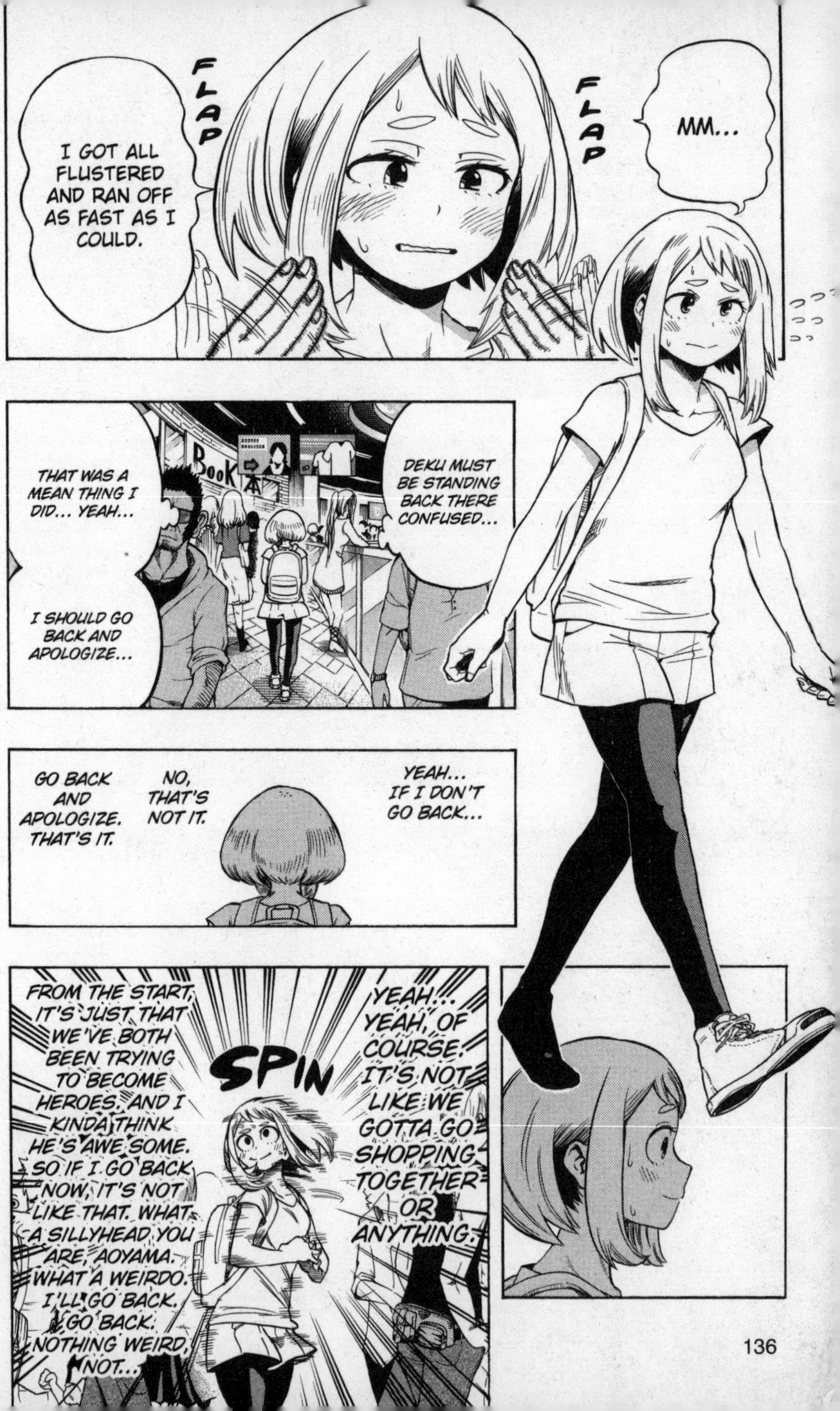
FLAP
MM...
FLAP
I GOT ALL FLUSTERED AND RAN OFF AS FAST AS I COULD.
DEKU MUST BE STANDING BACK THERE CONFUSED...
THAT WAS A MEAN THING I DID... YEAH...
I SHOULD GO BACK AND APOLOGIZE...
YEAH... IF I DON'T GO BACK...
NO, THAT'S NOT IT.
GO BACK AND APOLOGIZE. THAT'S IT.
YEAH... YEAH, OF COURSE. IT'S NOT LIKE WE GOTTA GO SHOPPING TOGETHER OR ANYTHING.
SPIN
FROM THE START, IT'S JUST THAT WE'VE BOTH BEEN TRYING TO BECOME HEROES, AND I KINDA THINK HE'S AWESOME. SO IF I GO BACK NOW, IT'S NOT LIKE THAT. WHAT A SILLYHEAD YOU ARE, AOYAMA. WHAT A WEIRDO. I'LL GO BACK. I GO BACK. NOTHING WEIRD, NOT...

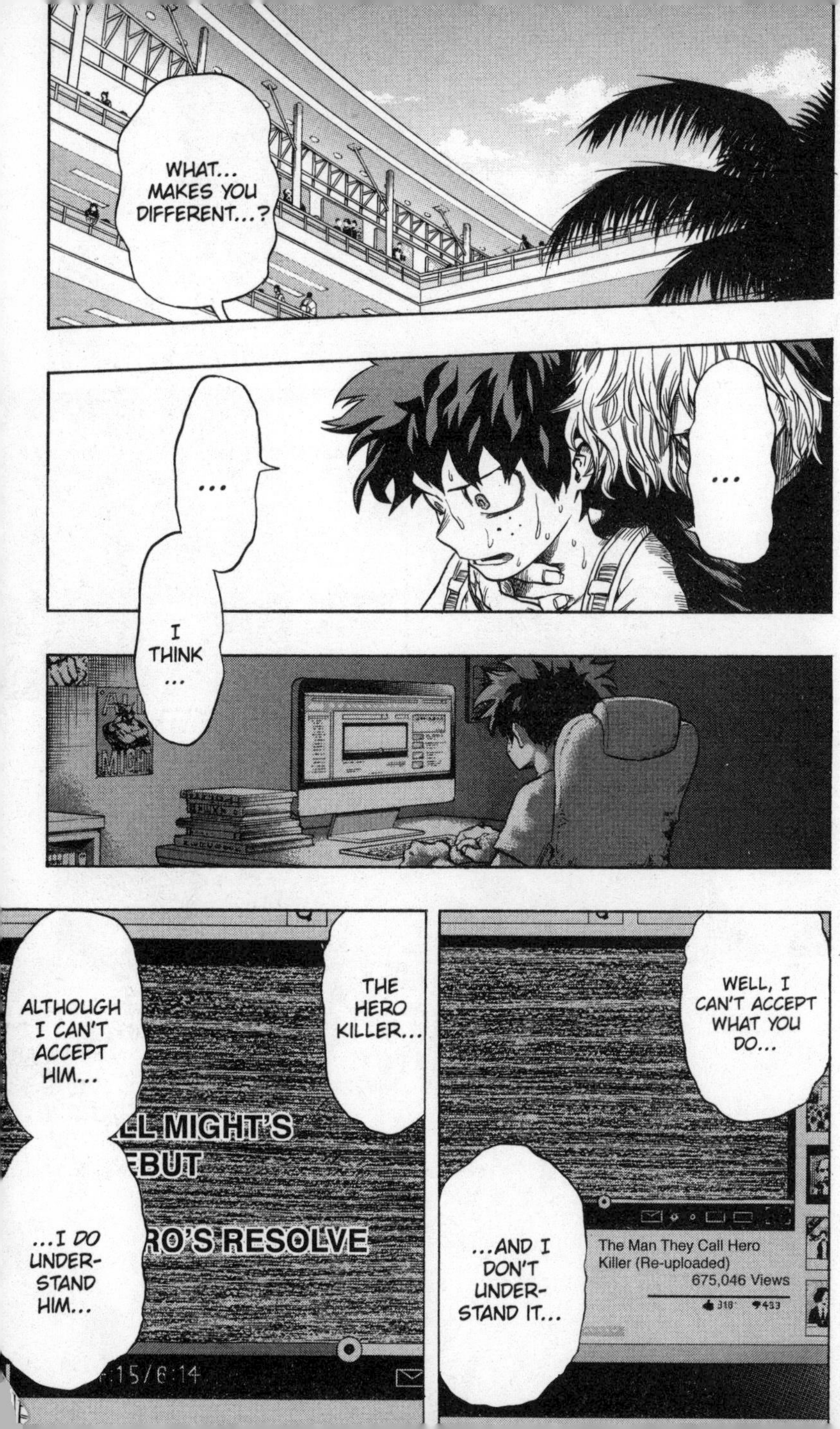
WHAT... MAKES YOU DIFFERENT...?
...
...
I THINK...
WELL, I CAN'T ACCEPT WHAT YOU DO...
...AND I DON'T UNDER-STAND IT...
The Man They Call Hero Killer (Re-uploaded)
675,046 Views
THE HERO KILLER...
ALTHOUGH I CAN'T ACCEPT HIM...
...I DO UNDER-STAND HIM...

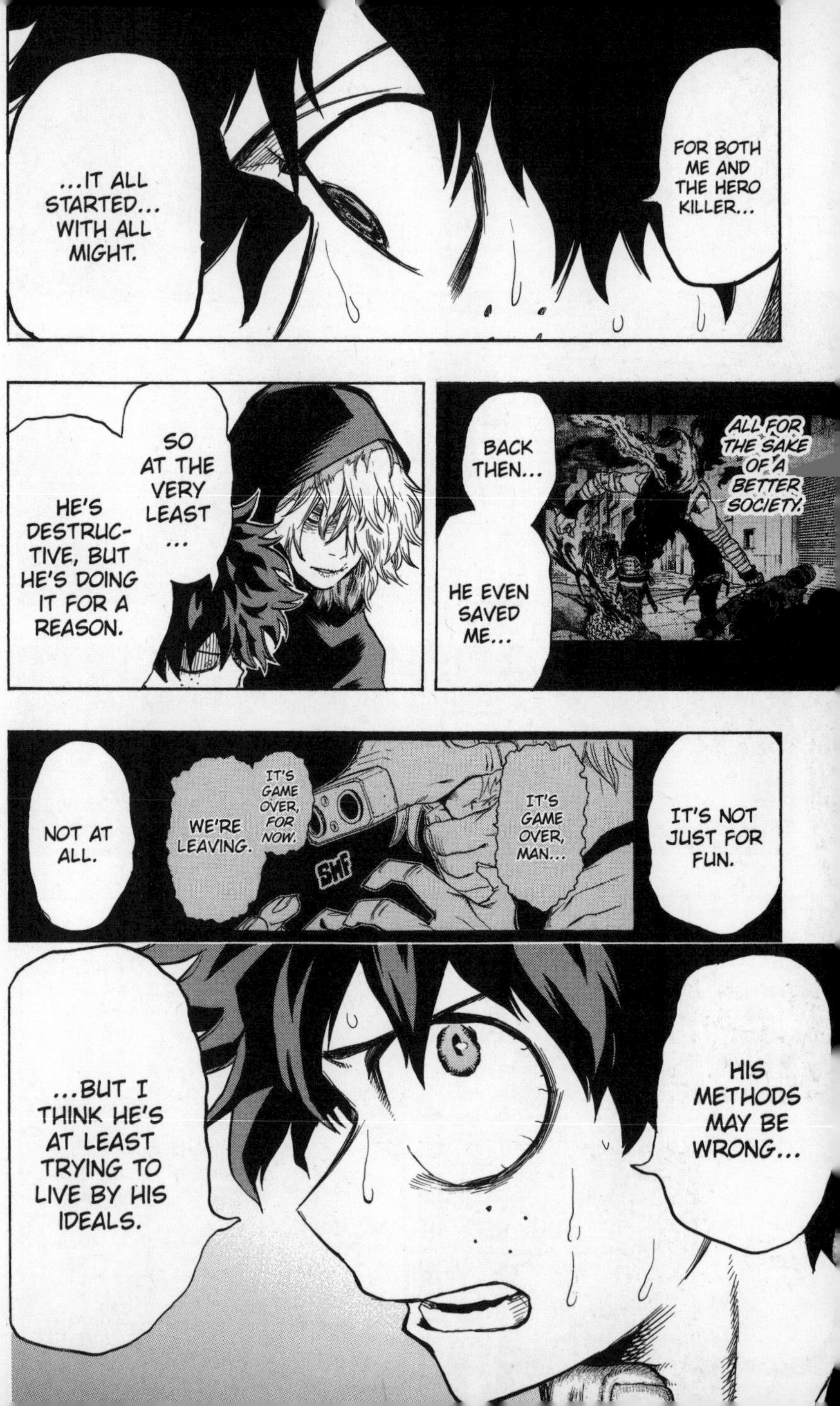
FOR BOTH ME AND THE HERO KILLER...
...IT ALL STARTED... WITH ALL MIGHT.
ALL FOR THE SAKE OF A BETTER SOCIETY.
BACK THEN...
HE EVEN SAVED ME...
SO AT THE VERY LEAST...
HE'S DESTRUC-TIVE, BUT HE'S DOING IT FOR A REASON.
IT'S NOT JUST FOR FUN.
IT'S GAME OVER, MAN...
IT'S GAME OVER, FOR NOW.
WE'RE LEAVING.
SMF
NOT AT ALL.
HIS METHODS MAY BE WRONG...
...BUT I THINK HE'S AT LEAST TRYING TO LIVE BY HIS IDEALS.

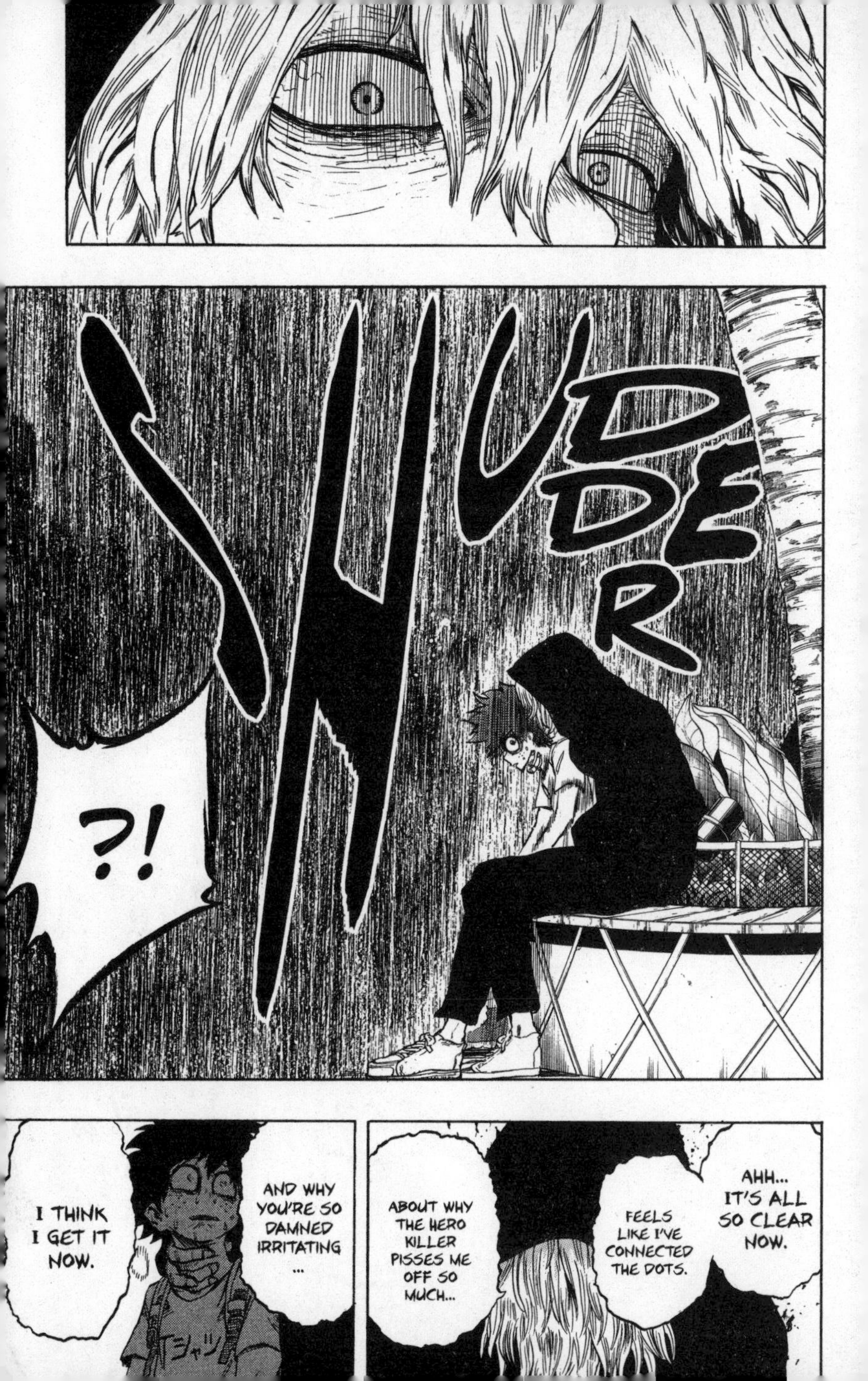
SHUDDER
?!
AHH... IT'S ALL SO CLEAR NOW.
FEELS LIKE I'VE CONNECTED THE DOTS.
ABOUT WHY THE HERO KILLER PISSES ME OFF SO MUCH...
AND WHY YOU'RE SO DAMNED IRRITATING...
I THINK I GET IT NOW.

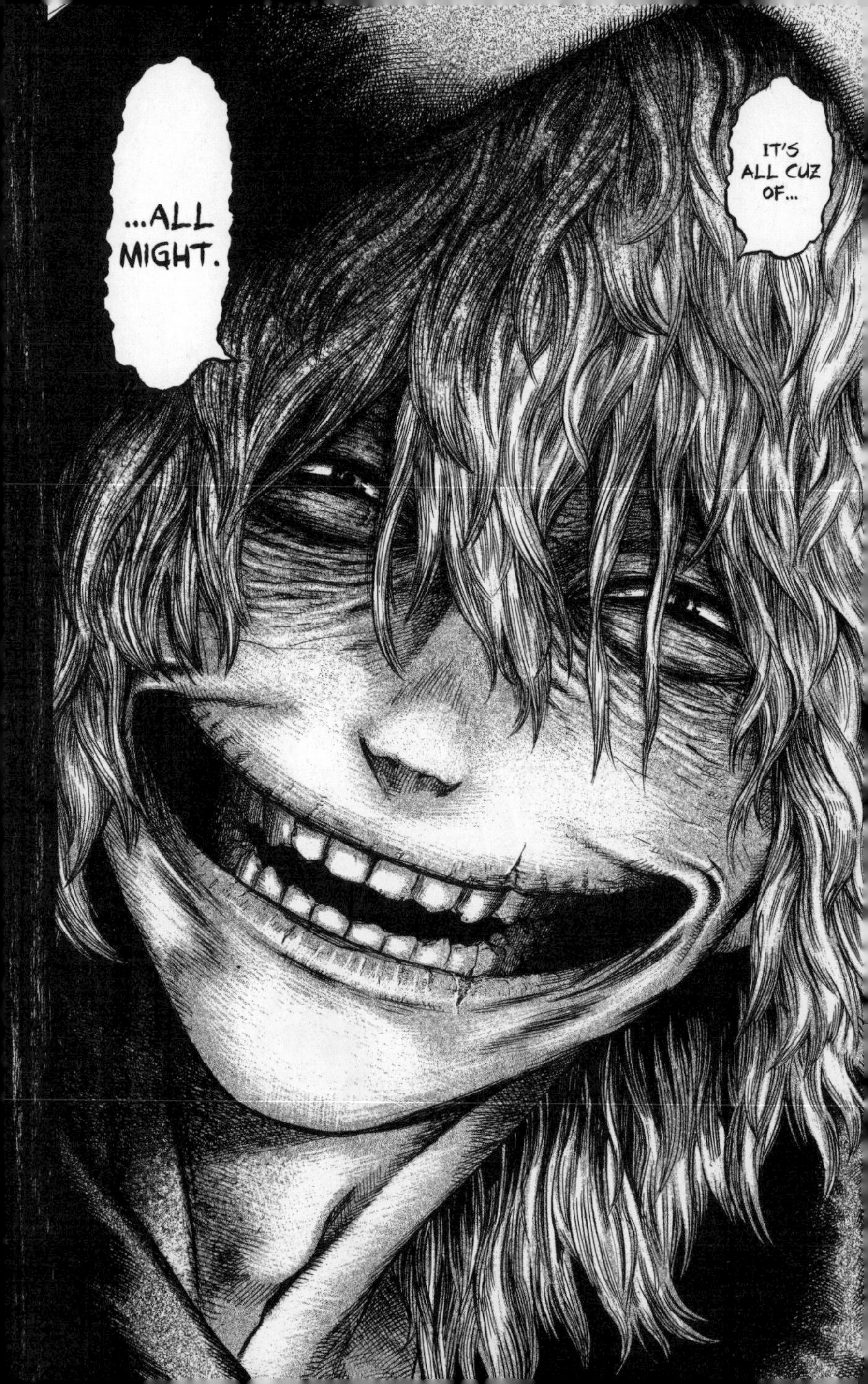
IT'S ALL CUZ OF...
...ALL MIGHT.

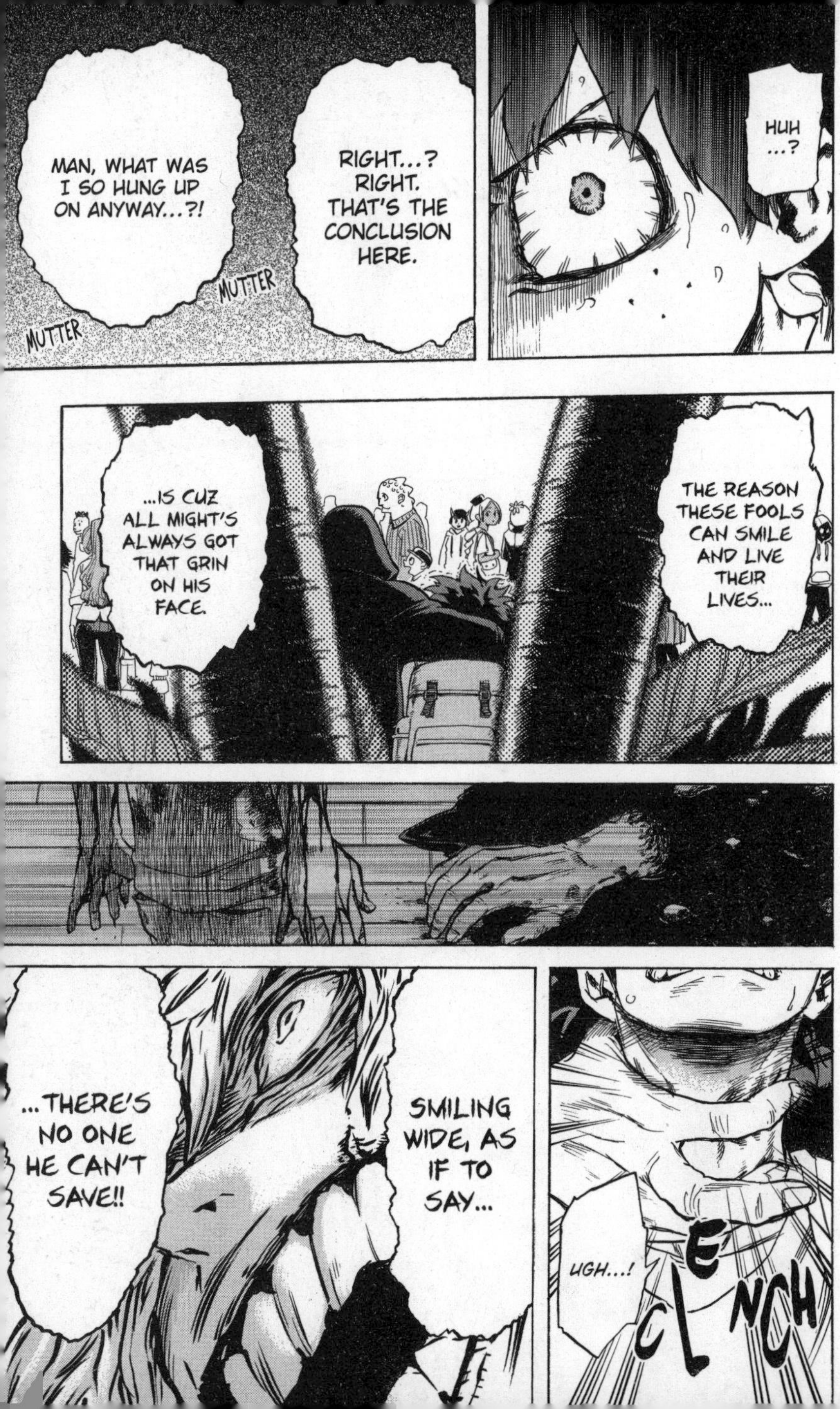
HUH ...?
RIGHT...? RIGHT. THAT'S THE CONCLUSION HERE.
MUTTER
MAN, WHAT WAS I SO HUNG UP ON ANYWAY...?!
MUTTER
THE REASON THESE FOOLS CAN SMILE AND LIVE THEIR LIVES...
...IS CUZ ALL MIGHT'S ALWAYS GOT THAT GRIN ON HIS FACE.
UGH...!
CLENCH
SMILING WIDE, AS IF TO SAY...
...THERE'S NO ONE HE CAN'T SAVE!!

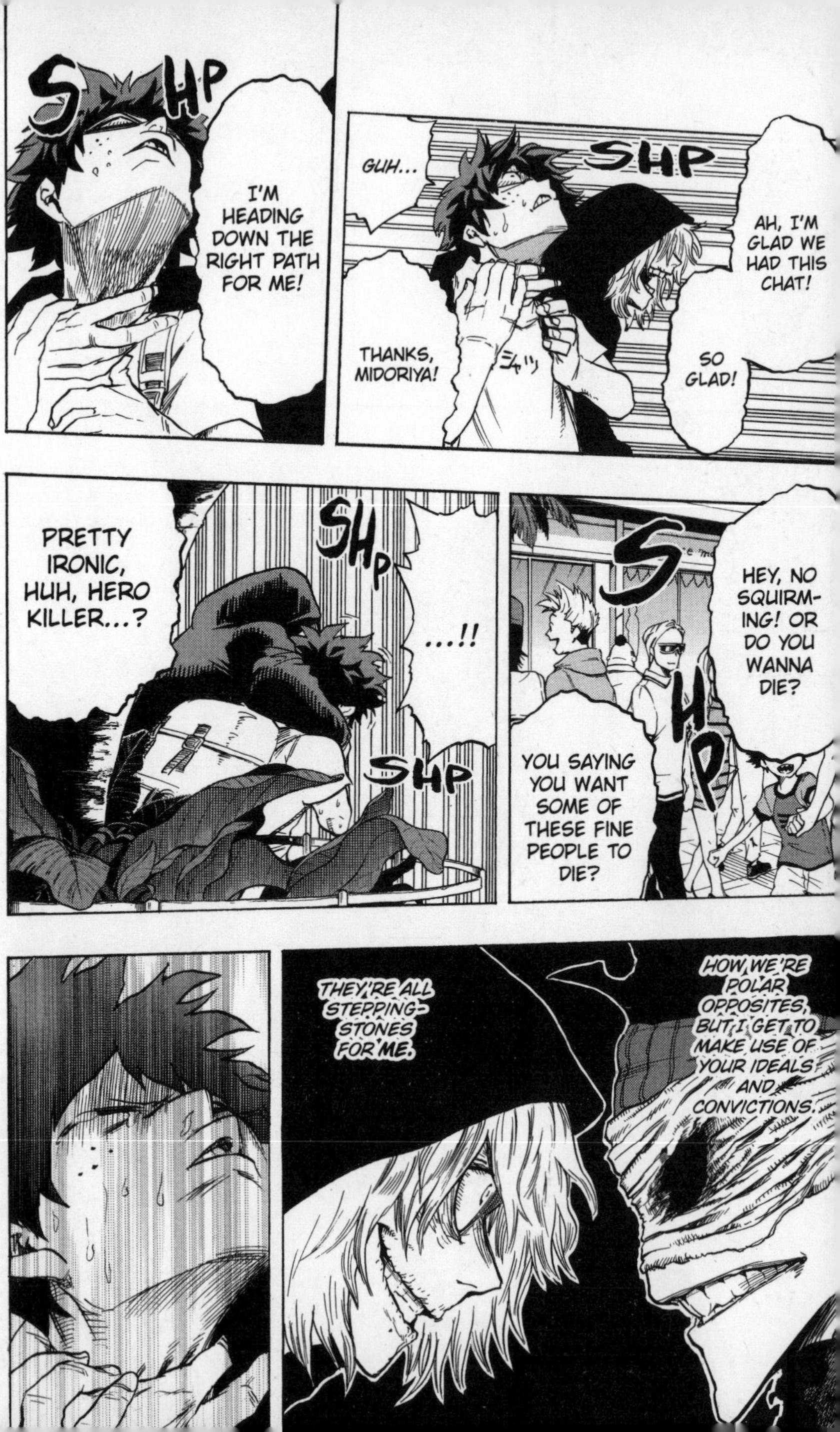
SHP
AH, I'M GLAD WE HAD THIS CHAT!
GUH...
SO GLAD!
THANKS, MIDORIYA!
ジャッ
SHP
I'M HEADING DOWN THE RIGHT PATH FOR ME!
SHP
HEY, NO SQUIRMING! OR DO YOU WANNA DIE?
YOU SAYING YOU WANT SOME OF THESE FINE PEOPLE TO DIE?
SHP
...!!
PRETTY IRONIC, HUH, HERO KILLER...?
SHP
HOW WE'RE POLAR OPPOSITES, BUT I GET TO MAKE USE OF YOUR IDEALS AND CONVICTIONS.
THEY'RE ALL STEPPING-STONES FOR ME.

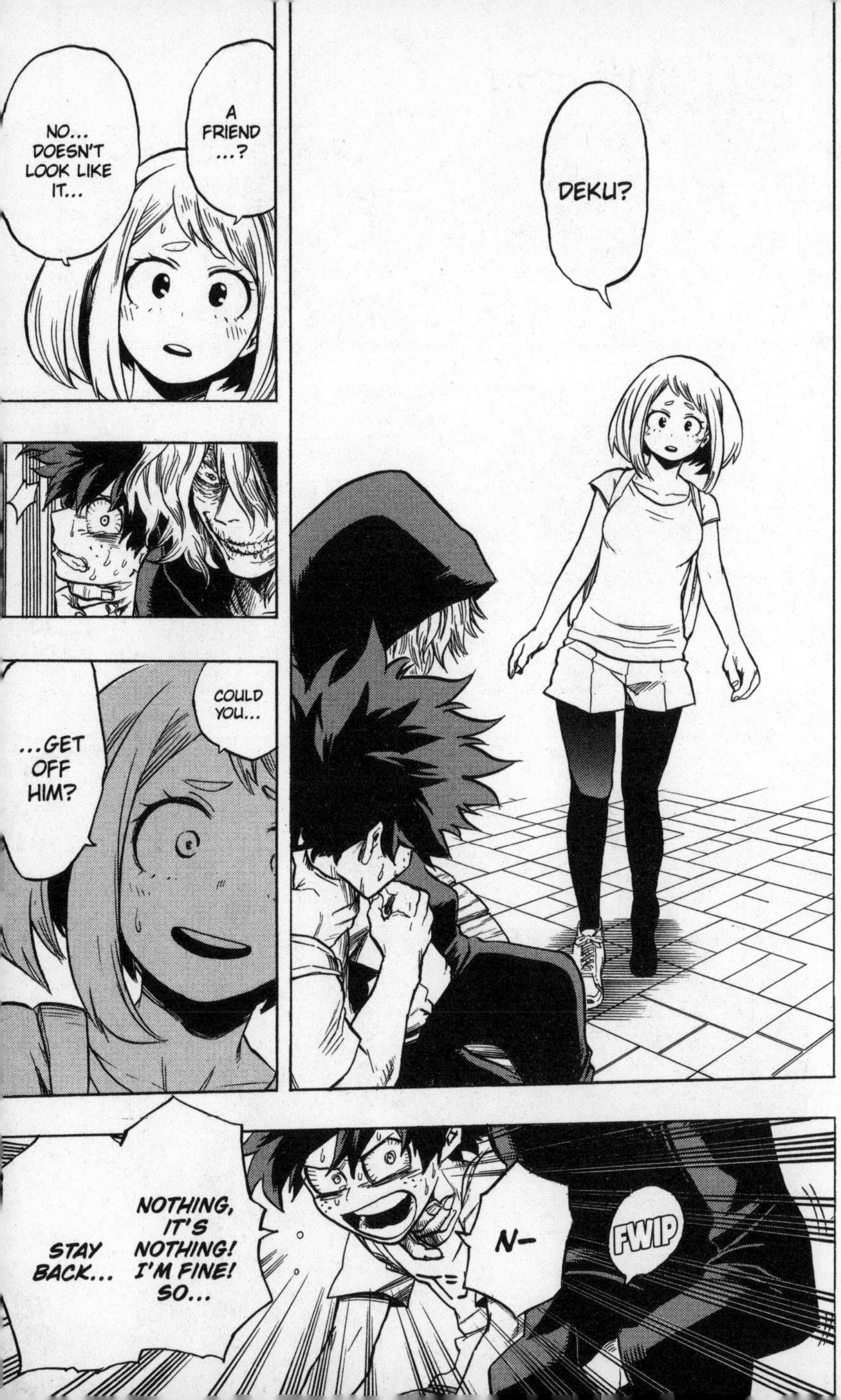
DEKU?
A FRIEND ...?
NO... DOESN'T LOOK LIKE IT...
COULD YOU...
...GET OFF HIM?
FWIP
N-
NOTHING, IT'S NOTHING! I'M FINE! SO...
STAY BACK...

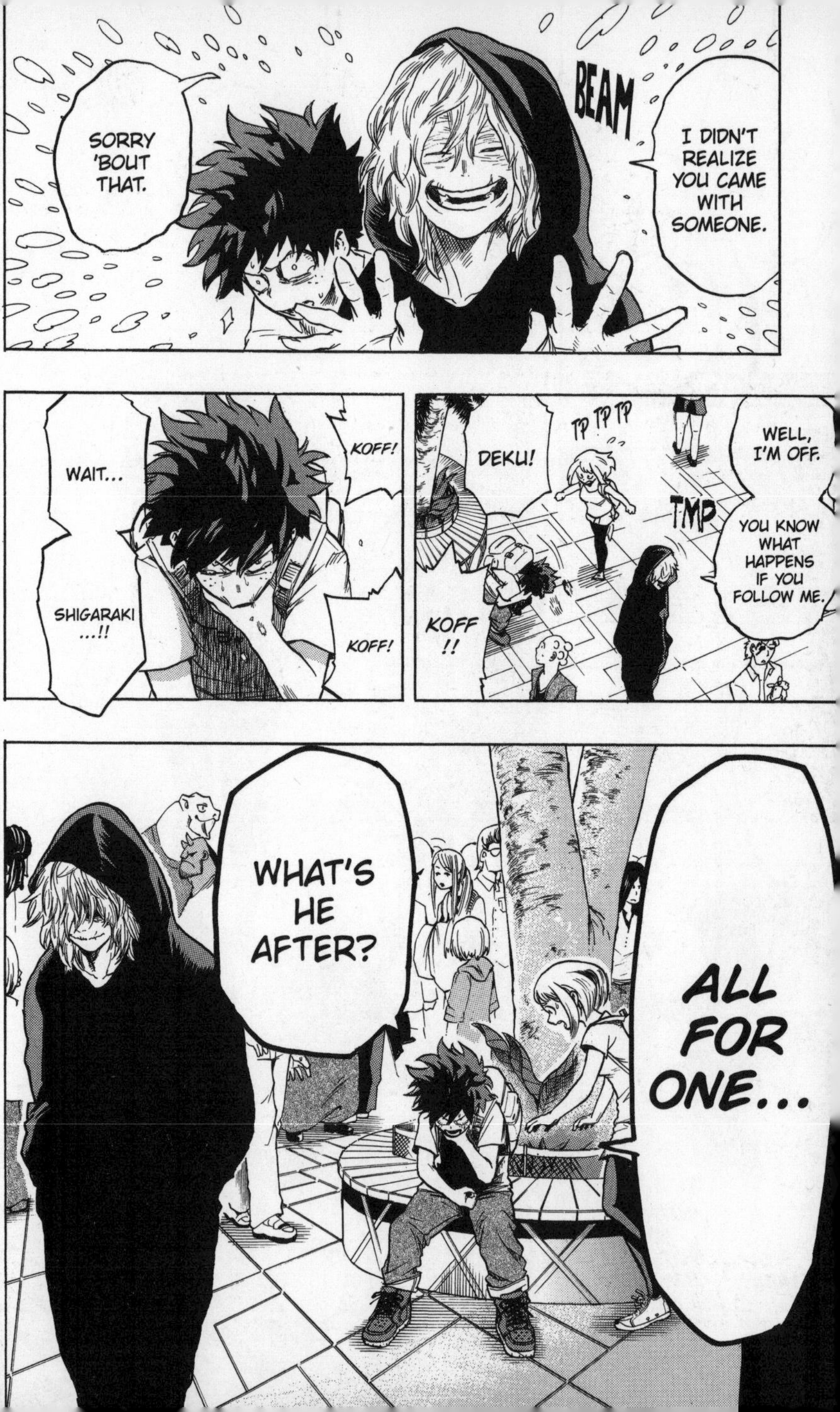
BEAM
I DIDN'T REALIZE YOU CAME WITH SOMEONE.
SORRY 'BOUT THAT.
WELL, I'M OFF.
TP TP TP
DEKU!
TMP
YOU KNOW WHAT HAPPENS IF YOU FOLLOW ME.
KOFF !!
KOFF!
WAIT...
SHIGARAKI ...!!
KOFF!
ALL FOR ONE...
WHAT'S HE AFTER?

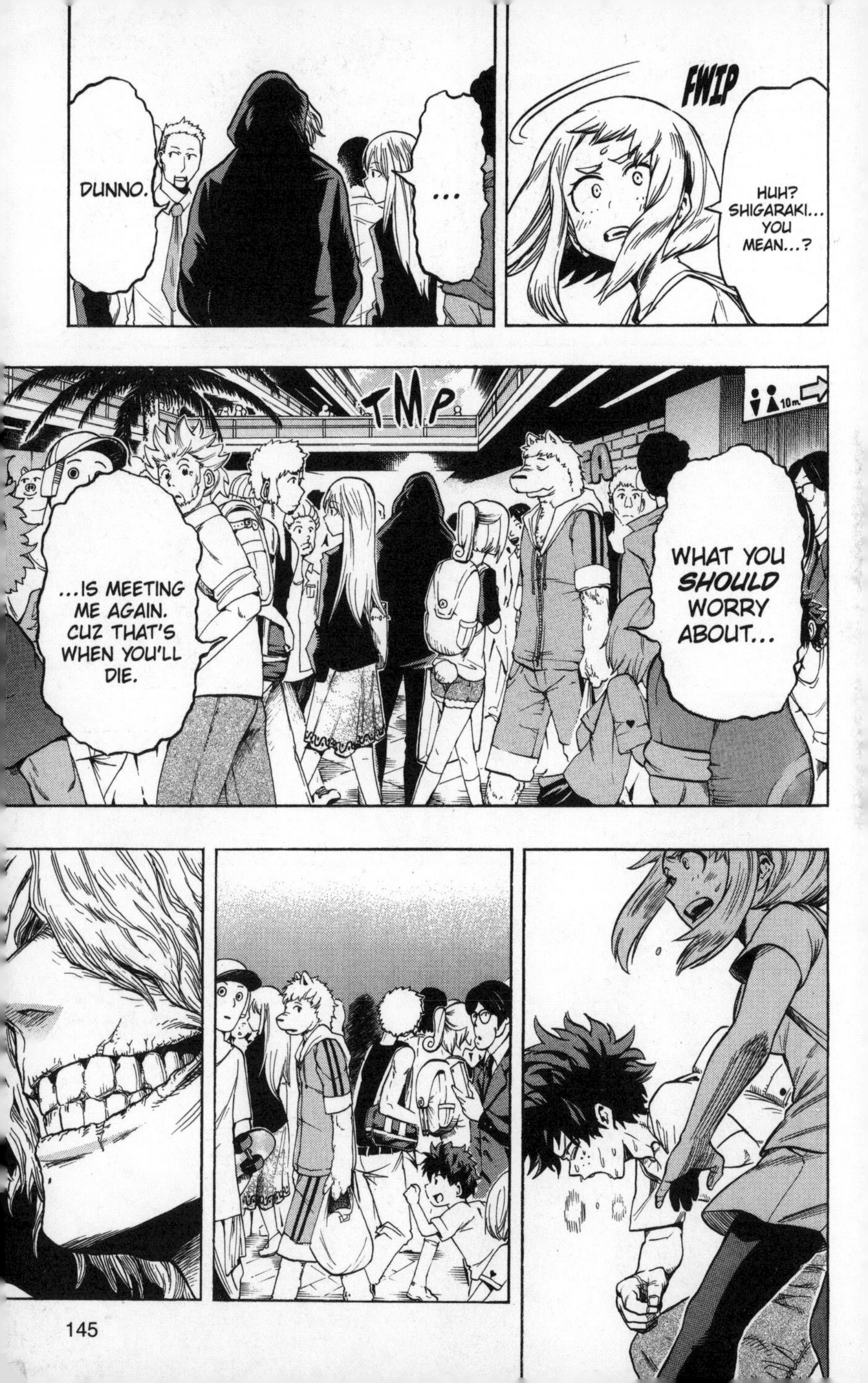
FWIP
HUH? SHIGARAKI... YOU MEAN...?
...
DUNNO.
TMP
WHAT YOU **SHOULD** WORRY ABOUT...
...IS MEETING ME AGAIN. CUZ THAT'S WHEN YOU'LL DIE.

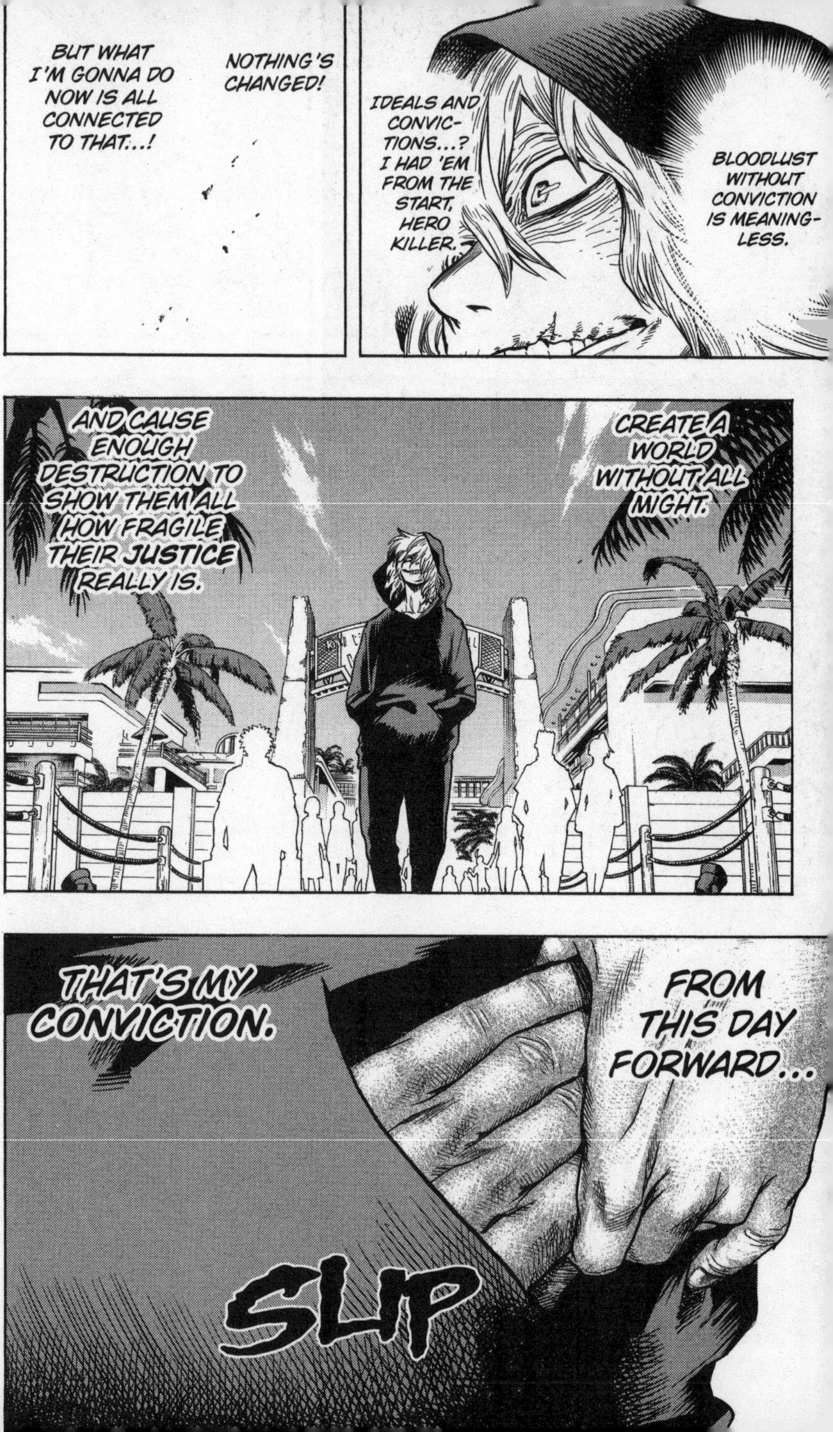
BLOODLUST WITHOUT CONVICTION IS MEANINGLESS.
IDEALS AND CONVICTIONS...? I HAD 'EM FROM THE START, HERO KILLER.
NOTHING'S CHANGED!
BUT WHAT I'M GONNA DO NOW IS ALL CONNECTED TO THAT...!
CREATE A WORLD WITHOUT ALL MIGHT.
AND CAUSE ENOUGH DESTRUCTION TO SHOW THEM ALL HOW FRAGILE THEIR JUSTICE REALLY IS.
FROM THIS DAY FORWARD...
THAT'S MY CONVICTION.
SLIP

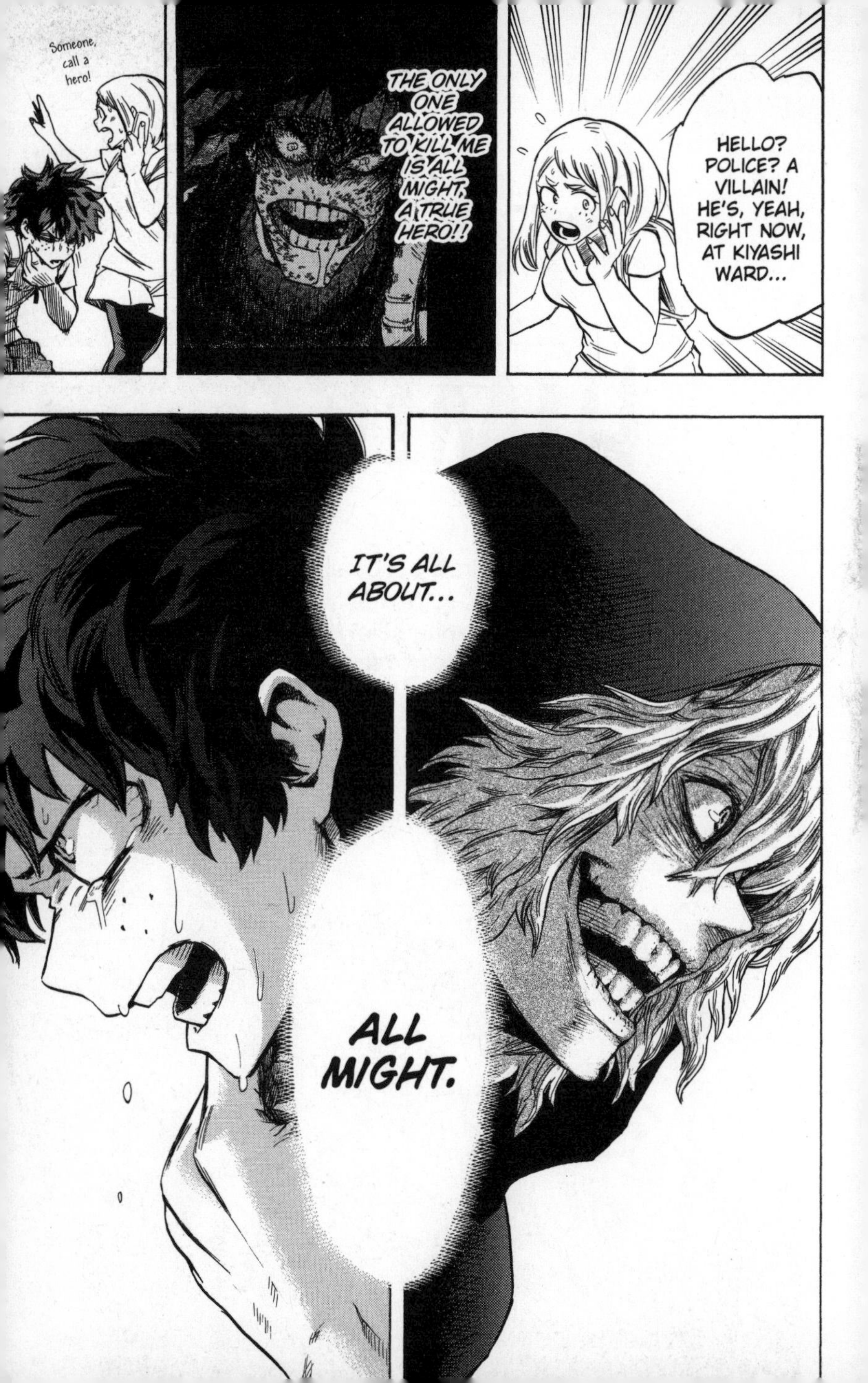
HELLO? POLICE? A VILLAIN! HE'S, YEAH, RIGHT NOW, AT KIYASHI WARD...
THE ONLY ONE ALLOWED TO KILL ME IS ALL MIGHT, A TRUE HERO!!
Someone, call a hero!
IT'S ALL ABOUT...
ALL MIGHT.

TOGA
HIMIKO

She's the hardest to draw out of all my female characters to date. Too hard, really. Especially her eyes and hair. The drawing below was done by my staff ↓. It's done beautifully. We're working hard.

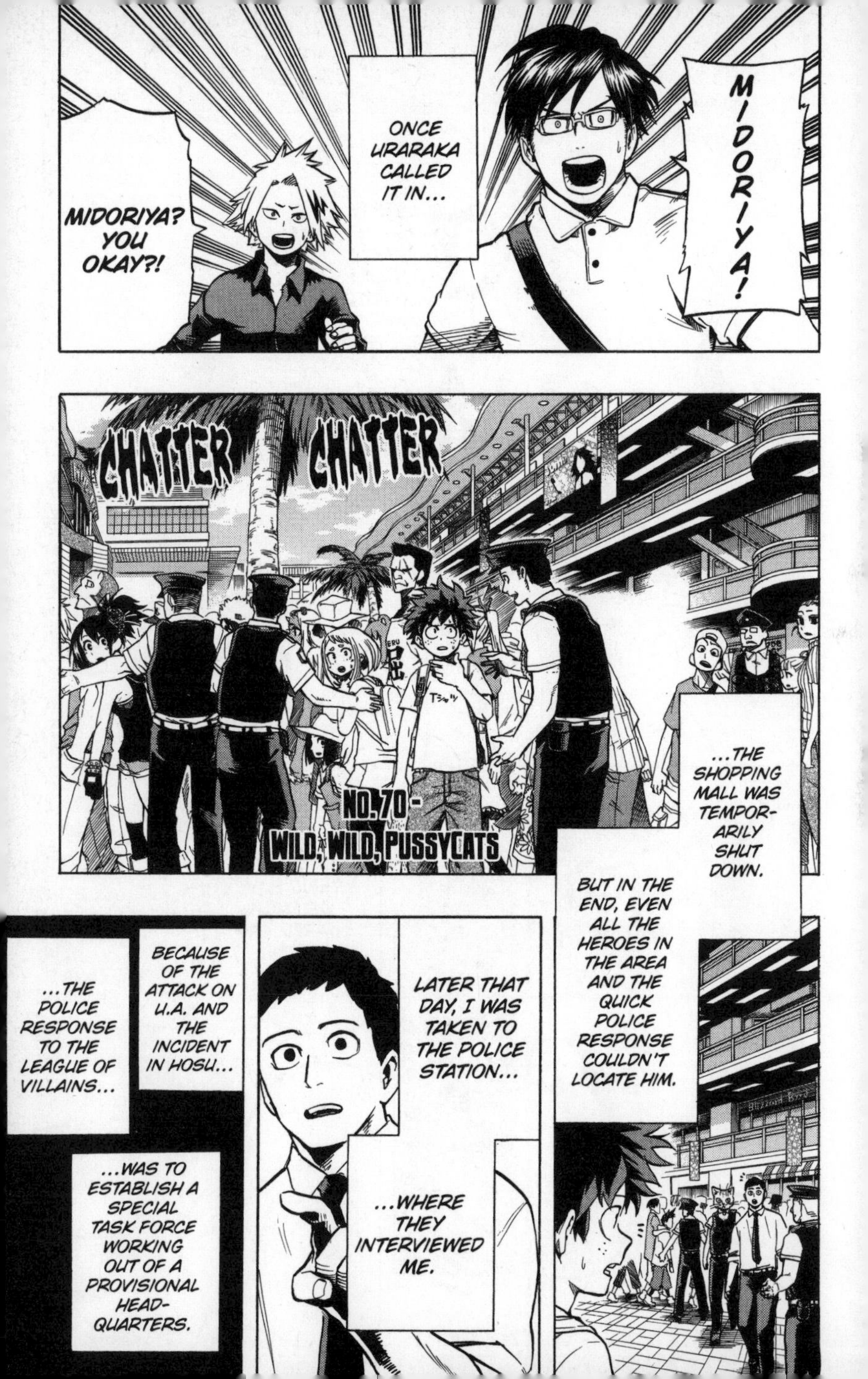
MIDORIYA!
ONCE URARAKA CALLED IT IN...
MIDORIYA? YOU OKAY?!
CHATTER CHATTER
...THE SHOPPING MALL WAS TEMPOR-ARILY SHUT DOWN.
NO. 70 - WILD, WILD, PUSSYCATS
BUT IN THE END, EVEN ALL THE HEROES IN THE AREA AND THE QUICK POLICE RESPONSE COULDN'T LOCATE HIM.
LATER THAT DAY, I WAS TAKEN TO THE POLICE STATION...
...WHERE THEY INTERVIEWED ME.
BECAUSE OF THE ATTACK ON U.A. AND THE INCIDENT IN HOSU...
...THE POLICE RESPONSE TO THE LEAGUE OF VILLAINS...
...WAS TO ESTABLISH A SPECIAL TASK FORCE WORKING OUT OF A PROVISIONAL HEAD-QUARTERS.

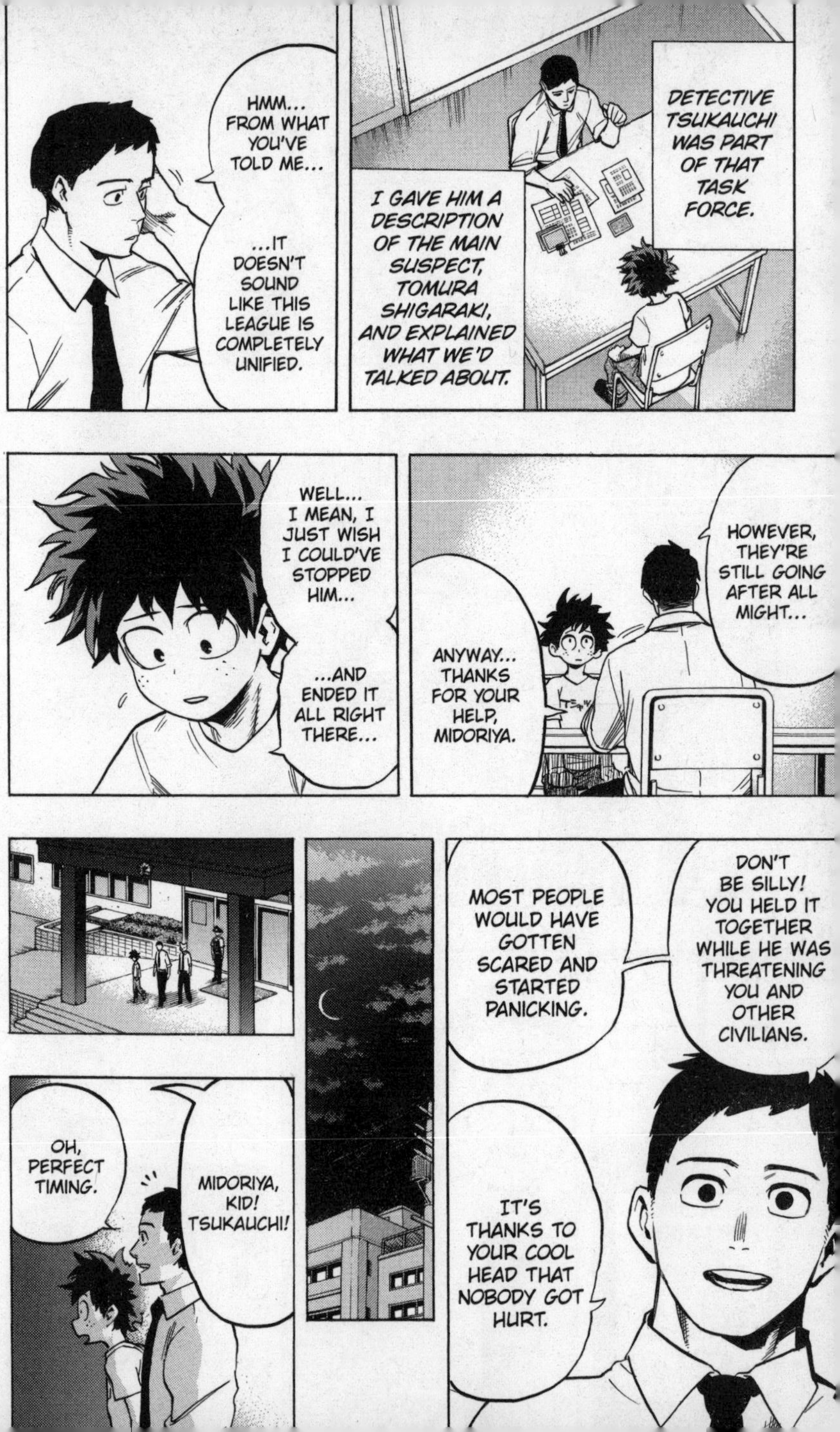
DETECTIVE TSUKAUCHI WAS PART OF THAT TASK FORCE.
I GAVE HIM A DESCRIPTION OF THE MAIN SUSPECT, TOMURA SHIGARAKI, AND EXPLAINED WHAT WE'D TALKED ABOUT.
HMM... FROM WHAT YOU'VE TOLD ME...
...IT DOESN'T SOUND LIKE THIS LEAGUE IS COMPLETELY UNIFIED.
HOWEVER, THEY'RE STILL GOING AFTER ALL MIGHT...
ANYWAY... THANKS FOR YOUR HELP, MIDORIYA.
WELL... I MEAN, I JUST WISH I COULD'VE STOPPED HIM...
...AND ENDED IT ALL RIGHT THERE...
DON'T BE SILLY! YOU HELD IT TOGETHER WHILE HE WAS THREATENING YOU AND OTHER CIVILIANS.
MOST PEOPLE WOULD HAVE GOTTEN SCARED AND STARTED PANICKING.
IT'S THANKS TO YOUR COOL HEAD THAT NOBODY GOT HURT.
MIDORIYA, KID! TSUKAUCHI!
OH, PERFECT TIMING.

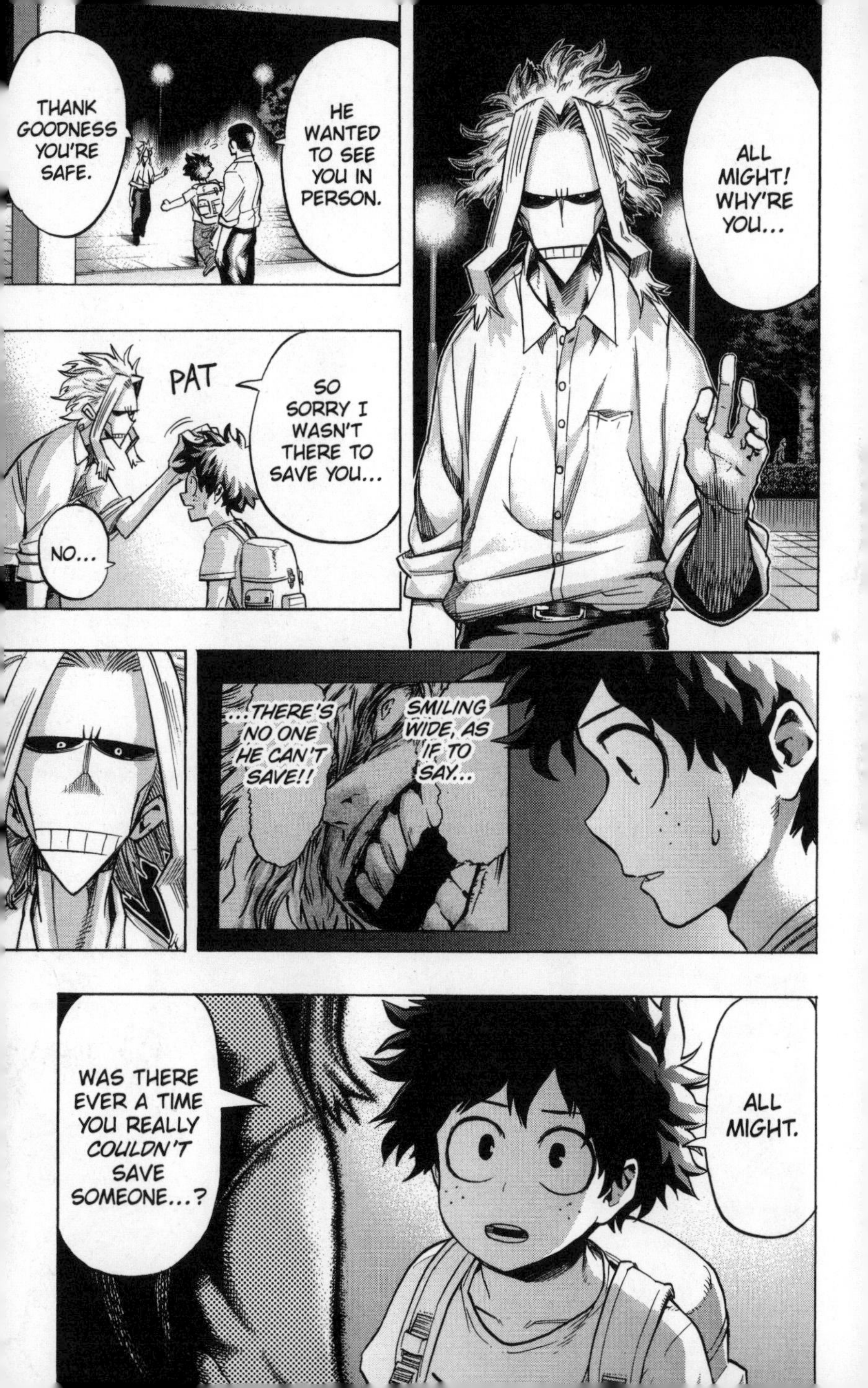
ALL MIGHT! WHY'RE YOU...
HE WANTED TO SEE YOU IN PERSON.
THANK GOODNESS YOU'RE SAFE.
SO SORRY I WASN'T THERE TO SAVE YOU...
PAT
NO...
SMILING WIDE, AS IF TO SAY...
...THERE'S NO ONE HE CAN'T SAVE!!
ALL MIGHT.
WAS THERE EVER A TIME YOU REALLY COULDN'T SAVE SOMEONE...?

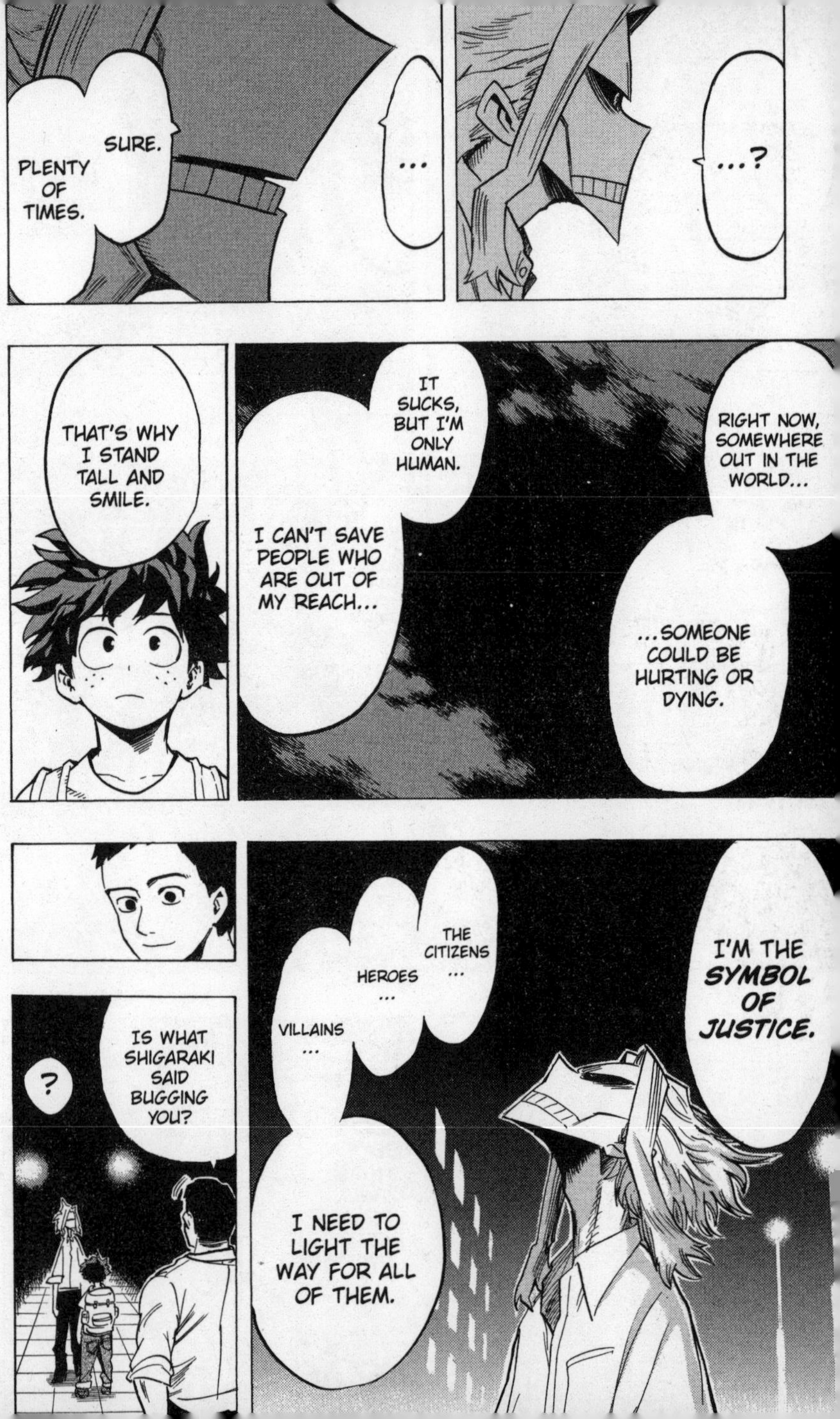
...?
...
SURE. PLENTY OF TIMES.
RIGHT NOW, SOMEWHERE OUT IN THE WORLD...
...SOMEONE COULD BE HURTING OR DYING.
IT SUCKS, BUT I'M ONLY HUMAN.
I CAN'T SAVE PEOPLE WHO ARE OUT OF MY REACH...
THAT'S WHY I STAND TALL AND SMILE.
I'M THE *SYMBOL OF JUSTICE.*
THE CITIZENS...
HEROES...
VILLAINS...
I NEED TO LIGHT THE WAY FOR ALL OF THEM.
IS WHAT SHIGARAKI SAID BUGGING YOU?
?

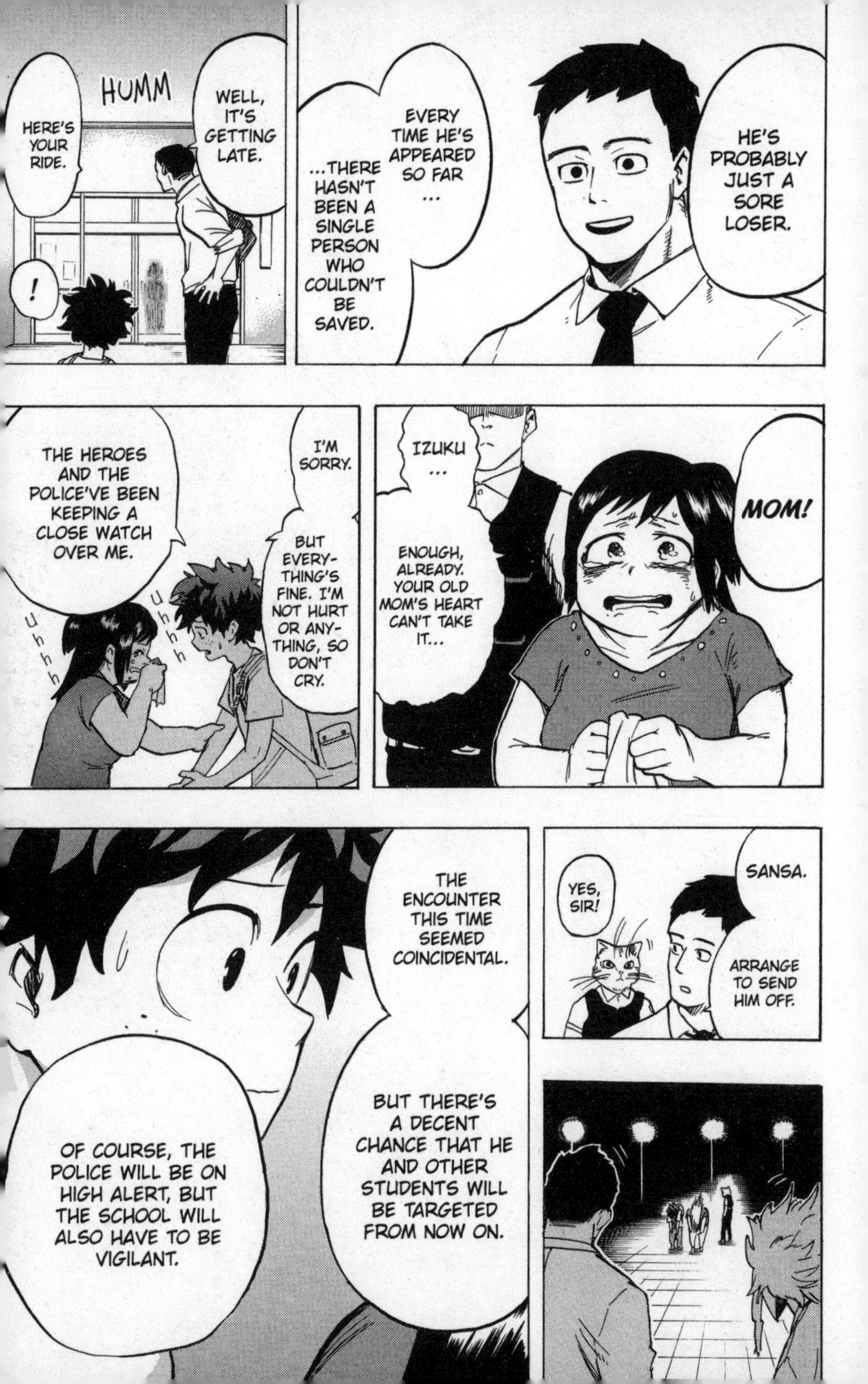
HE'S PROBABLY JUST A SORE LOSER.
EVERY TIME HE'S APPEARED SO FAR ...
...THERE HASN'T BEEN A SINGLE PERSON WHO COULDN'T BE SAVED.
WELL, IT'S GETTING LATE.
HUMM
HERE'S YOUR RIDE.
!
MOM!
IZUKU ...
ENOUGH, ALREADY. YOUR OLD MOM'S HEART CAN'T TAKE IT...
I'M SORRY.
BUT EVERY-THING'S FINE. I'M NOT HURT OR ANY-THING, SO DON'T CRY.
Uhhh
THE HEROES AND THE POLICE'VE BEEN KEEPING A CLOSE WATCH OVER ME.
Uhhh
SANSA.
YES, SIR!
ARRANGE TO SEND HIM OFF.
THE ENCOUNTER THIS TIME SEEMED COINCIDENTAL.
BUT THERE'S A DECENT CHANCE THAT HE AND OTHER STUDENTS WILL BE TARGETED FROM NOW ON.
OF COURSE, THE POLICE WILL BE ON HIGH ALERT, BUT THE SCHOOL WILL ALSO HAVE TO BE VIGILANT.

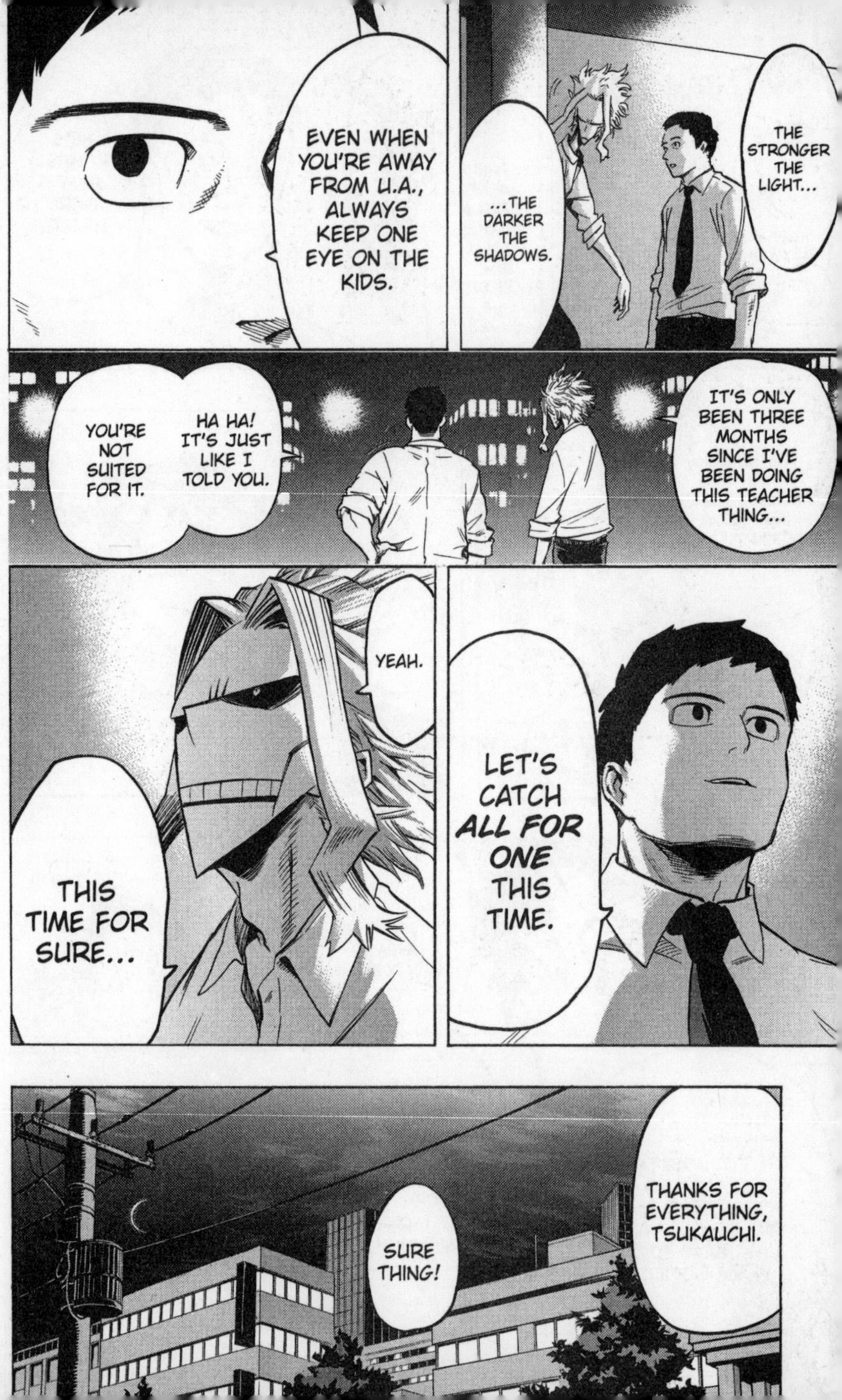
THE STRONGER THE LIGHT...
...THE DARKER THE SHADOWS.
EVEN WHEN YOU'RE AWAY FROM U.A., ALWAYS KEEP ONE EYE ON THE KIDS.
IT'S ONLY BEEN THREE MONTHS SINCE I'VE BEEN DOING THIS TEACHER THING...
HA HA! IT'S JUST LIKE I TOLD YOU.
YOU'RE NOT SUITED FOR IT.
LET'S CATCH *ALL FOR ONE* THIS TIME.
YEAH.
THIS TIME FOR SURE...
THANKS FOR EVERYTHING, TSUKAUCHI.
SURE THING!

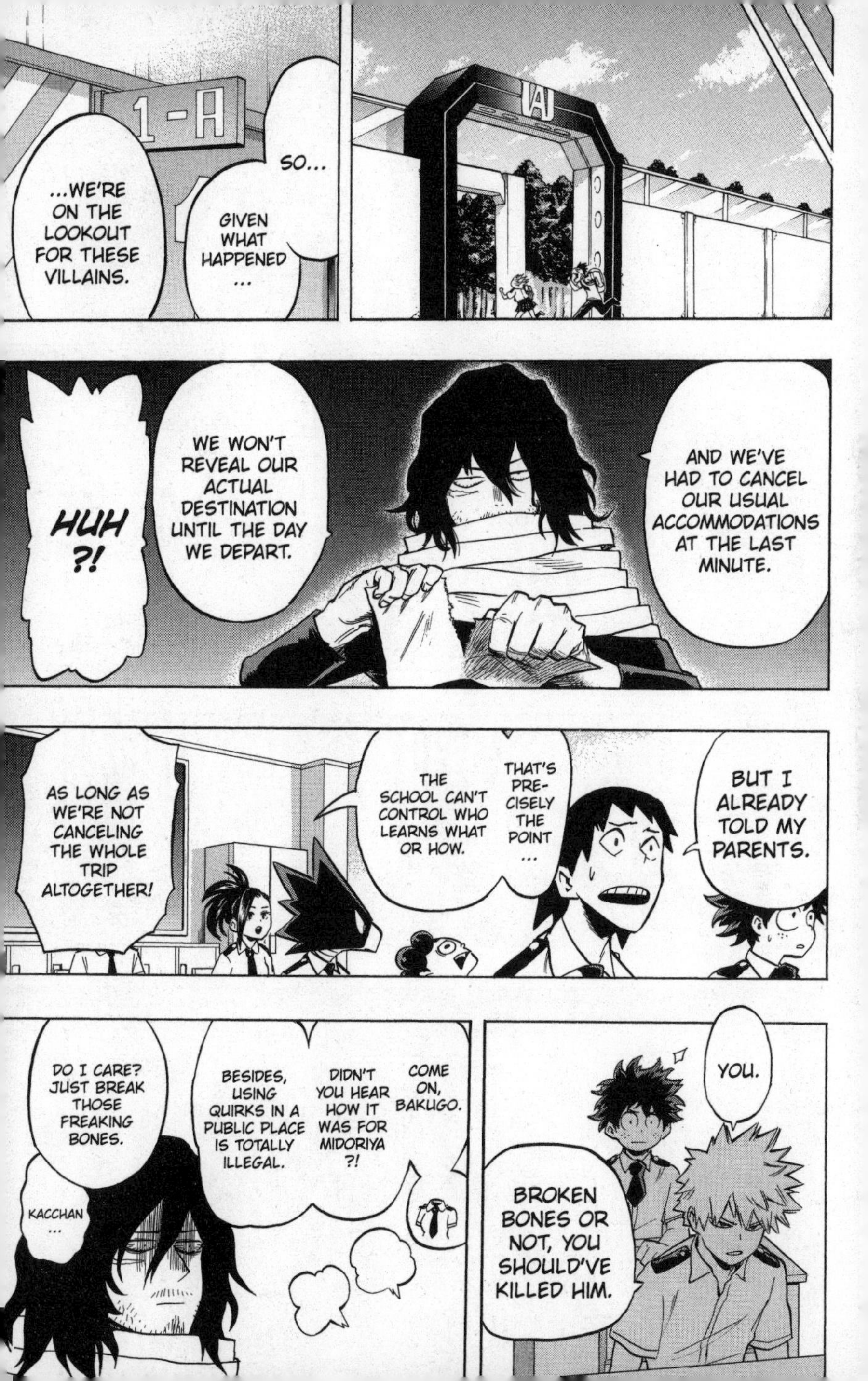
1-A
SO...
GIVEN WHAT HAPPENED...
...WE'RE ON THE LOOKOUT FOR THESE VILLAINS.
AND WE'VE HAD TO CANCEL OUR USUAL ACCOMMODATIONS AT THE LAST MINUTE.
WE WON'T REVEAL OUR ACTUAL DESTINATION UNTIL THE DAY WE DEPART.
HUH ?!
BUT I ALREADY TOLD MY PARENTS.
THAT'S PRECISELY THE POINT...
THE SCHOOL CAN'T CONTROL WHO LEARNS WHAT OR HOW.
AS LONG AS WE'RE NOT CANCELING THE WHOLE TRIP ALTOGETHER!
YOU.
BROKEN BONES OR NOT, YOU SHOULD'VE KILLED HIM.
COME ON, BAKUGO.
DIDN'T YOU HEAR HOW IT WAS FOR MIDORIYA ?!
BESIDES, USING QUIRKS IN A PUBLIC PLACE IS TOTALLY ILLEGAL.
DO I CARE? JUST BREAK THOSE FREAKING BONES.
KACCHAN...

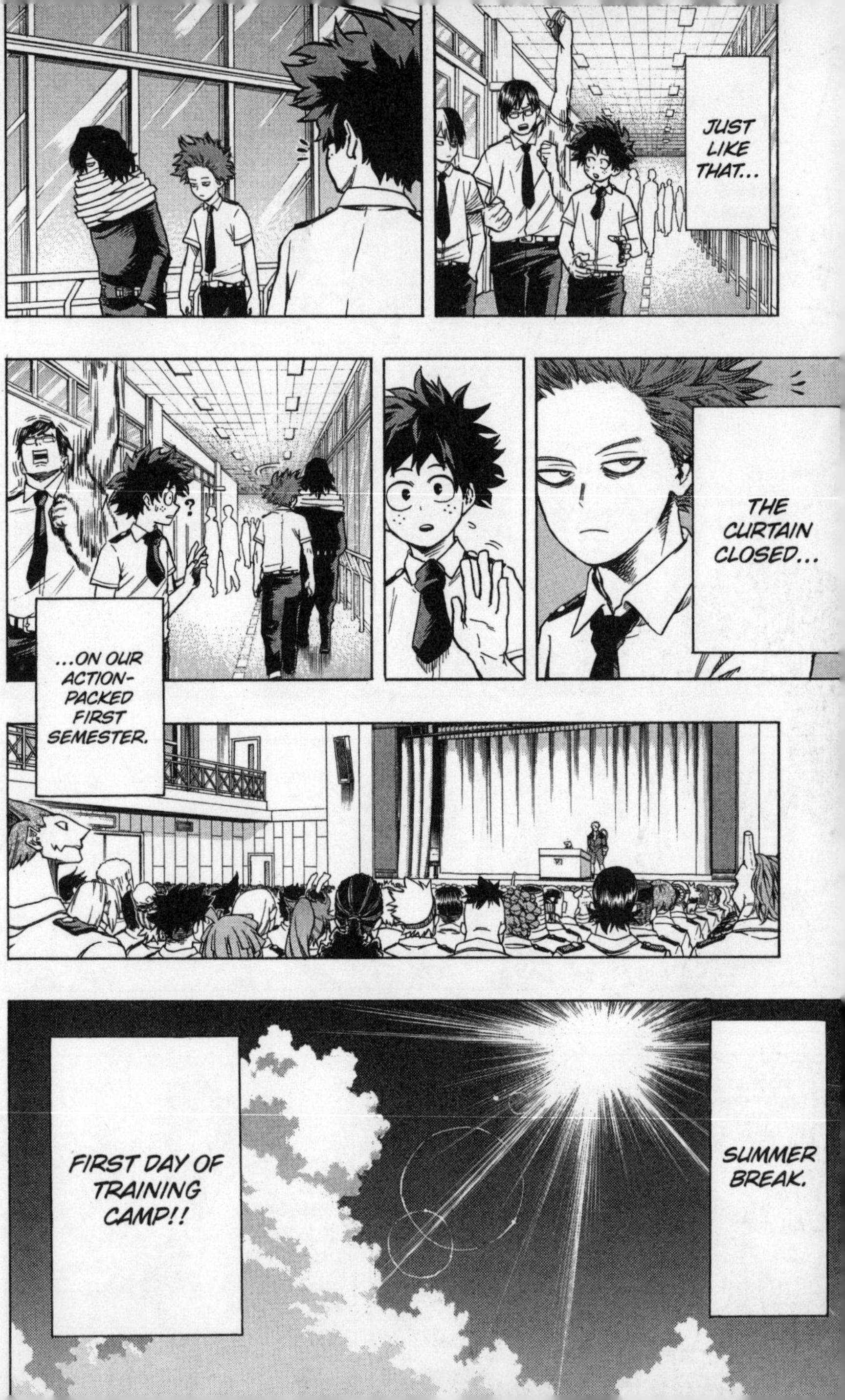
JUST LIKE THAT...
THE CURTAIN CLOSED...
...ON OUR ACTION-PACKED FIRST SEMESTER.
SUMMER BREAK.
FIRST DAY OF TRAINING CAMP!!

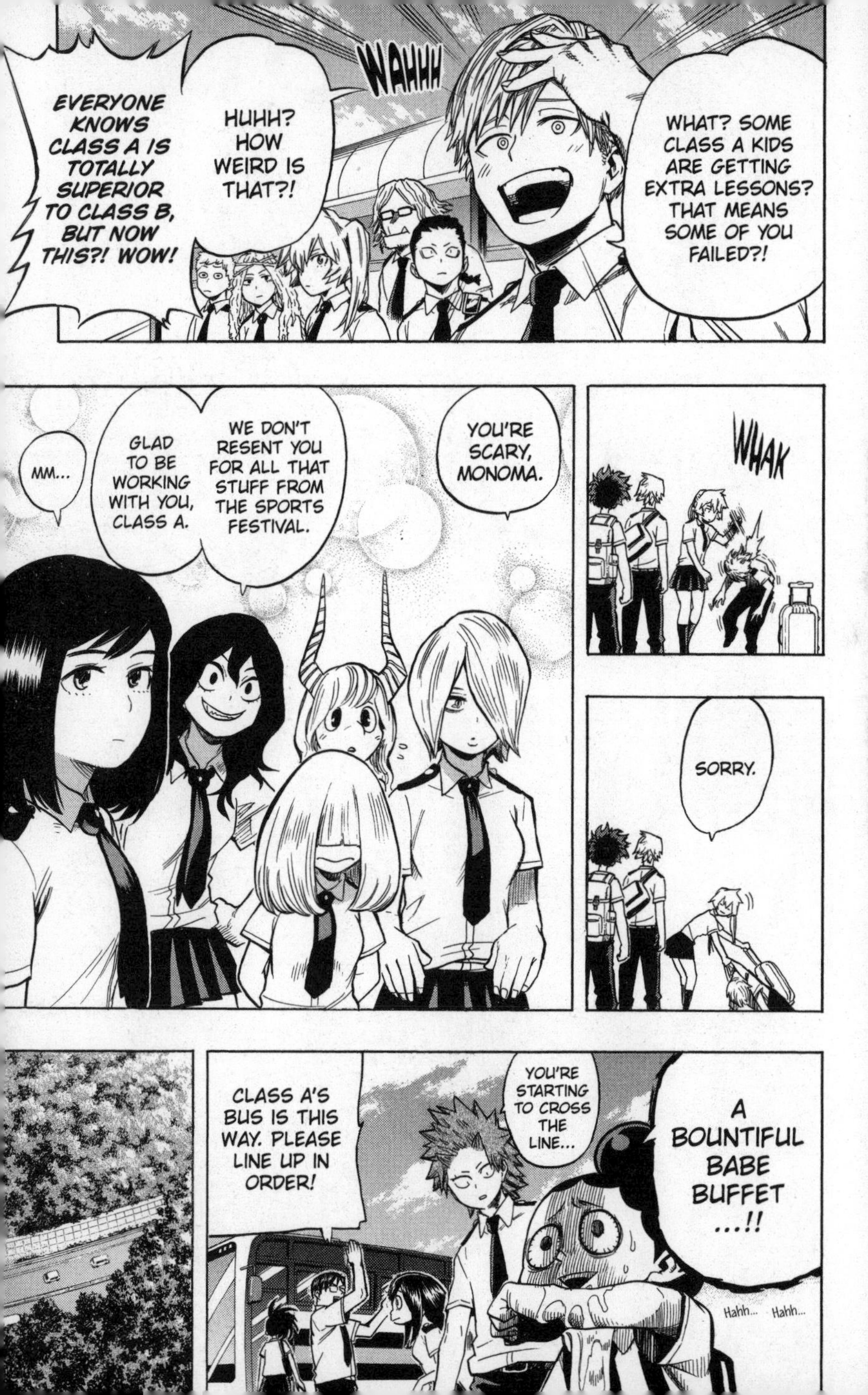
WHAT? SOME CLASS A KIDS ARE GETTING EXTRA LESSONS? THAT MEANS SOME OF YOU FAILED?!
WAHHH
HUHH? HOW WEIRD IS THAT?!
EVERYONE KNOWS CLASS A IS TOTALLY SUPERIOR TO CLASS B, BUT NOW THIS?! WOW!
WHAK
SORRY.
YOU'RE SCARY, MONOMA.
WE DON'T RESENT YOU FOR ALL THAT STUFF FROM THE SPORTS FESTIVAL.
GLAD TO BE WORKING WITH YOU, CLASS A.
MM...
A BOUNTIFUL BABE BUFFET ...!!
YOU'RE STARTING TO CROSS THE LINE...
CLASS A'S BUS IS THIS WAY. PLEASE LINE UP IN ORDER!
Hahh... Hahh...

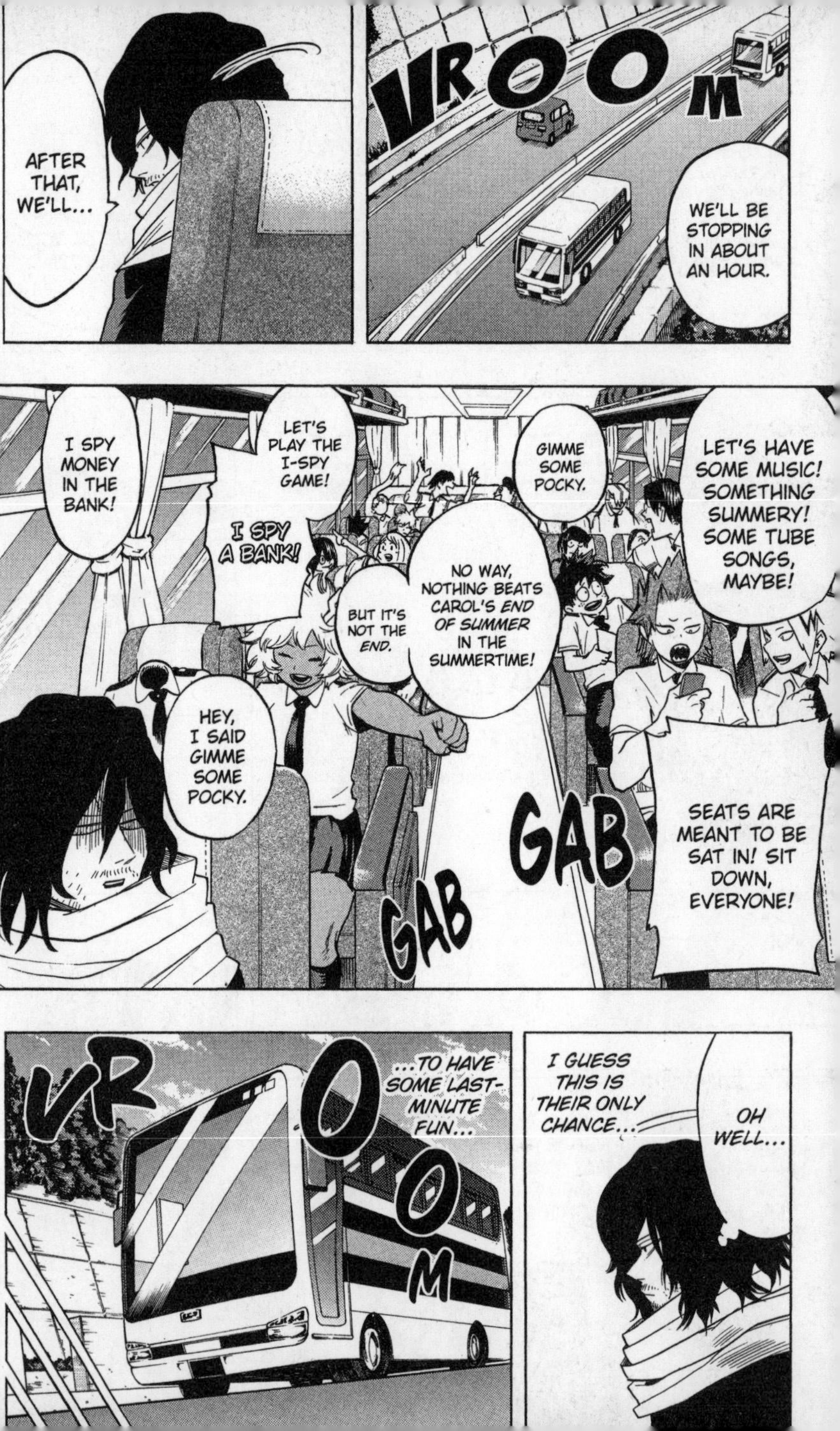
VROOOM
WE'LL BE STOPPING IN ABOUT AN HOUR.
AFTER THAT, WE'LL...
LET'S HAVE SOME MUSIC! SOMETHING SUMMERY! SOME TUBE SONGS, MAYBE!
GIMME SOME POCKY.
NO WAY, NOTHING BEATS CAROL'S *END OF SUMMER* IN THE SUMMERTIME!
BUT IT'S NOT THE *END*.
LET'S PLAY THE I-SPY GAME!
I SPY MONEY IN THE BANK!
I SPY A BANK!
SEATS ARE MEANT TO BE SAT IN! SIT DOWN, EVERYONE!
GAB
GAB
HEY, I SAID GIMME SOME POCKY.
I GUESS THIS IS THEIR ONLY CHANCE...
OH WELL...
...TO HAVE SOME LAST-MINUTE FUN...
VROOOM

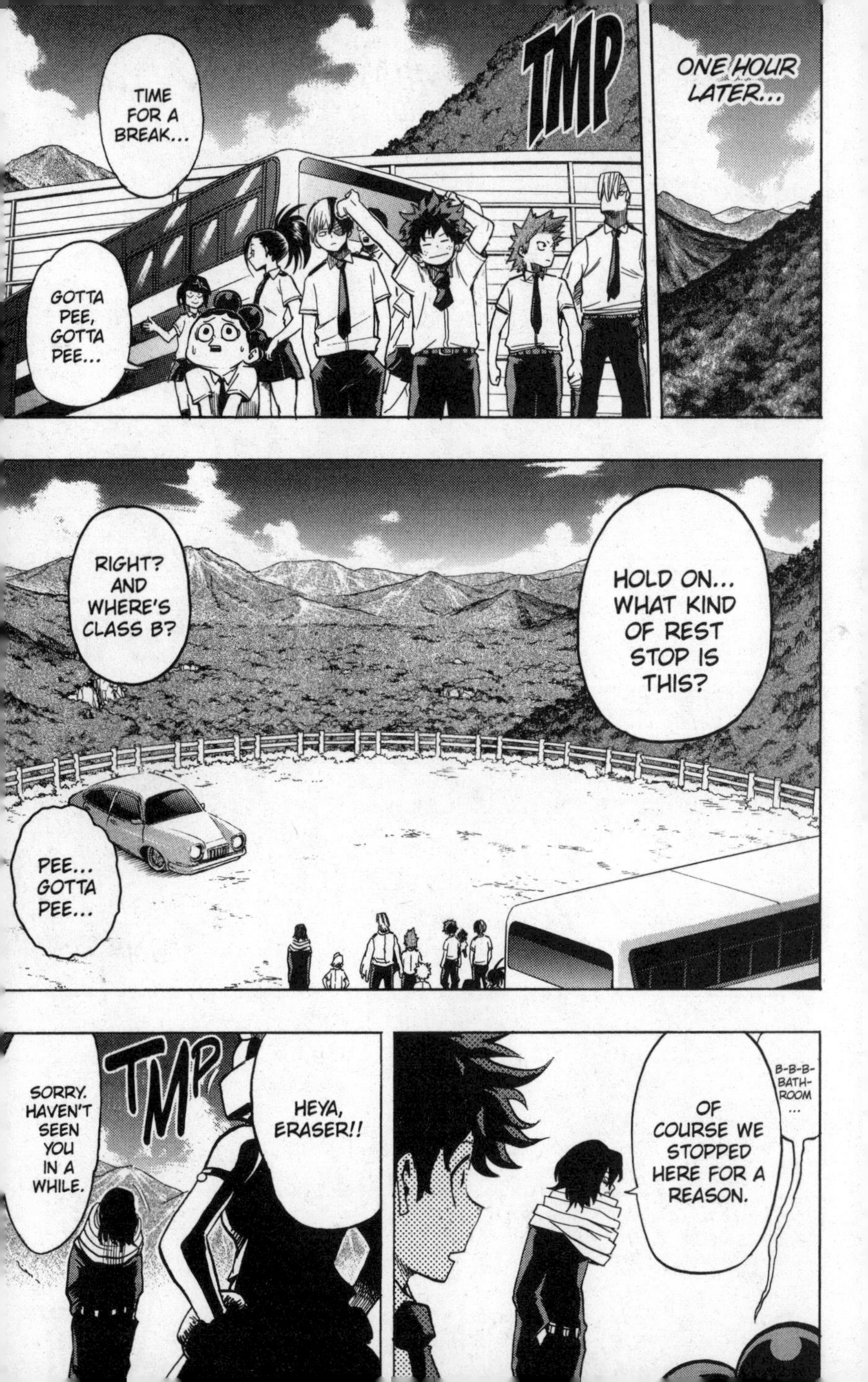
ONE HOUR LATER...
TMP
TIME FOR A BREAK...
GOTTA PEE, GOTTA PEE...
HOLD ON... WHAT KIND OF REST STOP IS THIS?
RIGHT? AND WHERE'S CLASS B?
PEE... GOTTA PEE...
B-B-B-BATHROOM...
OF COURSE WE STOPPED HERE FOR A REASON.
HEYA, ERASER!!
TMP
SORRY. HAVEN'T SEEN YOU IN A WHILE.

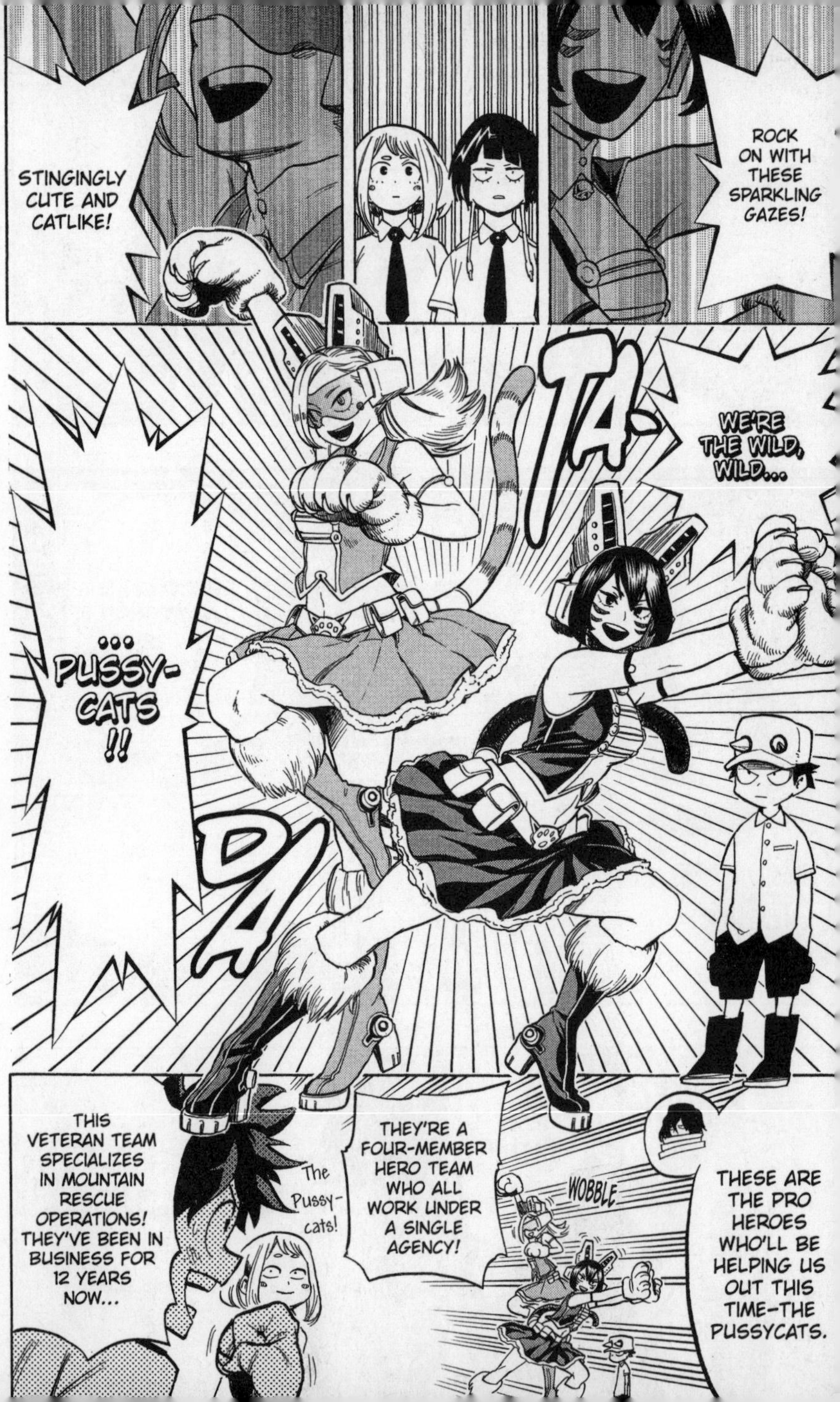
ROCK ON WITH THESE SPARKLING GAZES!
STINGINGLY CUTE AND CATLIKE!
WE'RE THE WILD, WILD...
TA-
...PUSSY-CATS!!
DA
THESE ARE THE PRO HEROES WHO'LL BE HELPING US OUT THIS TIME—THE PUSSYCATS.
WOBBLE
THEY'RE A FOUR-MEMBER HERO TEAM WHO ALL WORK UNDER A SINGLE AGENCY!
The Pussy-cats!
THIS VETERAN TEAM SPECIALIZES IN MOUNTAIN RESCUE OPERATIONS! THEY'VE BEEN IN BUSINESS FOR 12 YEARS NOW...

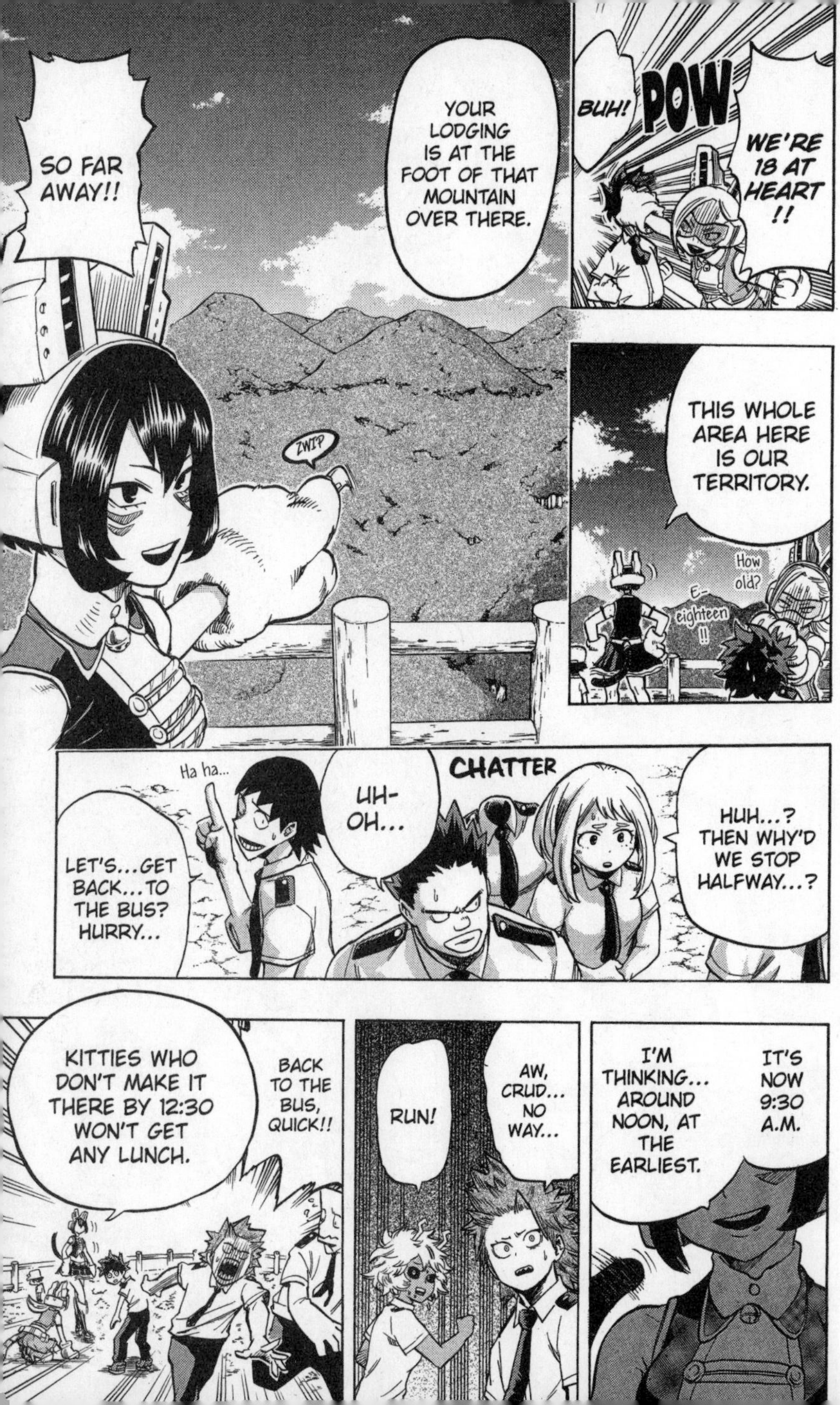
WE'RE 18 AT HEART!!
POW
BUH!
THIS WHOLE AREA HERE IS OUR TERRITORY.
How old?
E-eighteen!!
YOUR LODGING IS AT THE FOOT OF THAT MOUNTAIN OVER THERE.
ZWIP
SO FAR AWAY!!
HUH...? THEN WHY'D WE STOP HALFWAY...?
CHATTER
UH-OH...
Ha ha...
LET'S...GET BACK...TO THE BUS? HURRY...
IT'S NOW 9:30 A.M.
I'M THINKING... AROUND NOON, AT THE EARLIEST.
AW, CRUD... NO WAY...
RUN!
BACK TO THE BUS, QUICK!!
KITTIES WHO DON'T MAKE IT THERE BY 12:30 WON'T GET ANY LUNCH.

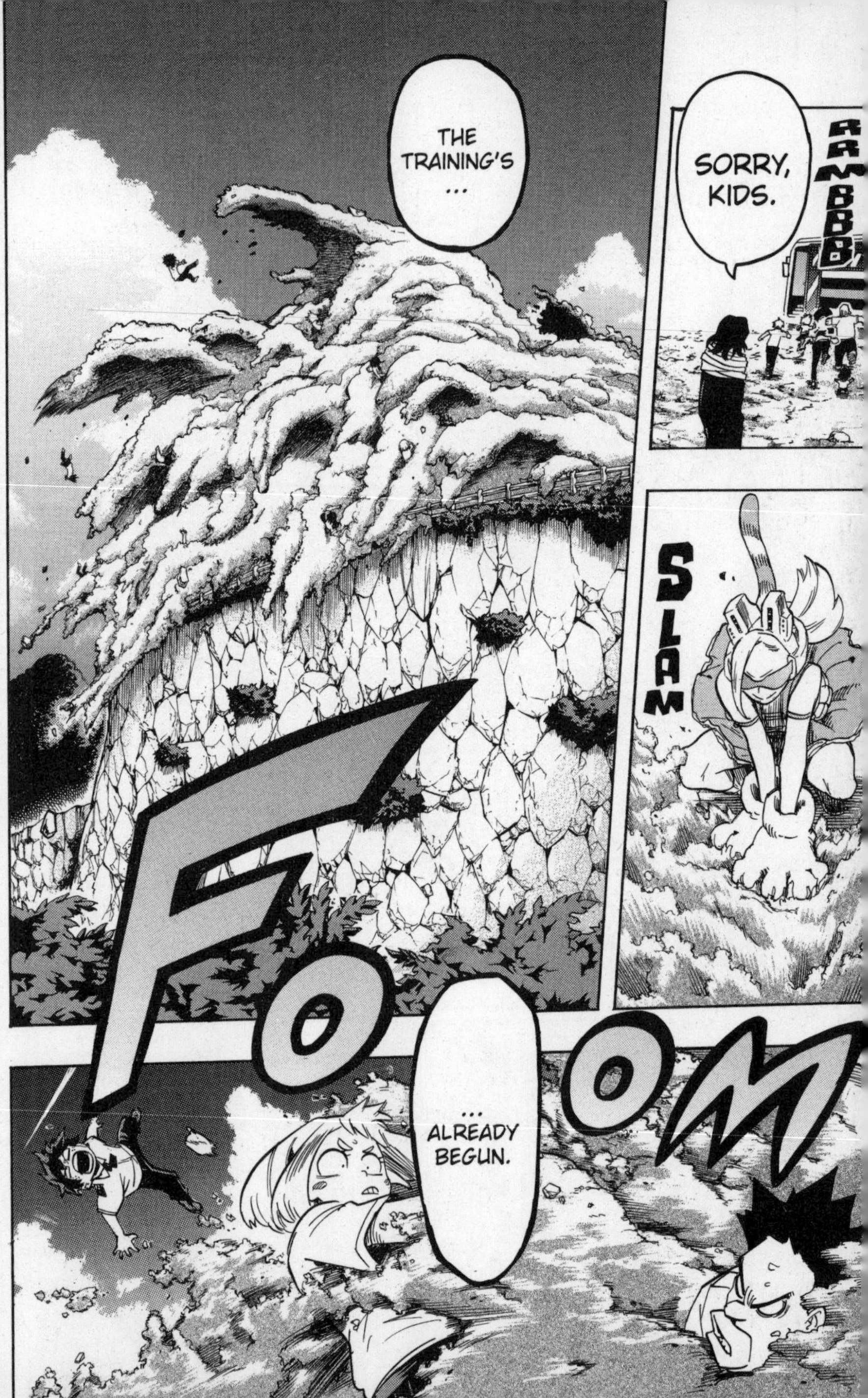
SORRY, KIDS.
RRMBBB
SLAM
THE TRAINING'S ...
FOOOM
... ALREADY BEGUN.

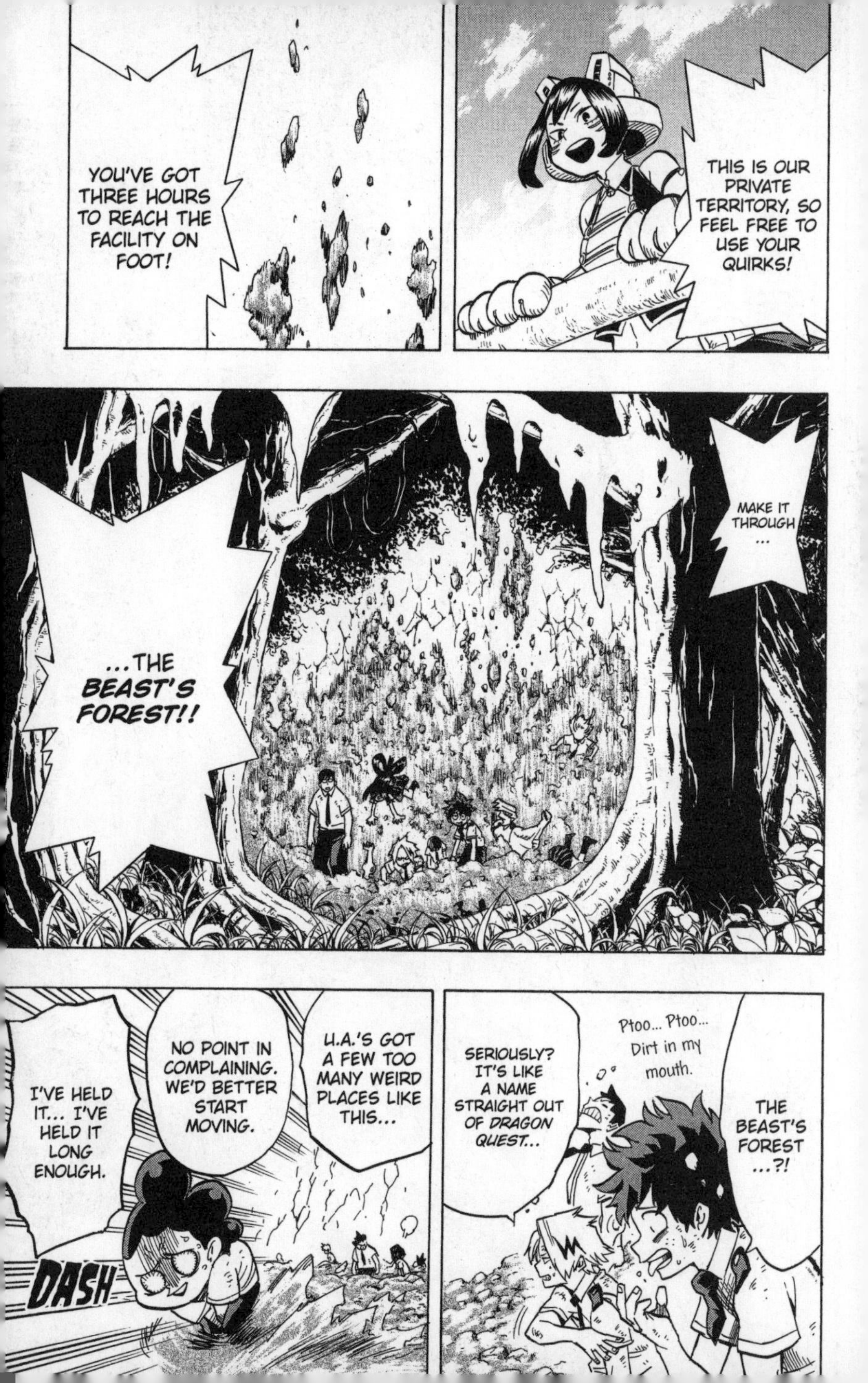
THIS IS OUR PRIVATE TERRITORY, SO FEEL FREE TO USE YOUR QUIRKS!
YOU'VE GOT THREE HOURS TO REACH THE FACILITY ON FOOT!
MAKE IT THROUGH...
...THE BEAST'S FOREST!!
THE BEAST'S FOREST...?!
Ptoo... Ptoo... Dirt in my mouth.
SERIOUSLY? IT'S LIKE A NAME STRAIGHT OUT OF DRAGON QUEST...
U.A.'S GOT A FEW TOO MANY WEIRD PLACES LIKE THIS...
NO POINT IN COMPLAINING. WE'D BETTER START MOVING.
I'VE HELD IT... I'VE HELD IT LONG ENOUGH.
DASH

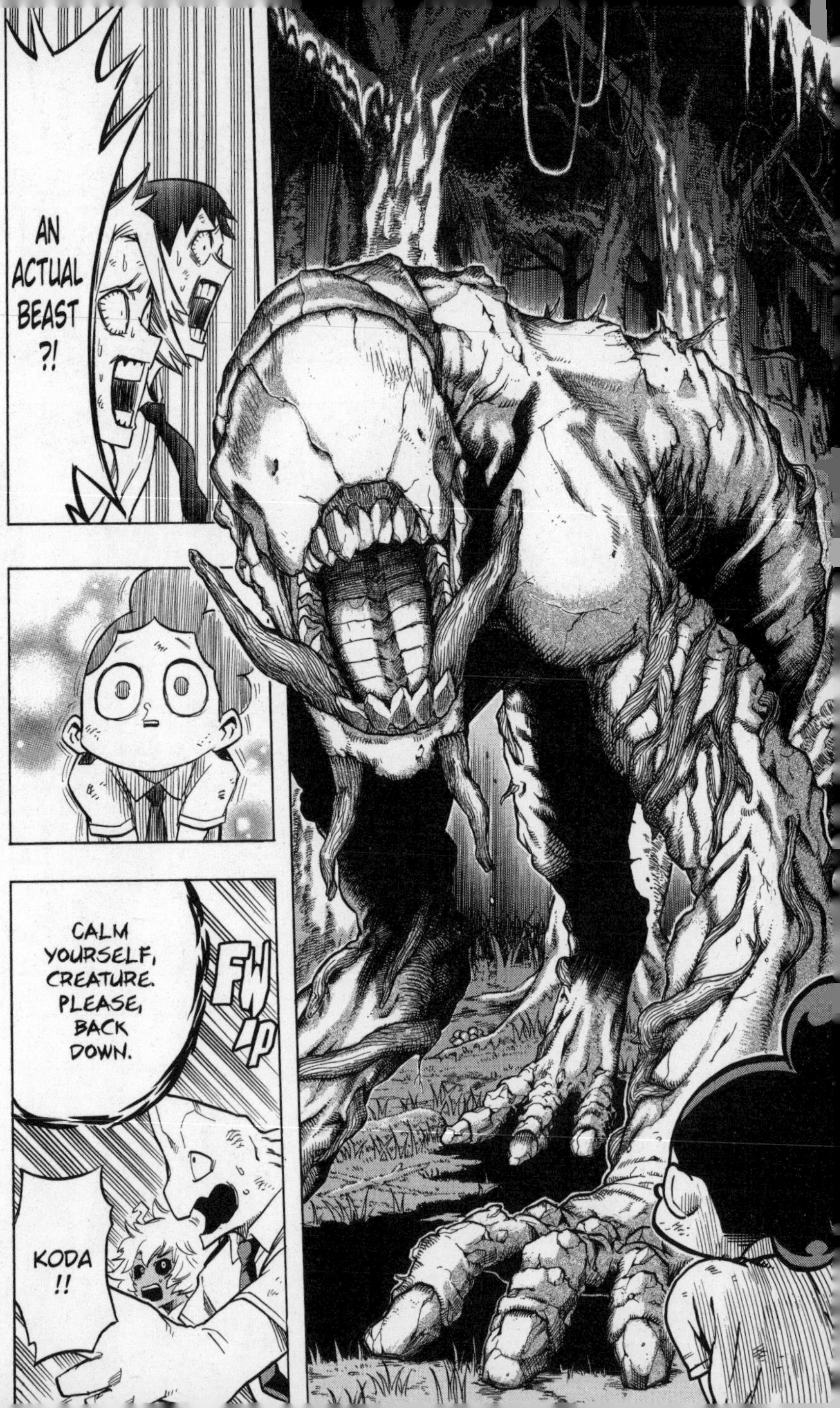
AN ACTUAL BEAST ?!
CALM YOURSELF, CREATURE. PLEASE, BACK DOWN.
FWIP
KODA !!

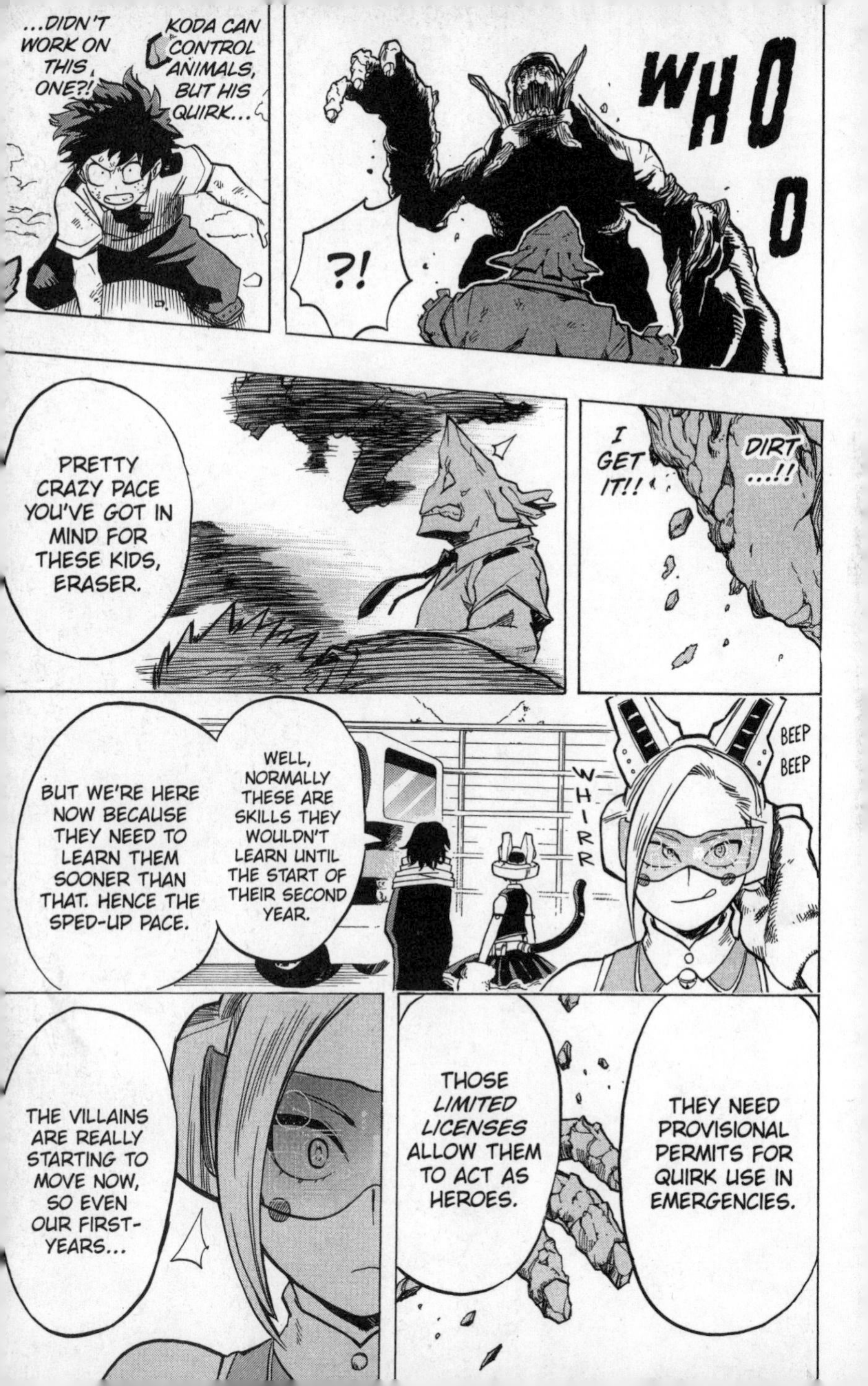
WHOOO
?!
KODA CAN CONTROL ANIMALS, BUT HIS QUIRK...
...DIDN'T WORK ON THIS ONE?!
DIRT ...!!
I GET IT!!
PRETTY CRAZY PACE YOU'VE GOT IN MIND FOR THESE KIDS, ERASER.
BEEP BEEP
WHIRR
WELL, NORMALLY THESE ARE SKILLS THEY WOULDN'T LEARN UNTIL THE START OF THEIR SECOND YEAR.
BUT WE'RE HERE NOW BECAUSE THEY NEED TO LEARN THEM SOONER THAN THAT. HENCE THE SPED-UP PACE.
THEY NEED PROVISIONAL PERMITS FOR QUIRK USE IN EMERGENCIES.
THOSE *LIMITED LICENSES* ALLOW THEM TO ACT AS HEROES.
THE VILLAINS ARE REALLY STARTING TO MOVE NOW, SO EVEN OUR FIRST-YEARS...

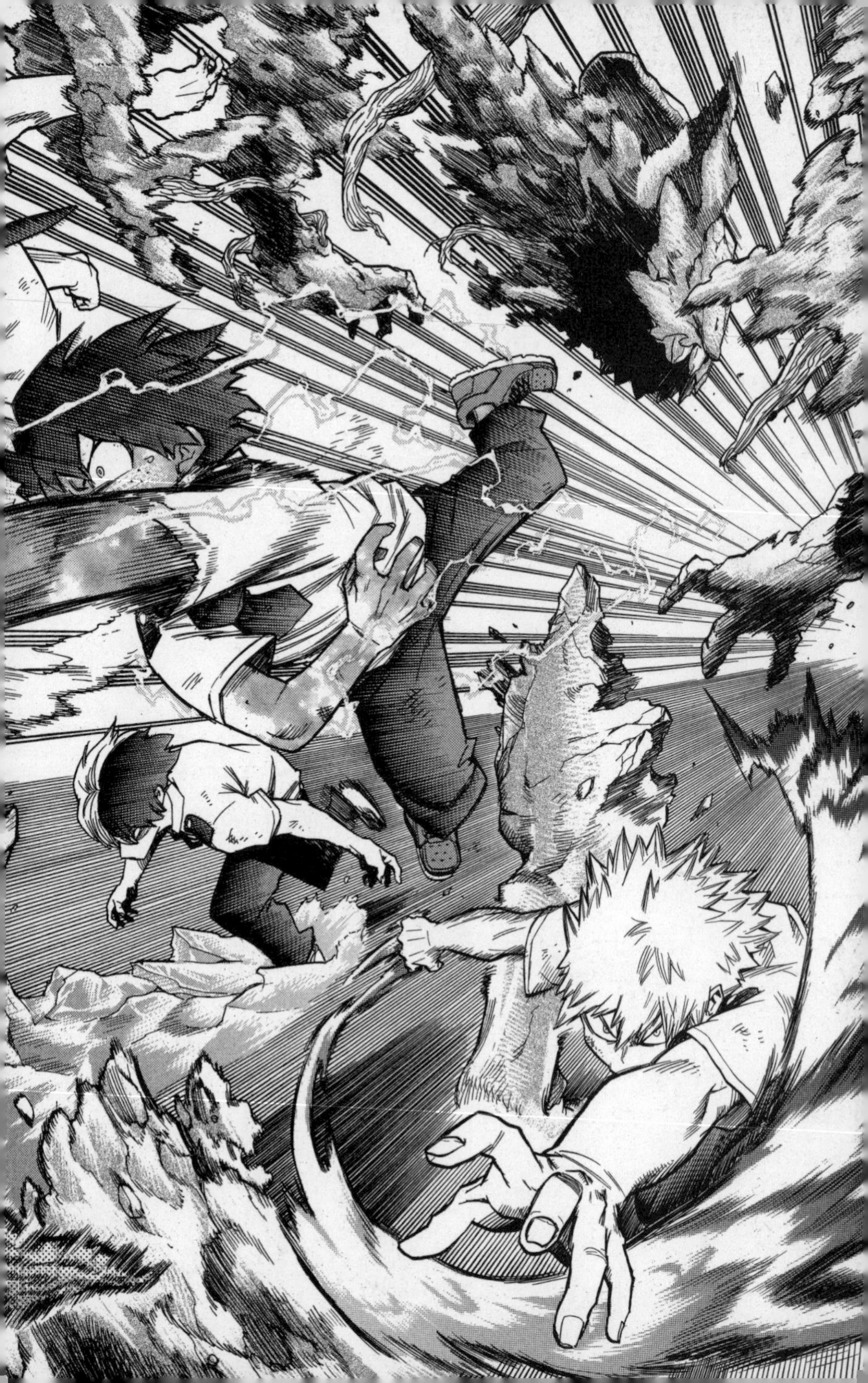

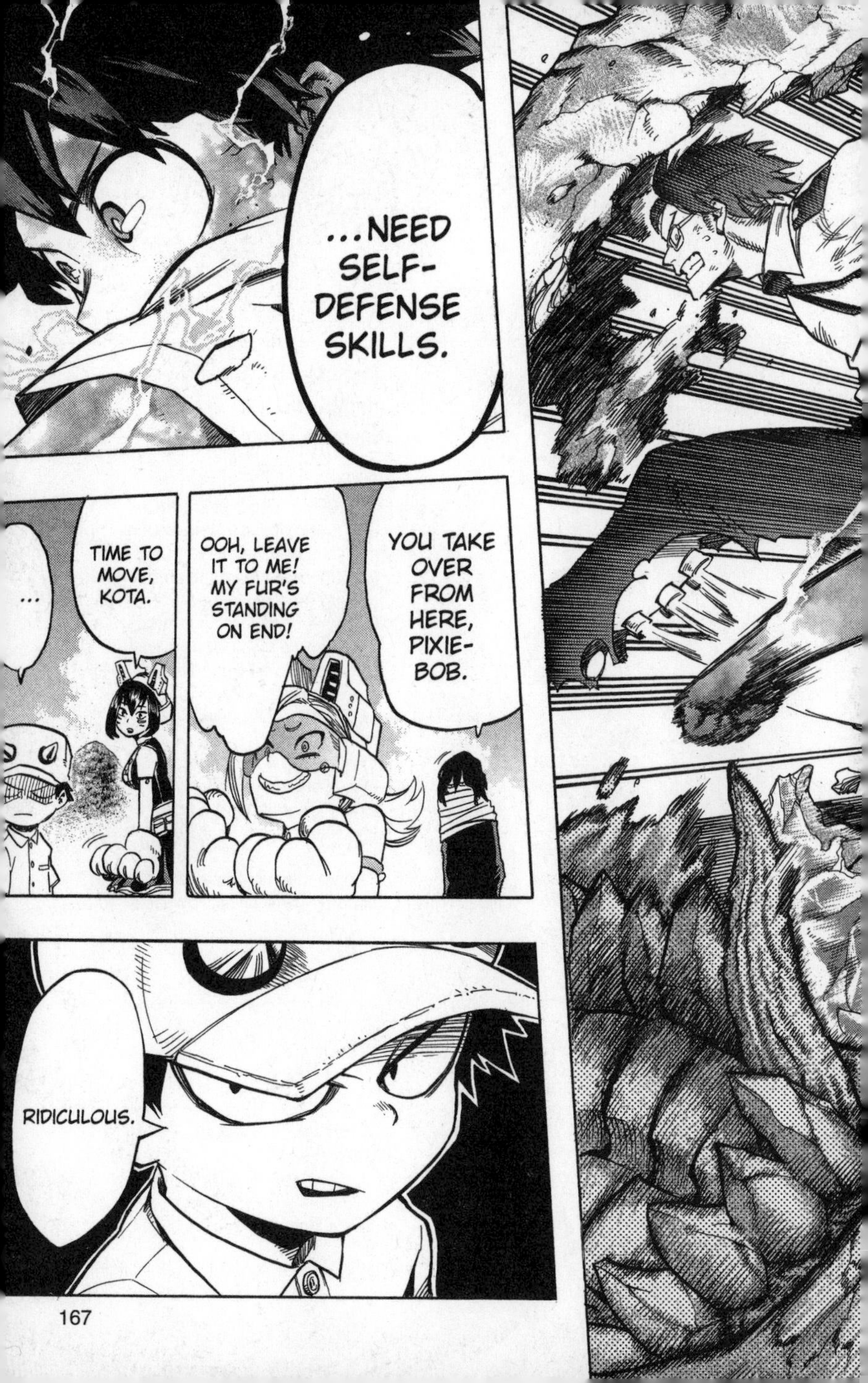
...NEED SELF-DEFENSE SKILLS.
YOU TAKE OVER FROM HERE, PIXIE-BOB.
OOH, LEAVE IT TO ME! MY FUR'S STANDING ON END!
TIME TO MOVE, KOTA.
...
RIDICULOUS.

HERO

WILD WILD PUSSYCATS:
PIXIE-BOB (31)
RYUKO TSUCHIKAWA

STREET CLOTHES

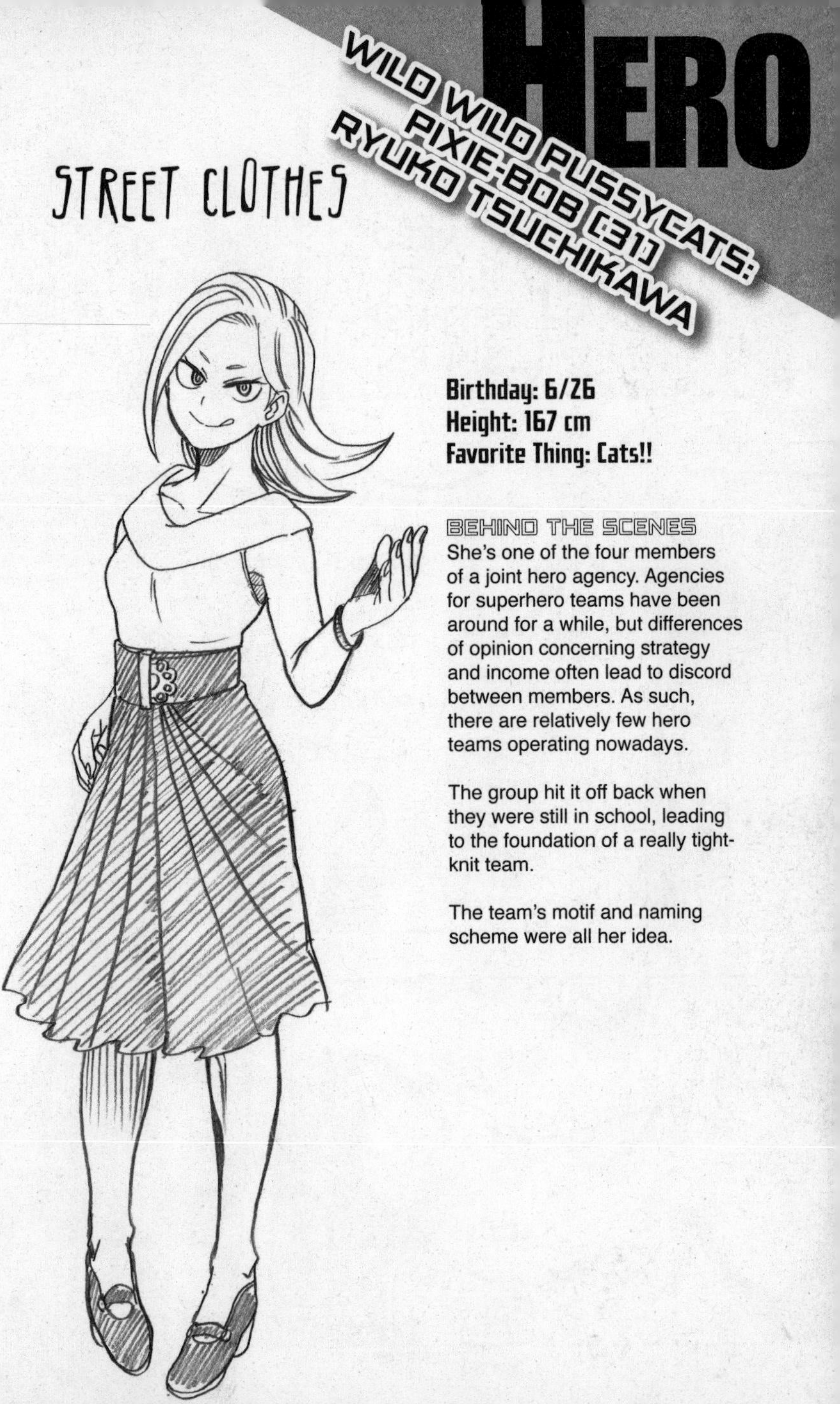

Birthday: 6/26
Height: 167 cm
Favorite Thing: Cats!!

BEHIND THE SCENES

She's one of the four members of a joint hero agency. Agencies for superhero teams have been around for a while, but differences of opinion concerning strategy and income often lead to discord between members. As such, there are relatively few hero teams operating nowadays.

The group hit it off back when they were still in school, leading to the foundation of a really tight-knit team.

The team's motif and naming scheme were all her idea.

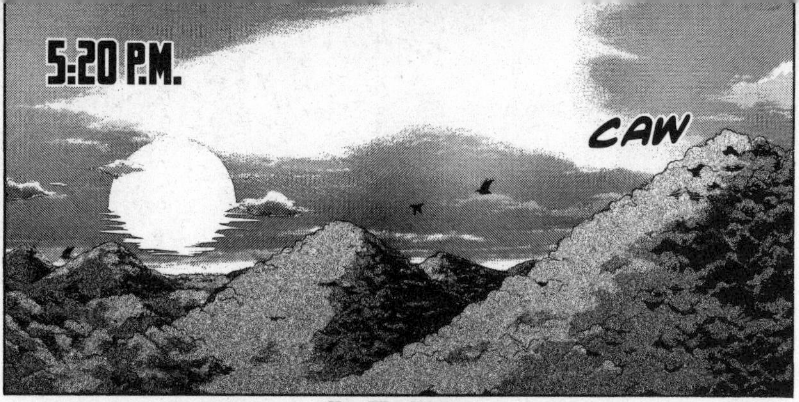
5:20 P.M.
CAW

NO. 71 - KOTA

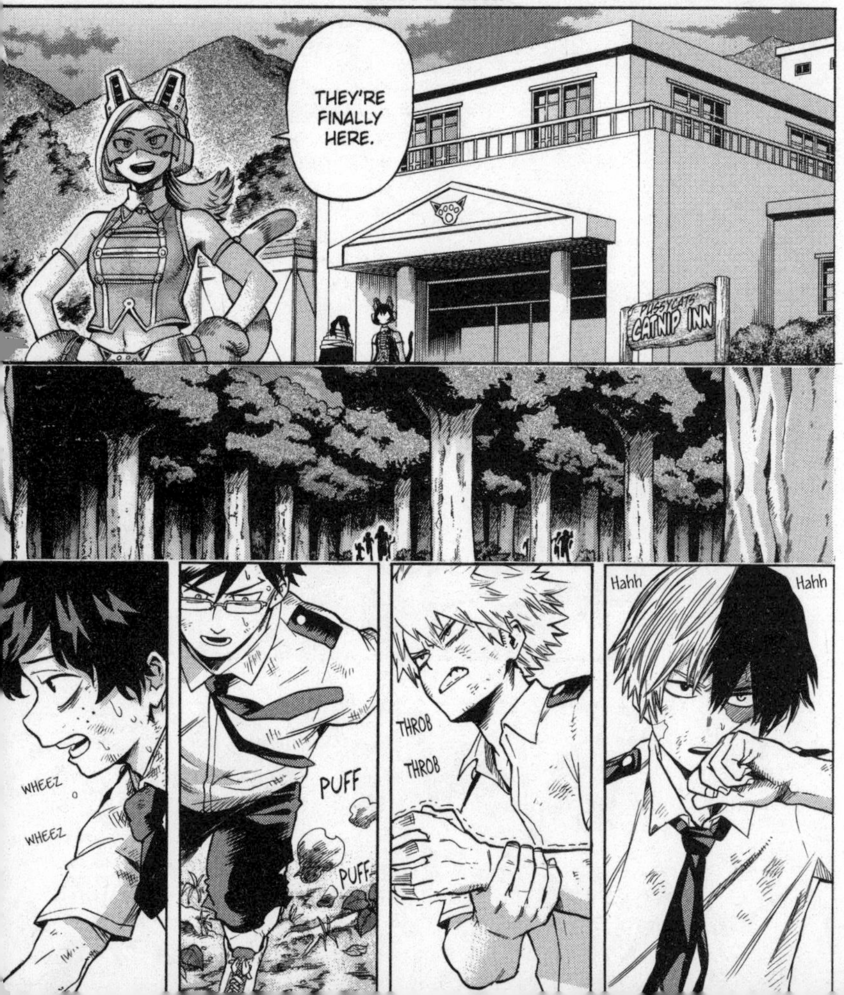
THEY'RE FINALLY HERE.
PUSSYCATS
CATNIP INN
Hahh
Hahh
THROB
THROB
PUFF
PUFF
WHEEZ
WHEEZ

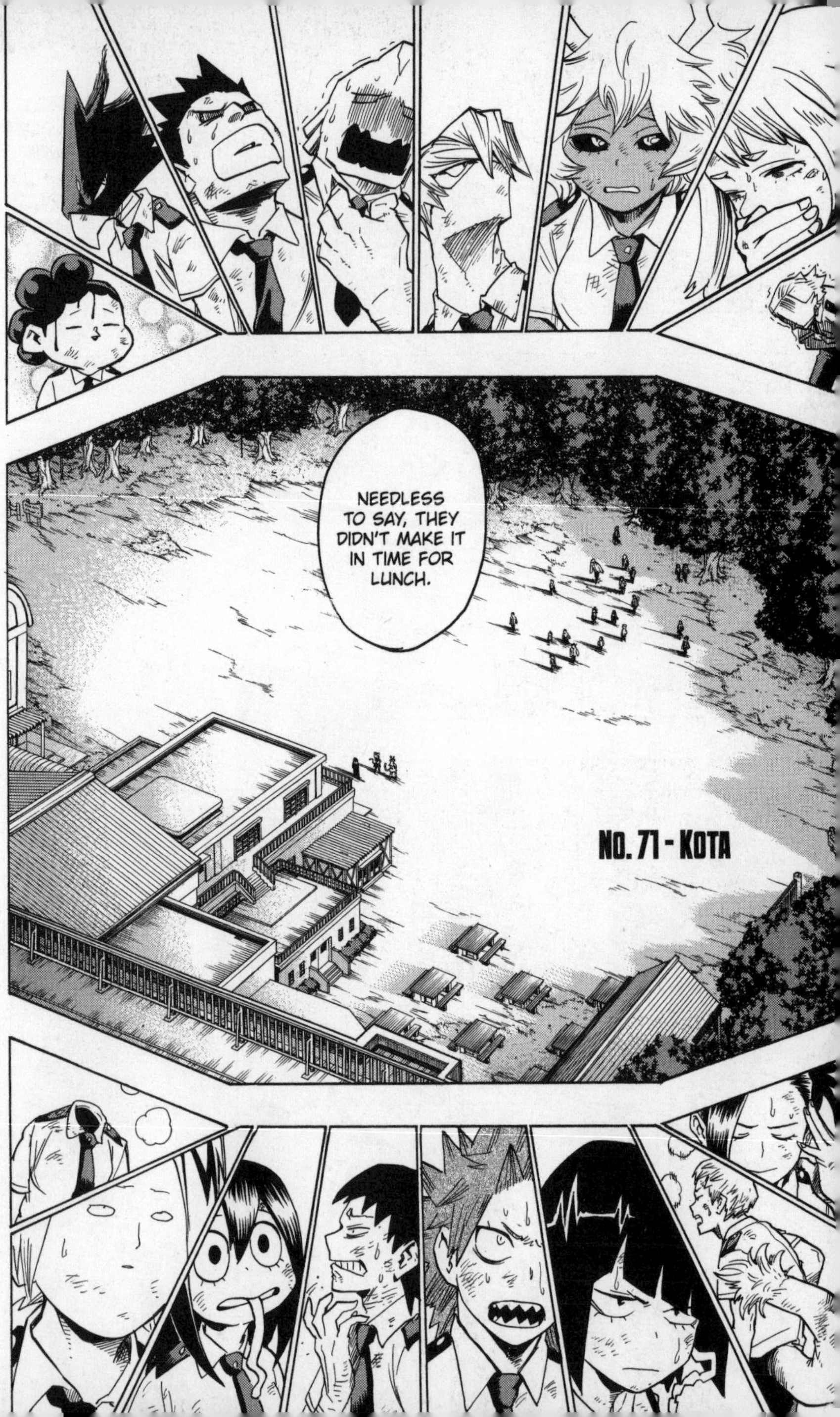
NEEDLESS TO SAY, THEY DIDN'T MAKE IT IN TIME FOR LUNCH.
NO. 71 - KOTA

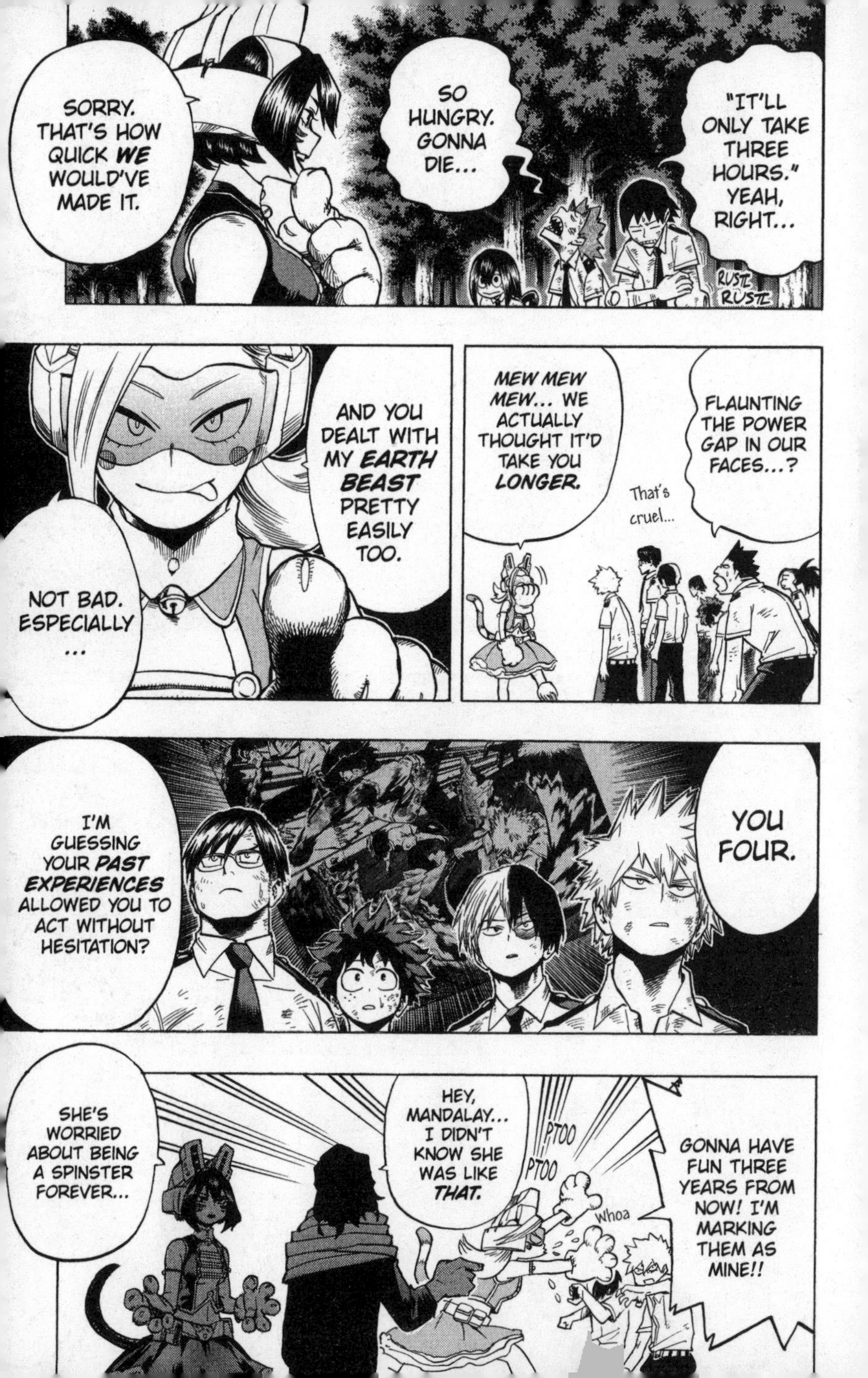
"IT'LL ONLY TAKE THREE HOURS." YEAH, RIGHT...
RUSTL RUSTL
SO HUNGRY. GONNA DIE...
SORRY. THAT'S HOW QUICK *WE* WOULD'VE MADE IT.
FLAUNTING THE POWER GAP IN OUR FACES...?
That's cruel...
MEW MEW MEW... WE ACTUALLY THOUGHT IT'D TAKE YOU *LONGER.*
AND YOU DEALT WITH MY *EARTH BEAST* PRETTY EASILY TOO.
NOT BAD. ESPECIALLY ...
YOU FOUR.
I'M GUESSING YOUR *PAST EXPERIENCES* ALLOWED YOU TO ACT WITHOUT HESITATION?
GONNA HAVE FUN THREE YEARS FROM NOW! I'M MARKING THEM AS MINE!!
PTOO
PTOO
Whoa
HEY, MANDALAY... I DIDN'T KNOW SHE WAS LIKE *THAT.*
SHE'S WORRIED ABOUT BEING A SPINSTER FOREVER...

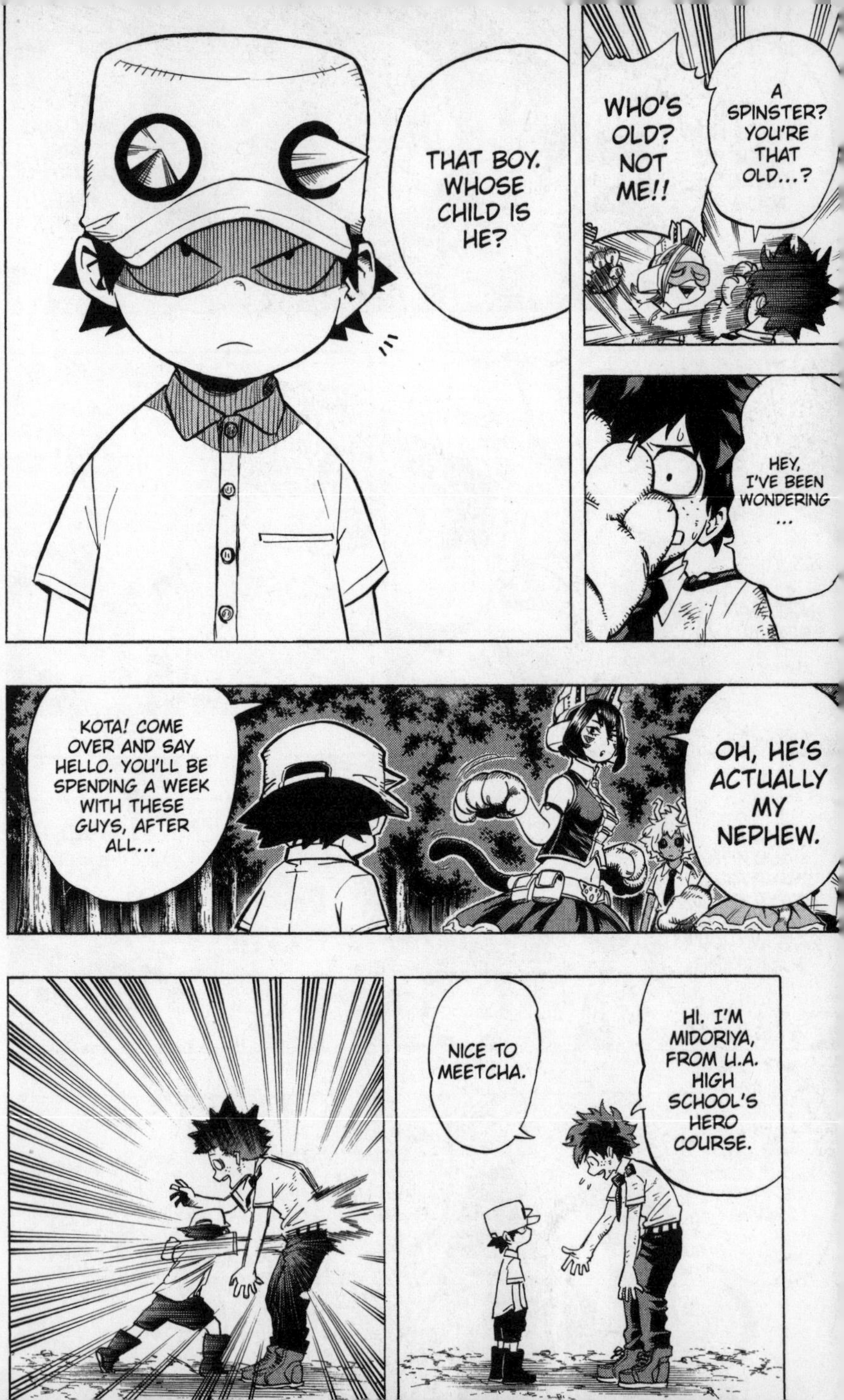
A SPINSTER? YOU'RE THAT OLD...?
WHO'S OLD? NOT ME!!
HEY, I'VE BEEN WONDERING ...
THAT BOY. WHOSE CHILD IS HE?
OH, HE'S ACTUALLY MY NEPHEW.
KOTA! COME OVER AND SAY HELLO. YOU'LL BE SPENDING A WEEK WITH THESE GUYS, AFTER ALL...
HI. I'M MIDORIYA, FROM U.A. HIGH SCHOOL'S HERO COURSE.
NICE TO MEETCHA.

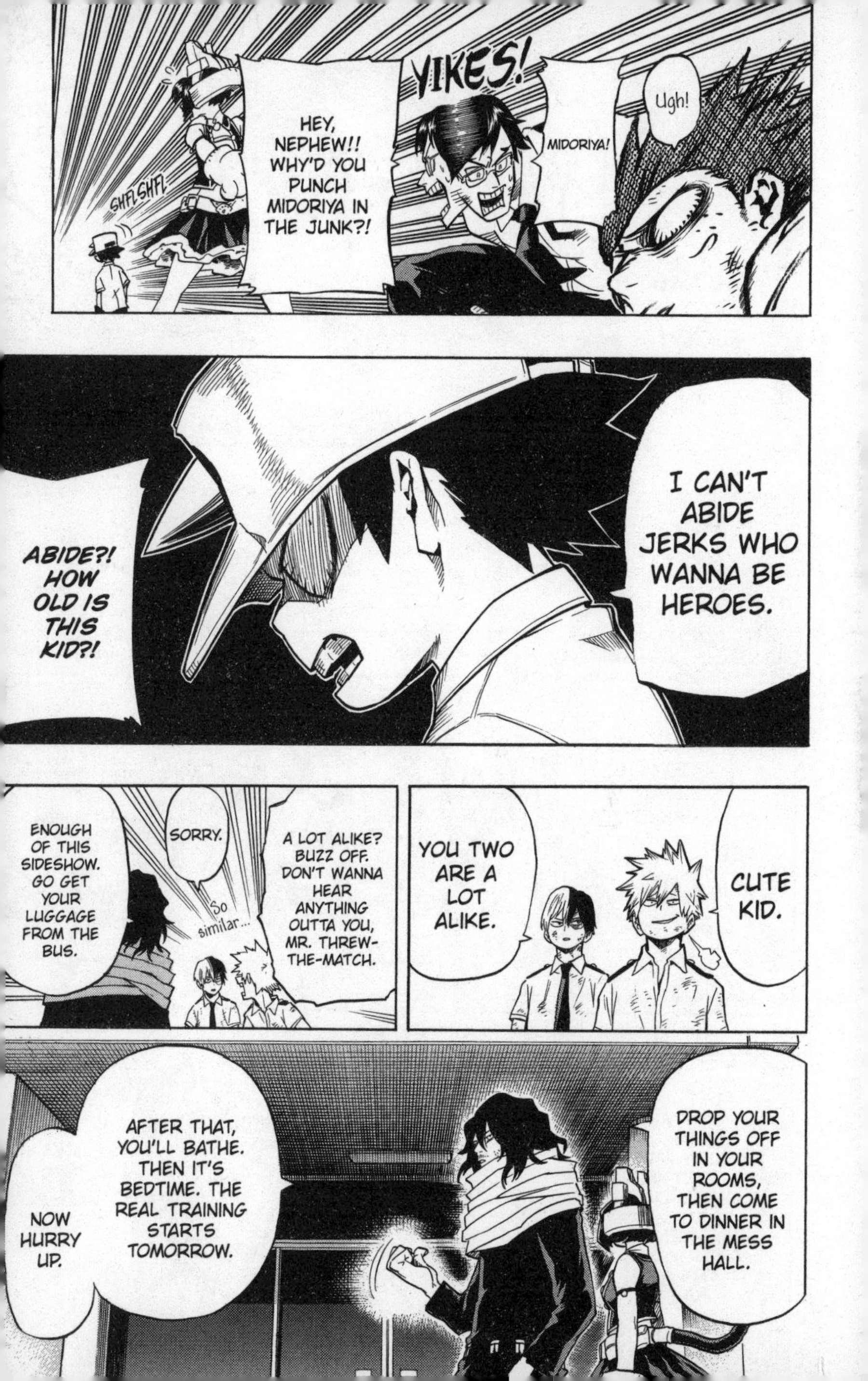
Ugh!
MIDORIYA!
YIKES!
HEY, NEPHEW!! WHY'D YOU PUNCH MIDORIYA IN THE JUNK?!
SHFL SHFL
I CAN'T ABIDE JERKS WHO WANNA BE HEROES.
ABIDE?! HOW OLD IS THIS KID?!
CUTE KID.
YOU TWO ARE A LOT ALIKE.
A LOT ALIKE? BUZZ OFF. DON'T WANNA HEAR ANYTHING OUTTA YOU, MR. THREW-THE-MATCH.
So similar...
SORRY.
ENOUGH OF THIS SIDESHOW. GO GET YOUR LUGGAGE FROM THE BUS.
DROP YOUR THINGS OFF IN YOUR ROOMS, THEN COME TO DINNER IN THE MESS HALL.
AFTER THAT, YOU'LL BATHE. THEN IT'S BEDTIME. THE REAL TRAINING STARTS TOMORROW.
NOW HURRY UP.

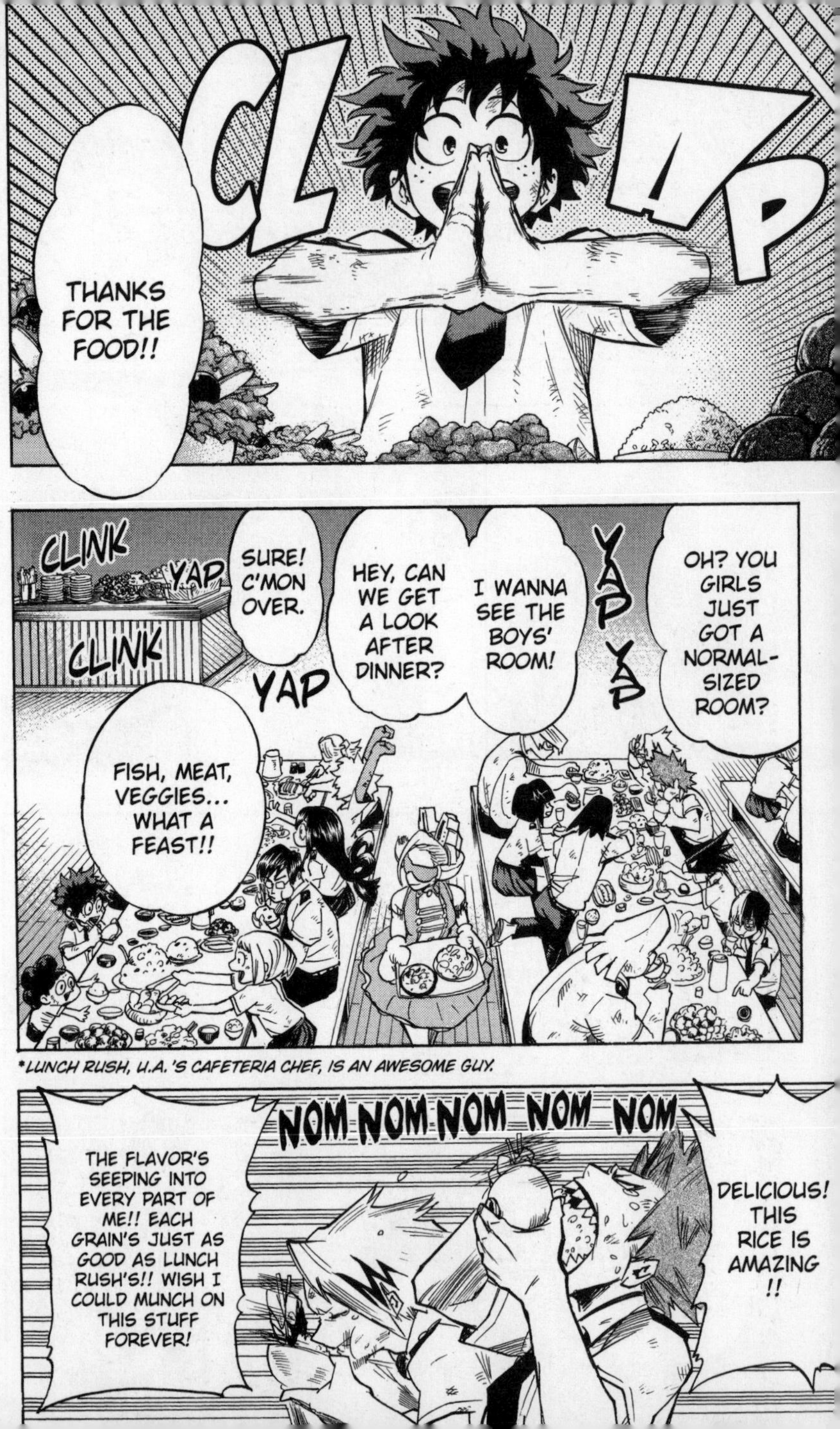
CLAP
THANKS FOR THE FOOD!!
OH? YOU GIRLS JUST GOT A NORMAL-SIZED ROOM?
YAP YAP
I WANNA SEE THE BOYS' ROOM!
HEY, CAN WE GET A LOOK AFTER DINNER?
SURE! C'MON OVER.
YAP
YAP
CLINK
CLINK
FISH, MEAT, VEGGIES... WHAT A FEAST!!
*LUNCH RUSH, U.A.'S CAFETERIA CHEF, IS AN AWESOME GUY.
DELICIOUS! THIS RICE IS AMAZING!!
NOM NOM NOM NOM NOM
THE FLAVOR'S SEEPING INTO EVERY PART OF ME!! EACH GRAIN'S JUST AS GOOD AS LUNCH RUSH'S!! WISH I COULD MUNCH ON THIS STUFF FOREVER!

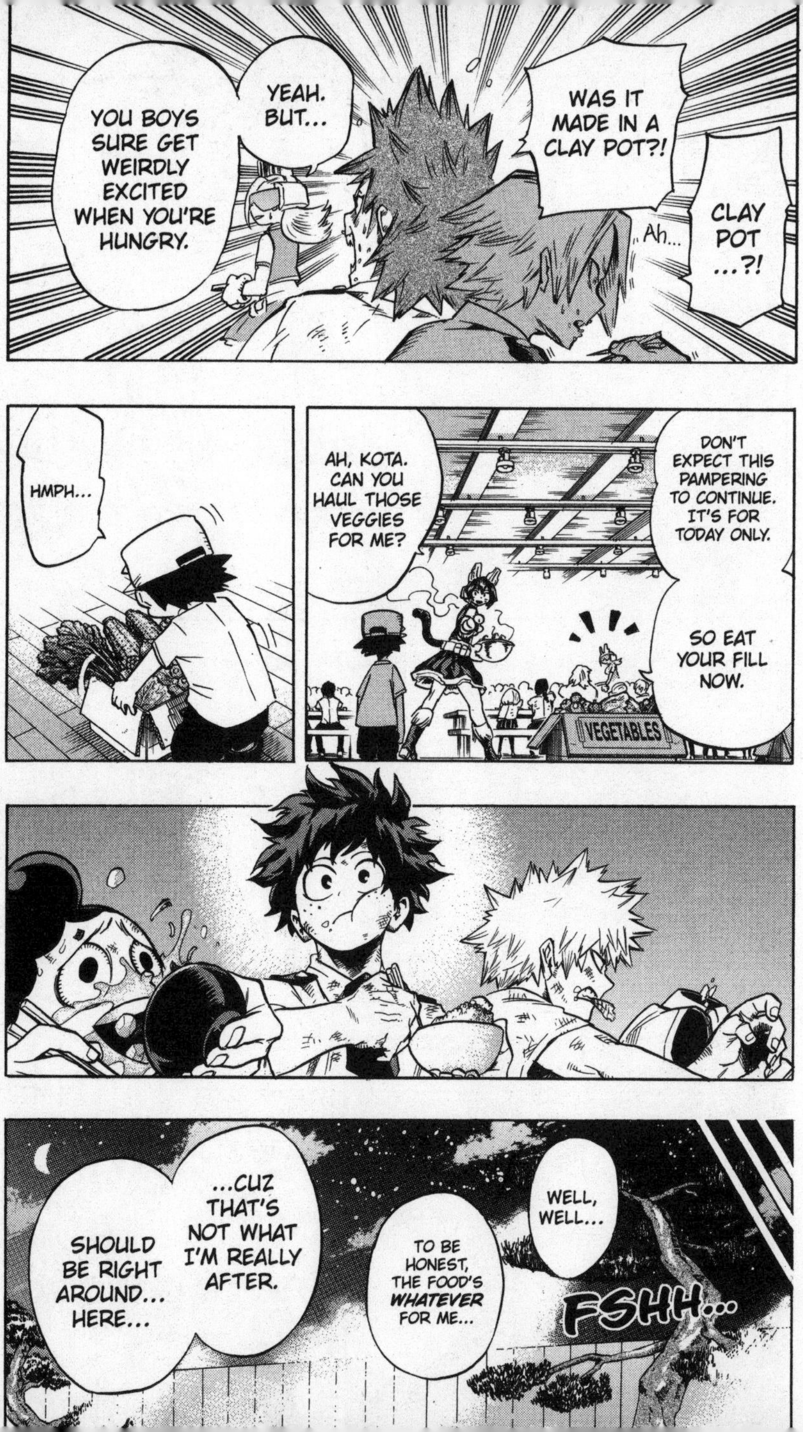
CLAY POT …?!
WAS IT MADE IN A CLAY POT?!
Ah…
YEAH. BUT…
YOU BOYS SURE GET WEIRDLY EXCITED WHEN YOU'RE HUNGRY.
DON'T EXPECT THIS PAMPERING TO CONTINUE. IT'S FOR TODAY ONLY.
SO EAT YOUR FILL NOW.
AH, KOTA. CAN YOU HAUL THOSE VEGGIES FOR ME?
VEGETABLES
HMPH…
FSHH…
WELL, WELL…
TO BE HONEST, THE FOOD'S *WHATEVER* FOR ME…
…CUZ THAT'S NOT WHAT I'M REALLY AFTER.
SHOULD BE RIGHT AROUND… HERE…

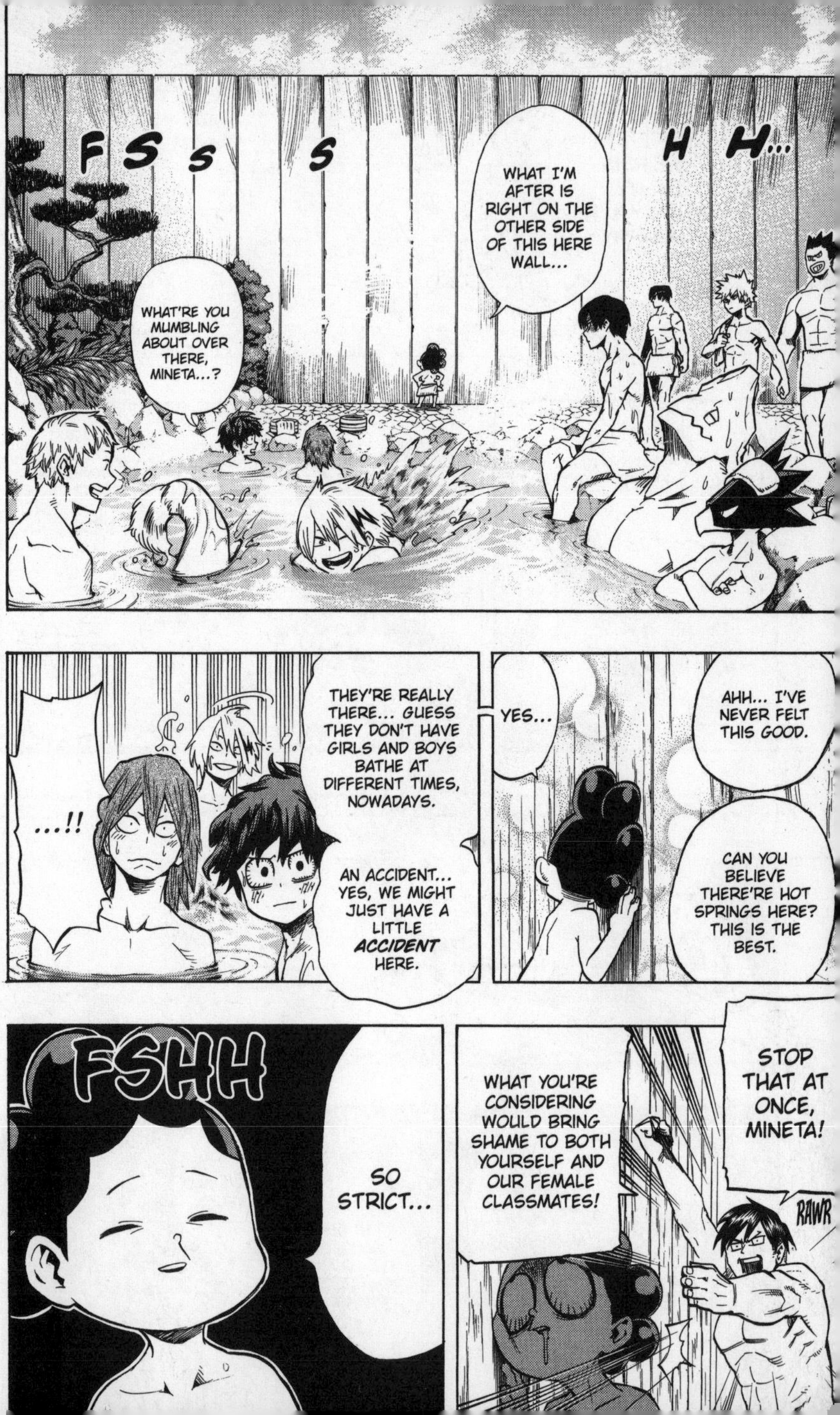
FSsss HH...
WHAT I'M AFTER IS RIGHT ON THE OTHER SIDE OF THIS HERE WALL...
WHAT'RE YOU MUMBLING ABOUT OVER THERE, MINETA...?
AHH... I'VE NEVER FELT THIS GOOD.
YES...
CAN YOU BELIEVE THERE'RE HOT SPRINGS HERE? THIS IS THE BEST.
THEY'RE REALLY THERE... GUESS THEY DON'T HAVE GIRLS AND BOYS BATHE AT DIFFERENT TIMES, NOWADAYS.
AN ACCIDENT... YES, WE MIGHT JUST HAVE A LITTLE *ACCIDENT* HERE.
...!!
STOP THAT AT ONCE, MINETA!
WHAT YOU'RE CONSIDERING WOULD BRING SHAME TO BOTH YOURSELF AND OUR FEMALE CLASSMATES!
RAWR
FSHH
SO STRICT...

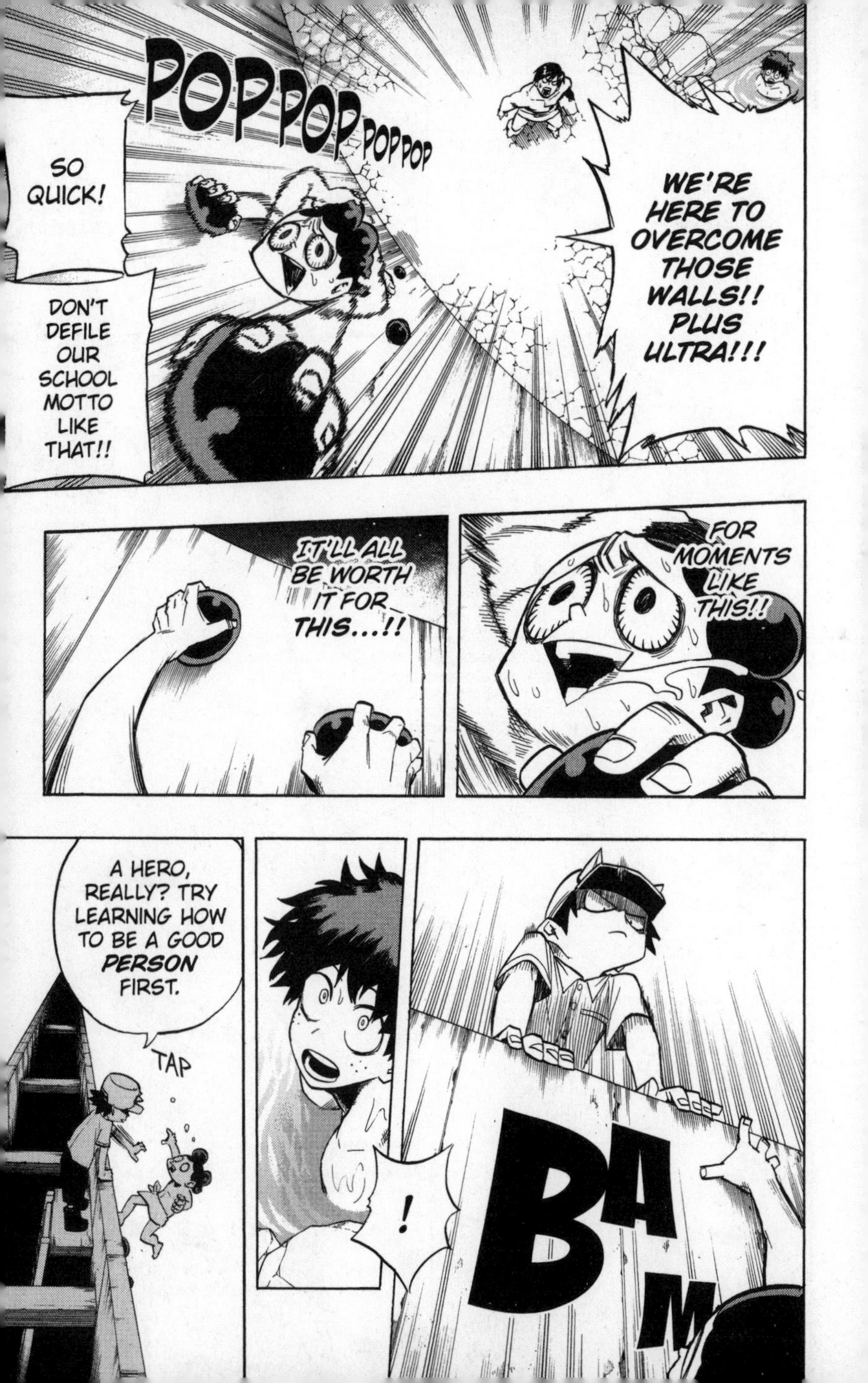
WE'RE HERE TO OVERCOME THOSE WALLS!! PLUS ULTRA!!!
POP POP POP POP POP
SO QUICK!
DON'T DEFILE OUR SCHOOL MOTTO LIKE THAT!!
FOR MOMENTS LIKE THIS!!
IT'LL ALL BE WORTH IT FOR THIS...!!
BAM
!
A HERO, REALLY? TRY LEARNING HOW TO BE A GOOD PERSON FIRST.
TAP

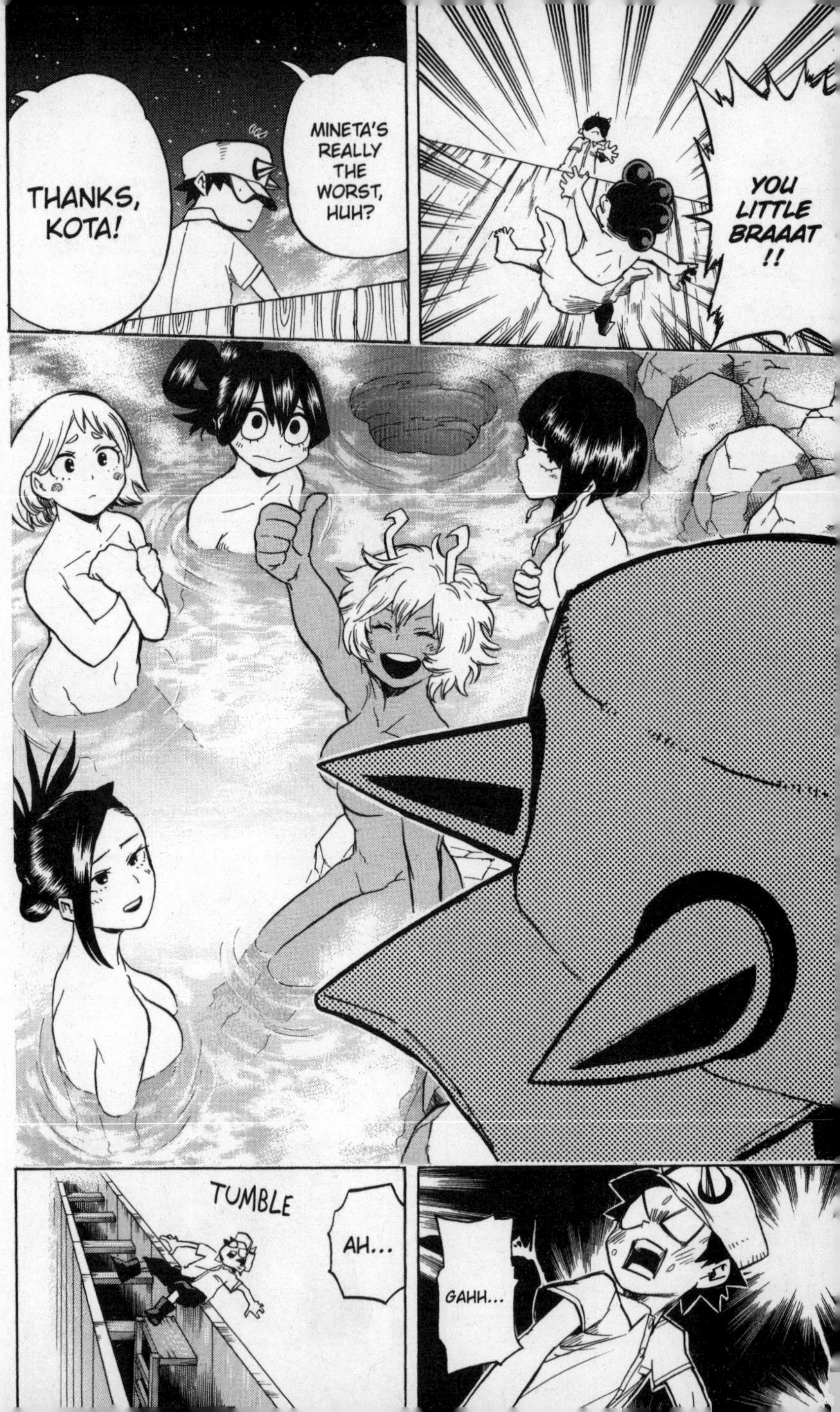
YOU LITTLE BRAAAT!!
MINETA'S REALLY THE WORST, HUH?
THANKS, KOTA!
GAHH...
AH...
TUMBLE

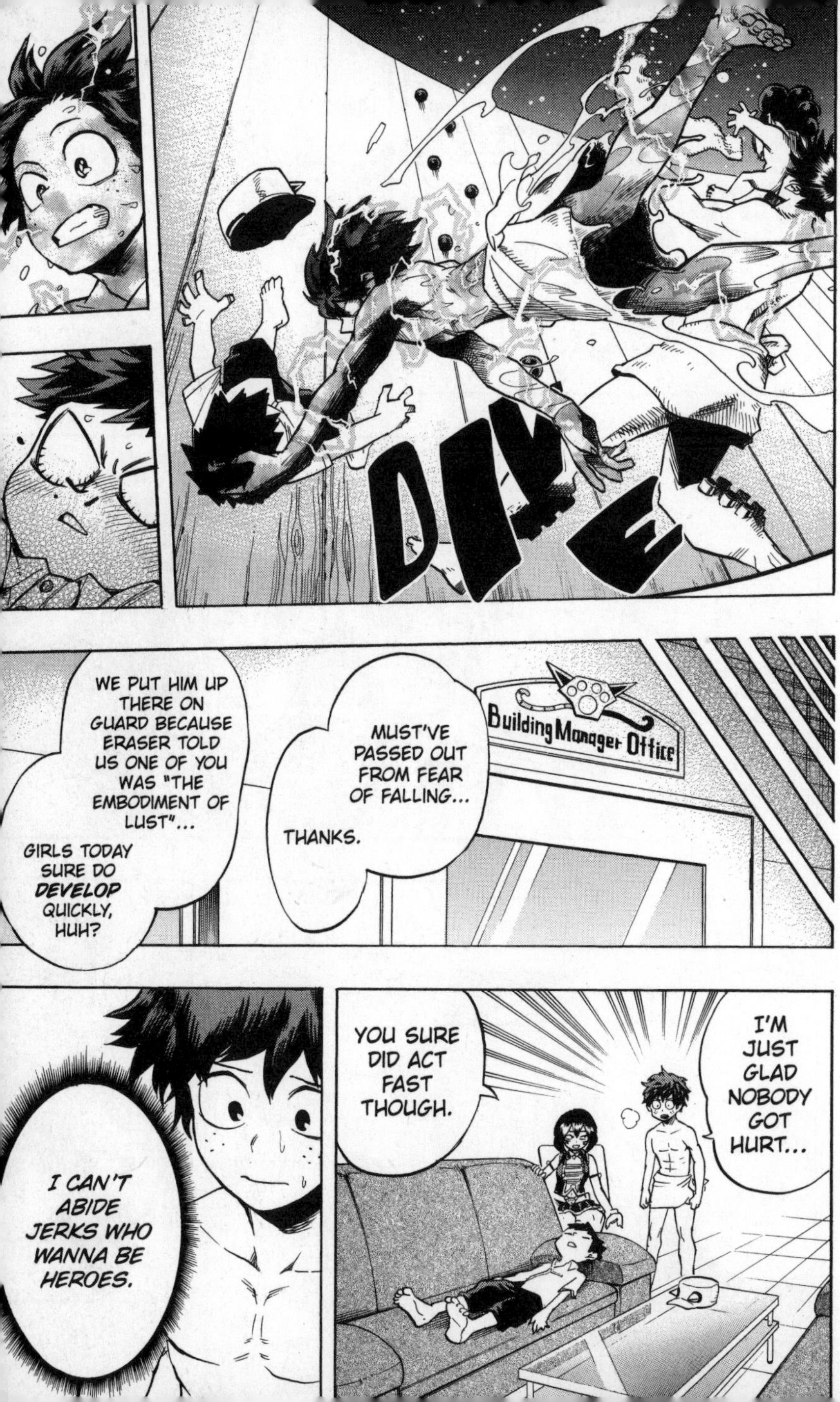
DIVE
Building Manager Office
MUST'VE PASSED OUT FROM FEAR OF FALLING...
THANKS.
WE PUT HIM UP THERE ON GUARD BECAUSE ERASER TOLD US ONE OF YOU WAS "THE EMBODIMENT OF LUST"...
GIRLS TODAY SURE DO *DEVELOP* QUICKLY, HUH?
I'M JUST GLAD NOBODY GOT HURT...
YOU SURE DID ACT FAST THOUGH.
I CAN'T ABIDE JERKS WHO WANNA BE HEROES.

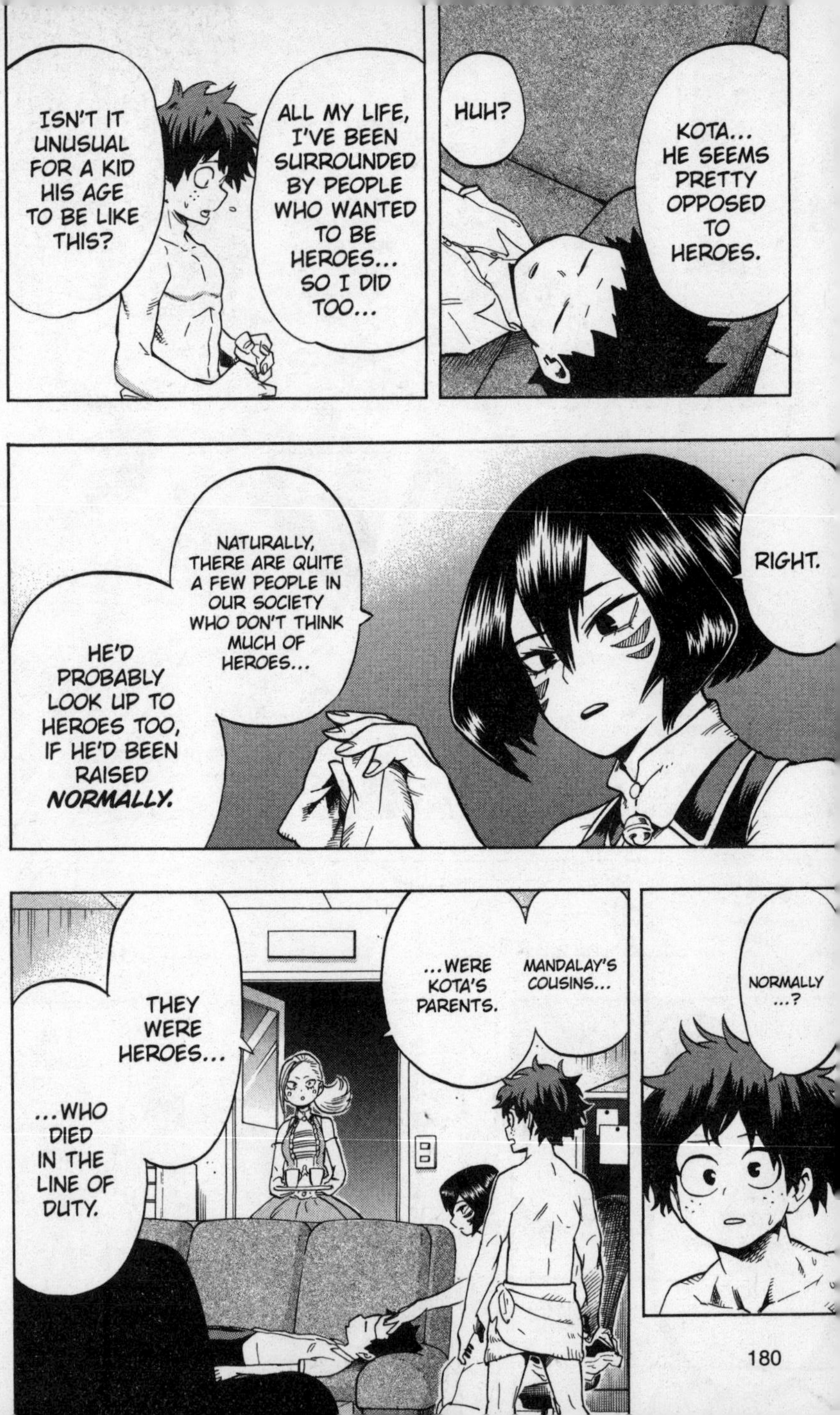
KOTA... HE SEEMS PRETTY OPPOSED TO HEROES.
HUH?
ALL MY LIFE, I'VE BEEN SURROUNDED BY PEOPLE WHO WANTED TO BE HEROES... SO I DID TOO...
ISN'T IT UNUSUAL FOR A KID HIS AGE TO BE LIKE THIS?
RIGHT.
NATURALLY, THERE ARE QUITE A FEW PEOPLE IN OUR SOCIETY WHO DON'T THINK MUCH OF HEROES...
HE'D PROBABLY LOOK UP TO HEROES TOO, IF HE'D BEEN RAISED NORMALLY.
NORMALLY...?
MANDALAY'S COUSINS...
...WERE KOTA'S PARENTS.
THEY WERE HEROES...
...WHO DIED IN THE LINE OF DUTY.

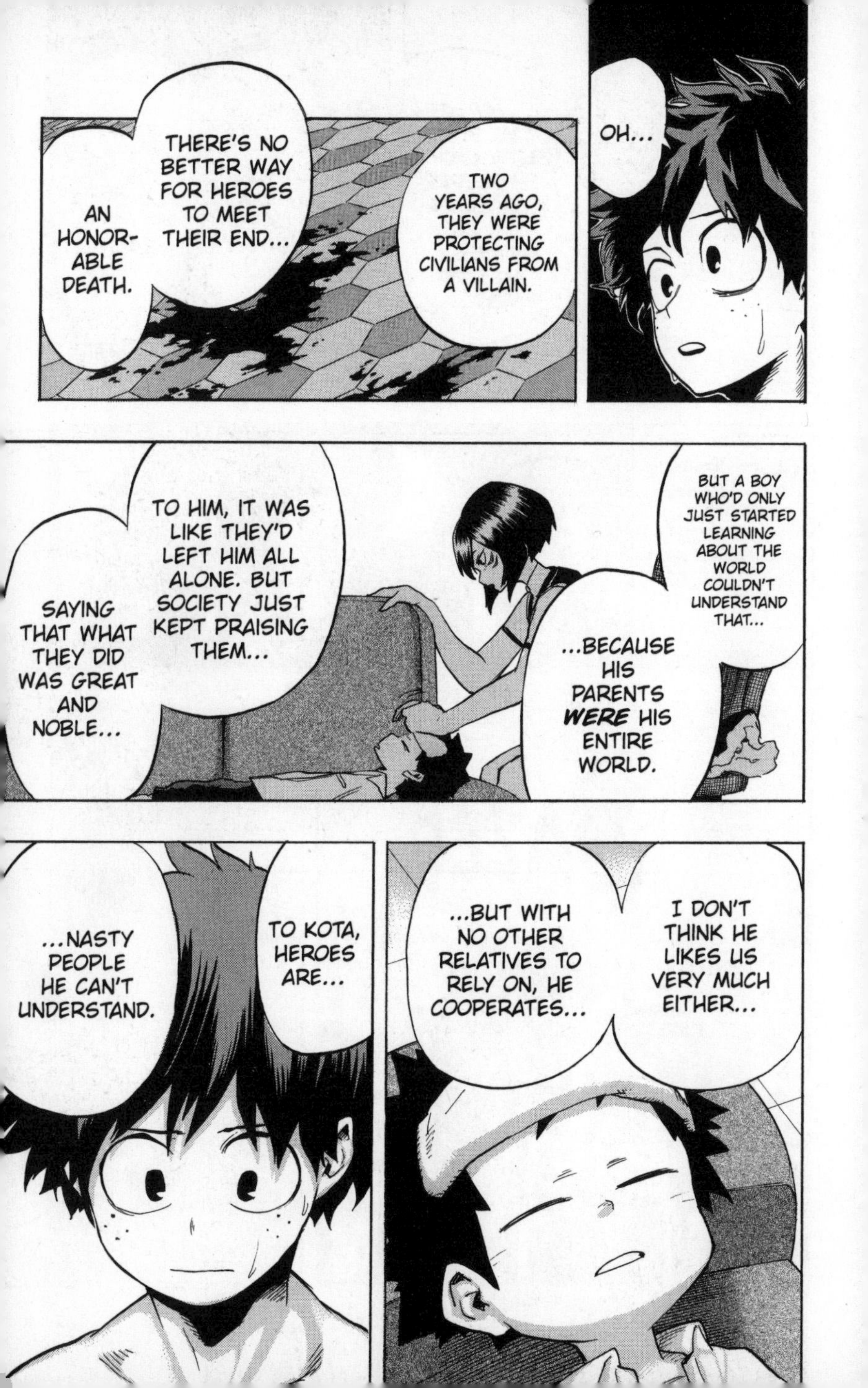
OH...
TWO YEARS AGO, THEY WERE PROTECTING CIVILIANS FROM A VILLAIN.
THERE'S NO BETTER WAY FOR HEROES TO MEET THEIR END...
AN HONOR-ABLE DEATH.
BUT A BOY WHO'D ONLY JUST STARTED LEARNING ABOUT THE WORLD COULDN'T UNDERSTAND THAT...
...BECAUSE HIS PARENTS *WERE* HIS ENTIRE WORLD.
TO HIM, IT WAS LIKE THEY'D LEFT HIM ALL ALONE. BUT SOCIETY JUST KEPT PRAISING THEM...
SAYING THAT WHAT THEY DID WAS GREAT AND NOBLE...
I DON'T THINK HE LIKES US VERY MUCH EITHER...
...BUT WITH NO OTHER RELATIVES TO RELY ON, HE COOPERATES...
TO KOTA, HEROES ARE...
...NASTY PEOPLE HE CAN'T UNDERSTAND.

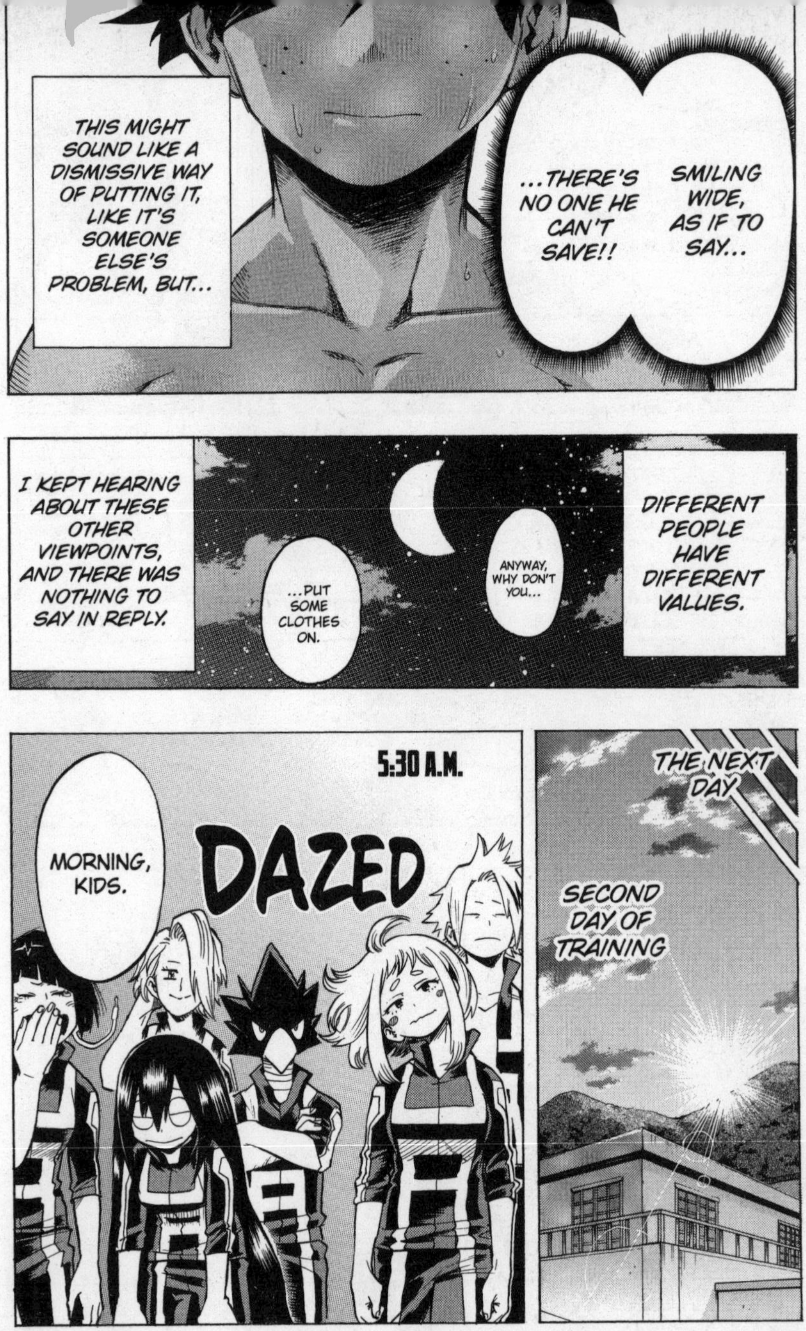
SMILING WIDE, AS IF TO SAY...
...THERE'S NO ONE HE CAN'T SAVE!!
THIS MIGHT SOUND LIKE A DISMISSIVE WAY OF PUTTING IT, LIKE IT'S SOMEONE ELSE'S PROBLEM, BUT...
DIFFERENT PEOPLE HAVE DIFFERENT VALUES.
ANYWAY, WHY DON'T YOU...
...PUT SOME CLOTHES ON.
I KEPT HEARING ABOUT THESE OTHER VIEWPOINTS, AND THERE WAS NOTHING TO SAY IN REPLY.
THE NEXT DAY
SECOND DAY OF TRAINING
5:30 A.M.
MORNING, KIDS.
DAZED

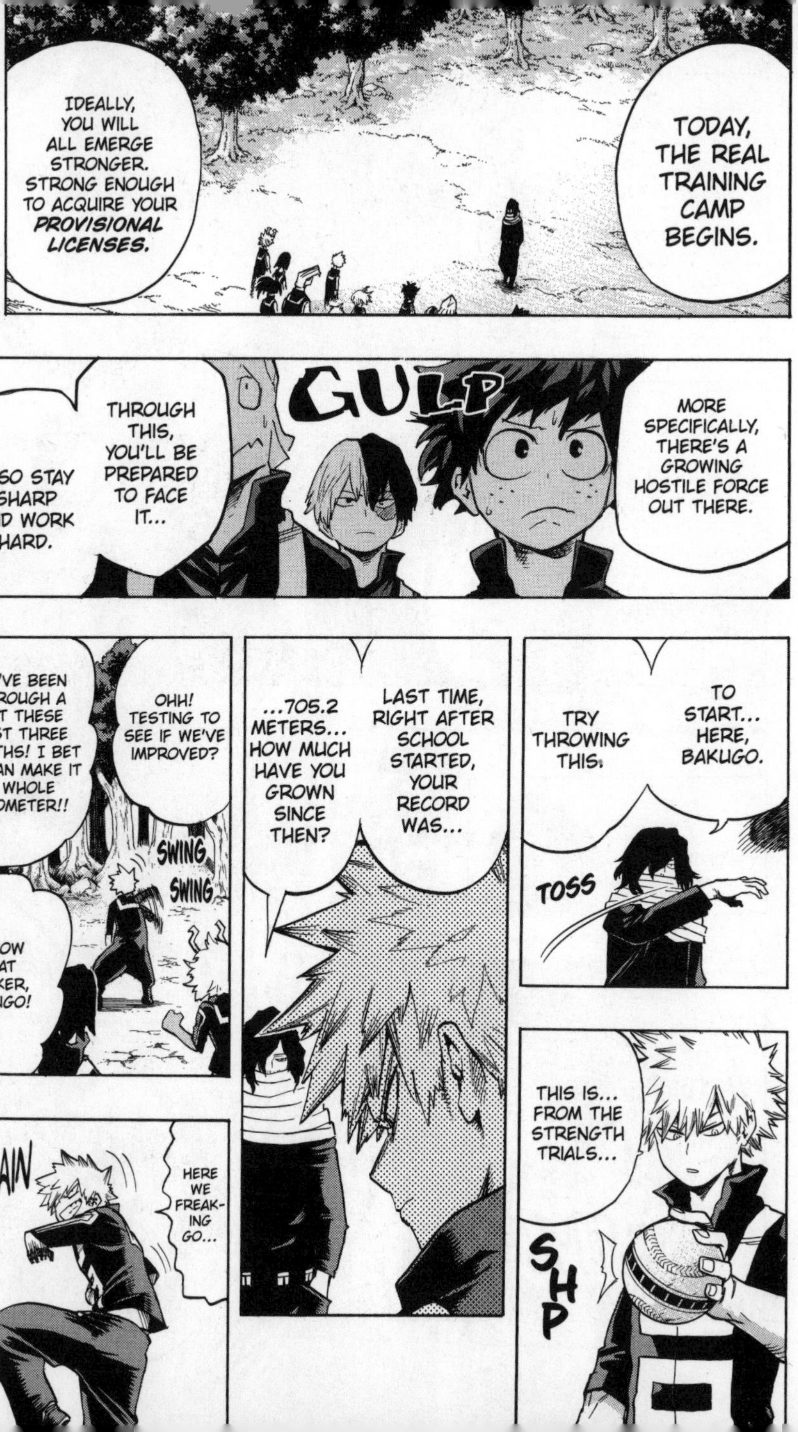
TODAY, THE REAL TRAINING CAMP BEGINS.
IDEALLY, YOU WILL ALL EMERGE STRONGER. STRONG ENOUGH TO ACQUIRE YOUR *PROVISIONAL LICENSES.*
MORE SPECIFICALLY, THERE'S A GROWING HOSTILE FORCE OUT THERE.
GULP
THROUGH THIS, YOU'LL BE PREPARED TO FACE IT...
...SO STAY SHARP AND WORK HARD.
TO START... HERE, BAKUGO.
TRY THROWING THIS.
TOSS
THIS IS... FROM THE STRENGTH TRIALS...
SHP
LAST TIME, RIGHT AFTER SCHOOL STARTED, YOUR RECORD WAS...
...705.2 METERS... HOW MUCH HAVE YOU GROWN SINCE THEN?
OHH! TESTING TO SEE IF WE'VE IMPROVED?
WE'VE BEEN THROUGH A LOT THESE PAST THREE MONTHS! I BET HE CAN MAKE IT A WHOLE KILOMETER!!
SWING
SWING
THROW THAT SUCKER, BAKUGO!
STRAIN
HERE WE FREAKING GO...

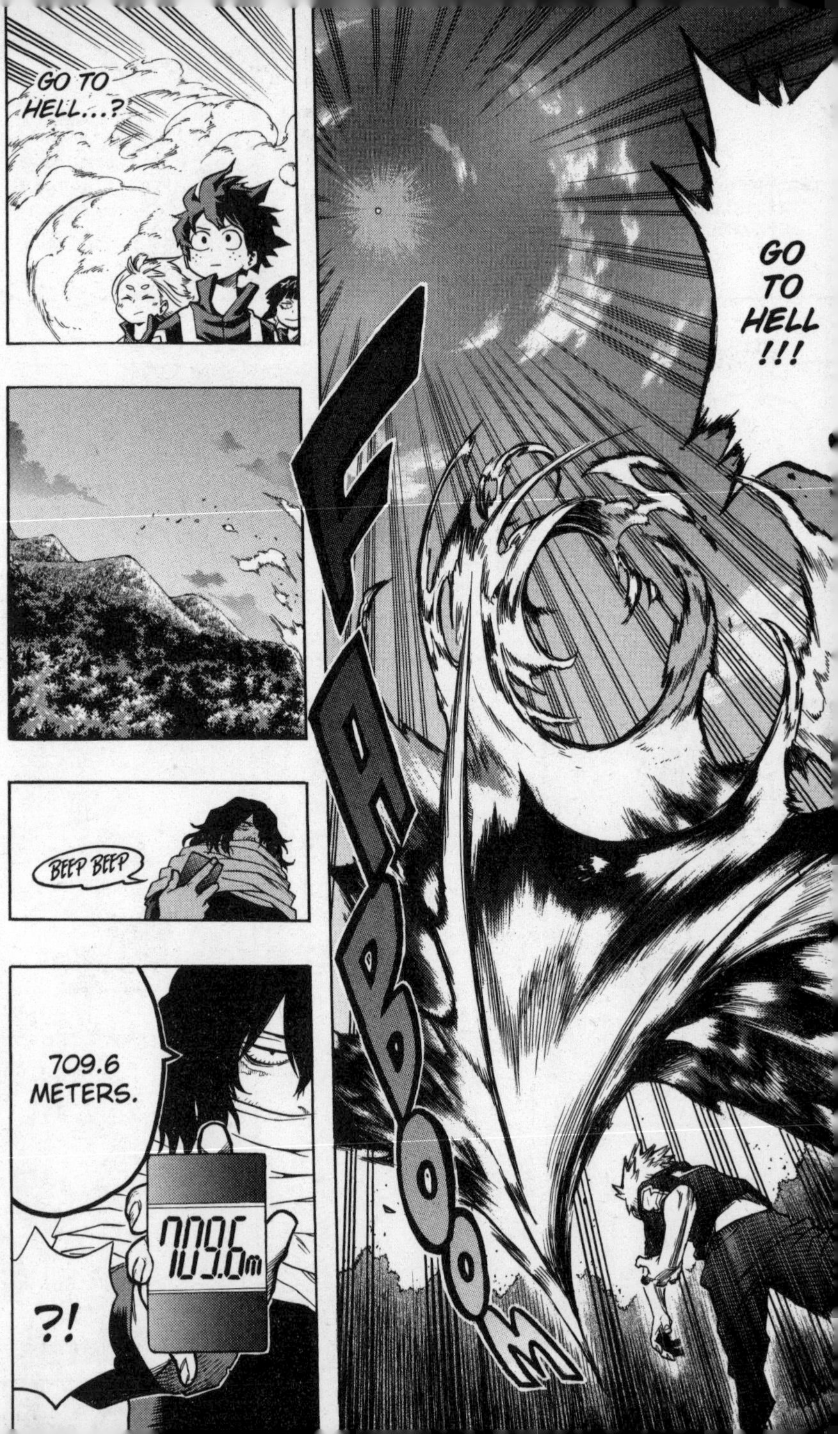
GO TO HELL!!!
GO TO HELL...?
BEEP BEEP
709.6 METERS.
709.6m
?!

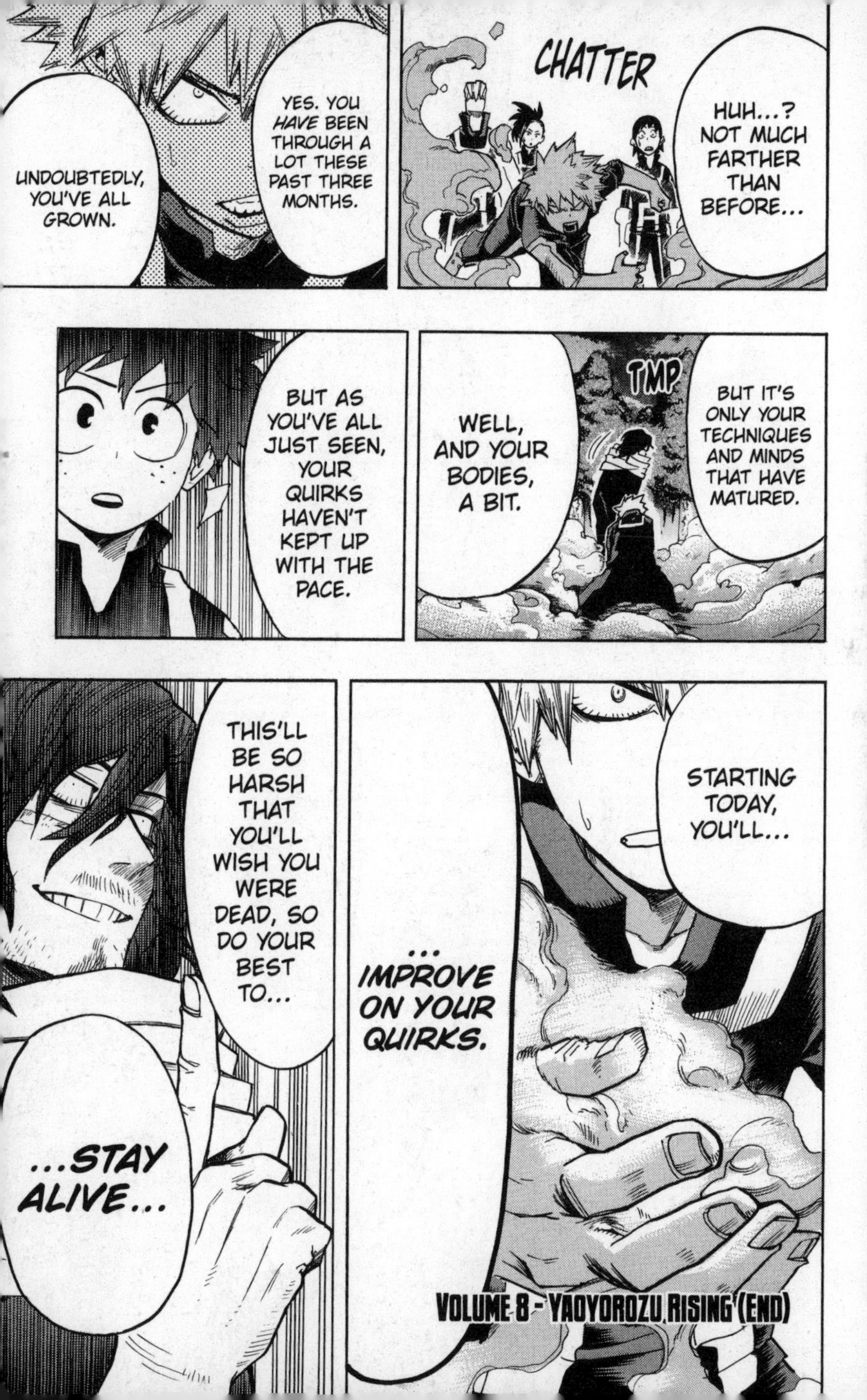
CHATTER
HUH...? NOT MUCH FARTHER THAN BEFORE...
YES. YOU *HAVE* BEEN THROUGH A LOT THESE PAST THREE MONTHS.
UNDOUBTEDLY, YOU'VE ALL GROWN.
TMP
BUT IT'S ONLY YOUR TECHNIQUES AND MINDS THAT HAVE MATURED.
WELL, AND YOUR BODIES, A BIT.
BUT AS YOU'VE ALL JUST SEEN, YOUR QUIRKS HAVEN'T KEPT UP WITH THE PACE.
STARTING TODAY, YOU'LL...
...IMPROVE ON YOUR QUIRKS.
THIS'LL BE SO HARSH THAT YOU'LL WISH YOU WERE DEAD, SO DO YOUR BEST TO...
...STAY ALIVE...
VOLUME 8 - YAOYOROZU RISING (END)

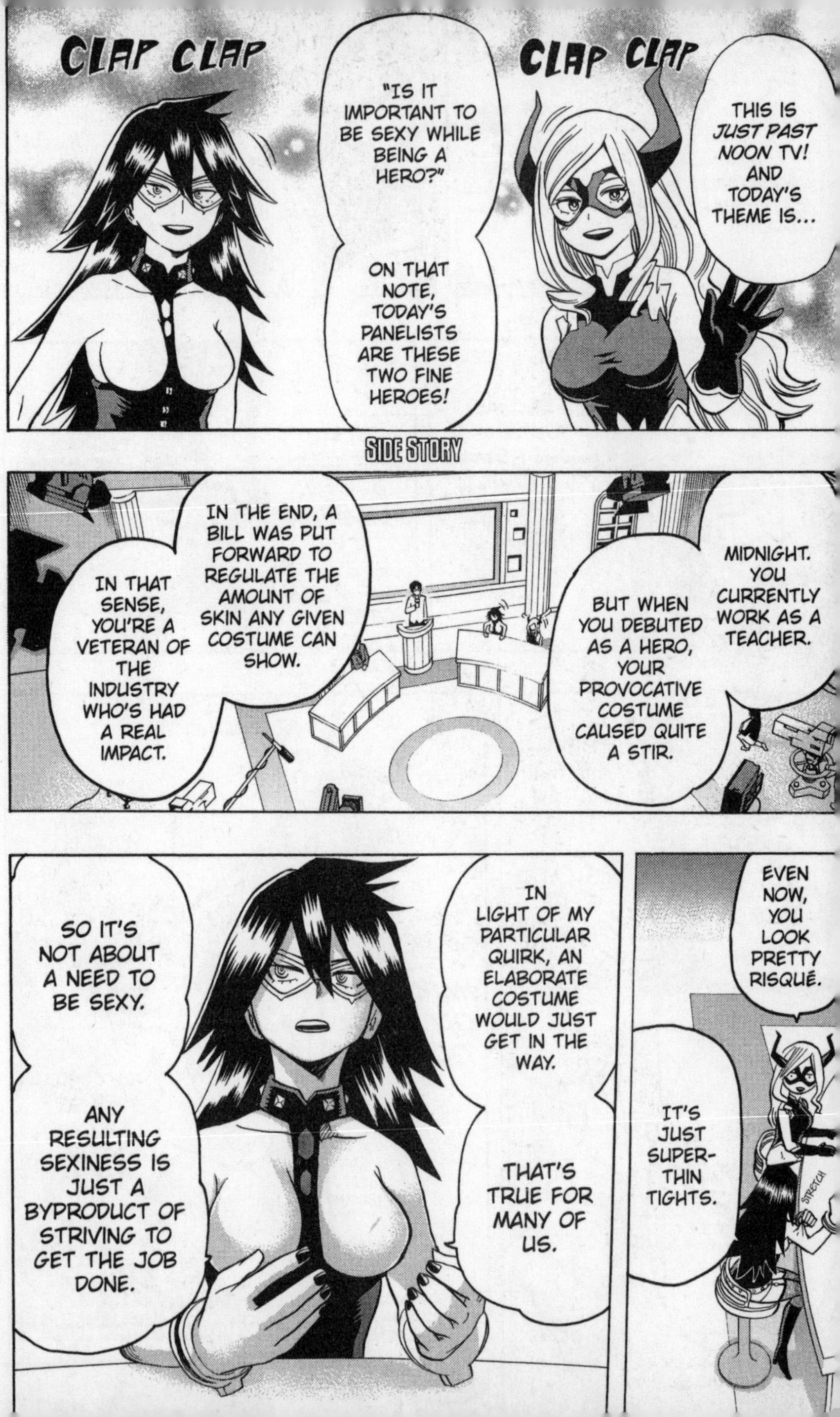
CLAP CLAP
CLAP CLAP
THIS IS JUST PAST NOON TV! AND TODAY'S THEME IS...
"IS IT IMPORTANT TO BE SEXY WHILE BEING A HERO?"
ON THAT NOTE, TODAY'S PANELISTS ARE THESE TWO FINE HEROES!
SIDE STORY
MIDNIGHT. YOU CURRENTLY WORK AS A TEACHER.
BUT WHEN YOU DEBUTED AS A HERO, YOUR PROVOCATIVE COSTUME CAUSED QUITE A STIR.
IN THE END, A BILL WAS PUT FORWARD TO REGULATE THE AMOUNT OF SKIN ANY GIVEN COSTUME CAN SHOW.
IN THAT SENSE, YOU'RE A VETERAN OF THE INDUSTRY WHO'S HAD A REAL IMPACT.
EVEN NOW, YOU LOOK PRETTY RISQUÉ.
IT'S JUST SUPER-THIN TIGHTS.
STRETCH
IN LIGHT OF MY PARTICULAR QUIRK, AN ELABORATE COSTUME WOULD JUST GET IN THE WAY.
THAT'S TRUE FOR MANY OF US.
SO IT'S NOT ABOUT A NEED TO BE SEXY.
ANY RESULTING SEXINESS IS JUST A BYPRODUCT OF STRIVING TO GET THE JOB DONE.

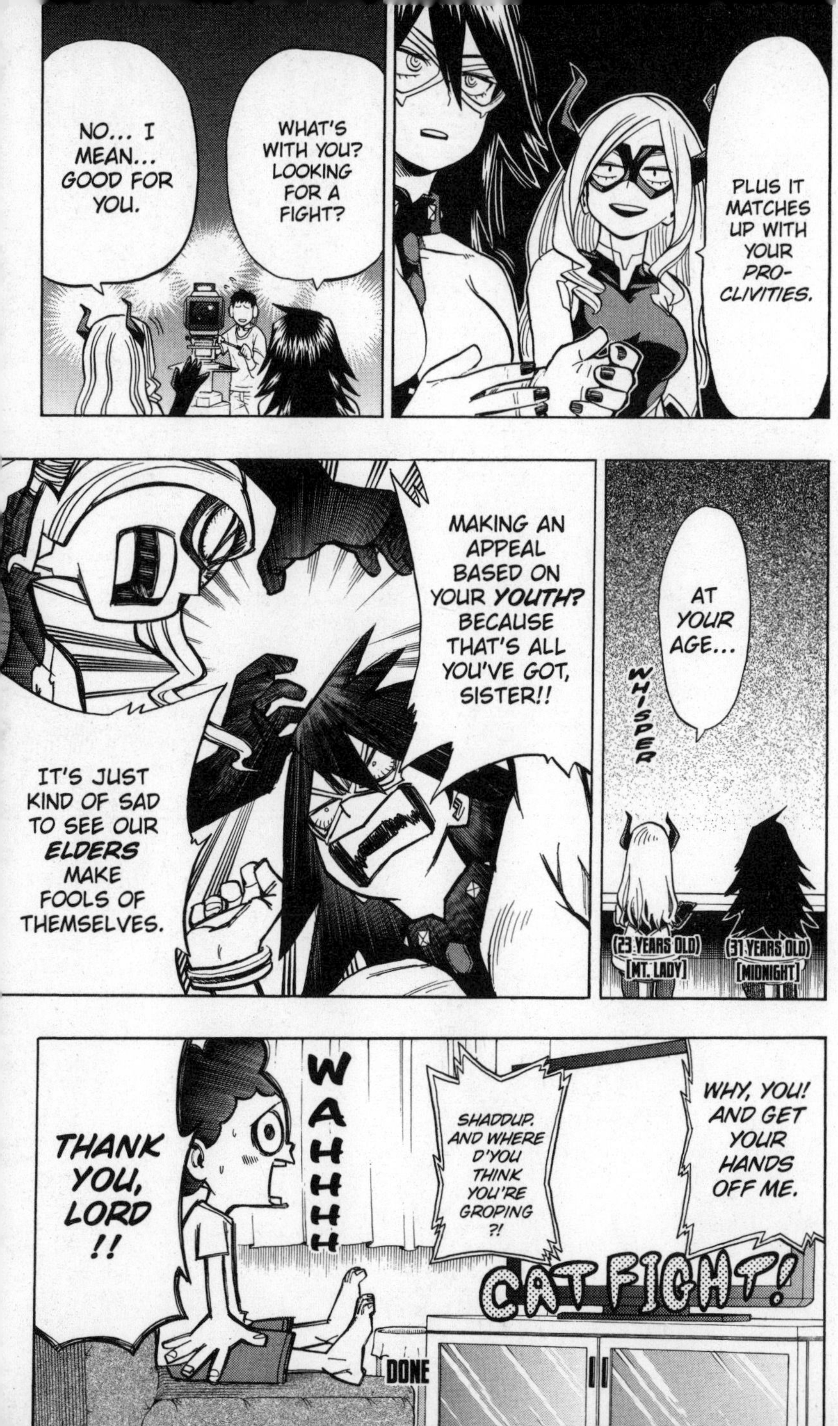
PLUS IT MATCHES UP WITH YOUR PRO-CLIVITIES.
WHAT'S WITH YOU? LOOKING FOR A FIGHT?
NO... I MEAN... GOOD FOR YOU.
AT YOUR AGE...
WHISPER
(23 YEARS OLD) [MT. LADY]
(31 YEARS OLD) [MIDNIGHT]
MAKING AN APPEAL BASED ON YOUR YOUTH? BECAUSE THAT'S ALL YOU'VE GOT, SISTER!!
IT'S JUST KIND OF SAD TO SEE OUR ELDERS MAKE FOOLS OF THEMSELVES.
WHY, YOU! AND GET YOUR HANDS OFF ME.
SHADDUP. AND WHERE D'YOU THINK YOU'RE GROPING?!
WAHHHH
THANK YOU, LORD!!
CAT FIGHT!
DONE

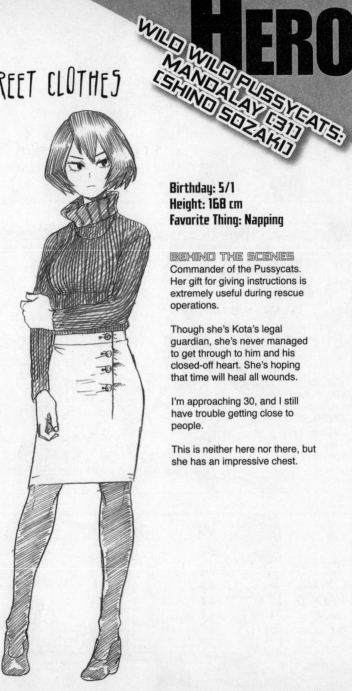

HERO

STREET CLOTHES

WILD WILD PUSSYCATS: MANDALAY [31] [SHINO SOZAKI]

Birthday: 5/1
Height: 168 cm
Favorite Thing: Napping

BEHIND THE SCENES
Commander of the Pussycats. Her gift for giving instructions is extremely useful during rescue operations.

Though she's Kota's legal guardian, she's never managed to get through to him and his closed-off heart. She's hoping that time will heal all wounds.

I'm approaching 30, and I still have trouble getting close to people.

This is neither here nor there, but she has an impressive chest.

BOY

STREET CLOTHES

Birthday: 12/12
Height: 107 cm
Favorite Thing: Being alone

BEHIND THE SCENES
He's a character who's tough to
deal with on all fronts.

YOUR HERO ACADEMIA: GRUDGE-FILLED TEARS

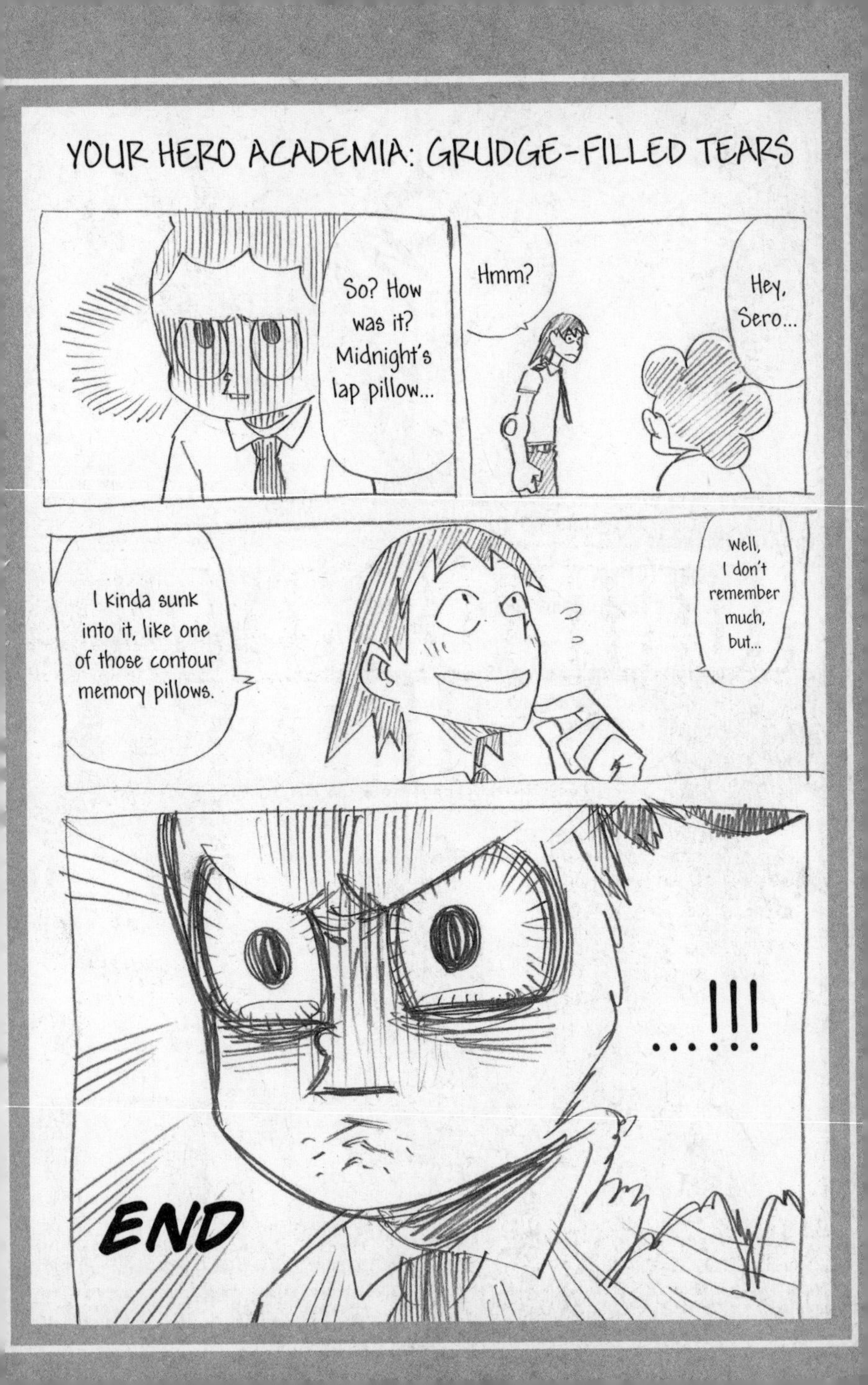
Hey, Sero...
Hmm?
So? How was it? Midnight's lap pillow...
Well, I don't remember much, but...
I kinda sunk into it, like one of those contour memory pillows.
...!!!
END

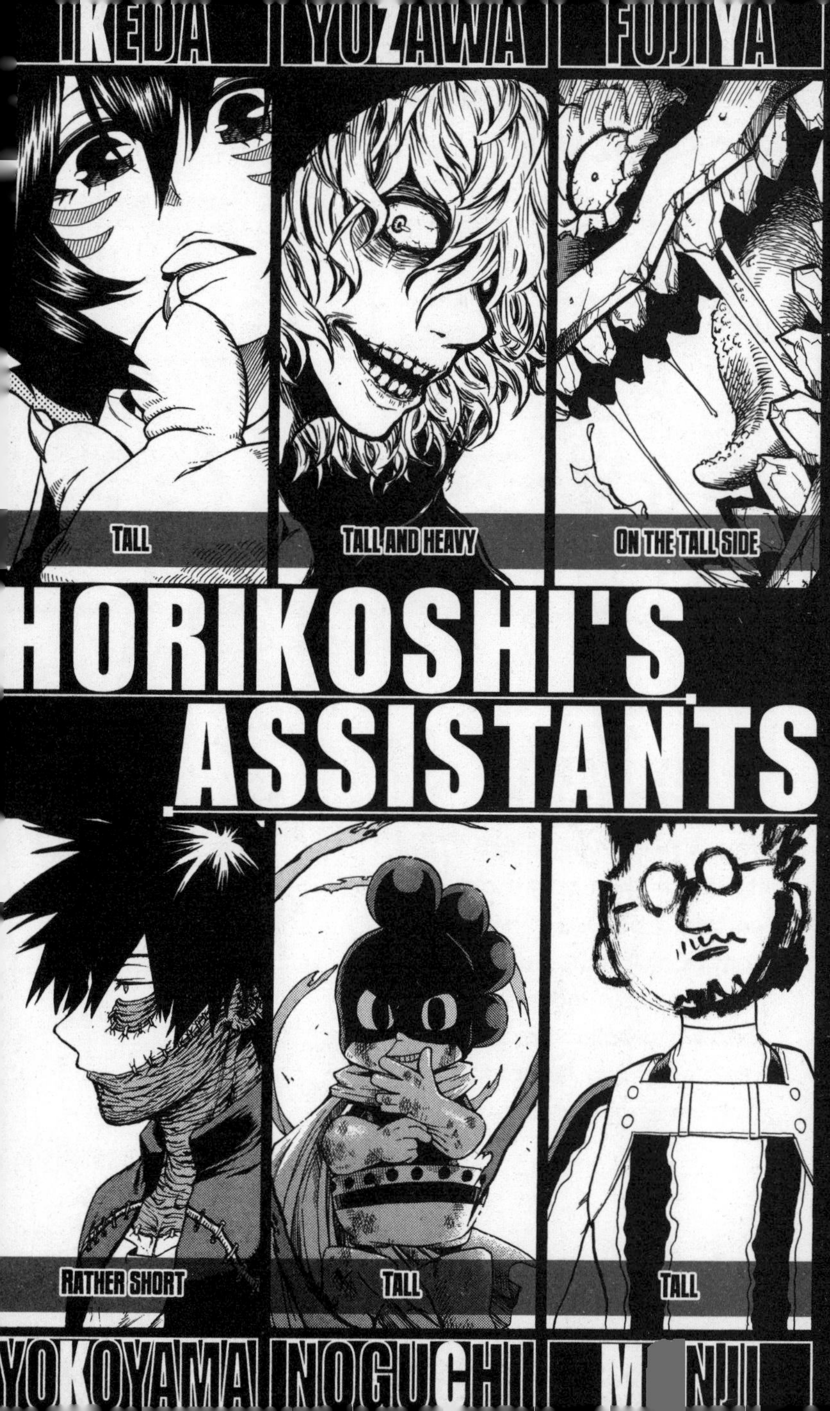
FUJIYA
ON THE TALL SIDE
YOZAWA
TALL AND HEAVY
IKEDA
TALL
HORIKOSHI'S ASSISTANTS
M[redacted]NJI
TALL
NOGUCHI
TALL
YOKOYAMA
RATHER SHORT

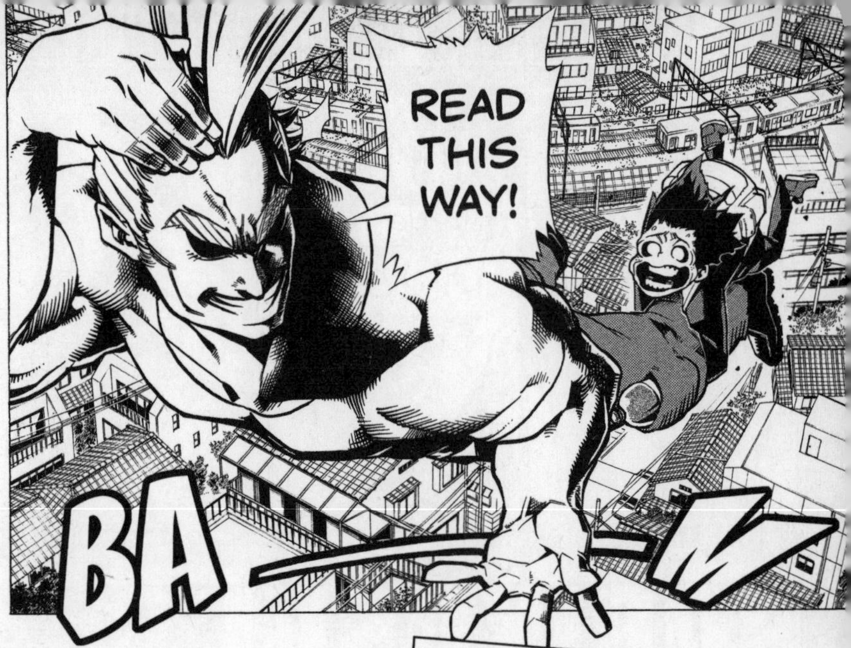
READ THIS WAY!
BA—M

MY HERO ACADEMIA

reads from right to left, starting in the upper-right corner. Japanese is read from right to left, meaning that action, sound effects and word-balloon order are completely reversed from English order.

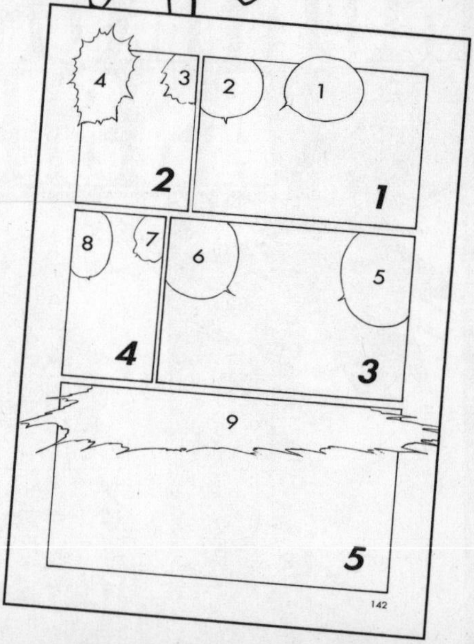
1
1
2
2
3
4
3
5
6
4
7
8
5
9
142